PEACE MOVEMENTS
WORLDWIDE

Recent Titles in Contemporary Psychology

Preventing Teen Violence: A Guide for Parents and Professionals
Sherri N. McCarthy and Claudio Simon Hutz

Making Enemies: Humiliation and International Conflict
Evelin Lindner

Collateral Damage: The Psychological Consequences of America's War on Terrorism
Paul R. Kimmel and Chris E. Stout, editors

Terror in the Promised Land: Inside the Anguish of the Israeli-Palestinian Conflict
Judy Kuriansky, editor

Trauma Psychology, Volumes 1 and 2
Elizabeth Carll, editor

Beyond Bullets and Bombs: Grassroots Peace Building between Israelis and Palestinians
Judy Kuriansky, editor

Who Benefits from Global Violence and War: Uncovering a Destructive System
Marc Pilisuk with Jennifer Achord Rountree

Right Brain/Left Brain Leadership: Shifting Style for Maximum Impact
Mary Lou Décosterd

Creating Young Martyrs: Conditions That Make Dying in a Terrorist Attack Seem Like a Good Idea
Alice LoCicero and Samuel J. Sinclair

Emotion and Conflict: How Human Rights Can Dignify Emotion and Help Us Wage Good Conflict
Evelin Lindner

Emotional Exorcism: Expelling the Psychological Demons That Make Us Relapse
Holly A. Hunt, Ph.D.

Gender, Humiliation, and Global Security: Dignifying Relationships from Love, Sex, and Parenthood to World Affairs
Evelin Lindner

PEACE MOVEMENTS WORLDWIDE

Volume 3: Peace Efforts That Work and Why

Marc Pilisuk and Michael N. Nagler, Editors

CONTEMPORARY PSYCHOLOGY
Chris E. Stout, Series Editor

 PRAEGER

AN IMPRINT OF ABC-CLIO, LLC
Santa Barbara, California • Denver, Colorado • Oxford, England

Library of Congress Cataloging-in-Publication Data

Peace movements worldwide / Marc Pilisuk and Michael N. Nagler, editors.
   p. cm. — (Contemporary psychology)
  Includes bibliographical references and index.
   ISBN 978-0-313-36478-5 (hard copy : alk. paper) — ISBN 978-0-313-36479-2
(e-book) — ISBN 978-0-313-36480-8 (vol. 1 hard copy : alk. paper) — ISBN 978-0-
313-36481-5 (vol. 1 e-book) — ISBN 978-0-313-36482-2 (vol. 2 hard copy : alk. paper) —
ISBN 978-0-313-36483-9 (vol. 2 e-book) — ISBN 978-0-313-36484-6 (vol. 3 hard copy :
alk. paper) — ISBN 978-0-313-36485-3 (vol. 3 e-book)
  1. Peace movements 2. Peace movements — History. I. Pilisuk, Marc. II. Nagler, Michael N.
  JZ5574.P44   2011
  303.6′6—dc22   2010037446

ISBN: 978-0-313-36478-5
EISBN: 978-0-313-36479-2

15 14 13 12 11   1 2 3 4 5

This book is also available on the World Wide Web as an eBook.
Visit www.abc-clio.com for details.

Praeger
An Imprint of ABC-CLIO, LLC

ABC-CLIO, LLC
130 Cremona Drive, P.O. Box 1911
Santa Barbara, California 93116-1911

This book is printed on acid-free paper ∞

Manufactured in the United States of America

CONTENTS

Contents

ACKNOWLEDGMENTS

The three volumes of this book were invited by our publisher, who saw, as we do, the value in an overview, as far as it was possible to take one, of the peace movement as a whole. First Debora Carvalko and then Lindsay Claire and Denise Stanley have been immensely supportive throughout. We soon found that the task of inviting, identifying, and editing selections from academics, officials, and activists from the varied aspects of the search for peace was a challenge to our time and organizational talents. To all of our contributors, some world renowned, all busy, we extend our thanks and appreciation for working with us, sometimes on short notice, to include their chapters. We remain amazed and grateful for the work for peace described in their contributions and the courage and persistence of the people they write about. The Metta Center for Nonviolence receives a special thanks for providing us with a welcoming place to meet.

This collection could never have seen the light of day without the dedicated involvement of a number of people. Gianina Pellegrini spent long hours beyond the few for which she was compensated to keep us on task, to communicate respectfully to hundreds of people through thousands of messages. She edited manuscripts, recruited other graduate students from Saybrook University to help, organized tasks and meetings, volunteered to write two chapters on her own that we truly needed, and fell behind in her own studies but never despaired or lost a chance to encourage others. Chris Johnnidis of the Metta Center provided initial help in setting up an interactive filing system. The project got a boost when Gianina spread the word at Saybrook University. Saybrook deserves thanks for finding some of the most talented and dedicated students anywhere. Rebecca Norlander provided endless hours of editing, evaluating, and reformatting chapters and is a co-author of an chapter. Angel Ryono likewise helped write, edit, and find authors to fill gaps, and is a co-author of two chapters. Other students whose generous help included becoming chapter authors. They are: Nikolas Larrow-Roberts, Rev. Jose M. Tirado, Ellen Gaddy, and Melissa Anderson-Hinn. Two other colleagues, Mitch Hall and Daniel J. Adamski, saw enough in the project to pitch in with major editing tasks and went on to be co-authors of chapters. Many others whom we were not able to include in the anthology helped us tremendously, sharing their specific expert knowledge and contacts to help us frame the task. These include Donna Nassor, Sandy Olleges, Kevin Bales, Curt Wand, Glen Martin, Byron Belitsos, Ethel Tobach, Douglas Fry, Ahmed Afzaal, Susan McKay, Joel Federman, Gail Ervin, Dan Christie, Jeff Pilisuk, and Josanne Korkinen.

Marc wants to express appreciation for the inspiration of two mentors, Anatol Rapaport and Kenneth Boulding; of his parents, who always valued peace and justice; and to his wife Phyllis who tolerated his sleep-deprived state for close to a year, understanding what he was trying to do. He thanks Michael Nagler for being a partner whose knowledge and belief in the peace movement is just amazing.

Michael wants to thank the staff at the Metta Center for giving him the space and the encouragement to see this task through; his friends and colleagues in the peace movement for stepping up with translation (especially Matthias Zeumer), ideas, and other contributions; Marc Pilisuk for inviting him on board in the first place; and above all his mentor and guide, Sri Eknath Easwaran of the Blue Mountain Center of Meditation, for showing him his life's path and never losing faith that he would follow it to the end.

SET INTRODUCTION

The only thing we can, and therefore must control, is the imagery in our
own mind.

           —Epictetus

We humans have great abilities to create images, and with them, to build a
significant part of our reality, and therefore to nurture or to destroy our
species and its surroundings. We have used these abilities creatively but not
always kindly, or wisely. As our science and technologies have made it possible to appreciate how our lives are part of one global world, they have also
provided us with the means to destroy Earth's capacity to support life. The
peace movement that is growing throughout the world gives recognition
and power to the first side of the balance, reacting against violence and war,
raising aloft a higher vision of harmony and peace. It provides us with a living history of the strength of people, communities, and tribes—and sometimes governments—to create social institutions and ideas that give peace
its chance to grow. It is in the search for peace, for a way to live in harmony
with each other and with the natural order, that we seem to come most alive
and closest to the meaning of our existence on this earth. The peace movement is likely the only undertaking that holds out a promise that the remarkable experiment of life can go on.

    We consider peace to include both the absence of unnecessary violence
and the pursuit of a world that offers deep contentment with the process of

life. We feel some dismay as we look at paths taken by humans toward large-scale violence. But the destruction and suffering we find is not the whole story. There is another and far more hopeful story, partly old, partly new, and partly yet to be written.

Peace connotes a world with harmony among people and between people and their environment. It is surely not a world without anger or one without conflict. But it is a world in which the fulfillment of human needs can occur without inflicting preventable violence and human beings can grow closer to one another in spirit, which, as Augustine said, is the ultimate purpose and underlying desire of our very nature (see Volume 1, Chapter 2). Like science, which has a capacity for change as new evidence emerges, the pursuit of peace is an ongoing process in which its adherents can and do learn from the past and continually make new discoveries. Like democracy, the pursuit of peace does not always produce a better world right away, but that pursuit unquestionably has the capacity to bring correctives into the directions of our evolution as a species. The peace movement is an exciting and empowering wave of worldwide change that can harness the power of each of us, individually and collectively, for love and for life.

There are many books about peace. In the three volumes of this anthology we have chosen not to be an encyclopedia of the efforts for peace,[1] or a history of worldwide efforts to realize it[2]—nor, for that matter, a celebration of a hopeful future. Rather, we have tried to present a mosaic that gives due recognition to the obstacles to be overcome while sampling the amazing creativity of what has been and is being done to overcome them. The doers are scientists and poets, professors and peasant women, intergovernmental agencies and community art projects, soldiers and pacifists, and environmentalists and defenders of human rights. Rather than force a rigid analysis on how all their efforts combine, we have tried mainly to let the voices be heard.

Volume 1 focuses on different ways people have looked at peace—to construct a theory of its nature and possibilities. We present a framework for peace studies set forth by Johan Galtung, who more than anyone living deserves to be considered the founder of the field (peace entered academic discourse as a discrete subject only very recently), and we go on to writings that examine the deeper meanings of peace. The ubiquity of human aggression and violence leads some to the despairing conclusion that we are inherently warlike. We report on the new perspectives in biology, anthropology, and psychology that paint a different picture of what humans are or are not constrained to do by our nature, and take issue with the prevalent concept that we are "wired" to fight—or even to cooperate—which implies a determinism that is denied by science and common experience. Because world peace will require some transformative changes in the way we view ourselves and our world, a section is devoted to the issue of human identity and the culture of peace. We look at the contribution of organized religion to the quest for peace. (Spirituality, as somewhat distinct from organized religion, and other broad topics are handled in Volume 3.) Volume 1 ends with chapters taking a hard look at the magnitude of change required for peace and the institutional, particularly economic and monetary, forces that need to be transformed if peace is to reign.

Volume 2 looks at what is being done in response to war and other forms of violent conflict. Moving along the chain of causality, we cite efforts to prevent mass killing by monitoring and controlling weapons that in some cases are capable not only of ending lives needlessly but of obliterating life as we know it, as well as the ongoing efforts to expose corporate beneficiaries of war and to invest instead in enterprises that promote human and environmental health. Then we examine the aftermath of violence—the trauma, the scars, and the all-important processes of reconciliation and healing. We end Volume 2 with accounts of select national and regional movements, the world over, that have grown in opposition to war.

Volume 3 is the proactive and constructive complement to the anti-war movements described in Volume 2. Here we illustrate efforts at building a peaceful world and its cultural infrastructure through peace education and reform of a media that at present does little to counter those powerful forces that promote a culture of violence and even instigate incidents of mass violence. We sample some highly creative ways that peace is being built at levels from courageous individuals to developing villages and on to international treaties and institutions. Then we examine, with examples, the process by which people can experience transformative change on a personal level that empowers participation in building a peaceful world.

When "peace" is taken in its full meaning, when one backs out from the simple cessation of one armed conflict or another to begin to sense the preconditions, the "dispositions" (as Erasmus says) that produced the outcome of conflict and its cessation, one begins to realize that the search for peace is almost coterminous with the evolution of human consciousness, of our destiny. Such a discussion obviously cannot be covered even in an anthology of this size. What one can do, and what we have tried to do, is sketch out a picture reasonably faithful to the variety, the intensity, and the unquenchable audacity of the men and women who have taken up this struggle from above (through law and policy), from below (from grassroots to civil society), and most characteristic of the present, from within (through personal transformation). For this goal, many have lain down their very lives. We come away from our survey of all this activity, dedication, and sacrifice with a combined sense of awe and inspiration.

At the end of the day, it is this inspiration that we wish to share with you. For as various writers in all three volumes have noted, all the ingredients for an evolutionary step forward toward this as-yet unrealized world are in place—some of them have been for some time. What is missing is the overview, the sense of the big picture, and the confidence in the heart of each one of us that we can make a difference. This we can do even in face of the apparently never-to-be-dislodged juggernaut of war: the mindset, the dehumanizing training, the institutions, the frightening technology. In face of that enormity, a countering awareness has arisen of the unquenchable drive for peace and what *it* has brought into being. The art, science, and practice of peace are having impacts on human understanding, institutions, and behaviors that are indispensable—if not for the courage to get engaged, at least for our sanity. But we hope for more; we hope you will come away from this set of books with re-fired determination to join this struggle, and a slightly sharper sense of where to make your best contribution. Nothing would please us more.

NOTES

1. Lazlo and Yoo, 1986; Kurtz and Turpin, 1999; Powers and Vogele, 1997.

2. Among many examples, see Chatfield and Kleidman, 1992; Chatfield, 1973; Beales 1971; and http://www.peacehistorysociety.org/. For conscientious objection worldwide, see the works of historian Peter Brock.

INTRODUCTION TO VOLUME 3

In this volume we take up proactive and constructive, often nonconfrontational activities aimed at the creation of peace and its institutions. These were, for Gandhi at least, the privileged "wing" of peace creation without which the direct resistance to injustice (essential activities to be sure) could at times dislodge regimes but would be unlikely by themselves to lead to lasting peace. This volume is thus about peace building, about making real the changes in our institutions—and our thinking—that will build an enduring peace. It is work that sets in place the conditions that make peace our normal expectation. At the same time, peace building does not remove the continuing need to resist injustice, to prevent outbreaks or spread of violence, or to heal the wounds of past violence. Each of these efforts, illustrated in Volume 2, repairs the fabric of life. As we pointed out in Volume 1, there is a great deal of this type of constructive activity going on, but some of its busy practitioners are by and large out of touch with the big picture that includes peace building at many levels; very often they also lack a sense of when it might be necessary to complement this constructive work with direct resistance.

It might be useful to think of this work in three categories: *remedial, restorative,* and *radical.* In remedial work we take care of victims of the system who are not going to be looked after (or even looked at) by the regime that has victimized them—displaced refugees, welfare mothers, illegal immigrants, the health uninsured, the homeless. All good work. And it has an *implicit* message that goes far beyond the help and comfort of those immediate victims: "these are human beings, precious of value; we care for them." This itself can be extremely important: think of Mother Teresa and her well-deserved Nobel Peace Prize. Yet on the other hand, it can actually facilitate the injustices of the regime. The aim of victimizers, remember, is not victimization per se: it is theft, exploitation of resources, and of people. When a financial boondoggle bankrupts a community (or a country: see the interview with John Perkins in Part III: Chapter 27 in this volume), for example, the manipulators walk off with their spoils and the existence of the "collaterally damaged" human beings is only an embarrassment to them. (This is not to say that on some level they could or would have a concern when they think as people and not as financiers or strategic gamesters.) Remove the embarrassment and you facilitate their work—and ease their conscience (which we believe they must have, on some level). This is why even those more exploitive and uncaring regimes, like the Bush/Cheney administration through which the United States has just passed, promote charitable work and nonprofit relief organizations. They'll look after the profits, thank you; and remedial work is too "downstream" to interfere with their exploitive systems.

Restorative work pushes further into the discomfort zone. A classic example, and one that we barely touched on in this book, is restorative justice. The overcrowded, dehumanizing prisons here in the United States, for example, are veritable madrasas (schools inculcating hostility and revenge) of future crime that entrap over 2 million Americans today. They both spring from and exacerbate a general culture of greed and dehumanization. The restorative justice movement and its various institutions—victim-offender reconciliation projects (VORP), Alternatives to Violence, meditation programs, and so on—are growing, but slowly in comparison to the retributive juggernaut that someday they hope to supplant. Here the counter-cultural message is a little louder, because it rehumanizes those whom society has not just victimized and ignored but condemned and rejected. I believe it was prison activist Bo Lozoff who pointed out that when society says to a lawbreaker, "Hey, get out of here," what we should be saying is more like, "get back in here."

Finally, what kind of activity could bring about deep, lasting, in other words, *radical*, change? We believe we can get at this question by asking, what do people in the exploiting class feel their identity, if not their very existence, depends on? And that the answer elaborated in Volume 1 is, profits and war.[1] Think of the rueful confession of General Smedley Butler that he fought wars to defend the likes of United Fruit Company and Standard Oil,[2] or the orchestrated downfall of leaders like Arbenz in Guatemala or Mosadegh in Iran when they sought to reclaim resources in their own countries for public benefit. The power of this exploitive elite can strike at leaders within their own country as well as in developing nations. Martin Luther King Jr. was assassinated (according to evidence that has not been refuted) not because he was advocating "mixing races"—not because of anything racial at all. He was assassinated, as was President Kennedy before him (again based on evidence not yet refuted), because he was threatening the war system.[3]

We would like to believe that such allegations, usually dismissed as conspiracy theories, are unfounded. But the absence of answers is disquieting, and in any case the extent of power that rests in the system of war and exploitation is real. Surely the most effective way to threaten the war system is not to rely solely on protesting it—we have seen to our dismay how that can be ignored—but by *building an alternative.* Precisely because peace building is nonconfrontational, and because it soothes rather than arouses fears, this approach just might get far enough that we could finally say to the world, "Look, we don't *need* to wage war; we can defend our country and accomplish anything we think war accomplishes by other means. And they work."

Joanna Macy, whose chapter on despair work appears in this volume, has proposed that shifting to a world peace paradigm (what she calls "the Great Turning") will call for work on three levels:

1. Stopping the worst of the damage.
2. Building new institutions.
3. Changing the culture.

Building institutions like Unarmed Civil Resistance (see Christine Schweitzer in Volume 2) answers to her second point; Macy further divides the third into *cognitive* and *spiritual* changes. All three of these volumes bring cognitive changes into play—how do we understand the potential, the challenges of peace, and the power of war? This volume also touches on the depth of change, whose power has only begun to be explored: replacing the emptiness of material life with the challenge of spiritual awareness, the chill of alienation with the sense of unity. While these efforts bubble up from the ground in locally inspired efforts, as transformative change for peace inhabits more hearts and as more people find ways to be heard, then a new set of more democratically responsive institutions for global governance gains a foothold and carves into stone some universal standards of decency. Then, starting with the most personal and local emergence of empowerment, the rules that have legalized predation also start to change.

We must be forgiven for believing that here we touch on the way to change that may be the most difficult, or at least the most misunderstood, but is quite possibly the most effective.

NOTES

1. Butler, 2003.
2. Pilisuk and Rountree, 2008.
3. Douglass, 2008 and forthcoming volumes on the assassinations of King and Gandhi.

PART I

PEACE FROM ABOVE

We have created a very complex world with institutions that often appear to have lives of their own. Massive organizational structures called corporations or government departments or military establishments are the bookends that often frame limits of what we can accomplish. There are too many of us humans on the planet and too many dangerous methods of killing and of exploiting resources for us to live without some form of large institutions and without enforceable universal standards. We no longer have the option to live in a simpler world without any such institutions, so we must instead restructure existing institutions and create new ones that are better designed to allow all people to enjoy freedom, meaningful security, and peace. Nation states with standing militaries (sometimes called "national security states") and corporate giants that can expand and exploit with minimal accountability are institutions that, for whatever good they may have served, are not able to step up quickly enough to prevent the unending wars and equally unending poverty that have beset our world. In Volume 1 David Korten made the case for why corporate domination must change if sustainability and peace are to be realized. In Volume 2 we included efforts through international treaties to prevent nations from continuing reliance on the weapons of war. Here we examine the emergence of institutions that are more responsive to real human needs.

Elise Boulding, who believed deeply that human institutions could grow to permit a healthier world died while this book was coming to fruition. Her life has been a testimony to the building of peacetime institutions. Here she writes of how much has been achieved, with very little notice or appreciation, in the many programs of the United Nations. Next, Kai Brand-Jacobsen describes the gradual process by which the institutional machinery of peace is coming of age and developing its place among other highly institutionalized forms of human endeavor, such as health care, agriculture, education, or the military.

In Volume 2 Jody Williams and Stephen Goose described a remarkable process used by the Coalition to Ban Landmines to engage separate citizen-based NGO efforts on the issue into a collaborative effort with nations and international bodies to push forward an agreement—an example of what can be achieved when forces from "below" and "above" collaborate. In this section, Maude Barlow deals with another issue that requires international regulation. It is the right to clean water, a fundamental human need and a gift of nature that is increasingly being treated as a commodity and becoming a major determinant of structural violence and of war. Here also, the structure of controls from above are coming largely as a result of actions by local groups seeking to preserve clean water, resisting its contamination and the attempt to have its availability determined by an unfair and often unfeeling marketplace. Her work reaffirms the association needed between local advocacy and international policies that protect the natural world that permits us to survive.

The effort to bring order and standards to the world of nation states is not new. Cris Toffolo offers an extremely useful and cautiously optimistic historical perspective on the evolution of international law. Ron Glossop then describes two of the milestones toward holding nations accountable and keeping the sovereignty of nations within boundaries consistent with the real demands of humanity. He describes the International Criminal Court (ICC) that has been approved by the United Nations General Assembly and the "Responsibility to Protect" principle that the General Assembly has approved, establishing that governments must protect the people within their borders from genocide, war crimes, ethnic cleansing, and crimes against humanity.

Finally, Richard Falk introduces us to the concept of a world federal government. In the current political climate the image seems as illusory as the prospect of ending all violence. But the current political climate may not be compatible with human survival and peace movements are changing that climate. Falk looks at the practical possibilities for moving beyond sovereign nation states vying for power under the law of the jungle, into an "international community" worthy of the name under a universal rule of law.

The practicality of a world federal government must be weighed against the dangers of the current system. One hundred and ninety-two autonomous sovereign nation states is a model for a war system. Real peace is established internally in countries when separate regions legislate their own rules and maintain autonomy over local matters but disputes between them are settled under rules by a central governmental authority. In such matters as the use of military violence, protecting universally recognized human rights, and issues of global climate collapse that affect all people, states relinquish the right to decide unilaterally to settle differences by force. Instead, they abide by the regulations of a federation. In this way, countries no longer go to war or attack neighbors but rather take their differences to court. Sometimes the people involved may apply conscious values of respect, forgiveness, and caring, making legal sanction unnecessary. At other times police actions may be needed to bring parties to judicial settlement. This may not be utopia, but it surely beats the mass killing associated with the present system.

—Marc Pilisuk and Michael N. Nagler

CHAPTER 1

New Understandings of Citizenship: Path to a Peaceful Future?

Elise Boulding

The world needs loving! Gaia herself, the Commonwealth of Life on the planet, needs loving. So do all 6 billion human beings, in our 10,000 societies[1] spread across 189 countries, with our 2,000 languages. The peoples of those 10,000 societies, remarkably enough, gathered together through their representatives well over 50 years ago to declare,

> *We the Peoples of the*
> *United Nations, Determined*
> to save succeeding generations from the scourge of war, which twice in our lifetime has brought untold sorrow to mankind, and
>
> To reaffirm faith in fundamental human rights, in the dignity and worth of the human person, in the equal rights of men and women and of nations large and small, and
>
> To establish conditions under which justice and respect for the obligations arising from treaties and other sources of international law can be maintained, and

---

This chapter originally appeared in *Hope in a Dark Time*, edited by David Krieger (Santa Barbara, CA: Capra Press, 2003).

The editors would like this brief chapter to stand as our loving tribute to Prof. Boulding, whose passing in June of 2010 was mourned by many others around the world.

To promote social progress and better standards of life in larger freedom, . . .
Have Resolved to Combine Our Efforts to Accomplish These Aims . . .

The result was the formation of the United Nations, and yes, the United Nations is part of this world's incredible diversity and needs loving, too.

The overlay of 190 sets of national boundaries on this world's diversity has left many ethnic, racial, and cultural identity groups, each with their own history, stripped of access to their traditional resources and excluded from opportunities to participate in the new life-ways of the new states in which they find themselves. Such identity groups include also the diasporas of immigrant communities and victims of past centuries of slave trade. The resulting struggles, fueled by a military technology that multiplies the availability of small arms to angry people and of high-level bombing power to a few major powers, almost makes the dream of putting an end to war seem obsolete.

Yet the capacity to envision a world at peace has been part of humankind's heritage over the millennia, and is with us still. So are the practical peacemaking skills of the 10,000 societies, present in memory and tradition but missing in practice because of fast-moving developments that outstripped possible strategies of adaptation. So is the capacity for developing and learning new peacemaking practices suited to the complexities of this rapidly changing world. The 20th century was a century of research and development of such practices, stimulated by The Hague Peace Conference of 1899. Today there are peace teams, the contemporary equivalent of Gandhi's Shanti Sena (peace army), at work in many conflict-torn areas. But too few and with too few resources. Military technology has outraced peace technology.

This outracing is the result of another type of heritage: recent centuries of colonial invasion of many of the territories of 10,000 societies and a large-scale drawing of maps that ignored their own traditional lands. Suddenly there were sovereign states with a ruling group that excluded other ethnic groups within their borders from economic and social opportunities in a world in which everything was changing. Diversity was deplored. Political modernization was all about assimilation and melting pots, but reality was about oppression and exclusion.

Only now, with the 21st century threatening ecological, economic, and social catastrophes, is there a dawning realization that diversity is valuable, that every language and every life-way includes some valuable knowledge and skills (as well as undesirable practices, such as clitoridectomy, which are certainly not to be cherished). UNESCO has played an important role in this realization, especially through its activity in declaring the World Cultural Development Decade (1988 to 1997),[2] which called the attention of all states to the riches of each other's many cultures. Ethnic groups are finding their voices again, and an increasing number of states, especially in Europe, are following the once-unique Swiss model of a federation of semi-autonomous provinces, each with their own language and culture but also a shared confederal system of governance. Africa, Asia, and the Americas all offer examples. On the European continent, the Council of Europe is encouraging this process through the Framework Convention for the Protection of National Minorities adopted in 1995. Scotland and Wales now have their own parliaments in the United Kingdom (the situation in Northern Ireland is still in process), with similar developments in Belgium, Spain, Italy, and Scandinavia.

A NEW MODEL OF CITIZENSHIP

In fact, a new model of citizenship is emerging for the states of the contemporary international community. This citizenship is rooted in love of one's own community, one's own culture, with a deep sense of civic responsibility for its well-being, but extends the feelings of community and civic responsibility to all those who live within the borders of one's country. It resonates to the symbols of citizenship—the flag, the constitutions, and the institutions and processes of governance of that country. This is different from the assimilation model of citizenship because it values and respects the sister identity groups within the borders of the country.

However, citizenship that limits its loyalties to those within its borders leaves us with 189 states each focused on maintaining sovereignty in relation to the other 188 states. This passion for sovereignty curbs the willingness of states to sign treaties limiting their freedom of action. And yet behavior-limiting treaties are essential if states are to deal with conflicting interests without going to war. How do we create a responsible system of mutually limited governance among sovereign states?

The new model of citizenship that hovers on the horizon is not only multicultural, involving respect for all groups of fellow citizens within the state, but is multinational and multidimensional: a three-fold citizenship. The first dimension, one's local community, has already been emphasized as a part of one's citizenship in the state, which in turn is the second dimension of citizenship. The third dimension of citizenship has yet to be recognized and explored: citizenship in the United Nations itself. The United Nations was formed as an association of "we, the peoples," as quoted at the beginning of this chapter, not as "we, the states." I do not mean to make this simply a play on words but, rather, to suggest that all 6 billion of us humans (and our fellow creatures in the biosphere) have a direct stake in the survival of the United Nations. The willingness of our national representatives to sign treaties to protect the security of all life is dependent on our civic activity in promotion of such treaties.

What weaves the local, national, and United Nations dimensions of our citizenship together in a common fabric is the existence of 25,000 international nongovernmental organizations (INGOs). These INGOs bring concerns for peace, justice, human rights, and the environment from our local chapters to the national and on the United Nations' level, with specific access points at the United Nations, including especially the UN conferences and commission hearings on critical world issues. These INGOs are new developments of the 20th century and are still in a learning mode, particularly in terms of learning how to relate international INGO offices to local situations, to *learn* from locals, and to learn from and cooperate with each other in this still new action sphere of international nongovernmental bodies. This is all part of a wider learning process as the new concept of citizenship evolves.

An important aspect of learning how to exercise that citizenship involves overcoming the vast public ignorance about the United Nations that exists in every country. The concept of national citizenship as encompassing active awareness of the diversity of peoples and needs within our own country already requires a major new educational effort, and the added challenge of learning how to work within the United Nations is daunting, to say the least. But if we want to enable the development of a workable United Nations system of governance to solve the many types of economic, cultural, and environmental conflicts already being faced within the international community of states, we have no alternative.

The body of existing conventions and treaties that binds the states of the United Nations together is the product of thousands of hours of citizens' time (in their role as representatives of INGOs) put into continuing dialogue with diplomats and representatives of Member States and United Nations officials over the nature of the problem to be solved, and what can be agreed to in the way of solutions that are in the common interest of states with different needs. This process, slow and frustrating as it is, brings into being new norms in the common human interest. The United Nations treaties on the law of the sea, the banning of landmines, and the establishment of the International Criminal Court are all recent achievements of this process.[3]

U.S. RESISTANCE TO INTERNATIONAL TREATIES

The United States, one of the original funding states of the United Nations itself, has in recent years been notably resistant to signing and ratifying many of these treaties, especially regarding arms limitations and the environment. It also withdrew from the United Nations Education, Science, and Culture

Organization (UNESCO) in the 1980s, in protest over the report of UNESCO's MacBride Commission on the New World Information Order (1980), which emphasized two-way information flows between countries of the North and the South to replace a one-way flow from North to South.

All citizens of the United States must share the blame for this withdrawal because we have not activated our citizenship in the United Nations itself to prevent the withdrawal. How could this be done? A specific opportunity at this time is to become involved in the United Nations Culture of Peace Decade, 2001 to 2010. Activities associated with this decade are strongly recommended to us by the collective voice of Nobel Peace Laureates. Since the theme is education for peace and nonviolence for the children of the world, educational materials have been developed for kindergarten through high school, for faith groups and community social action groups of all kinds.[4] Peace studies programs to support learning about peace building already exist in many colleges and universities in the United States and around the world and will contribute to the decade's work. This focus on peace education will help develop not only the skills of listening and dialogue but the skills of civic participation through grassroots organizations and INGOs. Educational materials about the United Nations itself are available directly from the United Nations Association of the United States (UNA–USA)[5](or from the UNA of any Member State).

Imagine how different the world would be if everyone read the quarterly UN Chronicle,[6] which reports on United Nations activities! Invisible as the United Nations is to the general public, there is a lot going on, on any particular day, in the United Nations system. Few realize what that system consists of: six major United Nations operating organs, 13 associated bodies, 16 specialized agencies, five regional commissions, and fluctuating numbers of peacekeeping and observer missions, as well as 20 research institutes, other divisions and special programs that continually evolve to meet new needs in various parts of the world, two United Nations Universities (one in Japan, one in Costa Rica), and about 50 worldwide information centers, plus special offices where new field programs are located. The research institutes publish their own newsletters and research reports. What a difference it could make if all disarmament activists read the reports of the United Nations Institute of Disarmament Research (UNIDIR), or development activists read the reports of the United Nations Research Institute on Social Development (UNRISD), to name just two valuable United Nations research bodies.[7] It is a tragedy that all the creativity and problem-solving activity that goes on in the United Nations, side by side with the more publicized bureaucratic inefficiency, is unknown to most civic activists. So many missed opportunities for support of important peace, human rights, development, and environment initiatives that, if carried out, would make the United Nations a more effective body!

RESTORATIVE JUSTICE

In activating the United Nations component of our citizenship, we are supporting principles of restorative justice that have been badly eroded by the evolution of punitive criminal justice systems in recent centuries of state-building. It is a very simplistic system: find the wrongdoers and punish them. The much older system of restorative justice, still practiced in many tribal groups, though outlawed by colonial occupiers, is far more complex. It involves identifying the wrongdoer, uncovering the circumstances of the wrongdoing and the full extent of the harm done, helping the wrongdoer take responsibility for the harm done, undertaking some form of restitution for the victim, and to the extent possible, restoring relationships, not only between the wrongdoer and the victim but between the wrongdoer and the community. When well-trained United Nations Peacekeepers are stationed in an area recovering from civil war, this is the kind of work that their special cadre of trained conflict mediators will undertake.

Soldiers without special training can only rely on force in areas of unrest. It is a sad fact that United Nations peacekeeping is severely handicapped by a great shortage of soldiers with special peacekeeping and peace building training and an equally severe shortage of civilian police officers for UNCIVPOL, the United Nations Civilian Police Force. The good news is that the United Nations Security Council has recently mandated that women be present in significant numbers in all United Nations peacekeeping missions.[8] Here are new career opportunities for the growing number of women entering into professional conflict mediation and conflict transformation work. But funding to support the missions is sadly lacking.

The Culture of Peace Decade could well be a decade of developing understandings of the meaning and possibility of United Nations citizenship for young people. Service in the United Nations Volunteers program gives young people and mid-career people the opportunity to participate in United Nations peacekeeping and development projects around the world (as well as in the national peace corps of Member States). Here is a way for young people to learn about the rich diversity of life-ways and languages around the planet, to explore the poetry and music and dance of human life, to thrill to the biodiversity of the rivers, mountains, valleys, and oceans, the deserts, and the plains—in short, to fall in love with the world that so badly needs loving.

The process that began with The Hague Peace Conference in 1899, when nations assembled to declare that war should no longer be used as a means to settle conflicts between states, is still alive. The 20th century saw the establishment of the World Court, the League of Nations, and finally the United Nations. The peace research movement brought social scientists together from every discipline to study the processes involved in conflicts and their resolution, and institutes to research and develop peace diplomacy were established on every continent. New professions of mediators and conflict transformation specialists developed. Social movements to end violence in all its forms arose, including the restorative justice movement to end the use of prisons for wrongdoing, and social movements to end all forms of economic and racial/ethnic oppression.

The United Nations began a long process of slowly crafting treaties that would limit the types of weapons used in war and move toward, first nuclear disarmament, and then, general and complete disarmament. Most of all, the treaties have aimed to protect civilians, who are increasingly becoming casualties of new military technologies used in war and of economic catastrophes in the form of slave-type sweatshops. But treaty-crafting is a slow process—states resist having their options limited. And the arms race never stopped—even more lethal military technologies are being developed, and World War II established the practice that it is okay to bomb cities; civilian casualties are just "collateral damage."

MORAL NUMBING

Who can say when the current process of moral numbing—a condition of moral and emotional unresponsiveness to human slaughter—first began? Did it begin with the bombing of Dresden? With the nuclear bombing of Hiroshima and Nagasaki? With the Gulf War? Or more recently with the bombing of Kosovo? Or has it, in fact, been an unnoticed byproduct of Western colonialism, the destruction of native peoples' life-ways and habitat, and the transatlantic slave trade? Is it not strange that a century noted for a growing awareness of human rights marked by the United Nations Declaration of Human Rights should not have brought that moral numbing process to a halt?

The horrified responses in the United States to the September 11 acts of terrorism gave a different kind of witness to that moral numbing. Yes, there were intense feelings of fear and vulnerability, deep sadness over the deaths, but a very rapid translation of those feelings into willingness to fight a vicious war against innocent civilians in the name of stamping out terrorism. The voices calling out in protest, "not in our name," are hard to hear. The media ignores them.

Yet the peace building initiatives of the previous century have not been in vain. There has been a steadily growing realization that cycles of vengeance and counter-vengeance can destroy the societies involved and must be stopped.

It is possible to create a social space between vengeance and forgiveness, so that those who have been enemies can learn to live together again. The first step was creating international criminal tribunals with justice as the primary objective. But gradually the concepts of the restorative justice movement have gained relevance as people consider how conflicting parties, whether tribal, clan-based, different ethnicities, faith communities, or primarily political groups, would be able to give each other room to get on with their lives after fighting stopped. The need to deal with feelings of injury, anger, and the desire for compensation was strong. And so it happened that the governments of some conflict-fractured states, working with grassroots organizations and national as well as transnational NGOs and the United Nations, worked to develop a new type of institution related to older concepts of folk law: the truth commission.

TRUTH COMMISSIONS

The South African Truth and Reconciliation Commission is the best known. The commission process is a long and tortuous one, but there are now between 15 and 20 states that have established some form of truth commission. A 1995 study[9] lists truth commission processes in Bolivia, Argentina, Uruguay, Uganda, Philippines, Chile, South Africa, Chad, Rwanda, El Salvador, Guatemala, Nicaragua, Brazil, Colombia, and Peru. They are sparse in Asia, with truth commission initiatives taking place in Sri Lanka and Cambodia, and certainly under consideration elsewhere.

The truth commission process involves an intensive examination of the meanings of citizenship and responsibility of conflicting groups for each other within a given country. How much forgiveness is possible? How much restitution can be made? By whom? How will healing take place? The United Nations has made important contributions to the truth commission process in a number of countries. Many trained helpers are needed in countries where there has been widespread killing and torture. Those involved in the violence must relearn their humanity. UNESCO's Culture of Peace program has worked with local peace centers to help reintegrate into local communities the former soldiers and guerillas who have engaged in widespread torture in countries such as Nicaragua.

Germany is the only European country that has had a commission to assess the consequences of war—in this case, focusing on the period of separation of East and West Germany. There has never been serious public discussion of a truth commission for the United States. The nuclear bombing of Hiroshima and Nagasaki, resulting in massive civilian deaths, has never been dealt with. Much of the information about the fate of the citizens of Hiroshima and Nagasaki remains classified to this day. The bombing is rationalized as having speeded the end of the war, although a 1998 study[10] indicates that capitulation was already under way. Government pressure stopped an effort by the Smithsonian Institute in Washington, DC, to hold a 50th anniversary exhibit about the bombing.

Failure to grieve over its own shortcomings is a serious problem for the United States and contributes to anti-American attitudes in the rest of the world. A new movement for United States reparations to African Americans for the harm done by slavery, and to Native Americans for harm done by driving them off their lands, may well link with the anti-bombing lobby and peace and disarmament groups to create a demand for a United States truth and reconciliation commission that could lead to public dialogue about the historical process of development in a country justly proud of its democracy, but not well enough aware of its history, and of the diversity of peoples who proudly call themselves Americans. This could give new meaning to American citizenship, as such truth and reconciliation commissions have given new meanings to citizenship in the countries that have worked through that healing process.

A MORE INCLUSIVE UNDERSTANDING OF CITIZENSHIP

I have been suggesting that a more multidimensional and inclusive understanding of citizenship, one that could make a peaceful world possible, has strong emotional components of involvement in one's own local community, in one's own country, and in the United Nations itself. Both the national and the United Nations components of citizenship involve respect for an empathy with the highly diverse Others with whom we share that citizenship, and a sense of identification with the world family, composed of identity groups and ethnicities scattered across 190 states. The United Nations represents us all. Can we love the United Nations flag as much as we love our country's flag?

This is the only planet we have, and the planet itself needs loving if the life it now supports is to continue into the future. And so I will close with a Sonnet by Kenneth Boulding, whose last words before he died in 1993 were, "I *love* the world."

Sonnet for the Turning Earth[11]
January 24, 1993

How good it is to live on Earth that turns,
That endlessly repeats the simple play
That gives us the great plot of night and day,
Sunrise, noontide, and sunset, and so earns
For us the precious skill that learns
To see the patterns in time's brave display
And so prevents our plans from going astray,
So we don't dash into a fire that burns.

Good it is too that Earth goes round the sun
In annual cycles, giving blessed seasons
So that we search successfully for reasons
Even though in some patterns we may see none.
So it is clear that what makes human worth
At least in part is learned from Mother Earth.

NOTES

1. The 10,000 societies is a term referring to the existence of thousands of ethnicities, and appears in UNESCO's 1996 report on "Our Creative Diversity". See also Ankerl, 2000.

2. See UNESCO, 1987.

3. A vivid description of citizen's involvement in the development of the law of the sea is found in Levering and Levering, 1999.

4. For more information about current developments with regard to peace culture and the involvement of INGOs in peace development work see Boulding, 2000. Also see David Adams, Vol. 1, Chapter 8 of this anthology.

5. The UN Association of the United States (UNA-USA) is located at 801 Second Avenue, New York, NY 10017–4706.

6. The United Nations Chronicle is published quarterly by the United Nations Department of Public Information, United Nations, Room DC20853, New York, NY 10017.

7. UNDIR and UNRISD are both located in the Palais des Nations, CH 1211, Geneva, Switzerland.

8. The resolution on the importance of women in peace building is Resolution 1325, adopted by the Security Council at its 4213 meeting, on October 31, 2000. Copies are available from International Alert, One Glyn St., London SE11, 5HT, England.

9. Kritz, 1995; Minow, 1998.

10. Bird and Lifschutz, 1998.

11. Boulding, 1994.

CHAPTER 2

PEACE BUILDING: TWELVE DYNAMICS

Kai Brand-Jacobsen

After the global demonstrations against war on February 15, 2003—said to be the largest internationally coordinated demonstrations by human beings in history—many went home and asked themselves "What next?" "What else can I do?" After the war began some weeks later on March 20, many more felt as if we had failed, as if those working for peace and to prevent the war from taking place had been defeated. Around the world, many of us, when faced with conflicts—whether in our own personal lives or conflicts, violence and wars in our communities, countries and globally—continue to feel powerless. Confronted by what we see presented to us in the media, some feel overwhelmed, sad, angry, frustrated, and often, disempowered.

Despite a rise in the number of peace studies programs at universities across the world, and despite organizations, networks, and institutions engaged in peace building, conflict transformation, alternative dispute resolution, nonviolence, social justice, sustainable community development and peace education, many, perhaps the majority of us, are often left with the feeling that conflicts and violence, global military and economic/political systems, are things over which we have little power and little say. It is clearly a time to reassess.

For thousands of years humanity has evolved its capacity for armed conflict and violence, to the point where today we have armies and weapons systems able to wreak extraordinary devastation and destruction. Yet as long as there have been conflicts, human communities have sought ways to deal with these conflicts constructively, and effectively, through peaceful means. In the last 20 years, peace building as a field has developed substantially. Today, more than ever before, from the local to the global level, we are *systematically* investing in and developing our capacities—as individuals, communities, countries, and globally—to deal with conflicts *without* violence.

We should not belittle or undermine what is actually happening. One of the challenges we often face is that people frequently do not see the wide range of activities and initiatives taking place, or their own power and ability to act. The number of organizations engaged in peace building and conflict transformation worldwide, for example, has increased significantly over the past 14 years. While many of those focused on by researchers and writers are larger institutions and nongovernmental organizations (NGOs) engaged in peace building and conflict transformation in war-affected countries, there are also organizations, networks, and groups within each of our communities and on every continent that are working to address and transform problems and challenges to a peaceful world.

Often the larger government agencies and donor-funded organizations that are extending help from afar, may be part of the challenge, sometimes negating local strengths and sometimes serving to re-enforce institutions that are at the root causes of war and violence. Some are unable or unwilling to challenge deeper roots and dynamics of war and the geo-political and strategic interests of their donors. They may be working to bring an end to "direct violence," but not touching deep structural or cultural violence and injustices, or their own home countries' contributions to wars. Just as often, however, the ties and networks we are forming across borders are helping us to better understand and learn from each other, and within our communities to deal with the contradictions and issues we face. Linking together we do more than we can apart. In this way we are going to both the root causes and the effects and impacts of war—direct, social, economic, cultural, and political—analyzing them and working to transcend them. These links are helping us to build networks and dialogues, exchanging experiences, and enriching ourselves through learning of each others' methods, the challenges and difficulties we face, and the many different ways in which we are addressing them. Together with these networks, peace studies, development organizations, UN agencies, and researchers have—systematically over the past 10 years but with roots even before that—begun gathering together best practices and lessons learned on everything from strengthening and supporting local capacities for peace, empowering communities to address and transcend violence, war to peace transitions, postwar reconciliation, recovery, healing, and economic viability.

We gain perspective and hope by examining 12 dynamics shaping the frontiers of peace building today. They do not tell the whole story, but they make visible a dimension of our work often not seen. Practitioners and policy makers most often work in-depth in *particular* areas of the field. The purpose here is to make visible a glance of the overall picture created as a result of that work.

When a bird's-eye view of the broad dynamics of the field is combined with a frog's-eye view looking at concrete, specific details, we see a field that is developing rapidly in necessary ways, enhancing our capacities to deal with conflicts effectively, and improving our abilities to prevent large-scale violence and armed conflicts. This chapter is both a presentation of some of those dynamics and an invitation to work together on developing them further.

TWELVE DYNAMICS

One: Growing, Broadening, Expanding

Peace building as a field has grown significantly over the past 20 years. There are more organizations involved. It is now a global field, replacing an earlier preponderance toward institutions and initiatives based in Western Europe and North America. A broader range of actors: governments, intergovernmental organizations, NGOs, local authorities, think tanks, media, and artists—each brings important contributions. Engagement is on a broader range of issues: mediation, early warning and prevention, civilian peacekeeping, post-war recovery, reconciliation and healing, gender and peace building, peace journalism, restorative justice, peace education, and building peace infrastructure. The field is continuing to expand.

Two: Improving Methodologies

Expansion is combined with gradually improving methods. It would take more space than we have here to list all the groundbreaking innovations of the last few years, in all corners of the world. A few institutions—Organization for Economic-Development Cooperation Directorate (OECD-DAC),[1] Collaborative for Development Action (CDA),[2] the Department of Peace Operations of the Romanian Peace Institute (PATRIR),[3] the Global Partnership for the Prevention of Armed Conflict (GPPAC)[4]—are in the forefront for describing them, but many local and regional networks of practitioners and organizations, working in their communities, nationally and internationally, are contributing. Such groups have been drawing together lessons from practitioners and organizations in the field and reflecting on how such information can help with future planning.[5] Current developments focus on cumulative impact assessments and are showing that peace building is not the result of any single engagement or intervention but comes about as a result of the cumulative impact of work done at many levels.[6]

Mediation as a method for resolving conflicts has been studied extensively and refined in important ways. We now have extensive study of the social psychological mechanisms that make it effective under diverse circumstances[7] and detailed examination of real cases providing guidelines for its use in rather difficult circumstances, some prepared by the U.S. Institute for Peace (USIP).[8] The UN Peace Building Portal[9] and Peacemaking Data Bank[10] Web sites are early steps toward online portals for knowledge, lessons identified, and experiences gained in the field.

An increasing number of quality programs are being implemented by organizations, agencies, and governments in the field at every level. Again, OECD-DAC is doing vital and pioneering work in conceptualizing a paradigm for policy development. Significant gaps remain, but the review of experiences is leading to improved methodologies and policies and contributing to the maturation of peace building.

Three: Development of Peace Building Policies

The third major dynamic is the creation of coherent government policies for peace building, crisis prevention, and post-war recovery, as well as the integrating of peace building into other related policy fields, including development, human rights, democratization, and gender equality. In reality there is often a major gap between policy and implementation. Yet overemphasis on what is missing can sometimes make us miss what is developing. Over the past 10 years, some governments have developed clear policies, practical proposals, and doctrines showing deep understanding of how governments can engage in peace building as well as how they can support regional and international organizations and civil society. Some good examples have been developed in the United Kingdom.[11]

Many more could be listed. The three cases cited are pioneering because they linked their proposals with the governments' significant operational and financial support for peace building. At the regional and global level, the United Nations, European Union, African Union, Organization of American States, Association of Southeast Asian Nations (ASEAN) Commonwealth Secretariat, Organization for Security and Cooperation in Europe (OSCE), and OECD are all developing or have developed policy and strategy papers, guidance notes, and operational toolkits for violence prevention, peace building and working with conflict.

Four: Peace Infrastructure

Policy needs to be linked with the institutional capacities and resources to enable effective implementation. Infrastructure refers to physical and organizational structures needed for the functioning of a societal function. In every field of human activity we have developed infrastructure to enhance operational capacity and effectiveness. Health care provides a useful illustration. Medical systems, ambulances, and cardiac intensive care units are not built the moment someone is having a heart attack. In the field of medicine and health, infrastructure and health systems include:

1. Health education in schools
2. Specialized training for nurses, doctors, psychotherapists, pharmacists, and other health professionals, as well as hospital administrators and researchers, with doctors on average receiving five to eight years of specialized training and one to three years of practice as residents
3. The physical buildings of hospitals and pharmacies and all they need to function
4. Government infrastructure, from local authorities to national level departments and ministries of health to ensure that services are accessible and affordable
5. Global infrastructure including the World Health Organization
6. National and international civil society organizations, health clinics, community-based health care services, the Red Cross/Red Crescent and Médecins sans Frontières
7. Infrastructure for rapid response, including ambulances, airlifts, and specifically trained personnel permanently available and ready to respond
8. Research and investment
9. Monitoring practices to improve service
10. Centers for disease control and prevention
11. Local, national, and international medical conferences and professional journals
12. Knowledge management systems that link what is learned and developed in medical practice with training and professional development of medical practitioners

Efforts to prevent illness include relationships with other areas of society: building codes, waste disposal, and design of cities, all influenced by what we have learned in health and medicine.

The infrastructure for war is similarly extensive. The military sector has extensive permanent resources, trained personnel, and support. Infrastructure for resolving conflicts and peace building is, by contrast, more similar to the approach to medicine taken in 14th-century Europe. Becoming sick and dying were considered unalterable parts of the human condition. The health care structures we have created mean that we now live longer, prevent some major epidemics, and cure diseases once viewed as incurable. The same can be true for treating the disease of war.

Violent conflict is still viewed by many as an inevitable part of the human condition. To move from aspiration for peace to realization, we need vision, policies, instruments, trained personnel, and a culture and practice of peace building. In comparison to other social functions, violence prevention, peace-making, peacekeeping, peace education, and peace building are in an early stage of development. Developing these tools is beginning to happen—and is essential—if we want to move from small-scale, ad hoc, sporadic, and often unsuccessful interventions and engagements, to effective peace building and to more enduring transformation of how conflicts are resolved.

The good news is that the infrastructure for peace is developing rapidly. Policy makers and practitioners, previously focused on responding to crises and dealing with the continual outbreak of different conflicts, are increasingly recognizing the need to enhance and improve systematic, standing, and effective capacities for peace building. Examples at the UN include the Peacebuilding Commission, Peace Support Office, Mediation Support Unit, Joint UNDP-DPA (Development Program-Department of Political Affairs) program for strengthening government capacities for conflict resolution, and UNDP's Bureau for Conflict Prevention and Recovery. A European Peace building Liaison Office has been created and the European Union and other regional organizations have set up programs. Many governments now have ministries or departments of peace. The Philippines, Sri Lanka, and Germany now have peace secretariats and commissioners and a Global Alliance for Ministries and Departments of Peace has been established.

Five: Conflict Intelligence

For policy, infrastructure, and operations to be effective in implementation, good conflict intelligence is an essential component. This means the link between understanding of conflict dynamics, root causes, proximate environment, drivers, and the full spectrum of operational conflict analysis; understanding, design, and development of appropriate and effective policy options; engagement strategies; and operational implementation. Coined by the Department of Peace Operations (PATRIR), conflict intelligence is the linking of conflict analysis and understanding with strategic and operational response and implementation of interventions/engagement to address the conflict.

In the last 10 years tools and methodologies for conflict analysis have developed substantially.[12] Some of these include the Department for International Development (DFID)'s *Conflict Assessments*,[13] USAID's *Conflict Vulnerability Index*,[14] the UNDESA's *Developing Capacity for Conflict Analysis and Early Response*,[15] *Working with Conflict: Skills and Strategies for Action*, compiled by the organization Responding to Conflict,[16] Clingendael's *Conflict and Policy Assessment Framework*,[17] the World Bank's *Conflict Analysis Framework*,[18] the Conflict Prevention and Post-Conflict Reconstruction (CPR) Network's[19] *Peace and Conflict Impact Assessment (PCIA) Handbook and Early Warning and Early Response Handbook*,[20] the Collaborative for Development Action's "Do No Harm" methodology,[21] and Swiss Peace's *FAST Methodology for Early Warning*.[22] Far too little has been done to review and compare these different methodologies, to identify strengths and gaps, and connect their methodologies with actual needs of policy makers and practitioners in conflict situations.

In practice today there is little linking between effective knowledge, understanding, and analysis of conflicts and planning and design of actual intervention and policies. Most governments, agencies, and organizations lack appropriate methodologies and processes for conflict intelligence. Improving conflict intelligence is essential to improving the effectiveness and relevance. The Department of Peace Operations' *Quick Reference Guides*,[23] the Clingendael Institute's *Conflict Policy Analysis Frameworks*,[24] DFID's *Guidance Note on Strategic Conflict Analysis*,[25] and the UK Prime Minister's Strategy Unit's *Investing in Prevention*[26] are all steps to link conflict analysis more effectively with development and design of policies and operational implementation. They are new, and have not yet had a significant impact, but they show an important direction of the field. Policies that were adopted, for example for Kosovo, Somalia, Rwanda, or Afghanistan, in many cases showed an absence of effective understanding of the conflict situation and dynamics in those areas, resulting in operations that had negative impacts. The impact of poorly designed interventions and strategies based on poor conflict analysis and understanding can be significant and often severe. Poor conflict intelligence hampers the work of almost all organizations and practitioners working in the field. Although it is one of the weakest areas of peace building today, the rapid and significant improvement in the quality of conflict analysis, mapping incipient incidents, and their potential spread, is one of the most dynamic areas of development in the field. It serves for peace building the absolutely vital function that epidemiology serves for combating disease. And like epidemiology, the link of this research and analysis to the work of practitioners on the ground is a key next step.

Six: Early Warning and Effective Prevention

A major development in the last 20 years has been the rise and improvement of early warning capacity, and the gradual linking of this with effective responses and prevention. We have some very well developed tools and systems. We know how to monitor conflicts to be able to know where and how they gradually escalate over time toward violence. A standard model for an early warning system is presented in David Nyheim's brilliant report for the OECD-DAC, *Can Violence, War, and State Collapse Be Prevented?*[27] The very real possibility of the war in Georgia in August 2008 was obvious for several months in advance. Its roots were evident even before that. The very probable and real possibility of the breakdown of the peace process in Sri Lanka could have been seen at least four years ahead of the renewed outbreak of fighting. In 2004 and again in 2007, discussions were held in Nairobi on the clear potential for violence around elections based on what was already clearly evident in the country at that time. Nyheim's report shows current and early initiatives for early warning systems in Africa, Asia, and Europe, to be poorly developed and not linked directly with existing response and prevention capacities.

The link between prevention and the institutions and capacity to address conflicts effectively is essential. It was often the missing component of earlier early warning systems. You can be warned that you're about to have a heart attack with a pacemaker, but we need people trained in how you respond to cardiac arrest and hospitals that can help if we want to transform "helping that person" to "saving their life." Standing institutional capacity, human resources, and a culture of prevention and peace building are essential components of effective early warning and prevention. The Nyheim report shows that knowledge and capacity to develop effective early warning and prevention systems has begun. We have placed human beings on the moon and cured diseases once thought to be incurable. Early warning and prevention is possible, but investment and commitment are needed to make it operational and effective.

Seven: Improved Training and Professional Development

More localized infrastructure, some NGO based, is clearly evident in training. Training for community-based mediation units and peace teams has expanded. In the last 15 years, the number of training organizations internationally and the number of training programs taking place has been increasing steeply. Notably, the number and variety of people taking these programs is also increasing: senior government officials, civil servants, aid and development practitioners and policy makers, UN staff and staff of national and international organizations, journalists and media professionals, teachers, current and former combatants and military personnel, mediators, and students. Programs range from the generic to highly specialized and advanced.

The growth in training is happening among college-and university-based peace studies and the number of degree programs, available today on all continents, has grown. Peace journals are flourishing and peace media have taken root, often electronically.

An essential ingredient of good educational programs is a close link with practical experience and operations in the field, and with the development of thinking at the operational and policy levels. Many peace studies programs still do not have this. Those who graduate should have knowledge, skills, and capacities to do peace building in practice much as we would expect from a graduating doctor or airplane pilot. Working with conflicts and preventing, stopping, or assisting in recovering from the visible and invisible impacts of war and violence are immeasurably more complicated than any disciplinary set of academic principles would suggest.

Increasingly, training academies, such as that of International Alert,[28] forumZFD,[29] and the International Peace and Development Training Centre (IPDTC),[30] are linking together, and working with organizations and agencies—state and non-state—that are deploying people to the field to improve the depth and quality of their preparation of adult professionals. An important aspect of this is mapping the competencies that people actually need when they carry out this work and seeing how to prepare them effectively and to assess them. The European Group on Training (EGT)[31] was also an important initiative to consolidate knowledge and experience of academies providing training for government officials in peace building, conflict transformation, and crisis management and prevention. As the quality of these programs improves, and as more people go through them, this will increasingly impact the quality and skills of those working in the field—leading to improved peace building in policy and practice.

Realism is needed, though. Two-day, five-day, or one-month trainings are not enough. Surgeons, architects, or scientists do not learn their fields in two-day, five-day, or one-month programs and practitioners overly reliant on limited methodologies may not be able to address effectively the range of settings they find. Learning the art of active listening is probably central to most programs. This has been fundamental for many of the best practitioners who have not actually gone through training programs, but have found other ways to train and to develop their knowledge, including constant practice, in-depth reflection, and assessment. Yet much has been learned and training can contribute to a more respectful, serious, and realistic approach to skills and professional development.

Eight: Improved Funding

While every experienced practitioner and policy maker has recognized a need for much more funding, the last 20 years have seen a marked improvement for the field. Still, many peacekeeping and peace building organizations face potential bankruptcy and constantly need to raise minimal resources to do essential work. Governments, the European Union, and the UN, however, together with private donors and foundations, are giving considerably more support than in the past 20 years. A key task now is to assess lessons learned from donor support for peace building to improve quality and effectiveness. The Utstein Report of the British, German, Norwegian, and Dutch governments[32] was an important step. Extensive evaluations have been done on country-by-country basis and of individual donor programs. What has not yet been carried out, is a more thorough, cross-country, cross-donor comparative assessment, engaging donors, practitioners, and policy makers in identifying how funding can be done more effectively to support peace building in practice. In the Progress Report of the Secretary-General of the United Nations on the Prevention of Armed Conflict,[33] then Secretary-General of the UN Kofi Annan importantly called on all member states to improve infrastructure and architecture for peace building, to improve coordination and cooperation among the different agencies and actors in the field, and to improve the scale of funding for peace building.

Nine: Improved Networking and Cooperation

There are considerable improvements in networking and cooperation. The Global Partnership for the Prevention of Armed Conflict (GPPAC),[34] along with its regional platforms, has played a major role. Across Asia, practitioners are linking together in the Asian Peace Builders Forums.[35] In many countries, national platforms linking organizations have been established. The European Network of Civil Peace Services[36] effectively links both existing peace services and national initiatives to establish professionally trained civil peace services across Europe, helping the organizations involved learn from each others' work. There are also specific associations for trainers, mediators, DDR experts, those working on gender and UN Resolution 1325, and organizations working to affect government policies on peace building. Researchers, academics, and others working anywhere in the world with access to the Internet can link together on the Peace and

Collaborative Development Network established by Craig Zelizer.[37] Those
working in the broad field of peace building are also improving collaboration
and cross-fertilization with people from other fields. Increasingly, cooperation is also happening across sectors—state and non-state, UN, governments, and NGOs.

Ten: A Collaborative Field

Peace building is becoming a collaborative field. Organizations, agencies,
practitioners, scholars, and the broad spectrum of those involved are often
working together. From the 1950s until today, there were many geniuses,
"giants," and gurus, who did incredible pioneering work, and a lot of people
looked at them like gods on mountains. They were seen as the sources of all
knowledge for anything to do with peace work. Today we are building on
their pioneering work by learning from and with each other. An increasingly
creative, committed, collaborative field is developing, with perhaps greater
respect and humility for the scale of the challenges we face, and a deeper willingness and commitment to build and work together authentically.

Eleven: Lessons Identified/Learned

At the heart of the field today is learning from experience. This is a complex and challenging task. So much is being carried out around the world that
a great deal of experience is never reflected on. Thousands of medical operations are conducted, and even though a great deal of experience is lost, an
awesome amount is gathered and transferred back into reflection in the field
and training and education of existing and new practitioners. Peace building
needs to do the same. The field as a whole is too sporadic, ad hoc, and does
not systematically learn from what has been done elsewhere. Even the shortcomings of modern medicine's over-reliance on technological fixes and failures
to recognize strengths and wisdom of patients and communities can ideally
provide one of the lessons for the field of peace building The last 10 years,
however, have seen the most significant advance of the field. The studies and
publications cited earlier are examples of efforts to gather and learn from
experiences. Governments, policy makers, and practitioners all need to understand the importance of committing space, time, and resources to the task.

Twelve: Streamlining and Coherence: Intrinsic Peace Building

A twelfth dynamic represents one of the most important developments
in the field. This is the transition from intervention-based/dependent peace

building and conflict transformation to intrinsic and systemic, or streamlined peace building. Examples of intervention-based approaches are local,
national, or external NGOs carrying out specific programs for peace education in schools; training teachers for peace education; facilitating interventions for justice or policing reform; or advocating for governments to adopt
more peace building-based approaches to conflicts. These are time-bound
(often framed as projects) and carried out by agents external to a sector trying to have an impact. The importance and need for this will remain. Intrinsic or streamlined peace building, however, is when the sectors and/or
systems have integrated and included peace building approaches and capacities into their basic knowledge, doctrine, and operating cultures, systems,
and practices; for example, when all teachers are trained in peace education
as part of the teacher training system; when courts, legal, and police systems have peace building, restorative justice, and effective, constructive
approaches to addressing conflicts built into them; and when governments
have standing, institutionalized peace building capacities and clear, coherent
peace building strategies, policies, and the political commitment and practice to use them.

Plus One

A final dynamic is the growing rejection of war and violence as an acceptable and/or legitimate means of addressing conflicts. Opposition comes
from local communities in war and violence-affected settings around the
world and was visible during the global demonstrations of millions of people against the war in Iraq. Politicians, policy and decision makers, doctors,
academics, military officers and soldiers, journalists, students, artists: people from all backgrounds and walks of life are increasingly recognizing that
violence—and the massive investment in military and war systems—produces incredible devastation, destruction, and misuse of human resources,
intelligence, capacities, and life. This chapter has tried to highlight some
key dynamics happening in the field today. It has also shown how some of
the essential building blocks for peace building, steps we have taken in
many other fields of human endeavor, have not yet advanced far enough into
the complex tasks of peace building, violence prevention, and post-war recovery. A paradigm shift is taking place. The doctrine that "If we wish for
peace, prepare for war" is increasingly recognized for what it is: a doctrine
that leads to increasing war and violence. It is being replaced, with a more
realistic understanding that "If we wish for peace, prepare for peace."
    Gaps and challenges remain, but the preparations already begun are
truly impressive. With all that is being done, how is it that wars such as

those in Iraq, Afghanistan, Israel-Palestine, Darfur, and the Congo continue? What have been identified are dynamics and/or trends—work that has been pioneered and that is beginning to reach new levels. They are some of the *frontiers* of peace building. The answer to the question of whether they develop to the point where they can become truly effective—to the point where wars such as those in Iraq, Afghanistan, Israel-Palestine, Darfur, and the Congo can be ended and, better still, prevented—depends on the choices we make.

NOTES

1. Development Co-operation Directorate.
2. CDA Collaborative Learning Project.
3. Patrir, Devastating Development – Costing Lives: The True Impacts of Armed Violence and the Cost of Not Investing in Prevention."
4. Global Partnership for the Prevention of Armed Conflict.
5. Reychler and Paffenholz, 2001; Lederach and Jenner, 2002.
6. "Reflecting on Peace Practice" (CDA); Anderson and Olsen, 2003; Lederach, 2005; Collaborative for Development Action's *Theories of Change*.
7. Deutch and Marcus, 2006.
8. Crocker, et al., 2001, 2004.
9. See "Peacebuilding Portal."
10. See United Nations Peacemaker.
11. See the UK Department for International Development (DFID), 2006; UK Government, 2007; "Investing in Prevention – A Prime Minister's Strategy Unit Report to the UK Government," 2005; In Germany see German Development Cooperation: Strategy for Peace-Building, 2005; In Sweden see Government Offices of Sweden. 2001.
12. For a listing of major conflict analysis tools and methodologies developed by a range of organizations and agencies in the field today see the Department of Peace Operations *Quick Reference Guide*, 8.
13. UK Department for International Development, 2002.
14. Stanley Samarasinghe, et al., 2001.
15. UN Department of Economic and Social Affairs, n,d.
16. Responding to Conflict.
17. Conflict Sensitivity Consortium, 2000.
18. Wam and Sardesai, 2005.
19. Conflict Prevention and Post-conflict Restoration Network.
20. Conflict Prevention and Post-conflict Restoration Network, 2005.
21. Collaborative for Development Action, n.d.
22. Anderson, 1999.
23. International Peace and Development Training Center (IPDTC).
24. Conflict Sensitivity Consortium, 2000.
25. Department for International Development, n,d.
26. Governance and Social Development Resource Centre, 2005.

27. Nyheim, 2008.
28. International Alert.
29. The European Network for Civil Peace Services (ENCPS).
30. Peace Action Training and Research Institute of Romania (PATRIR).
31. European Group on Training (EGT).
32. Smith, 2004.
33. UN General Assembly, 2006.
34. Global Partnership for the Prevention of Armed Conflict.
35. Action Asia.
36. The European Network for Civil Peace Services (ENCPS).
37. Peace and Collaborative Development Network.

CHAPTER 3

Our Water Commons: Toward a New Freshwater Narrative

Maude Barlow

The world's water crisis due to pollution, climate change and a surging population growth is of such magnitude that close to 2 billion people now live in water-stressed regions of the planet. By the year 2025, two-thirds of the world's population will face water scarcity. The global population tripled in the 20th century, but water consumption went up sevenfold. By 2050, after we add another three billion to the population, humans will need an 80 percent increase in water supplies just to feed ourselves. No one knows where this water is going to come from.

—*Blue Covenant: The Global Water Crisis and the*
Coming Battle for the Right to Water, 2007 [1]

There are two competing narratives about the Earth's freshwater resources being played out in the 21st century. On one side is a powerful clique of decision makers, heads of some powerful states, international trade and financial institutions and transnational corporations who do not view water as part of the global Commons or a public trust, but as a commodity, to be bought and sold on the open market. On the other is a global grassroots

A longer version of this article was first published by the Council of Canadians and The Commons in 2008.

movement of local communities, the poor and slum dwellers, women, indigenous peoples, peasants and small farmers working with environmentalists, human rights activists, progressive water managers, and experts in both the global North and the global South who see water as a Commons and seek to provide water for all of nature and all humans.

In recent years, some very important work has been done to create a renewed awareness of an ancient concept known as "the Commons." In most traditional societies, it was assumed that what belonged to one belonged to all. Many indigenous societies to this day cannot conceive of denying a person or a family basic access to food, air, land, water, and livelihood. Many modern societies extended the same concept of universal access to the notion of a social Commons, creating education, health care, and social security for all members of the community. Since adopting the Universal Declaration of Human Rights in 1948, governments are obliged to protect the human rights, cultural diversity, and food security of their citizens.

When governments do not adequately protect the Commons on our behalf, they fail us, the Commons, and future generations. Business exists to perform in the market and will do so until constrained by governments. The market and its values dominate over all sectors of society and the environment. This domination weakens communities and local economies, harnesses scientific inquiry for the advancement of private industry, undermines democracy, and proliferates an unsustainable global economy. The Commons need not result in tragedy if the right structures are put in place.

There is no better example of a runaway market engine than the corporate cartel now being created to own and profit from water. Private-sector interest in the world's dwindling water resources has been building for two decades, and has dramatically increased in recent years. Transnational corporations view water as a saleable and tradable commodity, not a Commons, and are set to create a cartel resembling the one that now controls every facet of energy, from exploration to production to distribution. Private, for-profit water companies now provide municipal water services in many parts of the world; put massive amounts of fresh water in bottles for sale; control vast quantities of water used in industrial farming, mining, energy production, computers, cars, and other water-intensive industries; own and operate many of the dams, pipelines, nanotechnology, water purification systems, and desalination plants government are looking to for the technological panacea to water shortages; provide infrastructure technologies to replace old municipal water systems; control the virtual trade in water; buy up groundwater rights and whole watersheds to own large quantities of water stock; and trade in shares in an industry set to increase its profits dramatically in the coming years.

The notion of water as a commodity did not happen in a vacuum. It was deliberately imposed on the global South by global institutions and water companies (and their governments) in an open attempt to capitalize on the desperate water crisis in poor countries. There was more than a little hypocrisy in foisting private water services on the South by countries that had been well served by public systems. In Europe and North America, public delivery of water helped to create the political stability and financial equity necessary for the great advances of the industrial age. As well, it was understood that public water and sanitation services protected public health and advanced national economic development. With few exceptions, these countries still understand the benefit of water as a Commons and continue to provide water as a public service. However, the World Bank and the big water companies set out to promote a major shift in water policy in the global South (a model they have gone on to try to sell in the North) by actively seeking the buy-in of nongovernmental organizations, think tanks, state agencies, the media, and the private sector to manufacture consent for the commodification of water. When the carrot of persuasion failed, the World Bank used the stick of financial compliance.

The privatization of water services has been a terrible failure in almost every community where it has been tried, and it is far from certain that privatization of the water Commons will accelerate at the same rate. Water commodification has left a legacy of corruption, sky-high water rates, cutoffs of water to millions of people, reduced water quality, nepotism, pollution, worker lay-offs, and broken promises. A multitude of studies has shown that private water companies have not brought new investments into the global South.[2] In fact, because both the lending banks and the development agencies of many wealthy countries assumed that privatization would bring in new water services investment, they pulled back on their own investments, resulting in a net loss in funding to provide water to the global South over the last 15 years—the very time when demand was exploding. Studies have also found that the big water transnationals have so much power with the World Bank and other regional development banks, that they actually often decide which countries and communities will receive bank aid, ensuring that poor countries with no possibility of profit for the companies are left behind.[3] The story is now repeating itself in municipalities in the global North that have opted for a for-profit water system.

Perhaps there is no better example of the enclosure of the water Commons than bottled water. Humans take free-flowing water from its natural state, put it in plastic bottles, and sell it to one another at exorbitant prices.

In the early 1970s, about 1 billion liters of bottled water were sold globally. In 2007, more than 200 billion liters (50 billion gallons) were consumed, and the bottled water industry is growing at over 10 percent a year. Because bottled water costs anywhere from 240 to 10,000 times more than tap water, depending on the brand, profits are very high in this sector. The bottled water industry is conservatively estimated to bring in $100 billion annually. There is a growing backlash against this form of enclosure of the water Commons. The bottled water industry is now understood to be one of the most polluting on Earth as well as one of the least regulated. Plastic water bottles are made up of chemicals and fossil fuels that leach into groundwater and human bodies. Nearly one-quarter of all bottled water crosses national borders to reach consumers, using enormous amounts of energy to transport. One million bottles of exported bottled water cause the emission of 18.2 tons of carbon dioxide. Fewer than 5 percent of bottled water containers are recycled. Water extraction for bottled water is draining communities all over the world, from the Great Lakes of North America to the rural villages of India. In most places, bottled water corporations pay little or no extraction fees, openly profiting from the local water Commons, and favored by governments over the needs of local communities.

A more recent form of water Commons enclosure is the practice of relying on high-technology solutions to the global water crisis instead of protecting the source waters of the water Commons. Far more attention is being paid (and billions of dollars annually invested) to cleaning up dirty water using expensive high water-reuse technology, than in stopping pollution and the destruction of the water Commons itself. The water industry's technology sector is growing at twice the rate of its utility sector and already accounts for more than one-quarter of all revenues. Desalination is one of the key technologies being touted. Global demand is expected to grow by 25 percent every year for decades, with capital investments of at least $60 billion in the next decade. There are 30 plants planned for the coast of California alone.[4] Due to the high-energy requirements of desalination, there are plans to build nuclear-powered desalination plants in several countries.[5]

There are three major problems with the abandonment of water as a Commons and the adoption of water as a commodity.

The first problem is that there is no profit in conservation. In fact, it is to the distinct advantage of the private water industry that the world's freshwater Commons are being polluted and destroyed. Even if individual corporate leaders do not take pleasure in the global water crisis, it is exactly this crisis that is driving profits in their industry. The market will favor those companies that maximize profit and, in the water business, that means taking advantage of a dwindling supply that cannot meet a growing demand.

Further, with governments, industries, and universities investing so heavily in the burgeoning water clean-up technology industry, there is less and less incentive at every level to emphasize source protection and conservation.

The second major concern around the commodification of water is that with no regulatory oversight or government control, there will be no protections for the natural world, and a need to safeguard integrated ecosystems from water plundering. As it is now in most parts of the world, governments have little knowledge of where their groundwater sources are located, or how much water they contain. Consequently, they have no idea how much pumping they can maintain or if current water mining operations are sustainable. The more private interests control water supplies, the less government and public interests have to say about them. The commodification of water is really the commodification of nature. If water in the future will only be accessible to those who can pay for it, who will buy it for nature?

The third problem with the commodification of water is that water, and water infrastructure—from drinking water and sanitation utilities services, to bottled water, clean-up technologies, and nuclear-powered desalination plants—will flow where the money is, not where it is needed. No corporation is in business to deliver water to the poor. That, say corporate leaders, is the job of governments. People who cannot pay do not get served. Already, wealthy countries like Saudi Arabia and Israel are dependent on expensive water purification technologies for their day-to-day living, while equally water-starved countries such as Namibia and Pakistan cannot afford such technology, and so their citizens suffer from severe water shortages. Bottled water is the exclusive prerogative of those who can pay for it, as is clean water from the tap in many parts of the world.

From thousands of local struggles for the basic right to water, galvanized through international resistance to the denial of rights, a highly organized and mature global water justice movement has been forged and is shaping the future of the world's water Commons. To the question, "who owns water?" they say, "no one—it belongs to the Earth, all species and future generations." The demands of the movement are simple but powerful: keep water public; keep it clean; keep it accessible to all. In other words, keep it in the Commons. The reclamation of the water Commons converges around three struggles.

THE COMMONS SOLUTION

This unparalleled environmental crisis can only be met and reversed through the lived affirmation that water is a Commons that belongs to everyone and therefore, any harm to water is a harm to the whole—Earth and humans alike. All over the world, groups and communities are confronting the twin engines of water pollution: industrial agriculture and industrial production for a global economy. The move to local, sustainable agriculture is growing everywhere as people question the wisdom of using fossil fuels to move food grown with chemicals and irradiated to prevent decay, over long distances to their dinner tables. The sales of organic food are soaring at about 20 percent a year, well ahead of the regular food industry, and the Slow Food Movement now claims 100,000 members in more than 100 countries. A survey done for the University of Surrey in Great Britain found that organic food consumers share the common (Commons) values of protection of their own health and the health of others, as well as of the environment at large. Community Supported Agriculture (CSA), where local families and communities support local farms, are growing daily. (One of the key goals of the network Our World Is Not For Sale in fighting the power of the World Trade Organization is to prevent the ability of transnational corporations to use trade rules to challenge local regulations and practices that favor the local, sustainable production of food, and therefore the protection of the local water Commons.)

One of the definitions of a Commons is that it is accessible to all without discrimination. The greatest indictment of our collective abandonment of the notion that water is a Commons is the water apartheid now suffered by the poor and disenfranchised of the global South.[6] Almost 2 billion people live in water-stressed regions of the planet; of those, 1.4 billion have little or no access to clean drinking water every day. Not surprisingly, most of these 1.4 billion live in poor countries in the global South and suffer unbearable hardships at the loss of their water Commons. Two-fifths of the world's people lack access to basic sanitation, leading to a return of communicable diseases like cholera and the plague, once thought extinct. Half the world's hospital beds are occupied by people with an easily preventable water-borne disease and the World Health Organization reports that contaminated water is implicated in 80 percent of all sickness and disease worldwide.[7] More children die every year from dirty water than war, malaria, HIV/AIDS, and traffic accidents together. In the last decade, the number of children killed by diarrhea exceeded the number of people killed in all armed conflicts since World War II. Every eight seconds, a child dies from water-borne disease. The average North American uses almost 600 liters (150 gallons) of water a day. The average African uses just six. A newborn baby in the global North consumes between 40 and 70 times more water than a baby in the global South.

Water apartheid will not end until we declare water to be a public Commons accessible to all. The global water justice movement is of one voice that water must be seen as a basic human right and must not be denied to anyone because of the inability to pay. In communities all around the world, local groups have resisted the privatization of their water services and won. For these tireless campaigners, the right to water and the concept of water as a Commons are one and the same. In response to intense public pressure under the leadership of a grassroots group called FEJUVE, the Bolivian government of Evo Morales recently ousted the private water company Suez from the capital, La Paz, after a disastrous 10-year contract to manage the city's water. In a ceremony marking the return of Bolivia's water to public ownership, President Morales said that water must remain a basic service so that everyone can have the water they need for life.

As well, citizens are not waiting for their governments in taking the lead on asserting the human right to water. On October 31, 2004, the citizens of Uruguay became the first in the world to vote for the right to water. Led by Friends of the Earth Uruguay and the National Commission in Defense of Water and Life, the groups first had to obtain almost 300,000 signatures on a plebiscite (which they delivered to Parliament as a "human river") to get a referendum placed on the ballot of the national election calling for a constitutional amendment on the right to water.

Several other countries have also passed right to water legislation. South Africa, Ecuador, Ethiopia, and Kenya also have references in their constitutions that describe water as a human right (but do not specify the need for public delivery). The Belgian Parliament passed a resolution in April 2005 seeking a constitutional amendment to recognize water as a human right and in September 2006, the French Senate adopted an amendment to its water bill that says each person has the right to access to clean water, but neither country makes reference to delivery. The only other country besides Uruguay to specify in its constitution that water must be publicly delivered is the Netherlands, which passed a law in 2003 restricting the delivery of drinking water to utilities that are entirely public and, in March 2008, announced its full support for a right-to-water constitutional amendment.

Other exciting initiatives are under way. In August 2006, the Indian Supreme Court ruled that protection of natural lakes and ponds is akin to honoring the right to life—the most fundamental right of all according to the Court. Activists in Nepal are going before their Supreme Court arguing that hiring a private firm to manage the drinking water system in Kathmandu violates the right to health guaranteed in the country's constitution. The Coalition Against Water Privatization in South Africa is challenging the practice of water metering before the Johannesburg High Court on the basis that it violates the human rights of Soweto's poor. Bolivian President Evo Morales has called for a "South American convention for human rights and access for all living beings to water" that would reject the market model imposed in trade agreements. At least a dozen countries have reacted positively to this call. Civil society groups are hard at work in many other countries to introduce constitutional amendments similar to that of Uruguay. Colombia's Ecofondo has launched a plebiscite toward a constitutional amendment similar to the Uruguayan amendment. They need at least 1.5 million signatures and face several court cases and a dangerous and hostile opposition. Dozens of groups in Mexico have joined COMDA, the Mexican Coalition for the Right to Water, in a national campaign for a Uruguayan-type constitutional guarantee to the right to water.

While these and countless other initiatives are taking place within a framework of the Commons, they are not yet seen by either all the groups themselves, or society at large, in a Commons context. Although most are using language that Commons pioneers cited in this chapter would identify as fully compatible with the notion of the Commons, the concept is still new for many in our world. A reframing of this work from a Commons perspective could help the work of the whole movement and act as a unifying force.

It is time for a new language of the Commons, one that claims water for people and nature for all time. A new water narrative could be based on the following 10 principles.

1. Declare Water to Be a Commons

Who owns water? That is the key question. A new water narrative must assert that no one owns water; rather, it belongs to the Earth and all species alike. As Vandana Shiva explains, because it is a flow resource necessary for life and ecosystem health, and because there is no substitute for it, water must be regarded as a public Commons and a public good and preserved as such for all time in law and practice.[8] The creation of a worldwide water cartel is wrong, ethically, environmentally, and socially and ensures that the decisions regarding the allocation of water are made based on commercial, not environmental or social, concerns. Private ownership of water cannot address itself to the issues of conservation, justice, or democracy—the underpinnings of a solution to the world's water crisis. Only citizens and their governments, acting on their behalf, can operate on these principles. Water companies thrive on pollution and scarcity and on the growing desperation for water in many parts of the world. Water must be understood to be part of the global Commons, but clearly subject to local, democratic, and public management.

No one has the right to appropriate water for personal profit while others are being denied access because of an inability to pay for it. Water should not be privatized, traded for profit, stored for future sale, or exported for commercial purposes. Governments must declare their domestic water Commons a public good and take responsibility for delivering clean, safe water as a public service to all their citizens. All decisions regarding the water Commons must be made transparently and with democratic oversight. This is not to say there is no place for the private sector in alleviating the global water crisis, as long as corporations are not running the water services directly. For instance, there is and will be a place for the private sector in providing water re-use technology and the building of water infrastructure. But all private sector activity must come under strict public oversight and government accountability, and would have to operate within a mandate where the goals are conservation and water justice. The high-tech water companies, in particular, need public oversight to ensure the wastewater returning to the water supply has met high quality assurance standards.

2. Adopt an Earth Democracy Narrative

Modern society has lost its reverence for water's sacred place in the cycle of life, as well as its centrality in the realm of the spirit. This loss of reverence for water has allowed humans to abuse the water Commons. Over time, we have come to believe that humanity, not nature, is at the center of the universe; whatever we run out of can be imported, replaced with something else, or fixed with sophisticated technology. We have forgotten that we are also a species of animal that needs water for life. Only by redefining our relationship to water and recognizing its essential and sacred place in nature can we begin to rectify the wrongs we have done. Only by considering the full impact of our decisions on the ecosystem can we ever hope to replenish depleted water systems and protect those that are still unharmed.

Albert Einstein said that no crisis can be solved with the same thinking that created it. It is likely impossible to assert a new water Commons narrative within the current global economic model. A system driven by the imperatives of market expansion, export competition, unlimited growth, and corporate power will not easily accommodate to a definition of water as a common good. To truly adopt the notion of water as a Commons requires a challenge to the tenets of economic globalization and the adoption of a new set of assumptions, values, and models for trade, commerce, development, and production. All systems now in place must be judged against their impact on the world's water resources. Growth in and of itself is anathema to the protection of the Earth's dwindling water supplies, and unregulated capitalism places far too much power in the hands of chief executive officers (CEOs) whose sole mandate is to generate profits. This system must be abandoned in favor of one based on the notions of cooperation, sustainability, equity, democratic control, and subsidiarity (if something can be grown, produced, or managed locally, it should be favored over a regional, national, or international solution). In this model, the private sector would be held to high standards and public scrutiny.

3. Protect Water through Conservation and Law

The most important demonstration of a new water narrative would be a commitment to protect and conserve the water Commons for all time. Water Commons sustainability means protecting source water at every level, reclaiming polluted water, and conserving water for the future. As American water pioneer Sandra Postel explains, we must learn to use very drop of water twice. Each generation must ensure that the abundance and quality of water is not diminished as a result of its activities. This will mean radically changing our habits, especially those of us who live in the global North. If we do not change our ways, any reluctance to share our water—even for sound environmental reasons—will rightly be called into question. The key is to stop polluting surface waters to allow local communities to return to the use of their rivers, lakes, and streams for the majority of their water needs, lifting the burden off groundwater supplies. Primary sewage treatment must be an international aid priority for the global South and infrastructure repair of leaking urban water systems everywhere must be implemented. The rule of law must be brought to bear on polluting industries at home and abroad. (Legislation would include penalties for domestic corporations that pollute on foreign soil. Such penalties could form part of a fund to pay for infrastructure repair.) Rigorous laws must be passed to control water pollution from industrial agriculture, municipal discharge, and industrial contaminants. Flood irrigation, which wastes massive amounts of water, must be replaced by drip irrigation and more sustainable water use. The rush to adopt water-guzzling industrial biofuels as an alternative to fossil fuels must be halted. Water abuse in oil and methane gas production must stop, requiring conservation of energy supplies and the adoption of alternative renewable energy sources. Water conservation practices must be adopted everywhere. Examples in the industrialized world include water-saving washing machines, low-flow shower faucets, and low-flush or composting toilets.

4. Treat Watersheds as a Commons

The mass transfer of water from wilderness and ecosystems, combined with the loss of water-retentive landscape, has displaced much habitat for the water Commons. Perhaps there is no greater right than the right of a drop of water to come back to the watersheds and water systems that nourish all life and maintain the integrity of the water Commons. Without this habitat, water cannot fulfill its ecosystem function and is lost as a nature Commons. Unless we protect water and its right to flow freely in nature, water will never be seen as a Commons, but rather a commodity to be moved around to serve industrialized humanity and our modern "needs." Nature put water where it belongs. Tampering with nature by moving large-scale water supplies from an ecosystem by pipeline or through virtual water exports has the potential to destroy whole watersheds and all that depend on watershed health, including indigenous peoples. By practicing bioregionalism—living within and adapting to the ecological constraints of a watershed—we honor the narrative of water as a Commons not only for humans, but also for nature and other species. One powerful example is the clear-cutting of mountains for timber or to build ski resorts and adult sports playgrounds. Mountains are the "water towers" of our world. They hold and retain water, snow, and ice that often provide the only water sources in a region. When their capacity to store water is reduced by the strip-mining of their trees and shrubs, people and nature alike suffer severe consequences. To protect watersheds and water sustainability, every human activity will have to be measured against its impact on the water Commons and water's natural habitat.

5. Assert Community Control over Local Water Sources

Another defining feature of water as a Commons is that its sustainable and equitable allocation depends on cooperation among community members. As a common good, water is managed with the community's solidarity and full democratic participation. This is very different from a corporate model of water distribution, which is based on individual ability to pay, not need. Local stewardship, not private business, expensive technology, or even government, is the best guardian of the water Commons. Local citizens and communities are the front-line "keepers" of the rivers, lakes, and groundwater supplies on which they depend for life. If reclamation projects or water delivery systems are not guided by the common sense and lived experience of the local community, they will not be sustained. The management models of indigenous populations and rural communities must be enhanced, as they have proved to be the real preserver of the water Commons. States must not only recognize these local rights, but also protect them in law, and provide the authority to local communities to exercise their stewardship effectively.

6. Maintain Water Sovereignty for Both Communities and Nation

Adopting (or re-adopting) the notion of a water Commons does not mean a free-for–all, or that anyone can help themselves to the water in others' territories. A basic principle of the water Commons (that is compatible with both watershed protection and local control) is that water is a sovereign good and cannot be taken from another country or community by force or by using economic dominance. Many countries are running out of water and the race is on to secure new water supplies. Before the new government of Evo Morales put a stop to it, the former government of Bolivia was planning to sell water to the foreign-based mining companies in Chile, a move strongly opposed by the majority of Bolivians. Israelis, who are supposed to share water resources with Palestinians, have access to five times as much water. Libya used its regional super-power status to build the biggest pipeline in the world to date to remove water from an aquifer under the Sahara Desert, water that should equally belong to Chad, Sudan, and Egypt. A plan to build a water pipeline from southern Nevada in the United States to Las Vegas has people in Nevada up in arms.

7. Adopt a Model of Water Justice, Not Charity

The water Commons narrative is based on a belief in justice, not charity. Although it is admirable that many people and groups from the global North assist the poor of the global South by building wells to link them up to groundwater sources, this is only a stop-gap measure. Billions of people live in countries that cannot provide clean water to their citizens not only because they are water poor, but because they are burdened by their debts to the North through loans from the World Bank and the International Monetary Fund. As a result, poor countries are forced to exploit both their people and their water resources. At least 62 countries currently need deep debt relief if the daily deaths of thousands of children are to end. Further, foreign aid in many wealthy countries is well below the recommended 0.7 percent of the gross domestic product (GDP). If the World Bank, the United Nations, and northern countries were serious about providing clean water for all, they would cancel or deeply cut the global South debt; substantively increase foreign aid; fund public, instead of private, services; tell their big bottling companies to stop draining poor countries dry; and invest in water reclamation programs to protect source water.

Special mention must be made of two groups feeling the brunt of water inequity: women and indigenous people. Women carry out 80 percent of water-related work throughout the world and therefore carry the greatest burden of water inequity. Ensuring water for all is a critical component of gender equality and women's empowerment, along with environmental security and poverty eradication. The more policy making about water is moved from local communities to a global level (the World Bank for instance), the less power women have to determine who gets it and under what circumstances. As the primary collectors of water throughout the world, women must be recognized as major stakeholders in the decision-making process. Indigenous people are particularly vulnerable to water theft and appropriation, and their proprietary rights to their land and water must be protected by governments.

8. Restore Public Delivery and Fair Pricing

A new water narrative must establish once and for all that water is a public Commons to be delivered as a public service by governments at a fair and accessible price. This means that the international financial agencies responsible for providing aid to poor countries for water development must shift their focus from public/private/partnerships (PPPs), which promote the big, private water utilities, to public/public/partnerships (PUPs), which transfer funding and expertise from successful public systems in the global North to provide local management and workers in the global South with the necessary funds and skills to deliver water on a not-for-profit basis to all their citizens. PUPs are a mechanism for providing capacity building for these countries, either through Water Operator Partnerships, whereby established public systems transfer expertise and skills to those in need, or through projects whereby public institutions such as public sector unions or public pension fund boards use their resources to support public water services in developing countries. The objective is to provide local management and workers with the necessary skills to deliver water and provide wastewater services to the public.

Examples of successful PUPs include partnerships between Stockholm and Helsinki water authorities and the former Soviet Union countries of Estonia, Latvia, and Lithuania and between Amsterdam Water and cities in Indonesia and Egypt. Public Services International asserts that if each effectively functioning public water utility in the world were to "adopt" just three cities in need, public/public/partnerships could operate on a global basis, and provide water to all those in need at a fraction of the cost now encountered supporting the private companies. This would also become a concrete example of how cooperation over water could be a uniting force for humanity. Financing public water in poor countries will need a combination of progressive central government taxation, micro-financing, and cooperatives to run the systems on a day-to-day basis.

9. Enshrine the Right to Water in Nation-State Constitutions and a UN Covenant

The new water narrative described here must be codified in law. It is finally time for the world to agree that water is not a "need," but a "right," codified at every level of government, from local municipal bylaws and nation-state constitutions, to a binding United Nations Covenant. The global water crisis cries out for good governance, and good governance needs a legal basis that rests on universally applicable human rights. A UN Covenant would set the framework for water as a social and cultural asset, not an economic commodity. It would establish the indispensable legal groundwork for a just system of distribution of the water Commons. It would serve as a common, coherent body of rules for all nations, rich and poor, and clarify that it is the role of the state to provide clean affordable water to all of its citizens. Such a Covenant would also safeguard already accepted human rights and environmental principles in other UN treaties and conventions. A UN Covenant would bind nations to an agreement not only to refrain from any action or policy that interferes with the right to water, but also would obligate them to prevent third parties, such as corporations, from interfering in that right. It would give ordinary citizens a powerful tool with which to argue their right to clean affordable water and put the spotlight on governments refusing to fulfill their obligations.

There are those in the water Commons community who question the value of working on the right to water, particularly at the level of the UN. One concern is that the UN, like the powerful governments that control it, has adopted a Western-style, individualist approach to rights that is contrary to the notion of collective rights embodied in the Commons. A second is that it is too human-centered and not rooted in an ecosystem framework. While both of these concerns are valid (and apparent in the reflections of some countries' UN delegations), a right-to-water Covenant does not have to reflect this worldview, but could be written to promote a more holistic one. Well constructed, it could enshrine the sovereignty of local communities over their natural heritage and therefore the management of their water Commons, including watersheds and aquifers. As Friends of the Earth Paraguay explains, "The very mention of the supposed conflict, water for human use versus water for nature, reflects a lack of consciousness of the essential fact that the very existence of water depends on the sustainable management and conservation of ecosystems." A third concern is that the right to water is not practical on a day-to-day basis for communities, particularly in the global South, struggling for water survival. But the citizen movements in many communities and countries in the South have already adopted, or are working to adopt, constitutional amendments to guarantee water as a right, with specific and immediately noticeable ramifications. The definition of the right to water need not belong to the same people who created economic globalization, but could be integral to the struggle of local people everywhere fighting for their water Commons.

10. Use and Expand the Public Trust Doctrine to Protect Water

Finally, the notion of a water Commons could be profoundly advanced if we had a body of law that recognized the inherent rights of the environment, other species, and water itself outside of their usefulness to humans. The move to create "wild law" comes to some extent out of the Public Trust Doctrine, first codified in 529 A.D. as Codex Justinianus, after the emperor of that period, who said, "By the laws of nature, these things are common to all mankind: the air, running water, the sea, and consequently the shores of the sea." This "common law" was repeated many ways and in many jurisdictions, including the Magna Carta, and has been a powerful legislative tool in the United States to provide for public access to seashores, lakeshores, and fisheries.

If the world is to save its freshwater resources, it is clearly necessary to create a counter-narrative to the dominant narrative currently governing water management thinking in powerful circles. Increasingly in the halls of government, business and international financial, and trade institutions, water is seen as a commodity to be put on the open market and sold and traded to the highest bidder. The right to water must be understood as a fundamental right. Let us commit to a water-secure future based on the principles of water protection and watershed renewal, equity, and justice, and the right of all living things to water for life.

A Commons approach and analysis could improve the quality of our research, communication, campaigning, and collaboration as well as promote alliance building with other Commons movements. To adopt and use the language of the Commons would give activists and writers a way of asserting common cause with allies in adjacent fields of action. The world is crying out for new vision and hope. This lens of the Commons, with its ancient beginnings and its infinite possibilities, could provide that vision and hope, as well as a way forward in these precarious times.

NOTES

1. Barlow, 2007.
2. Hall and Lobina, 2006.

3. Marsden, 2003.
4. Cook, 2009.
5. World Nuclear Association, 2008.
6. United Nations Development Program.
7. World Health Organization, 2000.
8. Shiva, 2002.

CHAPTER 4

Beyond Leviathan? The Historical Relationship between Peace Plans, International Law, and the Early Anglo-American Peace Movement

Cris Toffolo

As was indicated in the introduction, the editors hope this collection will explore not only movements that are working for a more peaceful world (that is, "the peace movement") but also strategies that embody "movement toward peace," in the sense of new attitudes, practices, policies, and institutions that have been created to prevent or resolve conflict in nonbelligerent ways. This chapter explores a central dialectic between these poles by examining the relationship between the development of early peace proposals, the development of international law, and the development of peace movements in the United States and Great Britain. It is hoped this information will inform contemporary thinking about strategies and tactics to advance the agenda of promoting peace, and ultimately ending war as a legitimate and very costly institution.

Long before there were social movements in the modern sense, pacifist-oriented thinkers were envisioning how to end war, either through outlawing its most barbaric features and/or by creating alternative methods of conflict resolution. Although these ideas did influence the development of international law early on, to some degree, more ambitious plans awaited the development of modern social movements.

As social movement theorists point out, one of the most important aspects of popular movements is that they open up existing political spaces to new actors, and sometimes they create new political terrain. The development of international law and alternative conflict resolution organizations at the international level are cases in point, with the result that today social movements can engage not only the nation state, corporations, and the institutions of organized religion, but also international courts, international bureaucracies, and international conferences. In other words, social movements were instrumental in creating new institutions that now provide them with new avenues through which to pressure states to further other peace movement goals.

International law organizations and other international organizations also provide alternative venues and methods of resolving interstate conflict. In this way the development of international law (with its corresponding machinery) is now part of "positive peace" that is helping to create a more transparent and accountable political dynamic. The impact of peace movements is thus greatly enhanced beyond their more noticed work on "negative peace" (that is, crises-driven work to stop a particular "hot" conflict). Additionally these sites, perhaps, are harder for national political and economic elites to capture (than the state and domestic economy). Therefore, power is more fluid and this can help keep pressure on domestic elites in a way that forces them to act more democratically and humanely.

In this chapter I review the early development of international law and peace plans, and show how the early peace movements were instrumental in setting up this new terrain that today is a main field in which social movements now operate.

EARLY VISIONS OF INTERNATIONAL LAW AND PEACE

As early as 3100 BCE, arbitration was used to settle a boundary dispute between two Mesopotamian cities. However, the modern international law regime within which peace movements today operate developed only a few hundred years ago within Europe, a context once so violent that nations were assumed to be at war unless they specifically entered into peace agreements, often guaranteed by hostage exchanges.

Only during periods when operative systems of states exist is interstate law needed: it had no place in the Roman Empire (which was governed by its own internal law), or in Europe's anarchic "dark ages," when raw force operated largely unchecked. However, gradually the disaggregated parts of the Roman Empire came to see themselves as discrete political communities, and eventually a minimum standard of conduct developed, understood in terms of rights and obligations. These ideas derived from that part of Roman law known as *jus gentium* (law based on universal ideals that originally covered controversies with non-Romans). During Europe's Middle Ages, *jus gentium* was reinterpreted by the church using the Stoic concept *jus naturale*, something God implanted in all humans so they could comprehend the unchangeable nature of justice and the universe. Another contribution of the church was canon law that included the conclusion of treaties, authority over territory, regulation of warfare, right of conquest, and papal arbitration as a desirable method of dispute resolution.

The legal implications of Europe's conquest of the Americas were theorized by a Spanish Dominican, Francisco De Vitoria, in *De Indis* and *The Law of War Made by the Spaniards on the Barbarians* (ca. 1539). These texts attempt to determine what makes a war just, the basis of Spanish authority in the Americas, and the relationship between Spaniards and the original inhabitants. In this same era the Pope, in the Treaty of Tordesillas, mediated a major dispute between Spain and Portugal over their respective "rights" to rule various portions of the "New World," thus averting a war between the two superpowers of that era.[1]

For precisely that reason, this era also demonstrates the limitations and weakness of international law as a method of attempting to establish a just peace. The very framework used to arbitrate the dominant conflict of that day created the legal grounds for the massive holocaust against native peoples around the globe who lost their lands, freedom, cultures, and right to be recognized as equally human based on the legal principles of "discovery" and *terra nullius*. It also, indirectly, led to the enslavement of Africans. These remain the basis of national laws that even today continue the ongoing disinheritance of native people around the world.[2]

This is also the era in which the pacifist humanist, Erasmus, worked in the arena of international law and wrote *Querela pacis* (*The Complaint of Peace*) in 1517, condemning war as an instrument of tyranny. His thesis: war and desire for empire had so degraded humanity that this most superior of all animals now routinely kills its own kind, and the only way to change this would be to henceforth use only reason, persuasion, and arbitration instead of war to settle disputes.

Despite being one of the people whose ideas inspired the Protestant Reformation, Erasmus, likely due to his measured approach to conflict resolution, refused to engage directly in this religio-political movement that culminated in the devastating Thirty Years War.

This conflict was actually a series of wars that raged between 1618 and 1648 in which the Habsburgs of Spain and Austria were opposed by various states, including France, the Netherlands, Denmark, and Sweden. It was also a German civil war complicated by the fact that Germany was the epicenter of the still-raging Protestant Reformation and thus various German groups supported either the Habsburgs or one of their opponents, at times switching allegiances. Although the Peace of Augsburg in 1555 had provided Lutheranism with official recognition, and allowed German princes to impose their religion on their subjects, this treaty did not settle all of the issues, because subsequently many German princes converted to Calvinism and thus were outside that peace agreement.

This conflict was finally brought to a close by the Peace (treaty) of Westphalia. It rendered governmental institutions religiously neutral and effectively ended papal authority over German princes as well as the common use of papal arbitration. And it led to the emergence of territorial "nation states" grounded on the principle of absolute, reciprocally recognized sovereignty, which remains a central tenet of international relations. For all of these reasons this treaty marks the beginning of the modern international system and law.

One document written in the midst of this horrendous conflict was Eméric Cruce's *The New Cineas* (a.k.a. Cyneas) (1623). It is considered to be the first peace proposal to include a general assembly. According to Cruce the four main causes of war are honor, profit, righting wrongs, and exercise. Religion that might seem like a main cause is only a pretext. Like Erasmus, Cruce addressed himself to rulers with the power to create peace from above, arguing states would be more secure if there was a universal peace, so rulers should strive to maintain justice and peace, rather than seek to aggrandize themselves through conquest. To that end sovereigns should shrink the size of their armies and not let militarists dominate decision making. Games and hunting should be used to release the tensions of aggressive men, who also should be put to work in agriculture and the trades.[3] In the place of armies, well-paid police and peace officers should be commissioned. Pirates and other rogues could be suppressed more economically by giving them land or the opportunity to work and it is the responsibility of the state to care for and feed the poor.[4] To overcome religious conflict princes should teach their subjects that human nature is universal, all religions have the same goal, and true piety does not incite hostility.[5] Cruce went on to propose an assembly of ambassadors from every country (including Persia, China, Ethiopia, and the East and West Indies) that would pass laws by majority vote and have the power to enforce peace using arms if necessary. Established boundaries would not be violated for any reason and all complaints would be presented to this assembly for decision.[6]

At the same time as Crucé was arguing for the creation of an international assembly as the alternative to war, Hugo Grotius elaborated rules to govern warfare. In his greatest work, *De Jure Belli ac Pacis (The Law of War and Peace)*, published in 1625, this "father of international law," drew on De Vitoria and other scholastics to argue that *jus gentium* is deliberately created by humans to serve their needs. Grotius theorized about both *jus ad bellu* (the beginnings of war), which he argues must be formally declared, and *jus in bello* (how to act during a war), delineating codes to protect noncombatants, as well as prohibitions against destroying property and certain types of indiscriminant weapons. He argued for the humane treatment of hostages and prisoners, as well as for moderation when dealing with the religions of defeated peoples. The work also provides advice for making truces and peace treaties to end war.[7]

EMERGENT LIBERALISM PROVIDES TERRAIN FOR MODERN PEACE MOVEMENTS

The Protestant Reformation gave rise to a new theory of the state, the earliest articulation of which is Thomas Hobbes's 1651 *Leviathan*, which argues the "state of nature" is equivalent to a "state of war" and the only way to leave such a dismal condition is to form a "social contract."[8] John Locke developed Hobbes's ideas in such a way that he provided the philosophical grounds to argue absolutist rule should be replaced by constitutional monarchy, which makes the rule of law paramount. Locke's argument is that a nation without a sovereign does not dissolve into a state of war (as Hobbes thought), rather the basic bonds among the populace remain, and hence regime change is possible, in fact advisable, in the face of tyranny, for all governments should rest on the will of the people. This idea of a "nation," plus the Treaty of Westphalia, created the nation states that today populate the international arena. This liberal framework, which puts law at the center of government, then became the vision for imagining an international order based on law instead of war.

In 1693, during the War of the League of Augsburg, the Quaker William Penn published a peace plan that was linked to the new ideas about international law. In *An Essay Towards the Present and Future Peace of Europe by the Establishment of a European Diet, Parliament, or Estate*, Penn argued individual states should disarm and create a European parliament that should include Russia and the Ottoman Empire. It should decide disputes collectively and unite in strength to enforce its decisions. In an argument that appears to owe something to Hobbes, Penn argues such an entity is necessary because there must be a sovereign authority greater than the conflicting parties to settle disputes; for just like individuals, states have difficulty objectively resolving their own disagreements.[9]

Two years later Abbé Saint-Pierre published his famous *Paix Perpetuelle*, which also advocates the creation of a European federation as a means to end war.[10] Following Hobbes, he believed the fear of violence must be used to enforce law and justice. Among the 12 main articles of this complex international treaty was one advocating that all of Europe's Christian princes unite to form a permanent union for peace and security, and together endeavor to make treaties with Muslim sovereigns. Second, the union should not interfere with the affairs of its members, except to preserve them from rebellions. Third, the union should have commissioners investigate revolts, and based on their reports, decide whether to send troops. Other critical articles stipulate no sovereign shall take up arms except against a declared enemy of the union, and a three-fourths majority should be needed to make all decisions, with unanimity needed to alter the treaty. Even though he was writing when states typically were governed by absolute sovereigns, and he argued the union should support existing regimes, Saint-Pierre believed different types of regimes could function together in this federation, and even included provisions for the union to deal with regime transitions.[11]

In 1761 Jean-Jacques Rousseau, a year before publishing his most famous works (that is, *The Social Contract* and *Emile*), published a loose translation of Saint-Pierre's essay that more clearly linked it to liberal political theory. Just as national governments have been instituted to control private wars, an international federation must unite nations under the authority of law to stop national wars that are so much worse than the private hostilities that occur within nations. A federation would be much more reliable than treaties to promote peace because the latter are temporary.

Such a federation would need several conditions to be successful: (1) all existing boundaries must be permanent; (2) all important powers must be members of the federation and none may quit; (3) the laws it creates must be binding and enforceable by coercive power; and (4) all conflicts should be settled by arbitration or judicial pronouncement. Defending this plan Rousseau argues that it addressed the six major causes of war (desire for conquest, fear of attack, attacking to weaken a powerful neighbor, attacking to maintain rights against an attacker, resolving a major conflict, or fulfilling a treaty obligation). The federation makes every purpose easier to accomplish except the first (that is, conquest), which it deters most effectively because it combines the powers of all other nations against an aggressor. Not only would security improve, and thus commerce flourish, but this arrangement would likely save each state half of its military budget.[12]

Of course it should not be forgotten that even as liberal ideals were transforming the terrain on which international relations was conducted in Europe, the nation states at the center of this theory were in the heyday of operating vast empires not governed by liberal principles. This fact was not lost on those interested in developing a peaceful alternative to international warfare (and was noted by Saint Pierre).

Jeremy Bentham's[13] 1789 *A Plan for a Universal and Perpetual Peace* argues the achievement of perpetual peace must rest on two fundamental grounds: (1) the reduction of troops; and (2) the "emancipation of the colonial dependencies of each state." Without colonies to protect, countries could reduce the size of their militaries, as all they would need would be a small navy to deter piracy. The plan's other major proposal was to create an international code of conduct (grounded on the "laws of peace"), and a Common Court of Judicature for deciding differences between states. Its proceedings should be public, and, in general, secrecy in international affairs should be curtailed, then people would learn the awful truth about war and naturally end their support for it. This court would not need a military to enforce its decisions but instead would rely on the power of public opinion.[14]

In 1795 Kant expanded on Bentham's critique of colonies, and deepened Rousseau's liberal reworking of Saint-Pierre, in his own plan for *Perpetual Peace*, arguing that in order for an international federation to work, its members must be free republics. For only this regime type is based on the will of the people and the rule of law, which are prerequisites to ending war, because only in such regimes is the consent of citizens required to declare war and they would "weigh the matter well before undertaking such a bad business." For in decreeing war, they would be resolving to bring all the miseries of war on themselves, as they would do the fighting themselves, pay for the war, and live with the devastation it leaves behind.[15]

In a contemporary-sounding passage, Kant argues that any successful plan must forbid rapacious international lending that encourages countries to take on massive debt (beyond what is required to develop infrastructure), for by this ingenious invention commercial states like England generated their great ability to make war, as the wealth that such a system generates the permits these countries to develop overwhelming military might. Not only do innocent states get entangled in their conflicts but it also causes them to go bankrupt.[16] Kant goes on to condemn "the inhospitable actions of Western countries that have conquered other lands and people with impunity," which has resulted in their oppression as well as widespread warfare, famine, and a whole litany of other evils.[17]

The solution to international warfare is analogues to the remedy for domestic conflict: just as the people form a national government to solve the problem of violence in a state of nature, so too states have an obligation to establish peace by creating a "league of nations" ("league of peace") because peace treaties are merely temporary truces that don't permanently solve the problem of war. Only a federation that unites all free republics can end "all wars forever." It does this by grounding itself strictly on existing state boundaries, which it is designed to defend, and devoting itself to maintaining the freedom and security of all members. Further, following William Penn, Kant proposes all states should abolish their standing armies, for armies menace other states by their constant readiness for war, and there ultimately is no limit to this.[18] Once this league is seen to work, all states will eventually join and this will create perpetual peace. If an enlightened people can make a republic, which by nature is inclined toward peace, this becomes the building block of a federation run by similar rules.[19] This faith in the power of ordinary people, which is part of the spirit that animated the Enlightenment and Liberalism, is a precursor to faith in the power of public opinion, which becomes an essential component in the development of modern social movements.

ABOLITION AND THE EMERGENCE OF MODERN PEACE MOVEMENTS

It was in the "Age of Revolution" that public opinion first became a real force in politics. It was part of the French Revolution and of the wars for independence in North and South America. But it was in the fight against the slave trade that an understanding of its importance became a catalyst to the development of modern peace movements. To understand how this occurred, it is important to know that Grotius's distinction between natural and customary law gave rise to different legal philosophies that in turn spawned public action.

The natural-law tradition of Vitoria, Gentili, and Grotius emphasizes the moral imperatives of law. In the 17th century positivist legal philosophy became ascendant, as scholars such as Zouche, Bynkershoek, and Vattel searched for the basis of international obligation. They argued that international law originates in actual state practices—in customs and treaties, and hence in the consent of states. Only positive law so assented to is true law. Vis-à-vis the slave trade, natural-law theorists saw it as an obvious violation of natural, and hence international, law. However, for positivists, who embraced state sovereignty and the necessity of ascertaining states' consent for rules, the issue was more complex. In a series of cases before American and British courts, where positivism dominated, the verdict was that the slave trade could only be suppressed if states agreed to do so.[20]

What arose to counter that position was the first modern social movement devoted to abolishing the international slave trade. It was led by committed Christians in England and the United States, and by ex-slaves. Although slavery had already been attacked by various enlightenment writers such as Montesquieu and Hume,[21] organized protests only started later, in Quaker communities. In response to severe persecution during the Seven Years War (1756 to 1763), which was interpreted as divine chastisement, Quakers sought self-purification. Part of that effort was to renounce slavery.[22] In 1758 the Philadelphia Yearly Meeting excluded members who were involved in the slave trade and began to pressure all its members to emancipate their slaves. In 1761 the London Yearly Meeting ruled all Quakers who owned slaves should be disowned.[23] Quakers also were instrumental in the founding of the London Society for Effecting the Abolition of the Slave Trade in 1787.[24]

In that same year William Wilberforce's diary records his pledge to devote his life to abolition and social reform. From then on, as a member of parliament, Wilberforce led the fight to change the law.[25] He also worked with Quakers (who could not hold public office due to their refusal to swear oaths) to convince the public that slavery was an obstacle to Christian morality, human progress, and modern economics.[26] Another key player, Thomas Clarkson, established local abolition groups across England, which were joined by Quakers, Baptists, Methodists, industrial workers, and women (who previously had been unpoliticized and had to hold separate meetings). African former slaves also participated, and the autobiography of a freed slave, Olaudah Equiano, which went through nine editions, was a key text that convinced people that ending slavery was a moral and political imperative, a message that was driven home by anti-slavery newspapers, other forms of mass propaganda, petitions, public meetings, lawsuits, and boycotts.[27]

This strategy of changing public opinion resulted in the passage of the 1807 Slave Trade Act in the British parliament that not only made it illegal to transport slaves, but also led to a shift in British naval policy, as the UK became the main force interdicting slave ships, a policy it pursued to level competition between its own domestic free-labor produced goods, and goods produced more cheaply using slave labor.[28]

The success of the abolitionist movement was a watershed for work toward international peace, for several reasons. First, once the battle against the slave trade was won, the same people who had worked on this project formed the first peace societies. Second, it led to a new understanding of the power of public opinion. Third, the international nature of the slave trade immediately raised awareness that although this battle had to be fought only in the British parliament, enforcement needed to be global. It was a short step to see that ending interstate wars would need a more audacious legal strategy, of international treaties, and/or entirely new venues of international law and organization.

If we frame this history using Johan Galtung's theory about the three-fold nature of violence, we see that the fight against direct violence (that is, war) was spawned by the fight against slavery, which though heavily reliant on direct violence, was primarily a system of structural and cultural violence. Even without the benefit of this theory, at the time the multifold character of violence led to debates about the best way to end the violence of slavery. This was especially true in the United States where a nascent anti-war movement, which was linked to the anti-slavery movement, was divided over this issue. One side argued the Civil War was a singular example of a just war; the other argued slavery was better ended by payment to slave holders (as Britain had done), which in the long run would be cheaper and less problematic.

Interestingly, 19th-century socialist and communist movements shared with liberals an anti-war agenda and a belief that elites, not the people, were the main cause of war. However, whereas the Liberal anti-war movement focused its ire at nondemocratic rulers and saw the solution in the development of democratically run international organizations and free trade, the former viewed the central cause of war as capitalistic exploitation of the working class, which must be ended first, as the means to ending war. In that view combating structural violence should take precedence over confronting direct violence, which is seen only as a symptom of a structurally exploitative capitalistic order. This debate is still with us today, reflected in contemporary discussions within the peace movement over whether to concentrate primarily on justice or peace (that is, structural/cultural or direct violence).

Interestingly both ideological camps in the 1800s regularly held international congresses to develop common principles and strategies to use back in their home countries. This is the first international coordination of national movements and also the first time those engaged in practical politics began to demand the creation of supra-national organizations to regulate national behavior of the kind theorized by the scholars noted above. Kant summed up the vision of that era by arguing that the "intercourse . . . which has been everywhere steadily increasing between the nations of the Earth, has now extended so enormously that a violation of rights in one part of the world is felt all over it. Hence the idea of a cosmopolitan right is no fantastical, high-flown notion . . . but a complement of the unwritten code of law—constitutional as well as international."[29]

FRUITS OF THE PEACE MOVEMENTS
FROM THE LATE 1800s TO WWII

During the 19th century, liberal peace efforts focused on developing international law and creating new international institutions. In terms of law, the focus was on limiting its increasing destructiveness, which was a result in part of the development, in the 18th century, of permanent professional military organizations. One of the first such efforts in this regard was the creation of domestic military courts empowered to try violations committed by soldiers during wartime. Particularly relevant here is Lincoln's promulgation, during the Civil War, of *Instructions for the Government of Armies of the United States in the Field*, which is the first codified law forbidding the killing of prisoners of war. Also known as the Lieber Code, it is the basis of U.S. army manuals and subsequent Hague and Geneva conventions, which are the foundations of modern humanitarian law (as the laws of war are called and denoting that such law is grounded in the "principle of humanity," which focuses on people as victims of war).[30] This point of view was first developed by Swiss businessman Henry Dunant, who organized the International Committee of the Red Cross and convinced the Swiss government to convene the 1864 conference that issued the First Geneva Convention, which was the first in a series of international laws focused on banning particular weapons and practices of war.

For its part the first Hague Peace Conference was focused on establishing an institutional alternative to warfare as a means of settling disputes, and as such the First (1899) Hague Convention established the still-existing Permanent Court of Arbitration, which, while not well known now, was an approach to ending war that was a major focus, especially of the early American peace movement.

Also signed at the end of the First Hague Convention were three "Declarations" prohibiting the use of certain weapons. In 1907 a Second Hague Convention addressed warfare at sea, an issue addressed further, in 1929, by the Second Geneva Convention. In 1925 the Geneva Protocol was added to the Second Hague Convention: it bans the use of all forms of chemical and biological warfare.[31] In 1929 a Third Geneva Convention addressed the treatment of war prisoners.[32]

Since World War I, the trend has been toward setting aside the original principle governing war, which stipulated that states have the right to use force. Specific statements of this trend began with the 1923 Treaty of Mutual Assistance and include the 1928 Pact of Paris, which renounced war as an instrument of national policy. While not successful in their own right, these documents formed the basis of the Nuremberg Tribunal's claim that aggressive war (a crime against peace) is illegal under general international law, and therefore its perpetrators can be tried for war crimes and other atrocities. This Tribunal informs Article 2 of the UN Charter that prohibits resorting to force, or even the threat of force.

Partly responsible for ushering in new international norms are the 1919 Treaty of Versailles and the 1920 Covenant of the League of Nations. For the first time since the end of the Holy Roman Empire, these treaties established bodies with arbitration powers that, at least theoretically, were above those of the nation state, thus bringing into being the institutions long argued for in the peace plans discussed above. These included not only the League, but also the Permanent Court of International Justice, formed in 1922.[33] The principle governing the League was that of collective security, which presupposed nations were at peace unless they declared war. This idea challenged traditional assumptions that war was a legitimate way to expand national power. With the creation of the UN in 1945 the traditional principle was further challenged by the UN's development of an "internationally organized collective defense," directed by the UN's Security Council (UNSC) and its Military Staff Committee. Thus, some argue that war and the use of force are illegal except in self-defense. Even this right is circumscribed once the UNSC establishes a dispute resolution mechanism, or takes collective security measures.[34]

Another development of the interbellum period was the incorporation into international law issues that affect ordinary people. This trend became much more pronounced after the Holocaust because the publicizing of that atrocity by the Allied powers shifted international law away from positivism and toward natural law. This trend was first expressed in the Nuremburg Tribunal and was confirmed in the Charter of the United Nations. Today the UN delves into all aspects of human cooperation, and the Universal Declaration of Human Rights (UDHR) places the protection of individual dignity alongside and equal to the principle of state sovereignty.

CONCLUSION

This chapter has highlighted several aspects of peace movements that are at the heart of social movement theory. The first is the power of movements to open up new political terrain (by creating a new realm of law and new international organizations). The second is the importance of reframing issues. Often anti-war movements are reactive national mobilizations against particular wars. The real question today, however, is whether we can reframe war in a way analogous to the reframing of slavery, as something immoral that retards progress and is against rational economics. Part of this task will be to articulate that war essentially is a (violent) method of conflict resolution, and demand that other more effective, less costly, and more righteous methods be used in the future. The third, making reference to Charles Tilly's concept, is that from the beginning the peace movement's "repertoire of contention"[35] has been aimed at developing international law and organizations because early activists understood that ending war is a function of creating a new and more peaceful international architecture. Today it is also understood that this new terrain can be effectively used to further other peace movement goals.

This will remain important, for no matter how much more international law and organizations are developed, a need will always remain for an active peace movement. This is perhaps best understood by reflecting on a line of poetry quoted by Heidegger about the dangers posed by technology: "where danger is grows the saving power also" (34). Following a tactic employed so brilliantly by Karl Marx, consider the inversion of this line: "where saving power is also lies the danger." Looking at international law in light of both lines, we can see that it can be used in the service of oppression, as was done historically to legitimize the slave trade and disinherit native peoples (and today in terms of undermining human rights in the service of a harsh national security doctrine after 9/11, and against immigrants, who increasingly are defined legally as criminals). This is to say, that in all institutional regimes, there is an inevitable gap between justice and law, such that law is not capable of fully articulating justice.[36] Nevertheless law is a necessary tool of all modern regimes, and is the central alternative to raw force. So it will always exist, and it will always be the work of social movements to keep an eye on this powerful tool (even as they also promote it as a means to create more peace and justice). Precisely because social movements are not routinized they provide a necessary corrective to the deadening effects of the very institutions they help to create.[37] Their genius is to articulate the conflicts that are generated by the injustices and contradictions within any established order in an extra-legal way so that these become issues that must be addressed. Social movements are the alternative to violent extra-legal ways to expose the contradictions and injustices of a given regime and/or legal order. Thus, as we think about the further development of the international law regime and institutions, it is clear that a vital place will always remain for international movements as a logical, if irregular, component.

NOTES

1. Amjad-Ali, 2007: 26.
2. Capeheart and Milovanovic, 2007: 108—124.
3. Crucé, 1972: 26–33.

4. Ibid., 155, 174.

5. Ibid., 50–51

6. Ibid., 78–79.

7. Other Grotian principles widely held today include the notion that subjects are responsible for the crimes of their sovereign if they consented to his acts or acted illegally under his command; therefore, "following orders" is not a valid defense, and treaties should bind successive regimes (thus debts incurred by one regime must be repaid by its successor).

8. In that text Hobbes also articulates a distinction between "natural rights" and "natural law" that became part of the basis for the modern notion of human rights.

9. Penn, 1693: 12.

10. In his original plan he included all the nations of the world but to get serious attention, in later versions he limited his plan to a confederation of European states. Saint-Pierre argued the existing confederations of the German and Helvetian states, as well as the United Provinces of the Netherlands could serve as models to demonstrate the practicality of his plan. He also argued no sovereign should keep more than 6,000 soldiers.

11. Abbé de Saint-Pierre, 1695: 411–414.

12. Rousseau, 1756: 95–131.

13. Bentham coined the term "international" in the 1780s, to discuss what then was called the "law of nations." See Van der Linden, 1987: 40.

14. Bentham; James Mill in his 1822 article "Law of Nations" argued for an international law code and court and rejected violent sanctions as the enforcement mechanism favoring instead "enforcement by public opinion." This argument was also made by William Ladd in 1827 when he argued "A peace extorted by force is no peace at all." See Van der Linden, 1987.

15. Kant, 1795: 186.

16. Ibid., 183.

17. Thus China and Japan wisely refused entry to western commercial states. See Kant, 1795.

18. Kant, 1795: 182.

19. Ibid., 189–191.

20. Interestingly, a British court in 1772 ruled slavery did not exist in England due to a lack of positive law on the subject, a ruling that was reconfirmed by other cases brought in that era.

21. Davis, 1984: 107.

22. Around the same time Quakers became involved in Granville Sharp's work to elevate the poverty of a growing community of American ex-slaves in London, which given the enormity of the need evolved into the Sierra Leone scheme. See Walvin, 1980: 149–162.

23. This was followed in 1773 by a Quaker request to the Lord of Trade to allow Virginia to levy taxes to stop further slave important. See Davis 1984: 108.

24. Davis, 1984: 108.

25. Walvin, 1980: 149–162.

26. Davis, 1984: 109.

27. Drescher, 1980: 43.

28. The United States outlawed the slave trade on January 1, 1808, but did not end slavery until 1865, with the Thirteenth Amendment to the U.S. constitution. The British had already outlawed slavery in 1832 through passage of the Abolition of Slavery Act that provided for the compensated emancipated of 780,000 colonial slaves by a payment of £20 million to slave owners. See Davis 1984.

29. Kant, 1795.

30. Today humanitarian law is mandatory on nations that have signed these treaties. There also is unwritten customary law that binds all nations, as was evident at the Nuremberg War Trials. Although the treaties that create positive humanitarian law are statements of general principles, lacking means of enforcement and penalties, much of their substance has been incorporated into military law in many countries.

31. This protocol was further augmented by the 1972 Biological Weapons Convention, the 1993 Chemical Weapons Convention, and the 1997 Ottawa Anti-Personnel Mine Ban Treaty and Conventions.

32. In 1949, a Fourth Geneva Convention was created to protect civilians in wartime. In 1977 "Protocols" were added. These documents also stipulate "rules of occupation;" these require an occupier to respect the rights, family honor, property, and religion of the population. Based on these rules the United Nations has repeatedly condemned Israel's conduct in the "Occupied Territories."

33. The International Labor Organization, established in 1919, also develops international law by promulgating international labor conventions.

34. Although these developments have made warfare largely illegal in principle, it continues to be a reality. This is important because international law is a fluid phenomenon, based always in part on current states' practices, which if sustained, create new customary law. In this regard actions taken by the United States since the terrorist attacks of September 11, 2001, may be seen as undermining aspects of international law. Most relevant in this regard are the United States' invasion of Iraq and its use of: preemptive strikes against "terrorists" in allied and neutral states; interrogation techniques that may constitute torture; extraordinary rendition; and holding uncharged "enemy combatants" offshore. The key issue now is whether other states will challenge, or mimic, these decisions. Future humanitarian and human-rights laws depend in part on those choices.

35. A repertoire of contention defines the ways people act together in pursuit of shared interests using a "limited set of routines that are learned, shared, and acted out through a relatively deliberate process of choice." See Tilly, 1995.

36. Capeheart and Milovanovic, 2007.

37. This, not incidentally, is related to an understanding of power that resides in consent not force or weapons. As societies become increasingly complex, as Durkheim theorized, solidarity comes to be grounded in a division of labor that makes social cohesion more a function of organization than force.

CHAPTER 5

The Good News: The ICC and the R2P Principle

Ronald J. Glossop

I want to discuss two movements of the last decade that are very promising in terms both of the ideals that motivate them and the progress they have been making in realizing their goals. That is, I want to direct our attention to the "good news"; that related to the International Criminal Court (ICC) and to the Responsibility to Protect (R2P) principle. I will conclude by noting why these developments are so important for the future of our global community.

THE INTERNATIONAL CRIMINAL COURT

The Establishment, Structure, and Personnel of the ICC

Less than 10 years ago, on July 17, 1998, an international conference in Rome approved by a vote of 120 to 7 (with 21 abstentions) a treaty to create a permanent International Criminal Court (ICC) as an alternative to relying on the ad hoc tribunals established by the UN Security Council after the crimes were committed in places such as the former Yugoslavia and Rwanda. Unlike the International Court of Justice (ICJ) or "World Court"

This chapter was originally a presentation for International Philosophers for Peace, Radford Univ., May 24–27, 2007.

that deals with disputes between national governments, the ICC can try and prosecute individuals for genocide, war crimes and crimes against humanity. Support for the treaty was led by the like-minded group that included countries such as Canada, Australia, Britain, Norway, Germany, and South Africa, cheered on by an 800-member international coalition of citizen groups. Opposition was led by the United States, even though up to the time of the Rome Conference it had supported the effort because it had assumed that the ICC would deal only with cases referred to it by the Security Council. With such an arrangement it would have been able to veto any cases involving Americans. The seven countries voting against the ICC treaty were China, Iraq, Israel, Libya, Qatar, Yemen, and the United States.

This treaty, known as the Rome Statute, stipulated that the jurisdiction of the ICC would begin on the first of the month 60 days after the 60th ratification. Enemies of the treaty were confident that it would be 10 to 25 years before that many ratifications would be acquired. But largely because of the efforts of a coalition of international nongovernment organizations (NGOs) called the Coalition for the International Criminal Court (CICC), the required 60th ratification of the Rome Statute was registered on April 11, 2002, only 45 months after the treaty was adopted. As a result the jurisdiction of the ICC began on July 1, 2002. The CICC can also take a lot of credit for the fact that as of March 21, 2007, the Rome Statute had already been ratified by 104 countries out of the 193 countries in the world. The most recent was Chad, now the home of many refugees from Darfur, Sudan. On March 24, the Yemeni House of Representatives voted to ratify the treaty, so it will soon become the 105th country. That activitist coalition, whose office is in New York City, now includes over 2,000 civil society organizations. Its Web site[1] is very useful. It also publishes an informative newspaper, *The International Criminal Court Monitor.* The national coalition of NGOs for the ICC in the United States is the American NGO Coalition for the International Criminal Court (AMICC).[2]

Representatives of countries that have ratified the treaty make up the Assembly of States Parties (ASP). The first meeting of this governing body for the ICC was held at UN Headquarters in New York, September 3 to 10, 2002. It called for nominations for the Prosecutor and the 18 judges of the Court before the first of December. The 18 judges were elected in February 2003, and they were sworn in on March 11 in The Hague, where the ICC will be located. Each judge must have established competence in criminal law and procedure or in relevant areas of international law. The judges are divided into three divisions, a Pre-Trial Division, a Trial Division, and an Appeals Division. The rules for electing judges ensure that they will come from different parts of the world and that a fair proportion of them will be women. Of the 18 judges selected in the first election, 7 were women. Their normal term of office is nine years, but after this first election they drew lots so that one-third had 3-year terms and one-third had 6-year terms.

Judge Philippe Kirsch of Canada was elected president of the ICC. In April 2003 the Assembly of States Parties elected Luis Moreno-Ocampo of Argentina to be the first Prosecutor, and he was sworn in on June 16, 2003. In June the ASP elected Bruno Cathala of France to be the first Registrar of the Court. His swearing in on July 3, 2003, marked the successful appointment of all the senior officers of the Court, just over a year after its jurisdiction began. In January 2006, elections were held for the six judges who had 3-year terms. Five of the six were re-elected and the sixth was a woman, so for a time there were eight women judges. But in December 2006, Judge Maureen Harding Clark of Ireland resigned to serve on the High Court of Ireland. Her replacement will be elected at the Fifth Assembly of States Parties to be held in December 2007.

In September 2003 the second Assembly of States Parties met in New York and elected five distinguished persons (two of them Nobel Peace Laureates) for 3-year terms to the Board of Directors for the Victims Trust Fund of the ICC. This fund ensures that the ICC will not only prosecute those guilty of committing crimes but will also assist those who have been injured. The five original members were Her Majesty Queen Rania Al-Abdullah of Jordan, former President Oscar Arias Sanchez of Costa Rica, former Prime Minister Tadekusz Mazowiecki of Poland, former President of the European Parliament Simone Veil of France, and Bishop Desmond Tutu of South Africa. The first two have resigned and have been replaced by Bulgaa Altangerel of Mongolia and Arthur Napoleon Raymond Robinson of Trinidad and Tobago.

In July 2004 a new supplemental treaty, the Agreement on the Privileges and Immunities of the ICC (APIC), entered into force. This treaty, which is essential for carrying out the work of the tribunal, gives employees of the ICC the same immunities and privileges granted to employees of the UN and other international organizations. As of February 1, 2007, this treaty providing immunity for ICC employees had been signed by 62 countries and ratified by 48.

One great value of the Rome Statute generally overlooked is the fact that nations that ratify the Statute are committed to bringing their own national laws into conformity with the international norms set up in the treaty. Consequently, many national legal systems are being modified to establish jurisdiction over the crimes of genocide, torture, ethnic cleansing, and rape.

An issue that everyone knew would require attention right from the time of the adoption of the Rome Statute is the matter of defining the crime of aggression as it applies to individuals. The Rome Statute gives the ICC jurisdiction over four kinds of crimes: (1) genocide, (2) war crimes, (3) crimes against humanity (which are clearly described in the statute itself), and (4) aggression. But it was decided in Rome that having jurisdiction on aggression would require a clear delineation of that crime. Discussion of this issue is being carried out by the Special Working Group of the Crime of Aggression (SWGCA), which held its third session June 8 to 11, 2006, at Princeton University. The aim is to have a proposal ready for action by the Review Council for the Rome Statute to be held in 2009. Issues involve not only defining aggression but also deciding whether jurisdiction of the Court should be restricted to the most clear-cut cases of aggression and determining the extent to which decisions of the UN Security Council, the UN General Assembly, and the International Court of Justice need to be taken into account.

The ICC and the UN in Africa and in the Rest of the World

On January 29, 2004, the ICC got its first case when the government of Uganda referred the situation in its northern region to the ICC. On April 19, 2004, the Court got its second case when the government of the Democratic Republic of the Congo called on the ICC to investigate crimes committed in that country since the Court's jurisdiction began July 1, 2002. Two months later Prosecutor Moreno-Ocampo announced the beginning of formal investigations in both these countries.

One of the most important events in the young history of the ICC occurred on March 31, 2005, when the UN Security Council adopted Resolution 1593 on the situation in the Darfur region of Sudan by a vote of 14 to 0, with one abstention, that of the United States. It was widely assumed that the United States would veto this measure because it included a section calling on the ICC to investigate the alleged crimes being committed in Sudan. Just over two months later, Prosecutor Moreno-Ocampo concluded that the requirements for initiating a formal investigation had been satisfied. The Prosecutor has reported to the Security Council on this matter four times, in June and December of 2005 and June and December of 2006. In the last two reports he called for more cooperation from national governments and other organizations.

One of the few times that the mainstream media has really focused attention on the ICC is related to its activity in Darfur. On Sunday, April 2, 2006, the cover story of the *New York Times* was "The Prosecutor of the World's Worst" by Elizabeth Rubin. The cover boldly presented this message:

> The UN is not going to stop the genocide in Darfur. The African Union is not going to stop the genocide in Darfur. The United States is not

going to stop the genocide in Darfur. NATO is not going to stop the genocide in Darfur. The European Union is not going to stop the genocide in Darfur. But someday, Luis Moreno-Ocampo is going to bring those who committed the genocide to justice.

This article provides a great deal of detail about how the leaders in Sudan are well aware of the work of the ICC and are actively doing all they can to prevent it from carrying on its work.

One reason the Sudanese government leaders don't want UN peacekeepers from countries that have ratified the Rome Statute is they might be arrested by them, especially now that as of April 27, 2007 (with the news being made public on May 2, 2007), warrants have been issued for the arrest of the former Minister of State for the Interior of the Government of Sudan Ahmad Muhammad Harun and Janjaweed militia leader Ali Kushbayd (real name: Ali Muhammad Al Abd-Al-Rahman). Nevertheless, the statement issued by the Office of the Prosecutor for the ICC notes that the government of Sudan itself has a legal duty to arrest these defendants. The Sudanese government has refused to accept these judgments of the ICC on grounds that it has not signed or ratified the Rome Statute, but that is irrelevant in this case because the UN Security Council has authorized the ICC to be involved. The question now is whether the UN or some countries in the UN will take action to back up the ICC judgments.

ICC President Kirsch has given reports to the UN General Assembly in November 2005 and October 2006. The ICC is a separate organization from the UN, but it reports annually to the General Assembly. This gives national representatives at the UN a chance to comment on the work of the ICC, and most of them have praised its work. A major theme of both the report itself and the responses from the General Assembly have focused on the need of national governments to assist the ICC, especially in the arresting of those indicted by the ICC such as Joseph Kony and four other leaders of the Lord's Resistance Army in Uganda. They were indicted on October 13, 2005, but have still not been arrested. A ticklish issue at present is whether these indicted leaders are going to be given amnesty as part of a peace agreement being negotiated at Juba, the capital of the regional government of southern Sudan. This possibility has evoked a loud cry of outrage from many human rights leaders.

On March 17, 2006, the ICC announced its first arrest. The defendant was Thomas Lubanga Dyilo, leader of a Congolese militia responsible for ethnic massacres, exploitation of child soldiers, rapes, and torture in the eastern part of the Democratic Republic of the Congo. He was turned over to the ICC by Congolese authorities aided by the French government and the UN Mission in the Congo (MONUC). The public hearing with Lubanga present was held on March 20, 2006, in The Hague.

The arrest of Lubanga along with investigations by the ICC resulted in an October 12, 2006, editorial in the *New York Times*. The editorial reads as follows:[3]

> Much good can come from the court's focus on child soldiers. The decision by the international tribunals for Rwanda and Yugoslavia to treat rape as one of the most serious international crimes has changed legal attitudes and practice worldwide. The International Criminal Court is now drawing attention to another widespread, yet widely ignored, horror. Guerrilla leaders in Colombia, Sri Lanka, West Africa and elsewhere, and government officials in Myanmar, should pay close attention.[4]

In fact, at least one has. Elizabeth Rubin, in her April 2 article mentioned earlier, notes that Prosecutor Moreno-Ocampo "holds up Carlos Castaño, one of Colombia's top paramilitary commanders, as an example of the court's potential reach" (p. 34). After Colombia ratified the ICC treaty, Castaño laid down his weapons because, according to his brother, he realized that he might become vulnerable to ICC prosecution.

Opposition of the Bush Administration to the ICC

The ICC has been progressing despite the efforts of the Bush administration to undermine it. President Clinton signed the treaty on December 31, 2000, the last day when a government could sign the treaty and not ratify it at the same time, something that would have been impossible in the United States. On May 6, 2002, the Bush administration announced that it had "nullified" the U.S. signature of the treaty, something not permitted by international law. It also launched a campaign against the ICC. A policy was adopted of trying to get other countries to sign Bilateral Immunity Agreements (BIAs) that indicated that no U.S. citizens would ever be sent to the ICC either for prosecution or even to testify. Economic assistance was to be cut off to any country that did not sign such an agreement. According to the U.S. administration, 101 nations have signed BIAs, but many of these cases are just executive agreements. Less than 40 percent have been ratified by parliaments. In addition 53 governments have publicly announced that they refuse to sign BIAs with the U.S. government. Several national governments in Eastern Europe have been squeezed by a U.S. policy threatening to cut off financial assistance to countries that won't sign a BIA while the European Union has indicated that any country that does sign a BIA can forget about becoming part of the European Union.

Another part of the U.S. campaign against the ICC is the legislation adopted by the U.S. Congress in August 2002 known as the American Servicemembers' Protection Act (ASPA). Its enemies refer to it as "The Hague Invasion Act" since it authorizes "any means necessary" to keep U.S. citizens from ICC custody in The Hague. A third U.S. effort against the ICC is the Nethercutt Amendment to the U.S. Foreign Appropriations Bill of December 2004. This measure goes further than the ASPA because it authorizes the end of Economic Support Funds to any country, including many key allies, that ratifies the Rome Statute but does not sign a BIA. The Nethercutt Amendment was reauthorized in the Joint Appropriations Bill for 2006.

A fourth element of the campaign against the ICC was to try to work through the UN to get immunity for all U.S. personnel involved in international peacekeeping efforts. The first effort in July 2002 succeeded. UN Security Council Resolution 1422 was adopted, granting immunity from the ICC during a one-year period for all personnel participating in missions authorized by the United Nations from countries who had not ratified the Rome Statute. Since that resolution stipulated only a one-year period, it came up for renewal the next year as UNSC Resolution 1487. It was passed again but with less support. In 2004 the U.S. wanted to renew this provision again, but withdrew it realizing that it would not be passed again.

On July 23, 2006, the *New York Times* published an op-ed piece by Mark Mazzetti entitled "U.S. Cuts in Africa Aid Said to Hurt War on Terror." He noted how the ASPA has led to the cutting off of millions of dollars in assistance to countries such as Kenya, Mali, Niger, and Tanzania, who had been assisting in efforts against Al Qaeda and other terrorist groups. He also mentioned the situation in Latin America where, as in Africa, the Chinese are moving in as the United States is cutting back on its economic assistance. He quoted Secretary of State Condoleezza Rice's comment in March 2006 that cutting military assistance because of ASPA is "sort of the same as shooting ourselves in the foot." He noted that the Pentagon's Quadrennial Defense Review issued in February 2006 called for the government to separate military funding from that anti-ICC law. He cited the opposition to the ASPA voiced by General Bantz J. Craddock of the U.S. Southern Command when testifying before the Senate in March 2006.

Such arguments may be having some effect. In October 2006, President Bush directed Secretary of State Rice to waive the prohibitions in the ASPA with respect to 21 countries. But the anti-ICC Nethercutt Amendment has not been revoked, and any changes in U.S. policy are motivated by concerns about the expanding influence of China, not by any readiness to support international law. What would be helpful would be a "sense of Congress" resolution saying that the policy of the U.S. government should be to support the ICC, including ratifying the Rome Statute so that this country can become a member of the Assembly of States Parties and so that U.S. citizens would be eligible to become judges on the Court.

THE RESPONSIBILITY TO PROTECT (R2P) PRINCIPLE

The Origins of the R2P Principle

The second part of the good news is the "Responsibility to Protect" movement (abbreviated as R2P). This movement has its origins in the report of the International Commission on Intervention and State Sovereignty published in December 2001 by the International Development Research Center in Ottawa, Canada.[5] Establishment of this commission was initiated by Lloyd Axworthy, former Foreign Affairs Minister of Canada, as a response to concerns about NATO intervention in Kosovo in 1999 without authorization by the UN Security Council on the one hand and the lack of international action to prevent the genocide in Rwanda on the other. UN Secretary-General Kofi Annan called for the international community to "forge unity" on the issue of how to deal with gross violations of human rights when international intervention seems to violate the principle of national sovereignty. The commission was appointed by the government of Canada and a group of major foundations, and its composition was announced to the UN General Assembly in September 2000. The co-chairs were Gareth Evans of Australia and Mohamed Sahnoun of Algeria while the other members were Giséle Coté-Harper of Canada, Lee Hamilton of the United States, Michael Ignatieff of Canada, Vladimir Lukin of Russia, Klaus Naumann of Germany, Cyril Ramaphosa of South Africa, Fidel Ramos of the Philippines, Cornelio Sommaruga of Switzerland, Eduardo Stein Barillas of Guatemala, and Ramesh Thakur of India.

The issues to be addressed by the Commission were: Does the international community ever have the right to intervene within the borders of a sovereign nation state? If so, under what conditions? What theoretical base could possibly justify such outside intervention? The Commission's answer in the report calls attention to the need of governments to preserve the "personal security" of their citizens as well as their "national security" in relations with other countries. It is argued that the notion of "state sovereignty implies a dual responsibility."[6] Each state not only has the responsibility "to respect the sovereignty of other states" but also has a responsibility "to respect the dignity and basic rights of people within the state."[7] The Commission says, "We prefer to talk not of a 'right to intervene' but of a 'responsibility to protect.'"[8] The key point is to shift focus from "sovereignty as control" to "sovereignty as responsibility."[9]

The Commission's report notes that the term *intervention* can be used to refer not only to military intervention but also to other coercive measures such as sanctions and criminal prosecutions of individuals.[10] At the same time the Commission deliberately refrains from using the term *humanitarian intervention* in deference to humanitarian groups who object to using that expression in any situation where military action is being employed.[11]

Sovereignty as responsibility means that leaders of national governments: (1) must protect their citizens and promote their welfare, (2) are responsible to their citizens and to the international community through the UN, and (3) can be held accountable for their acts of commission and omission.[12] Thus, not only do international criminal tribunals have a right to exert jurisdiction, but with regard to crimes like genocide where treaties provide for universal jurisdiction even other national governments can act. But the Commission cautions that "It is only when national systems of justice either cannot or will not act to judge crimes against humanity that universal jurisdiction and other international options should come into play."[13] Furthermore, the responsibility to protect includes (both for national governments and for the international community) not only the responsibility to react to human catastrophes but also to prevent them and to rebuild the community afterward.[14]

A great deal of the Commission's 85-page report deals with very specific and detailed commentary about specific situations organized in accord with specific topics such as the responsibility to protect individual citizens,[15] the responsibility to prevent catastrophes[16] (including how to deal with root causes to avoid the need for interventions), the responsibility to react to catastrophes,[17] the responsibility to rebuild the community after interventions,[18] the various roles of the UN in interventions,[19] the issue of how military interventions are to be carried out,[20] and what needs to be done in the future,[21] all with many references to specific past incidents such as Kosovo, Somalia, Rwanda, Haiti, Iraq, Sierra Leone, Liberia, Cambodia, and East Timor.

This report by the International Commission on Intervention and State Sovereignty aims "to strengthen, not weaken, the sovereignty of states" while also improving "the capacity of the international community to react decisively when states are either unable or unwilling to protect their own people."[22] It does this by proposing a re-interpretation of the notion of "national sovereignty" so that it includes the responsibility of a state to protect the security of its own citizens.

Official Adoption of the R2P Principle

Three years later, in December 2004, UN Secretary-General Kofi Annan's High-Level Panel on Threats, Challenges, and Change fully embraced and called for implementation of the Responsibility to Protect principle. The following year the Secretary-General's own report *In Larger Freedom: Toward Development, Security, and Human Rights for All* presented recommendations for action to the 60th session of the General Assembly including a reference to the "emerging norm of the Responsibility to Protect."

In September 2005, the UN General Assembly incorporated the Responsibility to Protect principle into the 2005 World Summit Outcome Document. Paragraph 138 reads:

> Each individual State has the responsibility to protect its populations from genocide, war crimes, ethnic cleansing, and crimes against humanity. This responsibility entails the prevention of such crimes, including their incitement, through appropriate and necessary means. We accept that responsibility and will act in accordance with it. The international community should, as appropriate, encourage and help States to exercise this responsibility and support the United Nations in establishing an early warning capability.[23]

Paragraph 139 of that document, addressing the issue of international intervention, says:

> The international community, through the United Nations, also has the responsibility to use appropriate diplomatic, humanitarian, and other peaceful means, in accordance with Chapters VI and VIII of the Charter, to help protect populations from genocide, war crimes, ethnic cleansing, and crimes against humanity. In this context, we are prepared to take collective action, in a timely and decisive manner, through the Security Council, in accordance with the Charter, including Chapter VII, on a case-by-case basis and in cooperation with relevant regional organizations as appropriate, should peaceful means be inadequate and national authorities manifestly fail to protect their populations from genocide, war crimes, ethnic cleansing, and crimes against humanity. We stress the need for the General Assembly to continue consideration of the responsibility to protect populations from genocide, war crimes, ethnic cleansing, and crimes against humanity and its implications, bearing in mind the principles of the Charter and international law. We also intend to commit ourselves, as necessary and appropriate, to helping States build capacity to protect their populations from genocide, war crimes, ethnic cleansing, and crimes against humanity and to assisting those which are under stress before crises and conflicts break out.[24]

On April 28, 2006, these two key paragraphs of the World Summit Outcome Document were affirmed unanimously by the UN Security Council when it adopted Resolution 1674 on the Protection of Civilians in Armed Conflict. It says: "The Security Council reaffirms the provisions of paragraphs 138 and 139 of the World Summit Outcome Document regarding the responsibility to protect populations from genocide, war crimes, ethnic cleansing, and crimes against humanity."

In March 2007, a report by the UN High-Level Mission of the Human Rights Commission concerning the situation in Darfur, led by Nobel Prize winner Jody Williams, disturbed by the failure of the May 2006 Darfur Peace Agreement to do much to improve the situation, called on the international community to take action, noting that the Responsibility to Protect principle required it. But the government of Sudan refused to allow the Mission to enter Sudan to carry on its investigation and objected to the use of the R2P framework in the report. The Human Rights Commission then appointed a new working group to work with the African Union and the Sudanese government on this issue.

As in the case of the ICC, civil society is pushing the national governments to act responsibly. In fact, the coordination of the NGOs in this effort is again in the hands of the World Federalist Movement-Institute for Global Policy (WFM-IGP) in New York. On this occasion they were asked to fulfill that task by the Canadian government that had sponsored the original report on the Responsibility to Protect. This coordination is being carried out under the name "Responsibility to Protect-Engaging Civil Society" or simply "r2p-cs" ("cs" is for "civil society").[25] One success for this civil society effort was the March 14, 2007, adoption by the Board of Supervisors of the City and County of San Francisco of a "Resolution Endorsing the United Nations Principle of the Responsibility to Protect."[26]

The results of a global public opinion poll released on April 5, 2007, by WorldPublicOpinion.org[27] and the Chicago Council on Global Affairs showed worldwide support for applying the R2P principle to the Darfur tragedy. Referring to that poll Andrew Stroehlein and Gareth Evans noted:

On the . . . question of whether the UN Security Council has the 'responsibility to authorize the use of military force to prevent severe human rights violations such as genocide, even against the will of their own government,' strong majorities in many countries replied favorably: 74 percent of Americans agreed, along with 69 percent of Palestinians, 66 percent of Armenians, 64 percent of Israelis, 54 percent of French and Poles, and 51 percent of Indians. And all populations polled were more in favor than opposed. . . . [T]he most surprising result emerged from China. Though its government has long been considered a staunch defender of state sovereignty under just about all circumstances, a full 76 percent of Chinese citizens agreed the Security Council had a responsibility to intervene when such mass crimes were taking place.[28]

Speaking on April 9, 2007, on the 13th anniversary of the Rwanda genocide, UN Secretary-General Ban Ki-Moon said: "All the world's governments have agreed in principle to the responsibility to protect. Our challenge now is to give real meaning to the concept, by taking steps to make it operational."[29] The Secretary-General then indicated that he was making his special adviser for the prevention of genocide (Juan Mendez of Argentina) a full-time post and that he was upgrading the UN Advisory Committee on Genocide Prevention.[30]

The situation is that there is plenty of theoretical support for the Responsibility to Protect principle both among national governments and the public, but how to implement it in particular circumstances has yet to be worked out. One relevant proposal is to establish a UN Emergency Peace Force made up of individuals employed directly by the UN that could be quickly moved into difficult situations like those in Darfur until the typical peacekeeping forces can be assembled and put in place.[31]

WHY THESE TWO DEVELOPMENTS ARE SO IMPORTANT

Let me conclude by noting why the creation and development of the ICC and the adoption of the Responsibility to Protect principle are so important. Both of them eliminate the notion of the unlimited sovereignty of national governments, a principle that has been used by ruthless national rulers to justify campaigns of violence against both other nations and those labeled "enemies" in their own country. The International Criminal Court establishes a permanent international institution to prosecute those individual high-ranking government officials and military officers responsible for genocide, war crimes, and crimes against humanity no matter where these are committed, while the Responsibility to Protect principle makes it clear that those committing these crimes can't hide behind the old notion of national sovereignty, the now-rejected view that national governments can do whatever they want within their own borders.

The creation of the ICC is a giant step forward in spreading the rule of law in the world. Professor Robert Johansen of Notre Dame University has noted that the creation of the ICC "could well be the most important institutional innovation [for the world] since the founding of the United Nations."[32] The adoption of the Responsibility to Protect principle is a gigantic step forward in protecting people from the murderous inhuman actions of their own national governments, something that in the last century has caused as many deaths as wars.[33] Human history shows that establishing judicial institutions and principles of law is an effective way of promoting peace and justice in the human community, just as important as repeated appeals to individuals to be more loving and less violent. We can be grateful that during our lifetimes the institutions and principles of law are being extended beyond the national level to the international level.

NOTES

1. Coalition for the International Criminal Court.
2. The American Non-Governmental Organization Coalition for the International Criminal Court.
3. Rubin, 2006: 42.
4. "Armies of Children," 2006.
5. The International Development Research Centre, 2001.
6. Ibid., 8.
7. Ibid.
8. Ibid., 11.
9. Ibid.
10. Ibid., 8.
11. Ibid., 9.
12. Ibid., 13.
13. Ibid., 14.
14. Ibid., 17.
15. Ibid., 11–18.
16. Ibid., 19–27.
17. Ibid., 29–37.
18. Ibid., 34–46.
19. Ibid., 47–55.
20. Ibid., 57–67.
21. Ibid., 69–75.
22. Ibid., 75.
23. World Summit Outcome Document, 2005.
24. Ibid.
25. International Coalition for the Responsibility to Protect (ICR2P)
26. Responsibility to Protect, 2007.
27. World Public Opinion, 2007.
28. Stroehlein and Evans, 2007.
29. UN Secretary General, 2007.
30. United Nations, 2007.
31. Johansen, 2006.
32. Joan B. Kroc Institute, 1997.
33. Rummel, 1994.

CHAPTER 6

TOWARD A *NECESSARY* UTOPIANISM: DEMOCRATIC GLOBAL GOVERNANCE

Richard Falk

URGENT REQUIREMENTS FOR A PEACEFUL WORLD ORDER

Not only the U.S. Department of Defense but practically every planning council among the developed nations and beyond is scurrying to plan for anticipated consequences of clearly visible trends producing hunger, environmental degradation, and violent conflict. Often the frameworks proposed fail to support institutions of international governance perceived as fair internationally. Too often the planning excludes the voices of those who are the first casualties. Unless the emergence of an effective form of global governance is adequately democratized it will not only reproduce existing acute inequities and exploitative patterns of present world order, but will almost certainly intensify these malevolent features. Such forebodings are based on the assessment of present global trends that document increasing disparities among peoples, races, and classes, but also call to our attention the growing struggle over dwindling oil supplies and the overall harmful effects of global warming and various associated forms of environmental

An earlier version of the ideas expressed in this chapter appeared in Richard A. Falk, *Achieving Human Rights*. New York: Routledge, 2009: 13–24.

deterioration.[1] Without drastic normative adjustments in the interaction of states and regions, as well as an accompanying social regulation of the world economy, global governance is almost certain to adopt highly coercive methods of stifling resistance from disadvantaged societies and social forces.

The presidency of George W. Bush in the United States brought to the fore an extremist leadership marked by preemptive military incursions and low respect for international law. This was subsequently repudiated by the American electorate, indicating some changes in the short run. But the tenets of the George W. Bush years may still be a crude forerunner of future hegemonic efforts by the United States to stabilize the unjust global status quo to the extent possible.[2]

There are no indications that President Obama, or any plausible new political leader on the horizon in the United States, will draw back the American militarization of the planet under its sovereign control, including oceans, space, the world network of military bases, global intelligence, and special forces presence.[3] Global governance under any such auspices, even if less manifestly dysfunctional than the failing neoconservative experiment to provide security for the world as administered from Washington, is almost certain to falter without ambitious moves to establish an inclusive consensual, cooperative, multilateral, and constitutional framework built around a truly operational global rule of law.[4]

At present, there seems to be grossly insufficient political agency available to support mounting a credible challenge along such transformative lines to existing world order arrangements. That is, the neoconservative American vision of global governance has been defeated by resistance, but as matters now stand there is no alternative, and signs indicate that this vision will be altered only to accommodate a more liberal style of promotion. It is due to this inability to depict a plausible path leading from the present reality of dysfunctional Westphalianism to a more democratically constituted and institutionally centralized global governance that makes any current call appear "utopian," that is, not attainable except imaginatively.

Against such a background the advocacy of world government seems constructive and responsive, yet I would argue that to push for world government at this time is dangerously premature. Such a post-Westphalian governmental restructuring of global authority, particularly in relation to war making, in the unlikely event that it were to become capable of enactment, would almost certainly produce a tyrannical world polity. Such a result seems almost certain unless the realization of world government was preceded by economic, social, and cultural developments that reduced dramatically current levels of material unevenness, poverty, and inter-civilizational antagonisms.

So long as this unevenness persists, any centralization of political authority is certain to be coercive, exploitative, and oppressive. Perhaps, in the decades ahead, the raw struggle for human survival may yield this kind of outcome misleadingly described as "world government," and may make it seem an acceptable or even the best attainable world order solution for the peoples of the world. This survival scenario is a rather realistic expectation, given the likelihood that pressures in relation to global warming and energy supplies and prices will soon reach emergency levels. What is politically possible in a circumstance of imminent catastrophe or at the early stages of an unfolding catastrophe cannot be foretold, but given our best understanding of present political realities, the present advocacy of world government is both utopian (unattainable) and dystopian (undesirable). If this is correct, then the contemplation of a benevolent world government is an idle daydream that we as humans concerned for the future can currently ill afford.

An alternative approach, suggested by a similar understanding of the same set of planetary circumstances, involves a focus on the preconditions for achieving a *humane* form of global governance. An early attempt to depict a post-Westphalian benevolent world order was made by Falk.[5] From this perspective the major premise of analysis is that without the emergence and eventual flourishing of global democracy the world seems assuredly heading for dystopia, if not irreversible catastrophe. Any reasonable approach to the future must exhibit an awareness of the probable relevance of crucial unanticipated developments.[6]

Given this outlook, it seems useful to distinguish among several horizons of possibility when contemplating the shape and viability of global governance in the relatively near-term future. Current policy debate, including mainstream reformist proposals and projections, takes place in a political space that seems consistent with *horizons of feasibility* (that is, policy goals attainable without substantial modification of structures of power, privilege, authority, and societal belief patterns); such horizons can shift abruptly during moments of crisis and emergency. In a negative manner, horizons of feasibility receded dramatically after the 9/11 attacks, making recourse to aggressive wars by the U.S. government much easier to justify, generating strong political backing at home.

A more positive illustration involved the establishment of the International Criminal Court in the aftermath of the Cold War despite the opposition of several leading governments. If such a project had been launched in the 1970s or 1980s it would have been quickly dismissed as utopian, yet in the late 1990s it became a realized goal of a group of moderate governments working in tandem with a coalition of transnational civil society actors. Horizons of feasibility shift and evolve, and not necessarily in a linear and incremental rhythm, but by jumps, discontinuities replete with contradictions.

It is not enough to ponder the future through calculations and assessments made by reference to horizons of feasibility. *We also require some sense
of preferred alternative ways of sustaining life on the planet along lines that accord
with scientific and professional judgments as to how to improve the material and
social quality of human life for all persons.* To do this is not just a technical
matter. It is also ethical, calling for special efforts on behalf of those now
poor, excluded, subordinated, and otherwise disadvantaged. It also presup-
poses that far longer term perspectives inform public policy at levels of
social integration than are now associated with domestic electoral cycles.
As well, the shaping of a democratic form of global governance cannot be
effectively or beneficially managed on the basis of either a world constituted
almost exclusively by territorial political communities enjoying sovereign
rights or a world that is controlled by either single or multiple hegemonic
centers of territorial power of global and regional scope or by market-based
global business and banking elites.[7]

To devise what will work to ensure a sustainable human future that does
not rest on naked force and entail grossly exploitative distributions of
wealth and income requires a scientifically and ethically informed vision of
what is needed, treated here as *horizons of necessity.*

*It is the gap between feasibility and necessity, as well as the fragility and com-
plexity of current world order, which largely explains what is appropriately
described as the deepening crisis of global governance.*

In this regard, the petroleum-based technologies of the 21st century,
military and otherwise, make the consequences of failure and breakdown so
much more consequential than earlier. This observation is particularly
obvious with regard to any assessment of the destructive impacts of major
wars fought with nuclear weapons as distinct from wars fought with bows
and arrows or machetes. But the same condition exists in many other
domains of international life, including, of course, the use of the global commons as a dump for greenhouse gas emissions, as for various other kinds of
waste disposal.

By itself this polarization of perspectives may not do more than help us
understand the gathering gloom about the future of humanity by focusing
our attention on what is needed, yet seemingly unattainable, rather than to
be content with what is feasible. With this consideration in mind, it seems
useful to look closely at what is desired and desirable with respect to the
multi-dimensional challenge of global governance.

In this respect, reflecting on *horizons of desire* is not entirely impractical,
but rather provides an inspirational foundation for the mobilizing energy
that will be required if horizons of necessity are to motivate action without
adding to human suffering. The emphasis on democracy as the ground on

which global governance must unfold, if it is to be successful and benevolent, is an acknowledgement, with risks attached, of the political significance of desire and the desirable.[8] As suggested, tyrannical forms of global governance might, although at great human costs, could more easily satisfy the imperatives of necessity, at least for some decades, but dystopicly.

The preferred alternative is to embrace the utopian possibility of conflating horizons of necessity and horizons of desire, which seems only imaginable if global governance is radically democratized in the near future. Whether that conflation would help fashion the political agency required to establish a credible political project of global democratic governance cannot be foretold. There is also some support, especially in American neoliberal and neoconservative circles, for embracing benevolent hegemony, even empire, as the most attainable form of effective global governance.[9] As with world government, hegemonic or imperial solutions, even if arguably responsive to horizons of necessity, should be rejected because they do not appear on the horizons of desire.[10]

Global democracy seems necessary and desirable, although its realization, assuming obstacles can be overcome, may turn out to be not altogether positive. Much can go wrong by way of implementation: corruption, militarism, even repression and exploitation could easily occur along the way, if the mechanisms of governance are not constrained by a robust regime of law that is itself responsive to the values and implementing procedures of a human rights culture and to demands for global justice. This regime of global law is particularly needed to offset to some extent the effects of gross inequality and disparity that currently exists, and seems built into the operational workings of the world economy.[11]

The final test of social justice globally conceived, recalling Gandhi's criterion of "the last man" and John Rawls's emphasis on the most disadvantaged elements in society, will be how those at the margins of human vulnerability are treated, including the impoverished, the unborn, the indigenous, and the deviant.

Procedural benchmarks will also be indicative of a more inclusive democracy that is not yet: progress toward accountability for wrongdoing by political actors, regulation of economic regimes to ensure the material and human well-being of all persons and groups, implementation of prohibitions on recourse to war as a political option, a dynamic of demilitarization, and behind everything, a rule of law as administered by an independent and available judiciary so that there is a growing impression that legal equals (for example, governments of sovereign states) are being treated equally.

In contrast, the present world order shocks the moral conscience by the extent to which powerful political actors are being given an exemption from criminal accountability while weaker figures are increasingly prosecuted and punished. Saddam Hussein or Slobodan Milosevic are prosecuted but George W. Bush, Tony Blair, and Vladimir Putin are de facto exempt from even indictment. More broadly, hegemonic actors enjoy an informal, yet fully effective, right of exception with respect to adherence to international law, expressed both by the veto given to permanent members of the UN Security Council and by the operational freedom of maneuver enjoyed by major states.

This chapter will not attempt to look at this entire global canvas of democratizing initiatives but limits itself to an inquiry that highlights the place of the individual as "citizen" of this unborn global polity and the creation of an institutional arena that can give meaningful expression to democratizing sentiments and express grievances that come from below. In this rendering, the spirit of democracy is derived from respect for the authority of the grassroots, giving some sort of preliminary outlet for legitimizing processes of popular sovereignty.[12] More concretely, attention will be given to **a futuristic conception of citizenship—the citizen pilgrim**—and to the establishment of a political forum for collective deliberation—a global peoples assembly or global peoples parliament.

It needs to be understood that both structural aspects of Westphalian world order, the horizontal juridical order encompassing the interplay of formally equal sovereign states and the vertical order exhibiting the geopolitical structure of grossly unequal states, now exhibit almost none of the characteristics of democratic governance.

The clearest embodiment of the horizontal juridical order may be seen in the functioning of the UN General Assembly. Governments are somewhat equal with respect to one another, but this body is denied the authority to decide or the power to enforce and there are no opportunities given for meaningful and direct participation by representatives of global civil society. The clearest expression of the vertical geopolitical order can be observed in the UN Security Council, where many sessions on crucial issues of peace and security are held in secret so that even transparency is absent in the context of debate. The UN is a quintessential Westphalian institution with respect to membership and operational responsibilities, although these realities are to some extent hidden behind the normative architecture of the UN Charter, which at least purports to impose major behavioral constraints on all states, including geopolitical actors.

A slightly deeper scrutiny discloses a veto power that almost completely nullifies the Charter constraints, and looking still deeper reveals an operational code in which the main hegemonic actor(s) overrides in almost all circumstances the autonomy of ordinary sovereign states, despite their formal rights of equality based on membership.

This presentation of current world order does not take account of the rise of non-state actors both as participants and challengers.[13] These post-Westphalian elements of world order are arrayed around market forces, humanitarian voluntary associations, and mobilized social forces. Characteristic arenas of activity for such actors included the World Economic Forum, conflict zones, and the World Social Forum. These actors, although outside the formal framework of interacting governments representing sovereign states, are also not subject to any consistent criteria of democratic governance. Their current main roles as gadflies or adjuncts to states make their absence of democratic practices of less present concern, but if their future contribution to the shaping of democratic global governance is to retain credibility, then appropriate forms of democratization of civil society actors need to be established.

CITIZENSHIP

Discussions of citizenship in the modern era focused mainly on the evolving relations of citizen and state in liberal democracies. This concept of citizenship in the last half of the 20th century became increasingly associated with a normative model of legitimate national governance, incorporating both the rise of international human rights and reliance on private sector economic growth. The authoritative character of this model was universalized, at least rhetorically, after the collapse of the Soviet Union, the entry of China into the World Trade Organization, and the emergence of a consensus among governments in support of neoliberalism as the foundation of national economic policy.

George W. Bush endorsed such an understanding of governance when he started his cover letter introducing the important document National Security Strategy 2002 of the United States of America with the following sentence: "The great struggles of the 20th century between liberty and totalitarianism ended with a decisive victory for the forces of freedom—and a single sustainable model for national success: freedom, democracy, and free enterprise."[14]

What is striking here is the regressive and revealing failure to mention any duty to protect those materially deprived by providing for basic human needs, as well as the arrogance associated with claiming to be the embodiment of the single model of societal success. To show respect for social and economic rights of individuals and groups was deliberately avoided in the Bush approach, presumably because it would be regarded as an acceptance of the welfare state, and might attract conservative criticism as a backdoor acceptance of socialism.[15] Although this American retreat from a conception of citizenship that includes the responsibility of the state for the material well-being of its citizenry has taken an extreme form, it does reflect a wider trend that is partly responsive to the supposed imperative of a neoliberal global economy, partly a reaction to the failures of state socialism as embodied in the Soviet Union, partly a consequence of a weakening labor movement in post-industrial societies, and partly reflective of a rightward swing throughout the industrial world in relation to state responsibility for the welfare of their citizenry.

Traditional forms of citizenship, then, at their best involved meaningful participation (rights and duties) within national political space, especially the enjoyment of civil and political rights (freedom), the opportunity to participate in an open political process that is framed by a constitutional document (rule of law), subsidized opportunities for education and health, the assured protection of private property and national and transnational entrepreneurial rights (trade and investment), and some measure of support in circumstances of material need. Such a view of what might be called Westphalian citizenship included a reciprocal series of duties; the most onerous involved obligations of loyalty and service to the state. The crime of treason, continues to be punished everywhere with great severity, legalizes a radical denial of a globalized moral conscience, presupposing that even if the state acts in defiance of international law, universal standards of morality, and self-destructive imprudence, it is a crime to lend aid and comfort to its enemy.

In this respect, there exists an unresolved tension between accountability of even government officials to international criminal law and the continuing claims made by governments to the unwavering, and essentially unchallengeable, allegiance of citizens. From the perspective of moral and legal globalization it seems like an opportune moment to advocate the abolition of "treason" as a crime. A serious debate on treason and conscience would serve the purpose of rethinking the proper vector of citizenship with respect to changing values, beliefs, and conditions, as well as to acknowledge the global and species context of human action. As matters now stand, the absolutizing of allegiance to the state that confers nationality and citizenship undermines both human solidarity and respect for norms claiming global applicability. Such an allegiance inculcates a tribalist ethos that anachronistically privileges the part over the whole at a historic moment when the parts that make up the whole increasingly depend on the well-being of the latter.

The Nuremberg ethos that held German and later Japanese leaders legally responsible for their official crimes almost obligates citizens of state embarked on a course of international criminality to advocate treason, and certainly requires a rejection of blind obedience to the orders and policies of a state. Of course, this Nuremberg legacy is ambiguous, starting out as victors' justice and persisting as a normative framework that effectively exempts geopolitical actors and their servants from all efforts to impose criminal responsibility on those who act on behalf of the state. The unsuccessful pursuit of the former American Secretary of Defense Donald Rumsfeld, for his role in authorizing torture, illustrates the de facto immunity of those who act on behalf of hegemonic states.

Beyond this, there is the question of citizenship that is not tied to the national space of the sovereign state. To some extent this has been formally recognized by the conferral of a secondary layer of European citizenship on persons living permanently within the countries belonging to the European Union.[16] This formal acknowledgement has a rudimentary corresponding structure of regional governance as especially embodied in such institutions as the European Court of Human Rights and the European Parliament.

More challenging, however, is the failure to take account of the partial disenfranchisement that has occurred globally both by the operations of the world economy and by the emergence of the United States as a global state, that is, exercising its authority as an override of both the sovereign rights of other states and through a self-decreed exemption from either the authority of the United Nations or of international law, especially in the areas of war and peace. This disenfranchisement has the effect of precluding the meaningful exercise of democracy on the level of the state for many countries, particularly in the ex-colonial countries. If we could imagine an adjustment by way of allowing persons outside the United States to challenge policy affecting their well-being by way of binding referenda or even by casting votes in national elections held within the United States, the leadership role of the United States in shaping global governance would likely be altered for the better (as measured by the principles of the UN Charter or by most accounts of global justice) in fundamental respects, and there would be a far better fit between the ideals of democracy and the benefits of citizenship. The Westphalian territorial grip on the political imagination remains so tight that such a recasting of electoral arrangements is almost unthinkable, conveying sentiments that have the ring of ultra-utopianism.

The ageing of the Westphalian structure of world order is exhibited by the emergence of new arenas of global policy formation that are more responsive to the influence of non-state actors.[17] For instance, the World Economic Forum (WEF), especially during the 1990s, provided global market forces, and their most important representatives, with an influential arena. The WEF was established after the Trilateral Commission, which was an elite-oriented private sector initiative that was supposed to offset the inter-governmental influence on world economic policy attributed to the Non-Aligned Movement, and its efforts in the early 1970s to achieve a new international economic order. In many respects the WEF shaped a policy climate that conditioned the behavior of governments and international financial institutions.

In reaction to this post-colonial West-centric nongovernmental continu-ing effort to steer the world economy in a manner that widened disparities between rich and poor within and among countries, civil society actors in the South formed the World Social Forum (WSF).

The respective ideological and geographical centers of gravity of these opposing initiatives were expressed by the WEF meeting annually in Davos, Switzerland, and the WSF meeting initially for several years in Puerto Allegre, Brazil. In a certain sense, these opposed initiatives repre-sented forms of self-created "global citizenship," established without the formal blessings of states or international institutions, and yet producing meaningful forms of participation by non-state global actors. Such partici-pation is quite likely more meaningful than what was possible through ei-ther individual or group participation in many national political processes. Of course, these two types of arenas are not necessarily contradictory when it comes to policy, and could be partially understood as complementary undertakings to overcome the limitations of a purely statist world order. Kofi Annan, while serving as UN Secretary-General, told the WEF at one of its annual gatherings that the UN would only remain relevant in the new century if it found ways to incorporate both market forces and civil society actors significantly into its activities.

Whether intended or not, the former UN Secretary-General was signal-ing the somewhat subversive opinion that the Westphalian era was over, or at least coming to an end, unless the purely statist structure of authority was modified at the UN, and presumably elsewhere in global policy arenas, to make room for certain non-state actors to take part in meaningful ways. Of course, these demands for access are not symmetrical. It is far easier for statist structures including the UN to accommodate private sector market forces, which already exert a huge influence thorough their strong repre-sentation in the upper echelons of officialdom in many governments. To varying degrees national governments have even been instrumentalized by domestic and global market forces.

This reality is accentuated by the fact that civil society actors are unrep-resented in governmental circles. It remains a rarity for activist representa-tives of civil society to exert any direct influence on governmental policy formation or operations. Such a generalization is particularly true with respect to peace, security, and foreign economic policy. In the humanitarian domain of conflict management, civil society actors often collaborate with governments.

This structural challenge to Westphalian conceptions of world order remains unmet, and has unleashed a statist backlash.[18] Annan's rather mild efforts to implement his views on the future of the UN, especially with regard to the role of civil society representatives were effectively rebuffed by statist forces, a story largely untold. For instance, Annan proposed having an assembly of representatives of NGOs hold a meeting, intended as perhaps the first of an annual event, at the UN as part of the millennium celebrations in the year 2000.

Even this largely symbolic gesture to civil society was opposed to such an extent behind the scenes by leading governments that the gathering had to be held in a diluted form outside UN premises and on the assurance that this meeting was a one-time event. This same Westphalian backlash has led the UN to abandon the format of highly visible world meetings on global policy issues, which became in the 1990s important opportunities for transnational social forces to organize and network globally, gain access to the world media, and to help shape the policy outcomes by influencing Third World governments.[19]

The rise of non-state actors and the formation of non-state arenas seem to be reshaping the nature of citizenship in the 21st century as concept, as behavior, and as aspiration.[20] If modes of participation and psycho-political identities are shifting to take account of the realities of globalization, it is misleading to continue to reduce citizenship to a formal status granted by territorial governments of sovereign states, or even by such inter-governmental entities as the European Union. Such an opinion is not meant to deny that citizenship of the traditional variety continues to provide most individuals with their most vibrant and useful sense of connection to a political community, especially in determining entitlements and rights and duties, as well as accounting for dominant political identities. What is being claimed, however, is that additionally *informal* modes of belonging and participating should begin to be acknowledged, encouraged, and evaluated as integral aspects of "citizenship."

There is also an emerging new outlook on citizenship identity, and community. It reflects a growing preoccupation with the unsustainability of present civilizational lifestyle, and petroleum-based modernities. Putting this preoccupation more positively emphasizes the relevance of *time* to an adequate contemporary conception of citizenship. This acknowledges that discourses on citizenship, even if visionary, were essentially related to *space*, including those that articulated the ideal of "citizen of the world."

If concerns for unsustainability and of responsibilities to the unborn are added to the desirable, and possibly necessary, adoption of a pacifist geopolitics are the substantive facets of this future-oriented perspectives on citizenship, it would be useful to signal this enlargement of outlook by adopting the terminology of "citizen pilgrim."[21]

The pilgrim, although it has some misleading religious connotations associated with holy journeys, conveys the overriding sense that normative citizenship in the early 21st century involves a pilgrimage to a sustainable, equitable, humane, and peaceable future. The citizen pilgrim is on a journey through time, dedicated to what is being called here "a necessary utopianism." In contrast the traditional citizen is bound to her territorial space, and at most can call on her government to be sensitive to long-range considerations.

The calling of the citizen pilgrim is to act without regard to territorial boundaries or the priorities of national interest when these conflict with the human interest in a sustainable future. As well, the citizen pilgrim is engaged in the project of global democratization in any of a multitude of ways, including establishing positive connections of affection and appreciation based on human solidarity and shared destiny. Sustained by an ecumenical spirit, the citizen pilgrim rejects the secular/religious binary that supposedly separates the modern from the traditional, and finds spiritual as well as mundane wisdom and visionary hope embodied in all of the great world religions.[22]

GLOBAL PARLIAMENT

Democratizing global governance raises a variety of issues, including greater degrees of accountability, transparency, and equity throughout the United Nations System, as well as establishing spaces for non-state participation. The most promising and practical way to acknowledge the challenge and organize a response is to establish *in some form* a global parliament with the mandate to incorporate transnational and futurist non-state civil societal priorities.[23] I have collaborated for some years with Andrew Strauss in the development of support for this initiative.[24]

Such an innovative step has been prefigured by the existence for several decades of the European Parliament, as well as the far newer African Parliament. Although a bold challenge to Westphalian notions of world order based on exclusive international representation by the governments of sovereign states, a global parliament is a flexible format that can be initiated modestly. In conception, the establishment of such an institution is a less radical innovation than was the International Criminal Court that proposes a capacity to hold leaders of sovereign states accountable for certain enumerated crimes. Whether this mission will be fulfilled, especially with respect to leading states, seems doubtful at present, but the existence of the institution is a recognition of a principled approach to the uniform imposition of a global rule of law on all who act in the name of the state.

A global parliament is capable of evolving into a lawmaking institution, but its initial phase of operations would be primarily to give the peoples of the world a direct "voice" at the global level, with a strong networking potential of benefit to the strengthening of global civil society and an institutional embodiment of populist concerns.

There are many organizational mechanisms that could be used to establish such a global parliament.[25] Undoubtedly, the easiest approach would be to rely on national parliaments to designate a given number of representatives proportionate to the size of their population or reflective of some formula for civilizational distribution. But such a starting point, although likely the most manageable, would seem likely to reproduce Westphalian attitudes in such a way as to defeat the main purposes of the global parliament. More promising, although potentially cumbersome, would involve the voluntary decision by a given number of governments, say, 30, to agree by treaty to the establishment of a global parliament via direct elections arranged either nationally or regionally.

It has been encouraging to experience reactions of growing receptivity around the world to the whole project of establishing a global parliament. I believe this represents both a gradual globalization of political consciousness and the spread of the idea that global governance needs to avoid hegemonic solutions, which requires a variety of moves in the direction of global democracy.

The disappointing and alienating results of the American use of its unipolar geopolitical position has also contributed to this receptive atmosphere, as has the halting, yet cumulative progress toward the establishment of a European polity based on consent and an ethos of democracy. These developments suggest a slow merger of horizons of necessity and desire, as well as less remoteness from the horizon of feasibility. As a thought experiment the emergence of a global parliament seems in 2008 less unlikely than did the establishment of an International Criminal Court a decade before its establishment in 2002. Of course, what happens to such an institution to make it live up to the hopes of its sponsors involves an equally difficult struggle.

· *There now exists much support for the global parliament idea throughout global civil society whenever world order reform is at issue. What is needed is a campaign, perhaps modeled on the collaborative efforts between coalitions of moderate governments and civil society actors that were so successful in relation to the treaties banning anti-personnel landmines and establishing the International Criminal Court.*

The campaign for a global parliament could initially aim to achieve support for convening a treaty-making negotiating session that might itself break ground by combining governments of states with transnational civil society actors as negotiating partners. What would hopefully emerge from such a process would be a treaty that would not come into force until ratified by national constitutional processes and by referenda in participating societies, which need not necessarily be configured as "states."

As with the idea of citizen pilgrim so with the global parliament, much of the benefit would flow from the process itself. This process would shape a consensus as to organizational format, including membership, funding and constitutional status. A big issue is whether the global parliament would be formed as a subsidiary organ of the UN General Assembly or take some more autonomous character within the UN System. It might also turn out to be impossible to gain agreement for situating the global parliament within the UN, in which case it might be established for a trial period as a free-standing international institution, which is the case, for instance, for the World Trade Organization.

CONCLUSION

This chapter, and its recommendations, proceed from the belief that politics as the art of the possible cannot hope to cope with the multi-dimensional, intensifying crisis of global governance.

At the same time, it seeks to root its analysis and prescriptions as coherently and responsively as the imagination allows with respect to what has been called horizons of desire and necessity. Its main utopian element is to encourage a radical revisioning of citizenship that currently continues to serve mainly nationalist and even tribalist values.

To be a citizen pilgrim in such a global setting is to be a lonely voice in the wilderness, yet representing an ethically driven commitment to truthfulness, human and natural well-being, and an overall quest for sustainability and equity.

Similarly, to advocate a global parliament, given the structure of the United Nations and the resilience of statist geopolitics, is to whistle in the wind, but yet the wind can shift, allowing the impossible to become abruptly feasible. Again, the rationale for establishing a global parliament rests on desire and necessity, not feasibility.

This leaves the question as to whether such a framework for advocacy can ground the struggle for global democracy, and ultimately hope in the human future, under present world conditions of denial, strife, oppression, exploitation, and alienation.

NOTES

1. Kunstler, 2005.

2. For continuity of recent American hegemonic behavior see Neil Smith, 2005.

3. Johnson, 2004, 2006.

4. *National Security Strategy of the United States of America*, 2002, 2006; Muravchik, 2007.

5. Falk, 1995.

6. Taleb, 2007.

7. Knutsen, 1999; Falk, 1999.

8. For comprehensive treatment see Archibugi, 2008.

9. Furguson, 2004; Bacevich, 2002.

10. This position is most elaborately argued by Mandelbaum, 2002.

11. Harvey, 2003.

12. Kaldor, 2007.

13. Andreopoulos et al., 2006.

14. *National Security Strategy of the United States of America*, 2002.

15. See Marshall, 1950, on the evolution of Westphalian citizen rights.

16. Maastricht Treaty, 1992; Balibar, 2004.

17. Falk, 2004.

18. Ibid.

19. Pianta, 2003.

20. Keck, 1998; Andreopoulos, 2006.

21. Falk, 1995.

22. Hurd, 2008.

23. For range of views see Widener Symposium, 2007.

24. Strauss, 2007; Falk and Strauss, 2000, 2001, 2003; Falk, 2007.

25. Falk and Strauss, 2001, 2003.

PART II

PEACE FROM BELOW

Virtually every existing means of preventing and constraining war originated with the peace movement. International law, arbitration and mediation, the creation of international organizations, disarmament, decolonization, economic development, democratization, human rights, the protection of civilians—all were proposed by peace advocates well before they were adopted by governments.
—Charles Chatfield

When the newly elected President Obama took office and began a dialogue with his supporters in a new vein, he harkened back to a well-known remark President Roosevelt is said to have made to someone who had just urged him to pass an important piece of legislation. The President replied, "That's a great idea. Now go out and force me to do it." Similarly, it is not apocryphal that when President Johnson told Martin Luther King Jr. that it was not possible for him to grant King's urgent request for a voting rights act, the latter went out to the streets; and after some more months of nonviolent protest he found himself back in the White House as the President signed the bill into law.

Although it has always been true that "when the people lead, the leaders will follow," the truth has a special cogency today, for the characteristic of our times, as Paul Hawken and many others have pointed out, is that major institutions—financial, governmental, educational, media—are losing their grip and new forms of popular action are coming together. Many feel that this is a result of new technologies, especially the new "social media." We tend to believe, however, that causality is going the other way around—that humanity is impatient with the old forms of association and the cumbersome, formal, often top-down institutions our industrial culture has produced and yearns to rediscover itself in different terms. To give that new mode of association its voice, or, if you will, its nervous system, new technologies have been developed, or adapted.

"Never doubt that a small group of thoughtful people could change the world. Indeed, it's the only thing that ever has." These words of Margaret Mead are among the most widely quoted today, particularly in these electronic media. We should never doubt, either, that an unsuspected power of self-organization exists in people or groups that can emerge even under the darkest or most dangerous conditions (see, for example, Broz's chapter). A young doctor in New Orleans noticed this when he was stranded in a hospital with no power and water rising and had to evacuate several hundred elderly and infirm patients. As the Army trucks sloshed up to take them to safer ground, volunteers came "from nowhere" and without anyone to give orders organized themselves to save those patients, in some cases carrying them down six flights of stairs in a building without air conditioning (the Fahrenheit temperatures were in the low hundreds) or light.[1]

It is not a coincidence, then, that "Peace from Below" is the most populated part in these three volumes. That reflects the importance of this dimension of change toward a more peaceful order, and its newness: when you are on the edge of a new paradigm it is typically difficult to sort out and summarize its characteristics synoptically. Also typical is that the new understanding toward which we are moving is at present somewhat contradictory, in that we are reaching for a more global, but at the same time less centralized, kind of order.

Because of this fullness, we will not try to summarize here each of the chapters in this important section. Rather, we point out several dimensions of civil society or peace from below that represent them collectively. In no particular order, there are attempts to see the emerging big picture (Nagler, Hawken), the role of individual courage (Broz), glimpses of new civil society institutions (Lozano, McCarthy, Bernstein, Marks and Marks, and Slachmuijlder), particular peace movement campaigns (Baumann, Butigan), efforts to make knowledge about peace and information about activities favoring it a part of the media, the classroom, and the Internet (Phillips and Huff, Carter, and Temple), and finally three studies of the situation on the ground for indigenous people and some heartening successes in their severe struggles for dignity and justice (Lozano again, Tirado, and Rountree).

What is particularly striking is that some of these efforts occur with minimal resources and with the leadership coming from the ground rather than from experts. Moreover, the variety and creativity of local approaches leaves a difficult target for those who would like to suppress them. Third, as small, personal, or local as these efforts may be, they are now able to communicate through new outlets so they can be protected—and copied (think, for example, of the worldwide organizations of indigenous peoples and the global social forum in which many of them participate). Taken together, the efforts sampled here contribute a sense of hope and innovation that is much needed in the present discourse on peace.

—Marc Pilisuk and Michael N. Nagler

NOTE

1. This account was widely circulated on the Internet.

CHAPTER 7

I Am the Leader, You Are the Leader: Nonviolent Resistance in the Peace Community of San José de Apartadó, Colombia

Elizabeth Lozano

This chapter examines practices of nonviolent resistance of the Peace Community of San José de Apartadó in Colombia and the context of structural violence in which these practices occur. To do so, I draw on data derived from fieldwork and witness accounts, as well as from published and unpublished documents, including the database of the Colombian Center for Research and Popular Education (CINEP), a Jesuit-run Colombian think tank; and scholarly work by Colombian and U.S. experts.

San José de Apartadó (SJA) is a small town located in the Urabá region of northwest Colombia, a highly desirable stretch of land for many of those engaged in Colombia's 50-year-old armed conflict. A fertile zone rich in water, coal, wood, agriculture, and oil, Urabá has been a theater not only of "crushing violence" since the late 1970s but also of "powerful civil organization and resistance."[1] Examples of such resistance are the Afro-Colombian Community of Self-Determination of Cacarica, whose inhabitants were forced to flee in 1997 and returned in 2001, as well as the peasant Peace Community of San José de Apartadó (CDP-SJA).[2] There are more than 50 peace communities around the country that have declared themselves neutral in the Colombian war.[3] Aside from the Urabá initiatives, these peace communities include the Indigenous Guard of Northern Cauca in the Colombian southwest, the sovereign town of Mogotes in northeast Colombia, the Medellín Youth Network, the Women's Path of Peace, and the Children's Movement for Peace.[4]

OCTOBER 2003. 5:00 P.M. AT THE TOWN OF SAN JOSÉ DE APARTADÓ

On the road between San José de Apartadó and La Linda hamlet, an army unit detains three youths on their way back from work. The news spreads quickly. A group of about 80 peasants led by Patricio,[5] one of the members of the CDP's community council, catches up with the army unit and demands the liberation of the youths. The soldiers deny having any youths in their possession. The peasants state that they are not moving until the youths are returned. The officer in charge demands to speak with the leader of the group.

The officer asks, "Who is your leader?"

"I am," responds Patricio.

"He is lying," responds an elderly woman, stepping forward, "I am the leader."

"Not true," says a teenage boy, "I am the leader."

"You are lying," yells another man, approaching, "I am the leader."

The officer interrupts impatiently, saying, "You are wasting my time!" He agrees to return the youths, if a form is signed stating that no damage has been inflicted.

It has started to rain, so the officer needs to go inside a house to sign the form, but Patricio stops him and says, "You cannot go inside one of our houses holding a weapon."

The officer is astonished. "No civilian speaks to me this way," he says. He has never left his weapon unattended, particularly while on duty. Patricio insists, however, that he must do so. Baffled, the officer disarms and enters the house under the watchful eye of his subordinates and 80 peasants. The form is signed and the youth are returned.

This story was told to me by two people and, as often happens with witness accounts of what has become a legend, several versions of the story circulate. Gimena thinks the last person to speak was a little girl, whereas Patricio remembers a man. There is some disagreement as to what were the exact words of the officer. The written, legal account of the event mentions the detention and its outcome, but gives no details of the exchange,[6] which makes sense, for a legal account of abuse is a complaint, not a celebration of resourcefulness.

In spite of the differences, however, some aspects of the story do not vary. The army detained three youths, CDP members demanded their freedom, and the community group refused to have one person represent it and hide behind a single individual's fate or eloquence. In doing so, the group also refused to follow the rules of engagement being proposed by the army and, thereby, broke the principles of the power game being enacted. The group's action produced great disconcert among the soldiers and for the army officer, who, in this instance, gave into another kind of power. To use Boulding's terms,[7] the social actors involved in this situation did not follow the logic of "threat" power used by legal and illegal armed actors, and appealed, instead, to "integrative" power, a power born of a decade-old organized and conscious resistance against decades-old organized terror dissemination.[8] The officer could see in the eyes of this "leaderless" group an absolute willingness to face even death in the name of principles it held sacred.

AN ARCHIPELAGO OF CONFLICTS

To make sense of the situation in San José de Apartadó, one must understand the larger Colombian context in which that situation takes place, for Colombia has been engaged in an armed conflict that has lasted almost 50 years. Such conflict has been complex enough to generate its own academic subfield, "violentology"; its own manifestations in language and daily life; and its multifaceted expressions in the arts, from literature to film.

First, some scholars argue that Colombia is not one country but many countries, for it is characterized by disseminated power centers and deep class, regional, and social divisions. In 1999, the poorest 10 percent of the population controlled less than a 0.4 percent of the total wealth, whereas the richest 10 percent had access to 45 percent of the national wealth.[9] The Colombian upper class has more in common with the values and dreams of the Miami upper class than it has with the values and dreams of the Colombian peasants who grow cacao and bananas. For most Colombians, the "state" is an alien and puzzling entity, and "citizenship," at best, is a quaint concept, and at worst, a cynical proposition. Santos's concept of an "intimate" and "foreign" society illuminates this situation.[10] Specifically, the Colombian bourgeoisie has an "intimate" relationship with the state, whereas wide segments of the population have little to no access to the state. Most Colombians live, therefore, in a "foreign society," whose functioning principles are fundamentally unknown to them.

In addition to the complexity of the social panorama, oftentimes, "feudal" rhythms overlap with "modern" routines and "postmodern" aesthetics, creating a fusion of diverse cultural times lived simultaneously. San José de Apartadó is a case in point. Although horses and mules are its citizens' main mode of transportation, the CDP peasants also own televisions and cell phones, and have a community Web page and e-mail account. Hence, although the means of transportation have not changed radically in centuries, the means of communication have been revolutionized. A member of the Peace Community may have never finished primary school or visited the Atlantic coast, but she or he has access to information from around the world and directly or indirectly provides information to the world, as a participant in a local project of resistance that resonates internationally. In ways that seem paradoxical, the CDP may be better known in the progressive sectors of Italy, Portugal, the Netherlands, the United States, and Israel, than it is known in the upper-class neighborhoods of Bogotá and Cali. Such resonance is evidenced in the awards and recognitions the community has been given, including a nomination for the Nobel Peace Prize in 2007; the articles, Web sites, and news that circulate about the CDP; and the frequent visit of international delegations to its small and troubled territory. Though this dynamic seems paradoxical—why is a small Colombian town better known in San Francisco than in Bogotá?—it is, on the other hand, a very clear outcome of "people's" globalization. Virtual communities and postmodern nets of solidarity are emerging, which are not based on geographic proximity, or common cultural heritage, but on ideological, political, and existential affinity.

Finally, Colombia does not face an armed conflict but an "archipelago" of conflicts.[11] A 50-year-old protracted war between army and insurgency is reinforced by an armed conflict between paramilitaries and guerrillas. That confrontation exists side by side with a "social cleansing" project by paramilitaries, a "dirty war" against human rights advocates, a U.S.-supported "war on drugs" against narcotraffickers, and a "war on terrorism" apparently directed against all of the above. These manifestations of violence, in turn, produce a war on civilians caught between the army, guerrillas, warlords, paramilitaries, police, petty criminals, and their multiple hybrid combinations.

Additionally, and as stated by García Villegas and Santos,[12] the United States contributes constantly to the "reproduction" of the Colombian drug problem, not only because of its governmental prohibitions, but also because of its high share in the illegal market of cocaine and heroine. Given this situation, these authors argue that the United States is "the financial source of the main actors of the war in Colombia."[13] U.S. legal aid finances the army and the police; and U.S. illegal monies support the drug trade directly and the guerrillas indirectly.[14]

According to Alther et al. and other human rights observers, the far-right paramilitaries are responsible for 80 percent of the political killings in Colombia.[15] The army also has been found guilty of abuses, with the June 2009 report by the UN Special Rapporteur on extrajudicial executions expressing great concern about the army's handling of civilian deaths.[16] Of specific concern is the increased phenomenon of *falsos positivos* ("false positives"), a civilian murdered by the armed forces who is claimed to be a guerrilla killed in combat. There is some evidence that suggests soldiers are rewarded and earn points for guerrillas killed, a practice that encourages tampering with evidence to earn rewards by disguising acts of personal revenge, political silencing, or simple abuse of humble civilians (the most common victims are working-class men). The Colombia guerrillas, particularly the Revolutionary Armed Forces of Colombia (FARC), also have been responsible for what can justifiably be called despicable crimes against humanity, including the kidnapping of hundreds of people of various political, economic, and social backgrounds; and the massacres of Afro-Colombian and indigenous communities, such as the Bojayá massacre of 2002 and the 2009 killing of 17 Awá indigenous people.[17] San José de Apartadó has been no exception, often being a target of abuse by the FARC. Given the situation in Colombia, specific locales within that country, such as San José de Apartadó, thus are profoundly revelatory of ways in which conflict and resistance unfold locally but may resonate globally.

LA COMUNIDAD DE PAZ DE SAN JOSÉ DE APARTADÓ

San José de Apartadó declared itself a "Peace Community" in March 1997 for as long as "the internal conflict and war continue" in Colombia and in response to the human rights abuses of armed actors and the forced displacements that often happened as a consequence. Such displacements came "as a result of executions of peasants outside combat zones, the destruction and looting of their goods, and threats of renewed actions if they do not abandon their territories."[18] In addition, becoming a peace community was a mechanism by which the civil population could protect itself by appealing to the principles of international humanitarian law.

Currently, the peace community is located in three hamlets that are a few miles away from one another and in eight "humanitarian zones."[19] At one point, the center of the peace community was the town of San José de Apartadó, but the government-mandated installation of a police post in 2005 forced the group to relocate to a much smaller settlement, San Josesito de la Dignidad. Located 15 minutes away from San José, San Josesito is a refugee camp for 300 people, but knowing this did not prepare me well for what I saw when I visited in March 2009. "Refugee camp" conjures up images of disease, despair, chaos, dirt, hopeless suffering, and destitute poverty. What I found, instead, is beautifully implied in the name of the settlement: Little Saint Joseph of Dignity. The small camp holds tremendous dignity, pride, and upliftedness. The poverty is evident in every way, as there is no running water, paved streets, phone landlines, or sewage system. However, the public spaces are clean, the houses are lovingly decorated with lush flowers and plants, and the common spaces vibrate with children's activities, men playing pool, youth playing soccer, and dogs, pigs, and horses wandering around.

Four public houses and a ceremonial ground constitute the heart of the settlement. These are the communal kitchen, the primary school, the children's library, which has one of the two computers in town, and the open-air hut where the community's meetings take place. In the middle of the settlement, and constituting its symbolic and emotional center, stands a tall tree surrounded by painted stones, carefully positioned around the roots, and arranged in concentric circles. Every stone has a name on it, the name of a CDP victim of violence by the armed actors. Even in a situation of displacement, the community has carried with it its dead and made sure no one fades away from memory.

These public spaces represent, in material ways, the principles of the community, which include alternative education, horizontal leadership, economic autonomy, solidarity, unity, transparency, plurality, and celebration of each member's contribution, whether dead or alive. In short, SJA and its sister communities embody a key principle of nonviolent change that Gandhi established at the very beginning of his campaign,[20] Constructive Programme. In this it parallels the somewhat similar but much larger Landless Worker Movement in Brazil. Unlike in that movement, however, the people of SJA have, as we have seen, a more highly developed set of creative responses to the inevitable conflict that arises in response to, if not prior to, attempts by people to create positive, long-lasting change within their own communities, whether or not these attempts are explicitly part of a campaign of resistance as they were in Gandhi's India.

A Peace Declaration

Becoming a peace community entailed the signing of a "declaration" on December 23, 1997, which explicitly identified rules the members of the community vowed to live by, as well as the community's principles and goals. The declaration described the *Comunidad de Paz de San José de Apartadó* as "a peasant, noncombatant civil community intent in protecting itself from hostilities no matter their intensity." The declaration stated (my translation) the community's decision to:

1. Not partake of any activity related directly or indirectly to the military actions of any of the armed actors in the Colombian conflict, or support them strategically or tactically.
2. Abstain from having arms, munitions, or explosive materials.
3. Abstain from giving logistic support to the actors in the conflict and from seeking help in any personal matters from anyone related to the conflict. Accordingly, the community takes the necessary measures to control the transit of any persons who do not have permission to stay in the places of settlement of the community.
4. Work and make decisions collectively.
5. Create an internal council conformed by seven elected delegates from the community, and a prosecutor. The council makes autonomous decisions, but may search the advisory of one delegate from a national NGO.
6. Say no to injustice.

The October 2003 collective confrontation with the army, mentioned previously, is an appropriate exemplar of the way these six rules are practiced. The community derives its moral authority from its members' refusal to bear weapons of any kind or to use violent retaliation against violent action. The community also refuses to collaborate in any way with Colombian illegal and legal armed actors, including providing information to warring parties or acting in any way that may be seen as complicit. This rule is complemented by, and held in precarious balance with, a commitment to "support transparent dialogue" and to tell "the truth to the armed actors." This seemingly straightforward commitment is one of the most difficult principles chosen by the community, for a condition of widespread terror demands the constant disguise of "reality," be it people's opinions, actions, or whereabouts. However, the only way to gain a space of autonomy is to be true to the community's principles and, therefore, be willing to state the "truth" of neutrality and noncooperation in any situation, regardless of how unsavory it is. Not collaborating with any of those involved in the armed conflict has led the community to take some extreme measures, including not having stores in town, so that no one can unwillingly or unknowingly sell goods to uniformed men or civilians connected to the armed actors.

Finally, the encounter between the CDP and the army highlights the very communitarian nature of the CDP. The community owns the land collectively, there is very little private property, and the pronoun "we" far outweighs "I" in decision-making processes. As stated in the Principles, "Morally and ethically, the members of the community must think in terms of 'us' rather than 'you' or 'me.' "[21]

These communitarian practices have emerged over time and as responses to the specific challenges of the context.[22] Working in the fields, for example, is done in groups of four people, so that no one is caught alone coming or going. Being accompanied is one of the most important ways for community members to ensure that they are not murdered, kidnapped, disappeared, injured, or framed *without witnesses.* Being or becoming a witness is a cornerstone of the community's survival strategy. Willingly witnessing and naming abuse or insult is an act of solidarity and resistance. It is also a Christian and a Buddhist concept associated with peacemaking, compassion, and reconciliation.[23]

Practices of Violence and Nonviolent Responses

Choosing to resist, itself, is an act of provocation; a courageous (or deranged) decision to stand up and fight without deadly weapons. The Colombian armed actors were prompted to respond to such provocation. Between the years 1996 and 2009, the CDP has been the object of more than 700 "acts of terror," as defined by international law, including more than 180 assassinations, 20 of which were perpetrated by guerrillas and the rest by "direct" or "indirect" agents of the state.[24]

To understand the practices of nonviolent resistance, one needs to understand the nature of the violence enacted against those who resist it. The following pages examine some exemplars of both violence and resistance that loom particularly large in the collective imaginary of this one community in Colombia.

February 21, 2005. 8:00 A.M. at the Mulatos hamlet
Luis Eduardo Guerra Guerra, a beloved leader of the Peace Community, his new spouse, Bellanira (age 17), and his 11-year-old son, Andrés, are stopped by the army on their way to their cacao farm. They are clubbed to death, their bodies left on the field.

February 21, 2005, five hours later at the La Resbalosa hamlet (located one walking hour from Mulatos; five hours away from San José)
The army arrives at the house of Alfonso Bolívar Tuberquia, where he is having lunch with his wife, Sandra Milena (age 24); his children, Natalia Andrea (age 5) and Santiago (age 18 months); and four workers. The soldiers surround the house and start shooting, but Alfonso and the workers escape, leaving behind his wife and children. Alfonso returns an hour later, despite the pledges of others, stating

that he would rather die than leave behind his family. Alfonso and his family are killed, dismembered, and disemboweled. Their remains are thrown in two improvised graves.[25]

February 25, 2005, La Resbalosa and Mulatos

A delegation of 110 people from San José de Apartadó arrives at La Resbalosa hamlet to recover the cadavers of Tuberquia and his family, and to search for the yet-to-be-found remains of Guerra and his family. A religious funeral takes place three days later, with the presence of national and international observers.

An international outcry ensues and, as a consequence, the U.S. budget for the local 17th Brigade is reduced (information based on personal interviews). In 2007, Captain Guillermo Armando Gordillo Sánchez is arrested for the crime, and, in 2008, he confesses that 100 militaries and 50 paramilitaries took part in the operation (Capitán del ejército), the strongest legal evidence thus far of the close tie between the army and paramilitaries—a connection that has been systematically denied by the government.

March 20, 2005 at the 17th Brigade headquarters in Urabá

While visiting the headquarters of the 17th Brigade in the Urabá region, President Alvaro Uribe Vélez makes the following declaration:

> Peace communities have a right to install themselves in Colombia, thanks to our regimen of liberties. But they cannot, as San José de Apartadó does, obstruct justice, reject the Public Force, prohibit the trade of legal goods, and restrict the freedom of its residents [. . .]. There are good people in the community of San José de Apartadó. But some of its leaders, supporters, and defenders have been seriously accused, by people who reside there, of helping the FARC and of wanting to use the community to protect this terrorist organization.[26]

Uribe's declaration affirms that the CDP and the national and international organizations that accompany it engage in illicit activities (*Nueva arremetida*). The CDP has the support of Colombian nongovernmental organizations (NGOs), such as the Corporación Jurídica "Libertad," and the support of international NGOs, such as the Dutch Paix Christi, the Portuguese Tamera, the Italian Colomba, and the U.S. Fellowship of Reconciliation and Peace Brigades International. By being allies of the CDP, these NGOs become accomplices in a radical display of disobedience. On these grounds, President Uribe accused the CDP leadership of collaborating with the guerrillas, and threatened to deport international peace observers. Rhetorically speaking, Uribe's statements intend to show how the Peace

Community is not particularly peaceful and, therefore, attempt to dismantle the very grounds of the community's existence.

This situation is congruent with what Tate[27] described in her book, *Counting the Dead*. The widespread view of the Colombian military, according to Tate, is that human rights abuses denounced internationally are a guerrilla conspiracy. The NGO human rights are "simply the façade of the armed Communist left, cloaking the political war of the guerrillas in the acceptable language of international law."[28] In fact, some human rights advocates whose support has been crucial to the survival of the CDP are systematically accused of ties to the guerrillas. These people include the Jesuit and human rights advocate Javier Giraldo, and the former mayor of Apartadó, Gloria Cuartas. Giraldo and Cuartas have been *acompañantes* of the community from its inception, and both receive periodic and, by now, almost routine, death threats.[29] The latest public attack against Cuartas and Giraldo happened in May 2009, when a former commandant of the fifth Front of the FARC (aka SAMIR) accused them on a radio interview of, among others, keeping the peace community as a summer vacation spot for FARC guerrillas.[30]

The decision to become a peace community is, indeed, an act of civil disobedience and collective conscientious objection. Doing so highlights the rights of groups to actively dissent in the face of institutionalized injustice, simultaneously appealing to an arguably "larger power"—an international court of human rights. A peace declaration also transforms a community into a potential foe of the state and a transgressor of law and order, for it questions the legal power of the army and police to protect citizens and to uphold the law. By not allowing soldiers or police in its midst, the CDP is challenging the legitimate right of the state to monopolize force.

RESPONDING TO VIOLENCE

The instances presented above represent in a vivid manner the variety of practices of violence exercised to contain, disperse, and neutralize resistance. In the case of the CDP, these practices have included torture, illegal detentions, disappearances, massacres, forced displacements, *judicializaciones* ("judicializations"), *falsos positivos*, economic blockages, and propaganda. In some ways propaganda may be the more lethal form of attack, for by leaving no material traces of abuse, the public discrediting of the peace community may create enough confusion to discourage national and international support, and encourage the penalization of human rights advocates (*judicializaciones*).

To these practices of intimidation the community has responded with several methods of nonviolent resistance, which correspond to many of those listed by Sharp,[31] and which include noncooperation; alternative means of communication; and appeals to supporters, to the general public, and to attackers. These methods engage the community in actions that include a bodily dimension, as well as symbolic and discursive ones. These three dimensions of engagement were at play in the exemplars presented in this chapter and are particularly highlighted in the instances below:

Jesus Has Not Called in Sick

When I ask Patricio how he manages to keep fighting such an uphill battle against multiple sources of violence, he responds with a grin: "Jesus has not called in sick. Why should I?" In other words, his struggle for justice is based on a moral, ethical ground. There is no justification for giving up when one knows one's struggle is based on a fundamentally good and just cause, which is sought for in numerous places throughout the world. He is not alone; they are not alone. The appeal to Jesus, in other words, emphasizes the universal quality of the struggle and the "catholic" nature of its goodness (one may recall that originally "catholic" means "universal" and "open-minded").

We Laughed

"Ignacio del Mar," a longtime Council member, was once ambushed by 200 men, a mix of paramilitaries and army, and threatened with death if he did not confess that he was a guerrilla member. With a machete caressing his neck, he was asked to take the armed actors to a guerrilla's compound. He refused to confess to an alliance he did not have. He also refused to run, even though he was encouraged to do so. He argued that if they wanted to kill him, they needed to do it right there and not with a shot in the back (which would most probably transform him into a "false positive"). He was ordered to strip off his clothes. Threats were increased and renewed but Ignacio remained firm. The armed men finally left confused by their inability to intimidate Ignacio. He ran naked for a while, until he was found by Patricio and a community rescue party.

"Why do you think they did not kill you?" I asked.

"I do not know," he said, and stops rather pensive. "Maybe it was a miracle."

"How did you celebrate such an incredible outcome?" I asked, already imagining a ceremonial acknowledgment of divine intervention.

"We laughed."

"You laughed?"

"Yes, Patricio and the rest just kept laughing at how skinny and silly I looked running naked."

Instances like this highlight the ways in which systematic aggression and its resistance directly engage the body. Ignacio's body is displayed in front of a large group of camouflaged and armed men. Within this particular cultural context, one can see how this is an emasculating act that elicits shame, powerlessness, and increased fear. But Ignacio responds with just the same arrogance and righteousness he had while fully clothed. When Ignacio is found by a group of his buddies and safely walked home, his shame becomes collective and is transformed into a communal permission to laugh at his very exposed and fragile masculinity. His nakedness is not emasculating any more but just plain funny. In other words, Ignacio's shame has been "witnessed" collectively and transformed into an opportunity to laugh, unifying the sacred and the profane; the sacrality of a body that could have been mutilated and the profane impulse to laugh at dangling masculinity, so to speak.

You Cannot Kill Me: It's Up to Him.

Patricio is ambushed by 40 armed men. He is asked to provide information about guerrillas (by now the reader will be very acutely aware of the repetitive pattern of these episodes). Patricio responds to the man who has approached him with a machete threatening to kill him,

"You cannot kill me."

"What?"

"It's not up to you," says Patricio. "If He needs me, He will call me. You cannot kill me."

"I do not believe that," says the armed man.

"Well, I do. We do. He does not care if you believe or not. It's just how it is."

Grunting, the man with the machete withdraws.

It does not matter if there is, literally, a Divine Being overlooking the scene. What does matter is that this appeal to a Divine Will takes the power *away* from the man using threat, for it makes him a tool in somebody else's plan, "God's plan." "God gave you life and only God can take it away," states the principle to which Patricio is appealing. Most of the power of threat resides in its ability to control somebody else's actions. But when that someone refuses to grant that control, the threat loses its power and needs to be either executed or withdrawn. Evidently, killing Patricio was not the aim of the ambush. Extracting information was the goal, and the threat was, therefore, completely ineffective. Patricio has effectively, and probably unconsciously, appealed rhetorically to a common ground between him and his attackers. Regardless of whether the attacker "believes," he participates of the same catholic semantic universe and cultural context, and thus, the appeal to the divine has worked and disempowered his threat. As such, the religious appeal is an appropriate tool in an arsenal of resistance, for it empowers those who choose to fight with no weapons, while it disarms those who choose to act "like God."

One can say that the CDP is "not religious at all," as a former U.S. Fellowship of Reconciliation (U.S. FOR) *acompañante* told me. There is, however, a fundamental "faith" in a threefold source of power, which resides neither in the individual nor in the collective, but in their interconnection.[32] This threefold power is constituted by (1) the community, as a body larger than the individual but nonexistent without the individual body; (2) the community's written principles and rules of resistance, which become a unifying discourse and a text which is observed, memorized, and cited; and (3) the ethical and moral grounds on which these principles rest. In the words of the CDP, the group "seeks to generate relations and attitudes based on new values: liberty, equality, respect, solidarity, and dialogue. This is a response to a form of thinking that has generated dehumanization, manifested, among others, in a lust for power that disregards everything else."

CONCLUDING REMARKS: METHODS OF RESISTANCE

Gene Sharp proposes a very helpful and detailed list of methods of nonviolent resistance.[33] The CDP employs several of these methods, including,

1. Formal declarations, such as the "Declaración" and "Los Principios" that have been amply discussed in this chapter.
2. Communication with the larger public, through the group's symbols, such as a flag, an icon, and welcoming billboards; several Web sites; and books by organizations such as Colombian CINEP and Italian "Colombia vive!" (for example, *San Josesito de Apartadó; Sembrando vida y dignidad*).
3. Tributes to the dead. As mentioned earlier, every single person who has been killed in the CDP is memorialized in San Josesito. At times, symbolic funerals are carried out, to remember those whose bodies

have not been found; and commemorative masses are celebrated at the places of massacres.

4. Personal noncooperation, as evidenced in the actions of the CDP members recounted in this chapter.

5. Economic noncooperation. The community grows organic products (cacao and bananas) and seeks to find an alternative, non-state sanctioned market for them. Additionally, the community is seeking food sovereignty and eco-sustainability.

6. Political noncooperation, expressed in a refusal to help the armed forces; obey official authority; accept being drafted; or follow traditional education. Very importantly, the CDP, in cooperation with other communities, is working on the creation of a Peasant University.

7. Creation of an alternative system of communication. This is particularly evidenced on the Internet, where the curious or concerned reader can find the community's Web site, as well as those of Gloria Cuartas and Javier Giraldo, SJ. Aside from these, the reader can find relevant information posted or produced by NGOs such as Amnesty International, FOR, PBI, Colombia Support Network, Chicagoans for a Peaceful Colombia, Tamera, Colombia Indymedia, and other Web sites dedicated to peace and nonviolence news and action.

8. Creation of new patterns of social engagement, as evidenced on a horizontal style of leadership; a commitment to use dialogue instead of force; and a moral rejection of state oppression and coercion.

Refusing to Cooperate . . .

An act of terror has a magnifying threatening effect such that it can weaken and disperse a population that knows itself to be fragile and unprotected (which was the outcome of attacks prior to the peace declaration). But terror can also strengthen resistance, if the group, in strong alliance with others—locally, regionally, and internationally—can challenge, name, and make visible its logic and patterns. Even the bloodiest dictatorship requires the cooperation of its citizens.[34] Even the grossest form of threat requires some sort communication common ground. Thus, a cornerstone of the CDP resistance resides in responding publicly to every single act of intimidation, and refusing to *accept* terror as a viable form of conversation. Therefore, when in 2005 the CDP lost a charismatic leader, faced the atrocious dismemberment of three children (accused of being guerrillas, nonetheless), and was directly attacked by the head of state, all within weeks, the community still *refused to be intimidated into silence*. By not lowering its profile or disbanding, the community may prove terror a very cost-ineffective strategy.

. . . And Multiplying

Being able to hold its ground would not be possible if the community did not have international accompaniment, such as that provided by the U.S. FOR. An international presence makes the casual exercise of violence a more difficult affair and challenges, in its role as witness, its public justification. That was the case with the massacre of 2005, which FOR helped bring to the attention of the international community and of U.S. Congress in particular. The outcome was an international outcry and the subsequent U.S. budget cut for the local 17th brigade, which was found complicit in the crime. To date[35] there have been no more massacres, probably because the army and paramilitaries have found them too costly. There is no guarantee that a massacre will not happen again. But we must join in the celebration of its temporal cessation and do what we can to continue making them expensive, impractical, and inefficient, not to mention, of course, criminal. We must, in the words of the community, become *multiplicadores*, outsiders who, by our willingness to listen, understand, and speak up, become "multipliers" of a peace effort and spread it well beyond its geographic confines. In the very evocative words of activist Gloria Cuartas, the CDP is creating an "acupuncture of peace."[36] Acupuncture works by touching nodes in the body and activating, transforming, and redirecting energy throughout the body. It does not need to penetrate the entire body with needles to induce transformation. In the same manner, the CDP appeals to an international net of support whose "nodes" include places as varied as Chicago, Quito, Pisa, Madison, Chiapas, Palestine, and Nantes (Spain), and whose needles are every single individual who chooses to bear witness, speak, and act, whether as members of the CDP or as members of international peacemaking initiatives.[37] Therefore, the "needle" of this peace activism is infinitely small, but its outcomes are large and reverberating.'

Cuartas seems to be alluding to a practice of power that is neither vertical nor horizontal, but web-like, and capable of extending and expanding in ways not directly connected to material or even symbolic might. This understanding is shared by other peace initiatives in Colombia, such as that of Feminine Grassroots Organization and of the indigenous Nasa.[38] For the Nasa, strategies of resistance are profoundly connected to strategies of communication, and both are done with the logic of an organic *tejido*: a woven material or fabric. Needling unites an infinite number of threads into a visible fabric. In the weaving of solidarity every single individual thread counts.

To the multiplicity of methods discussed and identified by Sharp, one may add, therefore, the crucial importance of grassroots solidarity across nations.[39] If both the Colombian and the U.S. states are profoundly complicit in the oppression of the Colombian peasants, both Colombian and U.S. grassroots are responsible for sustaining their resistance and imagining a more just and eco-sustainable future.

Acknowledgments: To the memory of Mildrey Dayana, Deiner Andrés, Santiago, Natalia Andrea, Duvalier, Felix Antonio, Luciano, Arturo, and all the children who have been assassinated by armed actors in the Peace Community of San José de Apartadó. To their parents, grandparents, and friends, who continue to resist in the name of dignity, self-determination, and life.

NOTES

1. Alther et al., 2004: 16–17.
2. For the remainder of this chapter, I refer to the peace community of San José de Apartadó by its Spanish acronym CDP.
3. FOR-Colombia, 2009.
4. Alther et al., 2004.
5. All names have been changed to protect the identity of the people involved.
6. Cronología, 2008: 26.
7. Boulding, 1989.
8. Ibid.; Nagler, 2004.
9. García-Villegas and Santos, 2004: 35.
10. Santos, 1995; García-Villegas and Santos, 2004.
11. García Villegas and Santos, 2004.
12. Ibid.
13. Ibid.
14. Ibid.
15. Alther et al., 2004.
16. Alston, 2009.
17. "Chain of Extermination," 2009; "The Bojayá Massacre," 2002.
On May 2, 2002, the FARC guerrillas threw a mortar on the roof of a church where 300 people from the Bojayá town had sought refuge from outside combat between paramilitaries and guerrillas, with 119 people dying as a result. According to a joint report by Witness for Peace and JUSTAPAZ, this was a "foretold," preventable tragedy, as warring guerillas and paramilitaries had been moving in closer to the town for about two weeks and were fighting for control of the zone ("The Bojayá Massacre"). The Indian Law Resource Center called the 2009 Awá tragedy a "foretold massacre" as well.
18. "Declaración"; my translation.
19. "Humanitarian zones" are hamlets that are not of the Peace Community but have sought its protection.

20. Nagler, 2004: 162.

21. *Nuestros principios*, 2009.

22. Uribe, 2004.

23. Glassman, 1998; Tate, 2007.

24. Comunidad de Paz de San José de Apartadó; See Giraldo, 2003, 2009.

25. Cronología, 2008: 84–85.

26. *El Colombiano;* My translation.

27. Tate.

28. Ibid, 266.

29. Viera, 2005.

30. Radio Interview with Fernando Londoño, May 28, 2009.

31. Sharp, 2005.

32. I would like to thank Larry Frye for his suggestion to consider the relationship between collective and individual dynamics in the life of this community.

33. Sharp, 2005: 201–210.

34. Ibid.

35. As of July 2009.

36. Personal interview, March 2009.

37. According to the Zen Peacemaking Order, peacemaking requires three principles: (1) Not knowing; (2) Bearing witness, and (3) Skillful action (which results from careful and multi-perspectival understanding). See Glassman, 1998.

38. Lozano, 2008.

39. Nagler, 2004.

CHAPTER 8

Peace Building Education: Responding to Contexts

Candice C. Carter

Education for peace is like a trek in the wilderness. Anticipation of peace includes thoughts about beauty and realities of violence. The trek involves observation of wonderful beings that sometimes do harmful things in fulfillment of their needs. Observation of the harm reveals opportunities for conflict analysis. Understanding of situated conflicts uncovers paths through them. Learning about the good in the world and how to preserve it, while calling attention to problems and needs, is a trek through education for peace. A collective foray for pools of peace where everyone can drink is a powerful transformer of conflict and a crucial lesson for nonviolence novices.

Peace movements, including education, have been responsive to the problems of people and the places they affect. Awareness of and sensitivity to harm, recognized as violence, has prompted responses from educators throughout time and across regions. The responses have had a wide range with a core goal of transforming current circumstances to bring about or increase peace. Often born of political strife between and in societies, education for peace identifies injustice in addition to other sources of structural conflict and violent responses to it. Like a walk in dark woods, peace educators identify past and potential sources of danger during their pursuit of coexistence without violence. This chapter briefly reviews the sources of education for peace, its domains, and contexts of activating those learning domains. It provides a few examples of instruction and programs before it summarizes current needs in the field of peace education.

The contextual responsiveness of education for peace renders it a dynamic field. Illustrative cases illuminate this characteristic. Government mandates in the United States ostensibly created for educational improvement proliferated sets of prescriptive instructional standards that did not include competencies of peace. Subsequently, researchers of peace education developed Voluntary Standards for Peace Education.[1] From different regions of the world, researchers of peace education have been contributing to that dynamic set of standards they created to legitimate this field and describe competencies of peace pedagogy. The continual use of those suggestions by organizations and teachers is evidence of the value of proactively responding to the omission of peace education in government mandates. Another related example occurred decades earlier, when educators throughout the United States developed guidelines for nuclear education. During that last decade of the Cold War, a plethora of educational efforts in school districts, universities, and nongovernmental organizations of the United States reflected the sentiment of their comrades, the citizens of the former Union of Socialist Soviet Republics (USSR), to find peaceful solutions to political conflicts, without construction of nuclear arsenals. Although the nuclear age curricula provided skills for analysis of political conflict, they variably included several other peace topics that their developers recognized as factors of peace building. Although peace researchers have clarified the contextual responsiveness of peace education,[2] its universality is evident in its philosophical foundation.

DIMENSIONS OF PEACE BUILDING EDUCATION

The dimensions of peace building education reflect the light of humanity's common hope for a good life. While the breadth and depth dimensions differ, the ideal of teaching about and for peace can be discerned in the theories that support peace pedagogy. The philosophical foundation of education for peace exists in spiritual notions across cultures that reject violence as well as in secular ideologies. Whereas this anthology elaborates philosophies that promote the pursuit of peace, briefly mentioned here are pedagogical theories that enable that pursuit.

Theoretical Markers

In the last century, peace pedagogy has been evident in secular schools as well as in faith-based education. Motivated by observations of social strife and inter-group tensions, a call resulted for education to ameliorate the situation. For example, Nobel Laureate Jane Addams advocated the full inclusion of immigrants in the public school system. In response to wars, Maria Montessori wrote extensively about the role of education in peace and she created an early form of global education. Additionally, she promoted the education of everyone, regardless of their disability characteristics that caused society to hide and ignore them. Her background as a physician and her extensive writing about human development legitimated an inclusion model of education. Unfortunately, the movements of global and inclusion education were slow to appear in U.S. schools and other nations outside of Eurasia. Subsequently, Elise Boulding, a Quaker sociologist, carried the call for intercultural education and advanced the notion of a global civic culture.[3] She posited the notion of global interdependence as a core concept for education and with her husband Kenneth, she demonstrated the importance of vision in pedagogy.[4] Additionally, she highlighted the developments of women and cultures of peace, both of which have been commonly omitted from published curriculum.[5] Betty Reardon[6] underscored the importance of teaching about female as well as male roles in change and development while she underscored the importance of including education for human rights. She emphasized the need for peace education to facilitate instruction about systemic violence and she emphasized the importance of teacher preparation for facilitating lessons about violence and peace. In Brazil, the work of lawyer Paulo Freire[7] demonstrated in adult education how instruction for literacy could include analysis of structural violence. He advanced a pedagogy that infused critical analysis of power during lessons of sanctioned subjects. Critical theorists demonstrated the role in education of power analysis to help teachers and their students identify antecedents of structural violence, for the purpose of its transformation.[8] Critical pedagogy and peace education share the concept of *agency*, which describes the knowledge and ability to act for collective as well as individual betterment.[9] The notion of communication *code*[10] supports discursive methods of transformation while awareness of *habitus*[11] facilitates understanding of interaction during conflict communication. Drawn from Buddhist traditions, the concept of mindfulness as a process aids awareness—a precursor of violence avoidance.[12]

Theories of nonviolence have supported pedagogies that promote conflict transformation through cooperative learning, conflict analysis, conflict mediation, and other forms of violence prevention.[13] Techniques developed for psychological analysis have enabled education not only about injustice, but also the processes of identity development.[14] In peace-oriented education, teachers learn these techniques for enhancement of their self-awareness and the development of their students. For example, Milton Bennett's theory of intercultural sensitivity provides a continuum that is useful for self-evaluation of one's ability to cognitively and behaviorally engage with other cultures.[15] Beyond cultural border crossing, theories about the influence of dispositions are core to peace building education. The roles of empathy and concern in an ethic of care are crucial.[16] Johan Galtung[17] theorized peace form as well as content in education, whereby teachers model peace processes for cultivation of their students' knowledge, skills, and dispositions. Theories of holistic education highlight the multidimensional nature of education for peace.[18]

Depth and Breadth

Depth

Two important dimensions in peace education are depth and breadth. The depth dimension ranges from violence or peace within the self to such interactions with others. Depth has three domains that are foci for analysis of conflict: intrapersonal, interpersonal, and systemic.[19] These constant domains have relational influences.[20] Peace, or the lack of it, in one domain affects the others—a ripple effect. Needed is instruction about all three of these domains. The one that has been most evident in secular education is interpersonal peace, involving interactions between people. Educators have primarily been teaching about human relations and how they can be improved through a range of contextually responsive strategies.[21] For example, students learn that cultural border crossing, with a disposition of acceptance and skills for successful interaction in another culture, can contribute to peace building. Lessons about interpersonal conflict and peace range from superficial approaches, such as learning about other cultures, to deep work in which students engage in problem-solving communication during their sustained cross-cultural interactions. The second most common domain in peace building education is intrapersonal. Lessons that teach students analysis and management of their emotions, identification of their unmet needs, and monitoring of their inner voice advance competencies of intrapersonal peace. Also construed as mindfulness, intrapersonal peace education ranges from awareness of personal responsibility to regular student practice with the associated skills. The third domain of peace building education is structural, also knows as systemic. It has been least present in schools' lessons. Education about structural peace involves recognition and understanding of widespread conflict throughout society. Lessons supporting structural peace building range from examination of a conflict across one society to its global evidence. For example, students identify, describe,

Table 8.1. Components of Peace Education

Competencies	Components
Knowledge	Inclusive history, sources of conflict, human rights, peace history, and strategies
Pluralistic acceptance	Multicultural participation and cooperation
Ethno relativism	Accommodation of and adaptation to different cultural norms
Self-management	Awareness and control of personal reactions to conflict
Peaceful discourse	Analysis of language for characteristics of violence or compassion
Proactive involvement	Participation in local to global conflict transformation
Restoration	Engagement in restorative human interactions
Stewardship	Responsibility for environmental preservation and reconstruction
Visioning	Picturing a peaceful society in the present and the future

© 2009 Candice C. Carter

and analyze institutional discrimination that is the root of social injustice, which causes interpersonal strife and intrapersonal conflict. The very limited facilitation of this instruction about structural conflict results from several factors, such as a lack of teacher preparation for this type of education and a lack of curricula provided for lessons about structural violence and peace.[22] Highly motivated teachers who facilitate such instruction have to develop or find resources for it. Educators often purchase from organizations the materials they need for such instruction. Organizations typically specialize in particular aspects of education. The types of instructional materials they offer evidence the problem to which they are responding. The lack of a comprehensive organization that provides curricula for the many strands of peace education is related to a problem with breadth in this field. Table 8.1 provides a succinct overview of strands that are currently evident in peace building education.

Breadth

The dimension of breadth includes a range of peace education components. Breadth fluctuates in peace building education with some components included for short durations while others are either sustained or missing. The reactionary nature of schools affects what is taught. When direct violence in schools erupted in predominately white U.S. middle-class neighborhoods, districts throughout the nation reacted with violence-prevention techniques. However, those techniques lacked depth, a theoretical foundation, and more often than not they failed to include peace as an instructional goal. Beyond reactionary trends in education, research and corresponding development is another influential factor in breadth variability. Research findings that report success with instructional methods catalyze adoption of those techniques. For example, social-emotional learning became a cogent topic after presentation of research about it and formation of an organization with that mission.[23] Additionally influential in breadth of peace building education is transdisciplinarity. Adapted from peace building lessons in one discipline are techniques that school participants use for its possible instructional value. Recently, restorative justice techniques used in victim-offender programs have been brought into schools as restorative discipline. Another example of transdisciplinarity is the recent incorporation of yoga in U.S. primary and secondary schools. The aspirations of educators who bring into the schools peace-promoting techniques that other fields and cultures use are as inspiring as the goals of organizations whose mission statements have peace foci. Examples of nongovernmental organizations in the United States that have been recently contributing to peace building through education include the Anti-Defamation League, Teachers Without Borders, Educators for Social Responsibility, the Human Rights Education Association, the National Association for Multicultural Education, as well as the Collaborative for Social and Emotional Learning. Such institutions advance informal as well as formal learning for, and work in, peace development.

Informal and Formal Education

Even as peace education moves forward as a field, its enactment occurs in two types of contexts: informal and formal. While informal contexts are as omnipresent as conflict, formal ones exist in explicit instruction. Peace building actions people observe or join provide informal learning that has been crucial for self-efficacy as well as for collective success. Another source of informal peace education is in the everyday interactions of people with each other and their environment. Children and youth learn from their many observations of conflict responses in their families and societies.[24] Media observation has a strong role as an informal educator, which evidences the importance of discernment in selection of any visual and auditory programs.[25] Additionally, the interactions of youth with each other and with their activity facilitators in organizations are "pockets of peace" for tacit instruction.[26] Hence, there are ample opportunities for indirect instruction about and for peace.[27] Adults who remain mindful of the instructional influence of their decisions and actions in the face of conflict are important facilitators of peace education. When they think aloud for others to hear their management of their inner voice, the rationale for their actions, and their enthusiasm for peace building, their modeling is an optimal lesson for observers. Writing about their thinking is a further aid of informal education. Indeed, the writings of peace workers have been crucial in moving peace education forward. Literature about how peace has happened is valuable for informal education.[28] It appeals to humanity as a source of inspiration and solace during difficult times and as affirmation following resolution of conflicts. Such literature is also valuable in formal education.[29]

Formal instruction for peace building has become a desired path in the field of education. Whereas some schools have infused it as a reaction to direct internal or local violence, others established peace building foci in their mission statements. Additionally, faculty and students who were motivated to include peace as a topic of study cleared the way for that pursuit. Writers in this series, as well as this author, who established those opportunities in public universities that were funded with government money climbed political and economic mountains during their treks through bureaucracy. The tasks of rationalizing and facilitating development support for peace studies in publicly funded colleges and universities are less daunting with extant programs operating. During the current economic downturn, when nonlicensure programs are being eliminated, the value of formal education for peace has remained evident. The retention of peace studies reveals its importance even without government sanctioning through licensure. It remains to be seen if governments that have developed peace departments or programs will recognize the value of peace competencies. Formal education that offers certification in peace building techniques such as conflict transformation and degrees in fields such as comprehensive law may be precursors to that thrust forward.[30] However, skeptics are dubious of a government managing its peace programs, for several reasons including conflict of interest. When a government descends into the darkness of violence and sends its youth there, it leaves bomb craters in its peace building path. Orienting youth in school toward violent futures is counterproductive in peace building. More than ever, youth today turn to violence even without their service in war initiatives, due to their lack of long-term expectations for personal and societal peace. Hence, a crucial component of peace building education is the cultivation of their expectations for a long life in which people work through their conflicts without resorting to violence.

Peace building contributions of formal education wax and wane, and occasionally eclipse. Mandates and funding for such education sustain it as well as ideological foundations in schools with clear missions. For example, in Northern Ireland, the government endorsement of Education for Mutual Understanding opened a peace building path in primary and secondary as well as teacher education.[31] However, its subsequent replacement with the focus of "citizenship education" did not emphasize peace, especially to those whose republican interests were in liberation from membership in the United Kingdom. During the time that Education for Mutual Understanding was promoted and implemented, the lack of directives for it evidenced a wide range of approaches and different dimensions of motivation for accomplishing it. As with other peace building initiatives, teachers and their educators in Northern Ireland grappled with how to fit it into an exam-focused curriculum that did not include peace competencies.

COMPREHENSIVENESS

Where peace building education has been endorsed by government and facilitated with support of time and funding, it has been more comprehensive. For example, the unity focused program Education for Peace in Bosnia and Herzegovina garnered government support that enabled its use across primary and secondary schools for changing worldviews that affect perceptions and conflict management.[32] The widespread implementation of Education for Peace illuminated the interest of bureaucrats who recognized the value of a peace building program.[33] Unfortunately, such support is rarely sustained across a school district after the initial training and facilitation. Too often, that support for peace building programs, whether they have limited or comprehensive implementations, is limited to post-conflict zones that are healing from political upheaval or high levels of direct violence. In such cases, governments' mandates for integration of previously or currently contending populations occur, without prior preparation of teachers. In those situations, teacher educators are responsible for enacting peace education. Observations in post-apartheid South Africa, where university faculty prepare teacher candidates for instruction of populations with whom they lack prior experience due to continued social segregation, have highlighted the importance of peace building competence in higher education. The challenges teacher educators experience with their students who resist social-integration work evidences the need for preparation of university instructors for success in their crucial peace building roles.[34] Accreditation mandates for institutions that provide teacher certification programs have been crucial to the inclusion of at least the diversity strand of peace building education. To renew their accreditation, the institutions must evidence how teacher candidates experience the mandated preparation. Potentially more effective than accreditation mandates that have limited strands of peace building through universities are current government recommendations for instruction oriented to peace. For example, the National Council of Educational Research under the Ministry of Human Resource Development in India declared the importance of peace education that resulted with its inclusion in a curriculum framework that ensured corresponding teacher preparation.[35]

Research on peace building education has the greatest potential for positively influencing government recommendations to provide that instruction. For that reason among others, there is a great need now for studies of current and new programs.

Needed to expand the research base of this field are studies that examine contextually responsive programs as well as sustained instruction. For instance, research could describe and analyze how students with different cultural and psychological characteristics and various types of conflicts experience restorative discipline and other techniques.[36] Studies could identify the effect-ranges of stewardship and sustainability instruction for children.[37] Case studies of arts-based peace education in different regions can show student and teacher needs as well as illustrate their perceptions of conflicts, especially those that may not be addressed in their schools.[38] There are many other research foci for studies of peace building education. All of the investigations should include information about contextual responsiveness, which is the foundation of peace construction. Rigorous research and its findings provide this field with a crucial compass for trekkers in search of peace building possibilities. Advancement of their pursuits may have ramifications for everyone.

ADVANCEMENT OPPORTUNITIES

Forging and extending paths of peace building education may have profound effects in human relations and all other elements of humanity's reach. Accordingly, it could be fortuitous to forecast its forward routes. Palpable projections of this field include substantial research, expanded scope, and responsive instruction. While describing the need for more research, Monisha Bajaj[39] emphasizes the importance of refocusing on "critical" peace education that identifies power imbalances. By naming the sites and sources of power disparities, educators will be better equipped for lessons that help students see and respond to structural conflicts. This is a needed turn for education that has been increasingly focused on interpersonal conflicts while decreasing analysis of their systemic antecedents. Researchers as well as educators in this field are responsible for advancing and protecting, especially in classrooms, inclusive conversations about power—who has it and who needs it. While looking from the peaks of power to the valleys of violence, several domains of peace building need to be noticed.

EXPANDED SCOPE

Although scholarship identifies components of peace building education, and programs variably provide education about and experience in different realms, opportunities abound for their expansion. Nonfiction literature and research have evidenced areas that need investigation and consideration in particular contexts. Outside of realms that have been more frequently seen, such as norms of communication, there are less-focused elements of conflict in other circumstances.[40] Another rationale for broadening the realms of peace building is stimulation of perspective diversity that aids analysis of problems and stimulates creativity for solving them. Informal peace building documented in true stories evidence strategies that have been useful in multiple realms that many programs do not include. For example, the role of persistence in transforming conflicts has been crucial, yet it is underemphasized in formal education.[41] Regular inclusion of identity domains in this field can uncover otherwise obscure paths to peace. Writings by under-represented or marginalized peoples offer insights about distinct cultural practices that positively respond to conflicts or promote the notion of peace.[42] For instance, Sharra[43] describes the importance of indigenous concepts for peace building, such as *uMunthu*, as well as the value of autobiography that illuminates and documents peace processes. Instruction that incorporates local concepts and includes all voices shows evidence of needed responsiveness.

RESPONSIVE INSTRUCTION

An open pedagogy that leaves room for students' ideas and time for incorporation of them, with development of their peace building skills, is crucial in this field. The form of instruction has importance that is too often overlooked with a focus on content. Although educators should expect content to vary due to changing circumstances that need consideration, such as current events as well as new revelations that generate new topics, the form of optimal instruction is less variable. It evidences compassionate concern, acceptance of differences, and mutual respect that results from honesty through considerate communication.[44] It is not linear or hierarchical. The latter quality is challenging within most educational institutions, because they reify authoritarian norms in teaching and prescribe requisite course contents. Maintenance of unresponsive instruction is a form of structural violence through oppression.[45] Educators who maintain status quo in such contexts counter, instead of contribute, to peace building. Hence, the importance of teacher reflection about their agency as peace developers. As role models, teachers contribute to peace building through demonstration of their awareness of and responsiveness to self, others, and nature. One approach to this pedagogical volcano in "traditional" school environments is the notion of partnership education[46] that includes voices and participation of all members in a school and its community. In that facilitation, the worldview of "unity in diversity" reveals the value of differences for collective success.[47]

CONCLUSION

Peace building education is a maturing field that evidences vigor in its responsiveness to contexts and research. It ranges from informal education that occurs through observations of and experiences with peace work to formal instruction that organizations and institutions provide. While its breadth varies, its depth uncovers unvarying domains of peacemaking and peace building. Whereas circumstances of conflict change, sources of peace with each of them are steadfast. Peace building education enables students to see how the capacities they develop can have positive effects in analysis of problems and creation of solutions, now and in their future. Their heightened awareness of conflict and antecedents of violence, along with opportunities for preventing harm, are relevant to all aspects of their lives. On the streets of reconstruction as well as in open classroom discussions, students experience peace building form even as they contribute to and encounter contextually relevant curriculum. Their educational trek can seem wild, characterized by unpredictability and affect, which stimulate interest in a cyclical process of learning.

NOTES

1. Carter 2008.
2. Haavelsrud, 1996; Salomon and Nevo, 2002.
3. Boulding, 1988.
4. Boulding and Boulding, 1995.
5. Boulding, 1976, 2000.
6. Reardon, 2001.
7. Freire, 1998.
8. Apple, 1995.
9. Giroux, 1988; Vongalis-Macrow, 2006.
10. Bernstein, 2000.

11. Bourdieu, 1977.

12. Greene, 1988.

13. Johnson and Johnson, 1995; Prothrow-Smith, 2005; Raider, Coleman, and Gerson, 2006.

14. Cross, 1993.

15. Bennett, 1996.

16. Noddings, 2008.

17. Galtung, 2008.

18. Eisler and Miller, 2004.

19. Galtung, 2004.

20. Carter, 2010.

21. Harris and Morrison, 2003.

22. Carter April, 2009; Jenkins, 2007.

23. Collaborative for Academic, Social Emotional and Learning, 2009.

24. Carter, 2003.

25. Cortes, 2000.

26. Carter, 2004.

27. Carter, 2003.

28. Canfield et al., 2005.

29. Carter and Clay-Robison, 2009.

30. Carter, 2010.

31. Carter, "Teacher Preparation for Peacebuilding," 2007.

32. Clarke-Habibi, 2005.

33. Education for Peace, 2009.

34. Carter and Vandeyar, 2009; Jansen, 2004.

35. De Paul, 2010.

36. International Institute for Restorative Practices, 2009.

37. Wenden, 2004.

38. Brunson, et al., 2002; Carter, 2007.

39. Bajaj, 2009.

40. Oetzel and Ting-Toomey, 2006.

41. *Journal of Peace Education,* 2007.

42. Hoppers, 2000.

43. Sharra, 2006.

44. Whang and Nash, 2005; Rosenberg, 2003.

45. Finley, 2004.

46. Eisler, 2000; Pierce, 2004.

47. Danesh and Clarke-Habibi, 2007.

CHAPTER 9

INSIDE THE MILITARY MEDIA INDUSTRIAL COMPLEX: IMPACTS ON MOVEMENTS FOR PEACE AND SOCIAL JUSTICE

Peter Phillips and Mickey S. Huff

Among the most important corporate media censored news stories of the past decade, one must be that over 1 million people have died because of the United States military invasion and occupation of Iraq. This, of course, does not include the number of deaths from the first Gulf War nor the ensuing sanctions placed on the country of Iraq that, combined, caused close to an additional 2 million Iraqi deaths. In the Iraq War, which began in March 2003, over 1 million people died violently primarily from U.S. bombings and neighborhood patrols. These were deaths in excess of the normal civilian death rate under the prior government. Among U.S. military leaders and policy elites, the issue of counting the dead was dismissed before the Iraqi invasion even began. In an interview with reporters in late March 2002, U.S. General Tommy Franks stated, "You know we don't do body counts."[1] Fortunately, for those concerned about humanitarian costs of war and empire, others do.

In a January 2008 report, the British polling group Opinion Research Business (ORB) reported that, "survey work confirms our earlier estimate

Appreciation is expressed for editing assistance by Rebecca Norlander and Ellen Gaddy.

that over 1 million Iraqi citizens have died as a result of the conflict which started in 2003. We now estimate that the death toll between March 2003 and August 2007 is likely to have been of the order of 1,033,000. If one takes into account the margin of error associated with survey data of this nature then the estimated range is between 946,000 and 1,120,000."[2]

The ORB report came on the heels of two earlier studies conducted by Dr. Les Roberts and colleagues at Johns Hopkins University and published in the medical journal *Lancet.* The first study from January 1, 2002, to March 18, 2003, confirmed civilian deaths at that time at over 100,000. The second study published in October 2006 documented over 650,000 civilian deaths in Iraq since the start of the U.S. invasion and confirmed that U.S. aerial bombing in civilian neighborhoods caused over a third of these deaths. Over half of the deaths were directly attributable to U.S. forces. The estimated 1.2 million dead six years into the war/occupation, included children, parents, grandparents, cab drivers, clerics, and schoolteachers. All manner of ordinary Iraqis have died because the United States decided to invade their country under false pretenses of undiscovered weapons of mass destruction and in violation of international law. An additional 4 to 5 million Iraqi refugees have fled. The corporate mainstream news would have the public believe many refugees are returning to Iraq, but independent journalist Dahr Jamail, reporting from the region, tells the opposite story.[3]

The magnitude of these million-plus deaths and creation of such a vast refugee crisis is undeniable. The continuing occupation by U.S. forces has guaranteed a monthly mass death rate of thousands of people—a carnage that ranks among the most heinous mass killings in world history. More tons of bombs have been dropped in Iraq than in all of World War II.[4] Six years later the casualties continue but the story, barely reported from the start, has vanished.

The American people face a serious moral dilemma. Murder and war crimes have been conducted in their name. Yet most Americans have no idea of the magnitude of deaths and tend to believe that they number in the thousands and are primarily Iraqis killing Iraqis. Corporate mainstream media are in large part to blame. The question then becomes how can this mass ignorance and corporate media deception exist in the United States and what impact does this have on peace and social justice movements in the country?[5]

TRUTH EMERGENCY AND MEDIA REFORM

In the United States today, the rift between reality and reporting has peaked. There is no longer a mere credibility gap, but rather a literal *truth emergency* in which the most important information affecting people is concealed from view. Many Americans, relying on the mainstream corporate media, have serious difficulty accessing the truth while still believing that the information they receive is the reality. A truth emergency reflects cumulative failures of the fourth estate to act as a truly free press. This truth emergency is seen in inadequate coverage of fraudulent elections, pseudo 9/11 investigations, illegal preemptive wars, torture camps, and doctored intelligence, but also in issues like domestic surveillance that intimately impact everyday lives. Reliable information on these issues is systematically missing in corporate media outlets, where the majority of the American people continue to turn for news and information.

Consider these items of noteworthy conditions. U.S. workers have been faced with a 35-year decline in real wages while the top few percent enjoy unparalleled wealth with strikingly low tax burdens. The United States has the highest infant mortality rate among industrialized nations, is falling behind in scientific research and education, leads the world as a debtor nation, and is seriously lacking in health care quality and coverage, which results in the deaths of 18,000 people a year. America has entered another Gilded Age. Someone should alert the media.[6]

The free press or media reform movement is a national effort to address mainstream media failures and the government policies that sanction them. During the 2008 National Conference for Media Reform (NCMR) in Minneapolis, Project Censored interns and faculty conducted a survey, completed by 376 randomly selected NCMR attendees out of the 3,500 people registered for the conference. This survey was designed to gauge participants' views on the state of the corporate news media and the effectiveness of the media reform movement. The survey also sought to determine the level of belief in a *truth emergency,* a systematic hiding of critical information in the United States. Not surprisingly, for a sample of independent media reform activists, majorities in the 90 percent-plus range agreed on most criticisms of mainstream media, that corporate media failed to keep the American people informed on important issues facing the nation and that a *truth emergency* does indeed exist in the United States. Regarding the reasons, 87 percent of the participants believed that a military-industrial-media complex exists in the United States for the promotion of the U.S. military domination of the world, and most agreed with research conclusions by Project Censored and others that a continuing powerful *global dominance group* inside the U.S. government, the U.S. media, and the national policy structure is responsible. What was clear from our survey is that media democracy activists strongly support not only aggressive reform efforts and policy changes but also the continuing development of independent, grassroots media as part of an overall media democracy movement.

While most progressive media activists do not believe in some omnipotent conspiracy, an overwhelming portion of NCMR participants believe the leadership class in the United States is *dominated* by a neo-conservative group of some several hundred people who share a goal of asserting U.S. military power worldwide. This Global Dominance Group continues under both Republican and Democratic rule. In cooperation with major military contractors, the corporate media, and conservative foundations, the GDM has become a powerful long-term force in military unilateralism and U.S. political processes.

THE GLOBAL DOMINANCE GROUP AND
INFORMATION CONTROL

A long thread of sociological research documents the existence of a dominant ruling class in the United States, which sets policy and determines national political priorities. C. Wright Mills, in his 1956 book *The Power Elite*, documented how World War II solidified a trinity of power in the United States that comprised corporate, military, and government elites in a centralized power structure working in unison through "higher circles" of contact and agreement.[7] This power has grown through the Cold War and, after 9/11, the global War on Terrorism.

At present, the global dominance agenda includes penetration into the boardrooms of the corporate media in the United States. Only 118 people comprise the membership on the boards of directors of the 10 big media giants. These 118 individuals in turn sit on the corporate boards of 288 national and international corporations. Four of the top 10 media corporations share board director positions with the major defense contractors including:

William Kennard: *New York Times*, Carlyle Group
Douglas Warner III: GE (NBC), Bechtel
John Bryson: Disney (ABC), Boeing
Alwyn Lewis: Disney (ABC), Halliburton
Douglas McCorkindale: Gannett, Lockheed-Martin

Given an interlocked media network of connections with defense and other economic sectors, big media in the United States effectively represent the interests of corporate America. Media critic and historian Norman Solomon described the close financial and social links between the boards of large media-related corporations and Washington's foreign-policy establishment: "One way or another, a military-industrial complex now extends to much of corporate media."[8] The Homeland Security Act Title II Section 201(d)(5) provides an example of the interlocked military-industrial-media complex.

This Act specifically asks the directorate to "develop a comprehensive plan for securing the key resources and critical infrastructure of the United States including information technology and telecommunications systems (including satellites) emergency preparedness communications systems."

The media elite, a key component of the Higher Circle Policy Elite in the United States, are the watchdogs of acceptable ideological messages, the controllers of news and information content, and the decision makers regarding media resources. Their goal is to create symbiotic global news distribution in a deliberate attempt to control the news and information available to society. The two most prominent methods used to accomplish this task are censorship and propaganda.

Sometimes the sensationalist and narrow media coverage of news is blamed on the need to meet a low level of public taste and thereby capture the eyes of a sufficient market to lure advertisers and to make a profit. But another goal of cornering the marketplace on what news and views will be aired is also prominent. Billionaire Rupert Murdoch loses $50 million a year on the *New York Post*, billionaire Richard Mellon Scaife loses $2 to $3 million a year on the *Pittsburgh Tribune-Review*, billionaire Philip Anschutz loses around $5 million a year on the *Weekly Standard*, and billionaire Sun Myung Moon has lost $2 to $3 billion on the *Washington Times*. The losses in supporting conservative media are part of a strategy. They also buy bulk quantities of ultra-conservative books, bringing them to the top of the *New York Times* bestseller list, and then give away copies to "subscribers" to their Web sites and publications. They fund conservative "think tanks" like Heritage and Cato with hundreds of millions of dollars a year. All this buys them respectability and a megaphone. Even though William Kristol's publication, the *Standard*, is a money-loser, his association with it has often gotten him on TV talk shows and a column with the *New York Times*. Sponsorships of groups like Norquist's anti-tax "Americans for Tax Reform" regularly get people like him front and center in any debate on taxation in the United States. This has contributed to extensive tax cuts for the wealthy and the most unfair tax laws of any industrialized country—all found acceptable by a public relying on sound bites about "big government." Hence, media corporation officials and others in the health care, energy, and weapons industries remain wealthier than ordinary people can imagine. Their expenditures for molding opinion are better understood as investments[9]

MODERN MEDIA CENSORSHIP AND PROPAGANDA

A broader definition of contemporary censorship needs to include any interference, deliberate or not, with the free flow of vital news information to the public. Modern censorship can be seen as the subtle yet constant and sophisticated manipulation of reality in our mass media outlets. On a daily basis, censorship refers to the intentional noninclusion of a news story—or piece of a news story—based on anything other than a desire to tell the truth. Such manipulation can take the form of political pressure (from government officials and powerful individuals), economic pressure (from advertisers and funders), and legal pressure (the threat of lawsuits from deep-pocket individuals, corporations, and institutions), or threats to reduce future access by a reporter. The following are a few examples of censorship and propaganda.

Omitted or Undercovered Stories

The failure of the corporate media to cover human consequences, like 1 million, mostly civilian deaths of Iraqis, reduces public response to the wars being conducted by the United States. Even when activists mobilize, the media coverage of anti-war demonstrations has been negligible and deni-grating from the start. When journalists of the so-called "free press" ignore the anti-war movement, they serve the interests of their masters in the military media industrial complex.[10]

Further, the corporate mainstream press continues to ignore the human cost of the U.S. war in Iraq with America's own veterans. Veteran care, wounded rates, mental disabilities, Veterans Administration claims, firsthand accounts of soldier experiences, and pictures of dead or limbless soldiers are rare. One of the most important stories missed by the corporate press concerned the Winter Soldier Congressional hearings in Washington, D.C. The hearings, with eyewitness testimony of U.S. soldiers relating their experiences on the battlefield and beyond, were only covered by a scant number of major media, and then only in passing. In contrast to the virtual corporate media blackout concerning U.S. soldiers' views of the war, the independent, listener-sponsored, community Pacifica Radio network covered the hearings at length.[11]

A common theme among the most censored stories over the past few years has been the systemic erosion of human rights and civil liberties in both the United States and the world at large. The corporate media has ignored the fact that habeas corpus can now be suspended for anyone by order of the President. With the approval of Congress, the Military Commissions Act (MCA) of 2006, signed by President Bush on October 17, 2006, allows for the suspension of habeas corpus for U.S. citizens and noncitizens alike. While media, including a lead editorial in the *New York Times* (October 19, 2006), have offered false comfort that American citizens will not be the victims, the Act is quite clear that "any person" can be targeted.[12]

Additionally, under the code-name Operation FALCON (Federal and Local Cops Organized Nationally), federally coordinated mass arrests have been occurring since April 2005 and netted over 54,000 arrests, a majority of whom were not violent criminals as was initially suggested. This unprecedented move of arresting tens of thousands of "fugitives" is the largest dragnet-style operation in the nation's history. The raids, coordinated by the Justice Department and Homeland Security, directly involved over 960 agencies (state, local, and federal) and mark the first time in U.S. history that all domestic police agencies have been put under the direct control of the federal government.[13]

All these events are significant in a democratic society that claims to cherish individual rights and due process of law. To have them occur is a tragedy. To have a "free" press not report them or pretend these issues do not matter to the populace is the foundation of censorship today.

Repetition of Slogans and Sound Bites

The corporate media in the United States present themselves as unbiased and accurate. The *New York Times* motto of "all the news that's fit to print" is a clear example, as is CNN's authoritative "most trusted name in news," and Fox's mantra of "fair and balanced." The slogans are examples of what linguist George Lakoff has referred to as *framing*. Through constant repetition, the metaphors and symbols that pervade our media turn into unquestioned beliefs. "Liberal media," "welfare cheaters," "war on terror," "illegal aliens," "tax burden," "support our troops," are all distorted images serving to conceal a transfer of wealth from people needing a safety net to corporations seeking military expansion.

Embedded Journalism

The media are increasingly dependent on governmental and corporate sources of news. Maintenance of continuous news shows requires a constant feed and an ever-entertaining supply of stimulating events and breaking news bites. The 24-hour news shows on MSNBC, Fox, and CNN maintain constant contact with the White House, Pentagon, and public relations companies representing both government and private corporations.

By the time of the Gulf War in 1991, retired colonels, generals, and admirals had become mainstays in network TV studios during wartime. Language such as "collateral damage" and "smart bombs" flowed effortlessly between journalists and military men, who shared perspectives on the occasionally mentioned but more rarely seen civilians killed by U.S.

firepower. This clearly foreshadowed the structure of "embedded" reporting in the second Iraq war, where mainstream corporate journalists literally lived with the troops and had to submit all reports to military censors.[14] A related militarization of news studies by Diane Farsetta at the Center for Media Democracy documented a related introduction of bias. These investigations showed Pentagon propaganda penetration on mainstream corporate news in the guise of retired Generals as "experts" or pundits who turned out to be nothing more than paid shills for government war policy.[15]

The problem then becomes more complex. What happens to a society that begins to believe such lies as truth? The run up to the 2003 war in Iraq concerning weapons of mass destruction (WMD) is a case in point. It not only illustrates the power of propaganda in creating public support for an ill-begotten war, but also reduces the possibility of a peace movement, even when fueled by the truth, to stop a war based on falsehoods. The current war in Iraq was the most globally protested war in recorded history. This did nothing to stop it and has done little to end it even under a Democratic president who promised such on the campaign trail. The candidate of "hope and change," with peace groups in tow, has proven to be dependent on the same interests in foreign policy that got the United States into war in the first place.[16]

THE PROGRESSIVE PRESS

Where the left progressive press may have covered some of the Winter Soldier issues, most did not cover the major story of Iraqi deaths. In *Manufacturing Consent*, Wharton School of Business Professor of Political Economy Edward Herman and MIT Institute Professor of Linguistics Noam Chomsky claim that because media are firmly embedded in the market system, they reflect the class values and concerns of their owners and advertisers. The corporate media maintain a class bias through five systemic filters: concentrated private ownership; a strict bottom-line profit orientation; over-reliance on governmental and corporate sources for news; a primary tendency to avoid offending the powerful; and an almost religious worship of the market economy. These filters limit what will become news in society and set parameters on acceptable coverage of daily events.[17]

The danger of these filters is that they make subtle and indirect censorship more difficult to combat. Owners and managers share class identity with the powerful and are motivated economically to please advertisers and viewers. Social backgrounds influence their conceptions of what is "newsworthy," and their views and values seem only "common sense." Journalists and editors are not immune to the influence of owners and managers.

Reporters want to see their stories approved for print or broadcast, and editors come to know the limits of their freedom to diverge from the "common sense" worldview of owners and managers. The self-discipline that this structure induces in journalists and editors comes to seem only "common sense" to them as well. Self-discipline becomes self-censorship—independence is restricted, the filtering process hidden, denied, or rationalized away.

Project Censored's analysis on the top 10 progressive left publications' and Web sites' coverage of key post-9/11 issues found considerable limitations on reporting of specific stories. The evidence supports the Chomsky and Herman understanding that the media barrage may well contribute to the news story selection process inside the left liberal media as well.[18] Even the left progressive media showed limited coverage of the human costs of the 9/11 wars.

The figure reported in summer 2007 documenting 1 million dead appeared in progressive Web sites and radio including *After Downing Street, Huffington Post, Counter Punch,* Alternet *Democracy Now!* and the *Nation,* but several took months to get to it. This lack of timely reporting on such a critical story on the humanitarian crisis of the U.S. occupation by the alternative press does not bode well for a strong, public peace movement. The United States is in dire need of a media democracy movement to address *truth emergency* concerns.

In response, the Truth Emergency Movement held its first national strategy summit in Santa Cruz, California, January 25 to 27, 2008. Organizers gathered key media constituencies to devise coherent decentralized models for distribution of suppressed news, synergistic truth-telling, and collaborative strategies to disclose, legitimize, and popularize deeper historical narratives on power and inequality in the United States. In sum, this truth movement is seeking to discover in this moment of constitutional crisis, ecological peril, and widening war, ways in which top investigative journalists, whistleblowers, and independent media activists can transform how Americans perceive and defend their world. We learn from grassroots actions in the United States but also from experiences of other countries. This requires us to transcend the stereotypes of other countries hammered by the corporate media. It is not by chance that two Latin American nations, both targets of U.S. efforts to remove their popular leaders by force, have been vilified by mainstream media. Both Cuba and Venezuela, however, have been experiments in local democratic participation in which voices of communities weigh heavily on social policy.

International Models of Media Democracy in Action: Venezuela

Democracy from the bottom is evolving as a 10-year social revolution in Venezuela. Led by President Hugo Chavez, the United Socialist Party of

Venezuela (PSUV) gained over 1.5 million voters in the November 2008 elections. "It was a wonderful victory," said Professor Carmen Carrero with the communications studies department of the Bolivarian University in Caracas. "We won 81 percent of the city mayor positions and 17 of 23 of the state governors," Carrero reported.

The Bolivarian University is housed in the former oil ministry building and now serves 8,000 students throughout Venezuela. The university (Universidad Bolivariana de Venezuela) is symbolic of the democratic socialist changes occurring throughout the country. Before the election of Hugo Chavez as president in 1998, college attendance was primarily for the rich in Venezuela. Today over 1,800,000 students attend college, three times the rate 10 years ago. "Our university was established to resist domination and imperialism," reported Principal (president) Marlene Yadira Cordova in an interview on November 10, 2008, "We are a university where we have a vision of life that the oppressed people have a place on this planet." The enthusiasm for learning and serious-thoughtful questions asked by students were certainly representative of a belief in the potential of positive social change for human betterment. The university offers a fully-staffed free health care clinic, free tuition, and basic no-cost food for students in the cafeteria, all paid for by the oil revenues now being democratically shared by the people.

Bottom-up democracy in Venezuela starts with the 25,000 community councils elected in every neighborhood in the country. "We establish the priority needs of our area," reported community council spokesperson Carmon Aponte, with the neighborhood council in the barrio Bombilla area of western Caracas. Community radio, TV, and newspapers are the voice of the people, where they describe the viewers/listeners as the "users" of media instead of the passive audiences.[19]

Democratic socialism has meant health care, jobs, food, and security, in neighborhoods where in many cases nothing but poverty existed 10 years ago. With unemployment down to a U.S. level, sharing the wealth has taken real meaning in Venezuela. Despite a 50 percent increase in the price of food last year, local Mercals offer government-subsidized cooking oil, corn meal, meat, and powdered milk at 30 to 50 percent off market price. Additionally, there are now 3,500 local communal banks with a $1.6 billion dollar budget offering neighborhood-based micro-financing loans for home improvements, small businesses, and personal emergencies.

"We have moved from a time of disdain [pre-revolution—when the upper classes saw working people as less than human] to a time of adjustment," proclaimed Ecuador's minister of Culture, Gallo Mora Witt, at the opening ceremonies of the Fourth International Book Fair in Caracas in

November 2007. Venezuela's Minister of Culture, Hector Soto, added, "We try not to leave anyone out . . . before the revolution the elites published only 60 to 80 books a year; we will publish 1,200 Venezuelan authors this year . . . the book will never stop being the important tool for cultural feelings." In fact, some 25 million books—classics by Victor Hugo and Miguel de Cervantes along with Cindy Sheehan's *Letter to George Bush*—were published in 2008 and are being distributed to the community councils nationwide. The theme of the International Book Fair was books as cultural support to the construction of the Bolivarian revolution and building socialism for the 21st century.

In Venezuela the corporate media are still owned by the elites. The five major TV networks and nine of 10 of the major newspapers maintain a continuing media effort to undermine Chavez and the socialist revolution. But despite the corporate media and $20 million annual support to the anti-Chavez opposition institutions from USAID and National Endowment for Democracy, two-thirds of the people in Venezuela continue to support President Hugo Chavez and the United Socialist Party of Venezuela. The democracies of South America are realizing that the neo-liberal formulas for capitalism are not working and that new forms of resource allocation are necessary for human betterment. It is a learning process for all involved and certainly a democratic effort from the bottom up.

International Models of Media Democracy in Action: Cuba

"You cannot kill truth by murdering journalists," said Tubal Páez, president of the Journalist Union of Cuba. In May 2008, 150 Cuban and South American journalists, ambassadors, politicians, and foreign guests gathered at the José Martí International Journalist Institute to honor the 50th anniversary of the death of Carlos Bastidas Arguello—the last journalist killed in Cuba. Carlos Bastidas was 23 years old when he was assassinated by Fulgencia Batista's secret police after having visited Fidel Castro's forces in the Sierra Maestra Mountains. Edmundo Bastidas, Carlos's brother, told about how a river of change flowed from the Maestra (teacher) mountains, symbolized by his brother's efforts to help secure a new future for Cuba.

The celebration in Havana was held in honor of World Press Freedom Day, which is observed every year in May. The UN first declared this day in 1993 to honor journalists who lost their lives reporting the news and to defend media freedom worldwide.

Cuban journalists share a common sense of a continuing counter-revolutionary threat by U.S.-financed Cuban Americans living in Miami. This is not an entirely unwarranted feeling in that many hundreds of terrorist actions against Cuba have occurred with U.S. backing over the past 50 years. In addition to the 1961 Bay of Pigs invasion, these attacks include the blowing up of a Cuban airlines plane in 1976 killing 73 people, the starting in 1981 of an epidemic of dengue fever that killed 158 people, and several hotel bombings in the 1990s, one of which resulted in the death of an Italian tourist.

In the context of this external threat, Cuban journalists quietly acknowledge that some self-censorship will undoubtedly occur regarding news stories that could be used by the "enemy" against the Cuban people. Nonetheless, Cuban journalists strongly value freedom of the press and there was no evidence of overt government control. Ricardo Alarcon, President of the National Assembly, noted that Cuba allows CNN, AP, and *Chicago Tribune* to maintain offices in Cuba, although the United States refuses to allow Cuban journalists to work in the United States.[20]

Cuban journalists complain that the U.S. corporate media is biased and refuses to cover the positive aspects of socialism in Cuba. Unknown to most Americans are the facts that Cuba is the number one country in percentage of organic foods produced in the world, has an impressive health care system with a lower infant mortality rate than the United States, trains doctors from all over the world, and has enjoyed a 43 percent increase in gross domestic product (GDP) between 2005 and 2008.

Neither Cuba nor Venezuela is a utopian society. Developing countries subject to continuing pressure by the United States may be cautious and suspicious of provocateurs who would incite violence or provoke U.S. military intervention. But in these countries, the ability of local media expressing voices of local communities is something from which media reformers can learn.

GRASSROOTS ANTIDOTES TO CORPORATE MEDIA PROPAGANDA

Tens of thousands in the United States engaged in various social justice issues constantly witness how corporate media marginalize, denigrate, or simply ignore their concerns. Activist groups working on issues like 9/11 truth, election fraud, impeachment in the Bush era, war propaganda, civil liberties abridgments, torture, the Wall Street meltdown, and corporate-caused environmental crises have been systematically excluded from mainstream news and the national conversation, leading to a genuine truth emergency in the country as a whole.

Now, however, a growing number of activists are finally saying "enough!" and joining forces to address this truth emergency by developing new journalistic systems and practices of their own. They are working to reveal the common corporate denominators behind the diverse crises we face and to develop networks of trustworthy news sources that tell people what is really going on. These activists know we need a journalism that moves beyond inquiries into particular crimes and atrocities, and exposes wider patterns of corruption, propaganda, and illicit political control by the military and corporate elite.

Recent efforts at national media reform through micro-power community radio—similar to the 400 people's radio stations in Venezuela—and campaign finance changes that would mandate access for all candidates on national media have been strongly resisted by the National Association of Broadcasters (NAB). NAB, considered one of the most powerful corporate lobby groups in Washington, works hard to protect over $200 billion dollars of annual advertising and the several hundred million dollars that political candidates spend in each election cycle.

The Truth Emergency movement now recognizes that corporate media's political power and failure to meet its First Amendment obligation to keep the public informed represents a huge task. Citizens must mobilize resources to redevelop news and information systems from the bottom up. Citizen journalists can expand distribution of news via small independent newspapers, local magazines, independent radio, and cable access TV. Using the Internet, the public can interconnect with like-minded grassroots news organizations to share important stories. These changes are already in progress.

BECOMING THE MEDIA: MEDIA FREEDOM INTERNATIONAL AND PROJECT CENSORED

In response to Truth Emergency conference, the Media Freedom Foundation and Project Censored launched an effort to both become a repository of independent news and information as well as a producer of content in validated independent news stories vetted by college and university professors and students around the world. As corporate media continue their entertainment agenda and the public relations (PR) industry—working for governments and corporations—increasingly dominates news content, there exists a socio-cultural opening to transform how the public receives and actually participates in the validation and creation of their own news.

Corporate media are increasingly irrelevant to working people and to democracy. People need to tell their own news stories from real experiences and perspectives, as an alternative to the hierarchically imposed and "official" top-down narrative. What better project in support of media democracy than for universities and colleges worldwide to support truth telling and validate news stories and independent news sources.

Only 5 percent of college students under the age of 30 read a daily newspaper. Most get their news from corporate television and increasingly on the Internet. One of the biggest problems with independent media sources on the Internet is a perception of inconsistent reliability. The public is often suspicious of the truthfulness and accuracy of news postings from noncorporate media sources. Over the past 10 years, in hundreds of presentations all over the United States, Project Censored staff has frequently been asked, "what are the best sources for news and whom can we trust?"

The goal of this effort is to encourage young people to use independent media as their primary sources of news and information and to learn about trustworthy news sources through the Media Freedom International News Research Affiliate Program. By the end of 2008, there were over 30 affiliate colleges and universities with plans to expand that participation several fold this. Through these institutions, validated independent news stories can be researched by students and scholars, then written, produced, and disseminated via the Web. In addition, on any given day at the Media Freedom Foundation Web site, one can view enough independent news stories from RSS (really simple syndication) feeds to fill nearly 50 written pages, more than even the largest U.S. newspapers. An informed electorate cannot remain passive consumers of corporate news. As aforementioned activist David Mathison suggested in his how-to manual, *Be the Media*, where he argues and instructs not only about how to build community media but how to build community *through* media.[21] Part of building community is developing an awareness about the type of world we want to participate in creating, and developing strategies for achieving change. New forms of media that promote widespread responsibility for both creating and disseminating information do not remove the need for people to protest, to demonstrate, to march, to boycott, and to demand entry into corporate offices. Rather it ensures that voices can be heard and, as shown in Howard Rheingold's *Smartmobbing Democracy*,[22] the power of new Internet communication technologies can be harnessed to mobilize more effectively. Contrasted with previous more limited technologies, Rheingold points out that now, "[m]obile and deskbound media such as blogs, listserves, and social networking sites allow for many-to-many communication." Technology has helped even the playing field by creating a virtual sphere where people can exchange ideas and instigate activism. Grassroots, bottom-up, peer-to-peer efforts have increased in influence and effectiveness due to the speed and breadth of new communication technologies. We are currently experiencing a potential for collective activism on a scale never before seen.

The continued expansion of independent Internet news sources allows for the mass political awareness of key issues and truth emergencies in the world.

The involvement of university and college professors and their students in validating news stories will be an important component of reliability verification of these sources. As we learn who we can trust in the independent news world, we will be in a stronger position for the continued development and expansion of democratic social movement/anti-war efforts in the future.

It is up to the people to unite and oppose the common oppressors manifested in a militarist and unresponsive government along with their corporate media courtiers and PR propagandists. Only then, when the public forms and controls its own information resources, will it be armed with the power that knowledge gives to move beyond the media-induced mindsets that limit change to modest reform. Grassroots media providing voice to those who would challenge elite domination are our best hope to create a truly vibrant democratic society that promises as well as delivers liberty, peace, and economic justice to all.

NOTES

1. U.S. General Tommy Franks as quoted in Epstein, 2002.
2. Phillips and Roth, 2008.
3. Holland, 2008.
4. Ibid.
5. Shenkman, 2008; Frank, 2004; Vidal, 2005; Kolb and Swords, 2003.
6. Mills, 2000; Habermas, 1962, 1981; Popper, 1945.
7. Habermas, 1991.
8. Solomon, 2005.
9. Uygur, 2009.
10. Milazzo, 2007.
11. Phillips and Roth, 2009.
12. Phillips, 2008.
13. Ibid.
14. Ibid.
15. See Farsetta, 2009 and the Center for Media and Democracy.
16. Stauber and Rampton, 2003; DiMaggio, 2008; Abele, 2009.
17. Herman and Chomsky, 1988, 2002; Chomsky, 2002.
18. Phillips, 2008.
19. Co-author Peter Phillips interviewed Carmon Aponte while visiting the Patare Community TV and radio station on a trip to Venezuela for a book fair in 2008. The station was one of 34 locally controlled community television stations and 400 radio stations now in the barrios throughout Venezuela.
20. Co-author Peter Phillips attended the major journalism conference in Cuba in 2008. About his experiences there, Phillips remarked,

During my five days in Havana, I met with dozens of journalists, communication studies faculty and students, union representatives, and politicians. The underlying theme of my visit was to determine the state of media freedom in Cuba and to build a better understanding between media democracy activists in the United States and those in Cuba. I toured the two main radio stations in Havana, Radio Rebelde and Radio Havana. Both have Internet access to multiple global news sources including CNN, Reuters, Associated Press, and BBC with several newscasters pulling stories for public broadcast. Over 90 municipalities in Cuba have their own locally run radio stations, and journalists report local news from every province.

During the course of several hours in each station I was interviewed on the air about media consolidation and censorship in the United States and was able to ask journalists about censorship in Cuba as well. Of the dozens I interviewed all said that they have complete freedom to write or broadcast any stories they choose. This was a far cry from the Stalinist media system so often depicted by U.S. interests.

21. Phillips, 2008; Mathison, 2009.
22. Rheingold, 2008.

CHAPTER 10

Renaissance 2.0: The Web's Potential for the Peaceful Transformation of Modern Society

Deva Temple

Throughout history new forms of mass media have transformed society by disseminating information and successfully enabling social movements to spread. Gutenberg's invention of the printing press eventually gave rise to the Renaissance and brought an end to the pervasive control of European society by the Church and kings who ruled by Divine Right.[1] The printing press would eventually contribute to the educational and infromational foundation for Habermas's bourgeoise public sphere,[2] further transforming global society through the spread of the Enlightenment, modernity, and the scientific method.

Later technologies also contributed to the transformation of society. Families gathered around the radio to listen to Franklin D. Roosevelt's *Fireside Chats,* creating support for New Deal legislation, transforming the relationship between American citizens and government, and building legal, economic, and environmental infrastructures that have served the United States for more than 75 years.[3] Television images coming out of Vietnam sparked the anti-war movement[4] and the civil rights movement was fueled when television images of marchers being attacked by police dogs and sprayed with fire hoses flooded into American living rooms.[5]

Telecommunications technologies have provided two-way communication while mass media provided a one-way medium for reaching large audiences. Both forms of communication technology brought people together in new ways and both were limited in their ability to move information from one person to another. Telecommunications, such as the telegraph and telephone, allowed for two-way communication and early forms of mass media provided for rapid information transfer to large audiences; however, because content creation remains centralized and expensive, mass media is easily used by powerful elites to promote their interests through the manipulation of information.[6] The power of the Internet is a result of synergies created by combining the preexisting mass media and telecommunications technologies. The Internet is, however, the first mass media technology that allows for more than one-way communication.

Early Internet technology, retrospectively called Web 1.0, was limited to informational Web sites and e-commerce sites. By comparison, second generation Web applications, also known as Web 2.0, are allowing users to connect and share in ways that mimic face-to-face social interactions. Web sites such as Twitter, MySpace, Tribe, Facebook and Meetup, among others, are allowing Internet users to interact with and expand entire social networks. Users who are interacting in virtual social networks are currently deciding the canon of a new religion, the fastest growing religion in New Zealand, the Jedi Church, fashioned after the peacekeeping Jedi heroes in the *Star Wars* movies.[7] If Gutenberg's printing press could be likened to Web 1.0, then Web 2.0 is the formation of Habermas's public sphere.

The Internet has been said to possess a great capacity for the promotion of peace and democracy worldwide[8] but this capacity will not be fulfilled without the conscious effort of dedicated individuals and organizations.[9,10] Web 2.0 provides a platform for the promotion of peace but it does not ensure that people will utilize it, or that they do so in a way that is nonviolent and leads to peace, democracy, or positive social transformation. The Internet can be used to organize violent terrorist activities, as well as to organize peace-focused, progressive political movements. What determines the difference in outcome is largely a result of differences in human inputs. Using a framework termed Technorganic Approaches to Peace, this chapter looks at ways that human agency can complement Web 2.0's potential to transform modern society, and to create a more peaceful world.

TECHNORGANIC APPROACHES TO PEACE

The Internet is a technological invention that has been said to mimic natural systems, particularly the brain.[11] The study of neural networks was integral to the development of computers and the Internet.[12] To be accurate, however, the Internet is not a true neural network because it remains incapable of synthesizing the information it possesses to solve problems. This task remains the domain and responsibility of human beings. The term *Technorganic* is used here to describe the melding of Internet technology with human agency to solve complex social problems. Contextually the term describes the ways in which humans can interface with Internet technology to promote peace, democracy, and social justice.

Technorganic approaches to peace rest on the theory of biomimicry, defined as "the science and art of emulating Nature's best biological ideas to solve human problems."[13] In much the same way that healthy, natural ecosystems are a result of diverse species engaging in symbiotic activities that work together to create dynamic states of health and resiliency, human social systems can be made healthy through the promotion of diversity and, in particular, the application of diverse approaches to solving complex human problems. By creating synergies between Internet technology and various types of human online and real-world activities, peace advocates, organizers, and political activists can multiply the power of individual human efforts. What follows is a brief exploration of technorganic approaches to peace, a three-part model that includes: personal transformation through education and interaction, communicating in 3D, and solidarity through online organizing.

PERSONAL TRANSFORMATION THROUGH EDUCATION AND INTERACTION

Personal transformation involves the transformation of the self so that one becomes more peaceful inwardly and in interpersonal interactions. Some say that peace cannot be achieved unless individuals transform themselves to become more peaceful, that peace cannot be achieved outwardly unless it is achieved first inwardly.[14,15] The Internet can facilitate personal transformation through two broad pathways: facilitating transformational learning through information dissemination, and facilitating interactions between individuals that lead to healing and personal transformation for the individuals involved. The first pathway could be accomplished using Web 1.0, but the second pathway is greatly enhanced by the advent of Web 2.0's social networking and interpersonal communications technologies.

Both pathways depend, however, on the synergistic function of 3D communication and solidarity through online organizing, discussed in greater detail below. The dissemination of information capable of contributing to personal transformation requires organized efforts among scholars, nonprofit organizations, educational institutions, businesses, communities, and governments. Healing and transformational interpersonal interactions require that participants engage in nonviolent, or 3D, communication. Web 2.0 makes it much easier for individuals and institutions to collaborate and share information and, as social networks grow, users have increased opportunities for the kind of human interaction that can lead to transformative experiences.

COMMUNICATING IN 3D: DIALOGUE, DISCOURSE, AND DEBATE

Communicating in 3D is a way of promoting peace from the bottom up through the use of nonviolent communication. The three patterns of communication included in 3D are: dialogue; discourse; and debate. *Dialogue* is defined as "a discussion between representatives of parties to a conflict that is aimed at resolution."[16] *Discourse* is defined as "formal and orderly and usually extended expression of thought on a subject, [or] a verbal exchange of ideas,"[17] often taking place in academic settings and applying a critical analysis to specific concepts and paradigms. *Debate* is a verbal communication pattern that involves carefully structured conflict, or "a regulated discussion of a proposition between two matched sides."[18] Dialogue is usually engaged in with the goal of furthering understanding among participants, whereas in discourse and debate there are increasing levels of conflict and the goal is often to convince others. As one moves from dialogue, to discourse, to debate, one encounters greater levels of conflict.

Movements and online structures that promote education in 3D communication techniques require concerted effort that is best accomplished when individuals, groups, and institutions work together. Online organizing can contribute to creating movements and institutions prepared to engage in such educational activities. Additionally, individuals who have engaged in personal transformation work are better prepared to engage in nonviolent communication.

SOLIDARITY THROUGH ONLINE ORGANIZING

The power of Web 2.0 technology provides a robust platform for the promotion of peace because of its power to assist coalition building and social justice activism through the enhanced sense of solidarity that arises from social networking. The Internet places the power of education, persuasion, and organizing in the hands of a wider segment of society than ever before in human history.[19] This empowers millions of people across the globe to impact the world in extraordinary ways. Many nongovernmental organizations (NGOs) have arisen and flourished as a result of the organizing power of the Internet. Individuals can be rallied to engage in letter-writing campaigns; to promote, attend, and participate in protests; to join in consumer boycotts; and to participate in various other acts of solidarity. Web 2.0 allows organizers of social justice movements to educate the public on the importance of key issues and to raise funds that help to further organizing activities in a more organic, self-assembling way. Political campaigns are able to draw together wider coalitions than with earlier Internet applications, in the process rewriting the rules of the game. Such online organizing benefits when individuals have done personal transformation work and are able to engage in nonviolent communication.

These three technorganic approaches to peace work synergistically with Web 2.0 technology to promote peace by organizing, empowering, and activating vast social networks. When the technorganic model is integrated successfully with Web 2.0, all three approaches work interdependently to produce synergistic results. Just as Habermas's public sphere could not have functioned properly without both the printed word and the gathering places, salons and coffee houses, The Internet fails to manifest its transformational potential if either component is missing. All of this requires, of course, intentional and well-informed action on the part of individuals and institutions.

ONLINE ORGANIZING

The Internet has provided a platform for several interesting political and social justice movements to emerge in recent years. This section considers the effectiveness of several high-profile online movements, assessing how well they were able to utilize the power of Web 2.0 technology by implementing the three technorganic approaches to peace.

THE WOMEN'S MOVEMENT FOR PEACE AND JUSTICE

The virtual space created by the Internet has been termed *virtual public spheres*[20] in reference to Habermas's theory concerning the role that previous, place-based public spheres played in the Enlightenment.[21] In the 1970s feminist consciousness-raising groups worked to create spaces for women to connect and share the stories of their experiences that led them to realize that they shared common systemic challenges. Only this time the spheres were not public but private. This process played a critical role in helping women to realize that many of the struggles they faced in their daily lives were not isolated, nor were they simply personal failings, but rather these systemic struggles became recognized as patriarchy.[22]

Modern feminists continue to utilize the technique of consciousness-raising but now place the practice into virtual public spheres. Sites such as Feministing and various public forums on popular social networking Web sites, such as Twitter, MySpace, and Facebook, among others, all serve as places of dialogue, discourse, and—more frequently—debate. The practice of nonviolent, 3D communication is sometimes absent from forums that are so large that they are difficult for moderators to police. However, many of these virtual public spheres provide a location in which critical discussions can take place and 3D communication could be implemented, but they do not all equally support the other two technorganic approaches to peace. According to Godin, what leads to cohesive groups, or *tribes* as he calls them, are shared vision, a set of tools, and opportunities to work together toward common goals.[23] Unfortunately, creating opportunities for communicators to work together toward common goals is not often the main focus on many of these Web sites. They do, however, serve a vital function as virtual public spheres where opportunities for personal transformation exist, where awareness can be raised, and beliefs deepened, transformed, or discarded.

CodePink is one very notable exception and provides a good example of an Internet-based movement that has successfully utilized technorganic approaches to Web 2.0 and mobilized followers to participate in direct democracy both in virtual space and on the streets. A communication analysis of CodePink Internet communications found that five main functions were accomplished: "the development of intrapublic consensus; improvements in group cohesion; the provision of a group medium for interaction; the mobilization of group action; and facilitation of broader access to the public sphere."[24] CodePink's successful accomplishment of these five functions is an example of what is possible when synergies between technorganic approaches to peace and Web 2.0 are achieved. The peaceful goals of CodePink, coupled with the provision of a virtual public sphere, serve to facilitate nonviolent communication that leads to consensus, group cohesion, and mobilization. The fact that CodePink is able to translate online communication and Web 2.0 networking tools into direct action often attracts media attention and thus reaches the consciousness of the general public and lawmakers. Had CodePink failed to capture these synergies, their consciousness-raising activities would have remained limited to group members and never have reached a wider audience.

THE ELECTION OF BARACK OBAMA

The historic election of Barack Obama could not have happened without the skillful use of Web 2.0 applications. Lessons learned from Howard Dean's

2003 primary campaign contributed to the design of Obama's successful Internet strategy, which included both the use of existing social networking sites and the creation of MyBarackObama.com, a Web 2.0 site that allowed the Obama campaign to quickly mobilize local campaign organizers, individual donors, and most importantly, voters. In addition, supporters were empowered by MyBarackObama.com to create their own campaign events, set their own fundraising goals, and quickly push information and fundraising requests out through their personal networks.[25] They were able to meet other supporters in cyberspace and to share ideas for successful campaign events and information on local fundraisers and caucus planning meetings, and to create a sense of camaraderie that continued after the election.[26]

Web 2.0 also played a role in creating transformative experiences, especially surrounding the Reverend Wright debacle, during which Candidate Obama made his historic speech on race that was featured on YouTube and widely circulated among users of social networking sites, which led many people to engage in online discussions around race issues in their own lives.[27]

Because the overall tone of the Obama campaign was notably cool and and his rhetoric was designed to be constructive and dialogical more than critical or combative.[28] By setting a calm, respectful tone, Obama helped guide his supporters to do the same. Obama supporters were encouraged to engage in respectful dialogues with friends, family, and with political opponents with this same spirit of respect and reconciliation.[29] In these ways, the Obama campaign utilized Web 2.0 coupled with thoughtful, conscious intent to achieve the synergy of technorganic approaches to peace.

By utilizing virtual public forums and creating new, networked opportunities for social activism and political engagement, the Obama campaign provided a best-case example of the marriage between Web 2.0 and technorganic approaches to peace. The number of young, progressive citizens pulled into the political process will continue to influence elections for years to come and the personal transformation, 3D communication, and online organizing skills acquired by Obama supporters as a result of their involvement with Obama's Web 2.0 campaign will allow them to be effective organizers of future politcal action.

THE IRANIAN INTERNET REVOLUTION

Protestors who gathered in Iran to challenge the results of the 2008 presidential elections engaged in the heavy use of social networking Web sites to organize protests and to disseminate information and images of the protests worldwide.[30] The locations of protests spread through sites like

Twitter and the streets of Iran soon filled with protesters, wearing green to show their solidarity in support of Mir Hossein Mousavi, the candidate challenging incumbent President Mahmoud Ahmadinejad. The Iranian government resorted to violence to quell the dissent and mainstream mass media outlets became dependent on online reports coming out of Iran as traditional journalists were forced to leave the country. Photos showing government violence were shown on a Facebook page dedicated to Mousavi, while a YouTube video of the death of 26-year-old philosophy student Neda Agha Sultan (who was not protesting but was nonetheless shot through the heart) made its way around the Internet and fostered worldwide empathy and support.[31]

The transformative impact of the widespread Web 2.0 reporting on the Iranian protests has served to transform the U.S. image of Iran and of the Iranian people. They have become human beings, struggling and dying in the streets to safeguard their democracy.[32] Because of Web 2.0, they have done this before our very eyes.

Whether the Iranian people had opportunities to become more personally peaceful or to learn nonviolent communication, it is clear that they have managed to utilize Web 2.0 applications to organize political movements. The fact that they have accomplished this much in a country where Internet access is so highly controlled, is an amazing feat in itself. It would be hard to imagine that the sense of solidarity and purpose created during the post-election unrest will soon fade.

CONCLUSION

The Internet is arguably the most powerful technology humans have ever created. The ability of Web 2.0 to provide information and multi-directional communication channels among the masses of the world's people is unparalleled. The ability of social networking to foster and assist social justice movements allows people to engage in acts of solidarity and direct democracy that have already made history and have the potential to change the course of the future. These capacities are ever-present in Web 2.0 technology, but their potential for creating peaceful, just, and democratic human societies must be fostered by the conscious intent of individuals and groups.

Without human agency, grounded in peaceful, competent, and organized solidarity, the Internet's capacity to promote peace is limited. Without a holistic, synergistic approach, the full potential of Web 2.0 remains to be manifested. Individual human beings must actively engage in personal transformation so that their capacity to engage in nonviolent problem solving is increased. People must also choose to engage in communication that is nonviolent and to join in movements that promote peace through social justice. All of these technorganic approaches to peace work together to achieve more than any of them would alone. In fact, they may all be essential elements of each other, just as we are all essential to each other—all a part of one shared solution that depends on the realization of our common humanity.

NOTES

1. Kreis, 2009.
2. Habermas, 1991.
3. National Archives, 2009.
4. Hallin, 2008.
5. Everet, 2009.
6. Chomsky, 2002.
7. Church, 2009.
8. Newmark, 2008.
9. Boyte, 2008.
10. Rheingold, 2008.
11. Stibel, 2008.
12. Naughton, 2000.
13. The Biomimicry Institute, 2009.
14. Kraft, 1992.
15. Toda Institute, 2008.
16. *Merriam Webster Dictionary*, 2009.
17. Ibid.
18. Ibid.
19. Rheingold, 2008.
20. Langman, 2005.
21. Habermas, 1991.
22. Kennedy, 2007.
23. Godin, 2008.
24. Simone, 2004.
25. Hill, 2009.
26. Ambi, 2009.
27. Ibid.
28. Powell, 2008.
29. Ambi, 2009.
30. Scola, 2009.
31. Kennedy, 2009.
32. Boal, 2009.

CHAPTER 11

BUILDING THE PEACE BY EXAMPLES OF CIVIL COURAGE DURING THE WAR

Svetlana Broz

When war broke out in Yugoslavia in the early 1990s, the only words spoken in conversations and read in newspapers in the capital, Belgrade, were words of the evil. The city where I had grown up, where I had completed my medical studies, and which I loved as a cosmopolitan and open city, had turned into a beehive in which each bee was building its own cell, carefully filling it with hatred. The worldwide coverage of the war was black-and-white. Even my friends who did not follow the news participated in those unremittingly crude conversations and I found that many relationships faltered on the question about whose contribution to evil was greater. The hive was not full of honey, but hatred, blame, and evil.

Refusing to believe that nothing human existed amid all the madness of war in Bosnia and Herzegovina, I searched for humanity behind the headlines. I started going to the war zones in January 1993, as a cardiologist, determined to help at least one human being denied normal medical care because of the war.

While providing care for the people of all three ethno-national backgrounds (Catholic Croats, Muslim Bosnians and Eastern Orthodox Christian Serbs), I felt their need to open their souls and talk without being questioned

---

The author expresses special thanks to Daniel Adamski for editorial assistance.

about their roles in the war. From their short, spontaneous confessions in the cardiology ward, I understood their need for truth, which in places where grenades were actually falling, was surprisingly subtle and refined compared to Belgrade's, and indeed the world's much more simplistic, black-and-white depictions of the Bosnian war zone.

I was told stories of people in Bosnia and Herzegovina who had the courage to stand up to crimes being committed against the innocent, even when they had no weapons to help them. These individuals served as genuine examples of the goodness, compassion, humanity and civil courage that continued to exist in these times of evil. They broke free from the identity of *bystander*, that person who chooses to look away, to ignore and to silently accept the suffering of others. Instead, these human beings provide compelling examples of what I call *upstanders*: people who stick to their moral convictions and norms and demonstrate great civil courage through their actions, even in a situation as horrific as the Bosnian war. My book, *Good People in an Evil Time*, is a collection of firsthand testimonies from people who survived the war: it illustrates the ways in which anonymous people were upstanders.

Some people may dismiss these stories, believing that wartime examples of violent behavior reveal far more about human nature. I disagree. Because they hold up a mirror and require us to examine our own acts and behavior, we must pay careful attention to these narratives. They clearly demonstrate the possibility of choice. When shared, these stories can, therefore, encourage more people to stand up and speak up against evil, and to act in accordance with their moral principles. The hundreds of interviews I've conducted, and the tens of thousands of people with whom I have shared these stories of humanity, repeatedly confirm this. Indeed, I've found that imparting evidence of upstanders' actions can have the very real and enduring effect of inspiring others to follow their example.

UPSTANDERS

Learning about upstanders and their motivations is not an easy, prescribed recipe that allows others to simply follow their traces. What defines the upstander cannot, for example, be captured in just a few words. His or her reasons for acting righteously are often personal and will depend on the circumstances, and finding what motivations upstanders might have in common is a question, unfortunately not for a cardiologist, but for psychologists, to debate. But we do not need to pin down general, abstract motivations to understand the function of these stories. These stories stir us. They appeal to us. They reach out and make us, readers and listeners, contemplate our own values and actions.

The upstander, thus, actively confronts the choice of whether to stand up against immorality and the degeneration of humanity, or keep quiet and accept things the way they are, as bystanders. The civil courage that characterizes the upstander is, in the words of Uwe Kitzinger, the courage of the rebel: it is the capacity to resist by thinking critically with one's own mind and the will to take part in life, instead of being a silent observer.

When so many other people chose to compromise their morals to survive, the upstander's actions suggest that we must not allow ourselves to be debased by circumstance: it is exactly to retain our dignity that we must sometimes refuse to live life at any cost. Hannah Arendt said: "It is always possible to say YES or NO." Upstanders are exactly those who want to make decisions about when to say "no" to evil.

Based on the anecdotal evidence of goodness I collected, I have found that upstanders are not extraordinary people. In fact, they are very often ordinary individuals. And regardless of their differences in age, gender, literacy, religious affiliation, ethnic identity, or wartime roles, what they shared was the bravery to sacrifice their lives rather than commit or be complicit in a crime. I had the opportunity to ask dozens of those who showed their civil courage during the war what motivated them to behave as they did and why they didn't follow the majority, who as bystanders either observed silently or participated actively in crimes. Their precise answers varied, but many spoke about the exemplary roles of their parents and forefathers and how they could not have acted differently, but only in accordance with their high moral norms. There is no predetermination that makes some upstanders and others not. It is a choice. It is the choice to refuse to live life *at any cost*. It is the choice to retain dignity and to value humanity when surrounded by evil.

Unfortunately, however, too often we only learn about upstanders through the stories told by others. This truth is brought to life in a story that a factory director from Central Bosnia told me.

Armed soldiers who were part of the Croatian Defense Council and men from paramilitary units took people, including me and my family, Muslim by nationality, from their apartments and houses and brought them to the elementary school that they had made over into a prison camp. After several days, they took 40 of the prisoners, including my wife, our five-year-old twin boys, and me and lined us up in a row. Then they brought over a civilian, a man who was Croatian like they were, but who was also my closest friend. They ordered him to choose a dozen of us from the lines and to decide how we would be killed. I was horrified—he knew all of us so well. Without a second thought he turned to the armed murderers and said, "You should be ashamed of yourselves! These people are innocent. Release them. Let them go home." Then he turned to us and looking right into our eyes, said, "I'm so sorry. This is all I can do. I know they will kill me tonight. I wish all of you the best." His soldiers dragged him off somewhere and took us back to the prison camp. My best friend was right. The criminal soldiers, his own people, killed him that night. We were luckier. After several months we were saved through an exchange of prisoners.

THE LEGACY OF THE UPSTANDER

I believe that the notion of the upstander has universal value and as their incidence is universal, so, too, is their significance. Stories like these about real, often anonymous, people whose selfless acts have influenced so many, make people everywhere from all backgrounds aware that they too have choices in life, and it is just this awareness of choice that enables them to stand up for the good.

For instance, a few years ago at a conference I attended, I heard Sami Adwan, a Palestinian psychologist, explain why he had chosen to dedicate his life to work for peaceful co-existence between Palestinians and Jews. As a young man he was held in an Israeli military prison. He suffered for three days with several other prisoners in a cell with no water because the commanding officer had ordered the soldiers guarding them not to give them any. On the fourth day, a soldier came into the cell, and after checking that none of his superiors was watching, he pulled out a canteen and gave it, without a word, to the prisoners. Several days later, the commanding officer beat Adwan for refusing to sign a document written in a language he didn't understand. After several blows he could hear the voice of the soldier guarding the officer, asking, "Aren't you ashamed of yourself for hitting this man just because he wouldn't sign something he couldn't read? I would never sign if I were in his place."

A man who lost most of his family during the Rwandan genocide, who survived only because he was studying abroad at the time, testified about the mother of one of the murderers. Every morning for four months, while her son went off to kill members of the other tribe, she brought into her home the entire family of the witness's aunt. The murderer's mother fed them, looked after their needs, and hid them, knowing no one would look for members of the enemy tribe at her house. Every evening, when her son returned from his bloody work, she hid the family in the bush near her home, where they slept. That family is the only remnant of the student's large clan thanks to this woman who found a way to oppose the actions of her own son.

All wars, everywhere in the world, contain this often-forgotten category of people: brave souls who say "No" in the face of a totalitarian regime, to nationalist doctrine, to ethnic cleansing, to persecution. Examples of good-ness that know no ethnic, religious, racial, or political bounds are important documentary material from the wars, and they also represent an axis around which it is possible to build a healthy future once the atrocities have halted. As such, they are of enormous social, cultural, and religious value. The effects of an upstander's behavior can also extend well beyond a single heroic act and across geographical boundaries, as the people who benefit from such acts try to emulate them. And as these individuals tell their own stories, the effects grow.

EDUCATION TOWARD CIVIL COURAGE

In the last three years, I have worked with more than 40,000 students from the Western Balkans who have heard me lecture on kindness, moral norms and civil courage. The process of listening and discussing, of engaging with these stories, seems to awake them from a deep sleep. They come to the lecture convinced that they cannot change anything, that they are not important as individuals, and that they are without influence over the societies in which they live. They feel completely on the margins of their worlds. They dream only about finishing their education and moving out of their country; according to statistics, 75 percent of the youth want to leave Bosnia and Herzegovina. But hearing about those who displayed kindness and civil courage, they suddenly wake up and want to become actively involved in the events around them. Loudly and clearly, they show that they are able to recognize negative authorities, and they often con-front them.

After one lecture, for example, students from Tuzla, in Bosnia and Her-zegovina, were inspired to form a movement demanding the introduction of sex education into secondary schools—an important but neglected public health issue. They collected signatures and sent a petition to the conserva-tive regional Minister of Education, announced their actions in the media, and were ready for demonstrations if their request was not met. The deci-sion is pending. Throughout Bosnia and Herzegovina, school directors who obstructed their students from attending my lecture on civil courage have been confronted afterward by these students, who demanded an explanation for this limitation of their freedom. Cases of corruption and even pedophilia in schools have been openly identified during public lectures at which media were present, thus finally bringing the problem into the public realm.

And even in the very peaceful Swedish city of Gothenburg, whose citizens can hardly remember when they last had a war, the topic of civil courage became very important for one student from the University of Gothenburg.

He sent me an e-mail in 2001 about an experience he had three days after hearing my lecture on civil courage:

> I was on the bus in Gothenburg (Sweden) and saw three enraged men physically abusing the bus driver who wanted them to leave the bus because they had lit cigarettes in their hands. He was covered in blood. I was turning to see the reactions of other passengers: all of them were looking out of the windows. I turned and looked through a window myself, but at that moment I saw your face and thought: what would you say if you could see me? What would all those who sacrificed their lives to protect someone who was unjustly persecuted do? So, I threw myself on those three attackers who broke my nose with the first blow, but I managed to enable the driver to call the police on his mobile phone.

This story demonstrates the young man's courage, as it also shows the impact of good education about civil courage. I believe, given the determination of this youth, such education can induce a critical mass of responsible individuals to practice civil courage until they make the world a better, more peaceful place. By learning about examples of unselfish human kindness and of those who acted in accordance with their deepest moral norms, young people become aware of the possibility of choice in their own lives. They ask themselves whether they will remain bystanders or upstanders in the world around them.

DOCUMENTING THE GOOD

Stories of goodness in the face of evil encourage tolerance. Because of their intrinsic moral value and because of their strong educational importance, they deserve to be archived and cherished. Documenting these personal narratives, in the form of books, in museums, and in other public spaces (which my NGO GARIWO is working on), offers important ethical resources for teachers and others to give both children and adults the chance to reflect on individual and group responsibility in the face of repressive regimes. Any place dedicated to civil courage can serve as a significant model for the implementation of restorative justice and the prevention of future conflicts. Stories of civil courage and kindness restore faith in humanity; they remind citizens that there are seeds of goodness in each of us, and that even if we have been unkind or unethical at one point, in the next moment we may find the strength to turn around. Goodness allows for the redemption of the individual and the collective self. It creates a sense of dignity and allows us to act from a more mature perspective. From this perspective peace can be achieved.

CHAPTER 12

Peace Can Be Taught

Colman McCarthy

As a journalist in Washington, D.C., since the mid-1960s, I've had lucky breaks landing interviews with some of the world's enduring peacemakers. Among them were Desmond Tutu from South Africa, Mairead Corrigan from Belfast, Adolfo Perez Esquivel from Buenos Aires, Mother Teresa from Calcutta, and Muhammad Yunus from Bangladesh: all Nobel Peace Prize winners. There were also those who deserved Nobel Prizes: Sargent and Eunice Shriver, Dorothy Day, Daniel and Philip Berrigan, Joan Baez, Jeannette Rankin, Philip Hart, Mark Hatfield, Mubarak Awad, and a long list of others. And let's include one of my heroes, Frank Kelly, a genuine peacemaker.

Toward the end of the interviews, which is often when you get the most candid answers, I would ask a pair of basic questions: What is peace? And how can each of us increase it while decreasing violence?

On the definitional question, agreement was reached. Peace is the result of love, and if love were easy we'd all be good at it.

The second question almost always had the same answer: go where people are. All that's happening is people and nations having conflicts—and solving them knowingly and morally with nonviolent force or unknowingly and immorally with violent force. No third way exists.

I heeded the peacemakers' advice: The sure place to find large numbers of people is in America's 78,000 elementary schools, 32,000 high schools, and more than 4,000 universities, colleges, and community colleges. In the early 1980s, I went to a public high school near my office at the *Washington Post* to ask the principal if I could teach a course on alternatives to violence. Give it a try, she said: but there's a problem, the school is poor and can't afford to pay you.

I didn't come for money, I said. I'll volunteer. That semester, 25 juniors and seniors at the School Without Walls enrolled in my course, "Alternatives to Violence." It wasn't difficult to teach. We started with the literature of peace, reading Gandhi, Tolstoy, Einstein, Thomas Merton, Jane Addams, Gene Sharp, A.J. Muste, Jesus, Francis, Amos, Isaiah, Buddha, Sojourner Truth, Addin Ballou, George Fox, Barbara Deming, Dorothy Day, John Woolman, and a long list of others. And that was on the first day! Then we really got into it!

After rattling off those names, unfailingly and often bafflingly, a student would call out, "How'd you ever hear of all those people? How come we haven't heard of them?"

They hadn't heard because they had gone to conventional schools where everything except peace is taught. To drive home the point, and drive it visually, I pulled out a $100 bill. I held it high and announced a spot quiz. Identify the following six people and you get the $100. Teenagers focus rather quickly when a try for easy money is offered. I began the quiz: Who is Robert E. Lee? Most hands rose. Then Ulysses S. Grant. Most hands again. The same for Paul Revere. By now, capitalistic fantasies of an after-school spending spree were rising.

Just three to go for the $100, I said. Who is Emily Balch? No hands go up. Who is Jeannette Rankin? Blanks on that one. Who is Ginetta Sagan. Silence.

I've given the $100-bill quiz before hundreds of high school and college audiences. I've done it before large audiences of teachers. No one has ever won the $100. I never worry about losing it. I can always count on American education and how it ensures that the young are well-informed about militarists who break the peace and ill-informed on those who make the peace.

The course went well that first year. Teaching peace was as easy as breathing. I went to another school, Bethesda-Chevy Chase High in suburban Washington, and then to Wilson High in the District of Columbia, again volunteering. Within a few years I found the time and energy to teach peace courses at Georgetown University Law Center, American University, the University of Maryland, and the Washington Center for Internships. Since 1982, I've had more than 7,000 students in my classes. Since leaving *The Post* in 1997, I teach at seven schools in the fall, six in the spring, and two in the summer.

That first school, by the way, was perhaps the poorest in America: it had no cafeteria, no gym, no auditorium, no athletic fields, no lockers, poor heating, and in recent years no clean drinking water. Something else was noteworthy: the poorest school in America was also the closest school to the White House. Five blocks away. We keep inviting presidents to come by. None has. George W. Bush was especially busy, traveling the land giving speeches on school reform, as in Leave No Child Untested. My students don't feel slighted. They aren't into big shots. They favor long shots, because they know that's what they are. So they work twice as hard to make it in life.

Peace education is in its infancy. In 1970, only one American college was offering a degree in Peace Studies: Manchester College, a Church of the Brethren school in Indiana. More than 70 colleges and universities currently offer undergraduate and graduate degrees in conflict resolution, with more than 300 offering minors and concentrations. Although the message is getting through that unless we teach our children peace someone else will teach them violence, no one should be deluded. The day is far away when the teaching of peace is given the academic attention that goes to conventional subjects. My high school students will graduate with only that one course in peace studies. Counting elementary school, they will have been in classrooms for 12 years. Would we ever let students go through 12 years of school with only one math course? Or only one science course? And yet, we keep telling the young that nothing is more important than peace. It's natural for them to be disbelieving, otherwise school boards would see that the study of peace was given as primary a place in the curriculum as any other essential subject.

Even muscling one course into one school takes some extraordinary flexing. A while back I was invited by a school board to speak about peace education. After 20 minutes, I thought I was making progress. Board members listened politely and asked relevant questions. My goal was to move the board to get one peace studies class into each of the county's 22 high schools. Just one course. One period a day. An elective for seniors. Nothing grandiose.

I was already a volunteer peace teacher at one of the county's high schools, so I wasn't whizzing in as a theorist with a lofty idea who lets someone else do the work. At the end of my talk, a board member confessed to having a problem. Peace studies, he said. Is there another phrase? The word studies was okay, but peace? It might raise concerns in the community. I envisioned a newspaper headline: "Peace Studies Proposal Threatens Stability in the County," with a sub-head, "School Board Nixes Bizarre Proposal." And this was in an allegedly liberal bluer than blue county.

Unable to rouse the school board, I tried the school system's curriculum office. It was an end-run, and there's always an end to run around if you look hard enough. I had edited a textbook, "Solutions to Violence," a

16-chapter collection of 90 essays that ranged from Gene Sharp's "The Technique of Nonviolent Action" to Dorothy Day's "Love Is the Measure." After some half-dozen meetings with assorted bureaucrats, papercrats, and educrats, as well as meetings with principals and social studies teachers at several high schools, I began to realize that public schools are government schools. Teachers are government workers. Caution prevails. It took six years to get the book approved. I'd already been using it in my own course all that time, slipping it in like contraband. Fittingly, I'd start each semester by reading and discussing Thoreau's essay "On the Duty of Civil Disobedience." Dutiful me.

Whether in the high school, college, or law school classes, students would usually divide into two groups. One would bond intellectually, and often quickly, with Gandhi's belief that "nonviolence is the weapon of the strong" and agree with Hannah Arendt that "violence, like all action, changes the world but the most probable change is to a more violent world." Another group came in loaded with doubts, which I encouraged them to express. Nonviolence and pacifism are beautiful theories, they said, but in the real world there are muggers on the streets and international despots on the prowl. So let's keep our fists cocked and our bomb bays opened.

All I asked of the skeptics was that they think about this: do you depend on violent force or nonviolent force to create peace not merely peace in some vague "out there," but, first off, in our homes. I had a student pull me aside on leaving class after we'd spent a week on Gandhi's essay "The Doctrine of the Sword." It's good to learn about that, she said, but what about the war zone in her home, where her mother and father regularly battle each other emotionally, verbally, and often physically. How do we stop that war?

It's a valid question. Perhaps if her parents had gone to schools where nonviolent conflict resolution skills and methods were systematically taught, the living room wars might never have erupted. The leading cause of physical injury to American women is being beaten by a man they are living with—husband or boyfriend, ex-husband or ex-boyfriend. The emotional violence between couples can only be imagined. I'm convinced much of it could be prevented if our schools taught the basic skills of mediation and nonviolent conflict resolution. It's easier to build a peaceful child than to repair a violent adult.

Peace teachers have no illusions that exposing students to the literature of peace and the methods of nonviolence will cause governments to start stockpiling plowshares, not swords, or that the young will instantly convert to Franciscan pacifism. But what isn't illusory is that effectively organized nonviolent force is far more powerful than the gun or bomb.

Where has it worked? In only the past quarter-century, at least six brutal regimes have been overthrown by people who had no weapons of steel but only what Einstein called "weapons of the spirit."

On February 26, 1986, a frightened Ferdinand Marcos, once a ruthless and U.S.-supported ruler of the Philippines but now just another powerless rogue, fled to exile in Hawaii. As staged by nuns, students, and human rights workers—many of them trained in Boston by Gene Sharp—a three-year nonviolent revolt brought him down.

On October 5, 1988, Chile's despot and another U.S. favorite, Gen. Augusto Pinochet, was driven from office after five years of strikes, boycotts, and other forms of nonviolent resistance. A Chilean organizer who led the demand for free elections said, "We didn't protest with arms. That gave us more power."

On August 24, 1989, in Poland, the Soviet puppet regime of Gen. Wojciech Jaruzelski fell. On that day it peacefully ceded power to a coalition government created by the Solidarity labor union that for a decade used nonviolent strategies to overthrow the communist dictator. Few resisters were killed in the nine-year struggle. The example of Poland's successful nonviolence spread, with the Soviet Union's collapse coming soon after. It wasn't oratory by Ronald Reagan or the Pope that first stoked the end of the Cold War. It was the heroic deeds of Lech Walesa and the nonviolent Poles he and others organized. They didn't bring the Soviets to their knees, they brought them to their senses.

On May 10, 1994, former prisoner Nelson Mandela became the president of South Africa. It was not armed combat that ended white supremacy. It was the moral force of organized nonviolent resistance that made it impossible for the racist government to control the justice-demanding population.

On April 1, 2001, in Yugoslavia, Serbian police arrested Slobodan Milosevic for his crimes while in office. In the two years that a student-led protest rallied citizens to defy the dictator, not one resister was killed by the government. The tyrant was put on trial in The Hague, but died before a verdict was reached.

On November 23, 2003, the bloodless "revolution of roses" toppled Georgian President Eduard Shevardnadze. Unlike during the country's civil war that marked the power struggles in the 1990s, no deaths or injuries occurred when tens of thousands of Georgians took to the streets of Tbilisi in the final surge to oust the government.

In the mid-1980s, who would have thought this possible? Yet it happened. Ruthless regimes, backed by torture chambers, were driven from power by citizens who had no guns, tanks, bombs, or armies. They had a superior arsenal: the moral power of justice, the strength of will, and the toughness of patience.

Yet we still see these victories as flukes. Theodore Roszak explains: "The usual pattern seems to be that people give nonviolence two weeks to solve their problems and then decide it has 'failed.' Then they go on with violence for the next hundred years and it seems never to fail or be rejected."

During these years of nonviolent successes, the failures of violence were rampant. The United States government, which Martin Luther King Jr., in his prophetic sermon on April 4, 1967, in Riverside Church in New York City, called the "world's greatest purveyor of violence," prowled the world trying to heal it with bullets and bullying. The pattern of dominance and intervention was set after World War II. As compiled by historian William Blum, these are the countries—and men, women, and children living in them—that American pilots have bombed since 1945: China (1945 to 1946), Korea (1950 to 1953), China (1950 to 1953), Guatemala (1954), Indonesia (1958), Cuba (1959 to 1960), Guatemala (1960), Congo (1964), Peru (1965), Laos (1964 to 1973), Vietnam (1961 to 1974), Cambodia (1969 to 1970), Guatemala (1967 to 1969), Libya (1986), Grenada (1983), El Salvador (1980s), Nicaragua (1980s), Panama (1989), Iraq (1991 to 2008), Sudan (1998), Afghanistan (1998 to 2008), and Yugoslavia (1999).

After discussing that list in my peace classes, I give the students a multiple choice quiz. In how many of those countries did a democratic government, respectful of human rights, occur as a direct result of the U.S. killing spree? Choose one: (a) none, (b) zero, (c) not a one, (d) naught, (e) a whole number between -1 and +1.

No one has ever flunked the quiz! Pick a, b, c, d, or e and it's a guaranteed A!

That's one way to give a lesson on the failures of violent conflict resolution. Another is to read the essay by Daniel Berrigan from his autobiography *To Dwell in Peace*:[1]

Blood and iron, nukes, and rifles. The leftists kill the rightists, the rightists kill the leftists, both, given time and occasion, kill the children, the aged, the ill, the suspects. Given time and occasion, both torture prisoners. Always, you understand, inadvertently, regretfully. Both sides, moreover, have excellent intentions, and call on God to witness them. And some god or other does witness them, if we can take the word of whatever bewitched church.

And of course, nothing changes. Nothing changes in Beirut, in Belfast, or in Galilee, as I have seen. Except that the living die. And that old, revered distinction between combatant and noncombatant, which was supposed to protect the innocent and helpless, goes down the nearest drain, along with the indistinguishable blood of any and all.

Alas, I have never seen anyone morally improved by killing—neither the one who aimed the bullet, nor the one who received it in his or her flesh.

A crucial part of peace education is to combine ideas with action. Conventional teachers, either through inertia or fear of not producing students who score well on the latest exam dreamed up by testocrats, keep pumping theories into the minds of students. The result? People who are theory-rich but experience-poor. They are unbalanced ones, and too often, grade mongers who have forgotten Walker Percy's line, "that you can make all A's in school and go out and flunk life."

One solution is service learning, the growing movement to move students out of classrooms and into the scenes of poverty and despair. I've taken my high school, college, and law classes into prisons, impoverished schools, shelters, and soup kitchens—sometimes to be of real service, other times merely to see, smell, and feel what it's like to be broke and broken. Those are the places to understand the truth of Sargent Shriver's call:[2] "The cure is care. Caring for others is the practice of peace. Caring becomes as important as curing. Caring produces the cure, not the reverse. Caring about nuclear war and its victims is the beginning of a cure for our obsession with war. Peace does not come through strength. Quite the opposite. Strength comes through peace."

I took my Georgetown law students recently to a women's shelter, about a mile from the school but economically a universe away. Some Carmelite nuns, skilled in the works of mercy and rescue, serve about 40 homeless women. I take my classes there often to see a sermon, rather than hear a sermon. When we arrived late one afternoon, we went to the dining room where the women were hunched over their soup and saltines. The class looked on in wonder. Who are these women? How did they fall to the streets? The law students, some quicker than others, got the picture. These are people outside the law. These are people for whom the law represents only one thing: the failure of love.

While speaking with one of the Carmelite nuns, I said that I'd like to help out: I'll go back to my neighborhood to collect some food and clothing for the homeless women, and bring it in next Saturday.

"Oh, how wonderful," said the nun. "I can't tell you how deeply touched I am. I love it when you NPR and C-SPAN liberals come around with your Volvos filled up with food and clothing. It moves my heart. It's indescribable." The good nun, I fear, had a cynical side, which occasionally flared. It was the beginning of Lent, so she was probably doing penance by eating lemons for dinner that put her in a foul mood right about then. But she recovered: "If you'd really like to help, just go talk to that lady in the corner." She pointed to a bedraggled, wrinkled-skinned woman, sitting alone. She had the misery of the Earth in her sunken eyes. "Just talk to her?" I asked. "That's all?" "Yes," the nun said. "You'll be doing plenty. We are doing fine with food and clothing but we don't have enough people who will just come in and talk with the women. The hardest thing about street life, especially for women, is the loneliness."

Many of the law students sat with the women that day, just to talk. Many went back on their own for regular visits, to learn these were human beings, not bag ladies. When I catch up with my law students 5, 10, or 20 years later, I ask them what they remember from my class. I expect they'll tell me about that brain-stretching day when we all discussed the nuances of the Ninth and Fourteenth Amendments. For some reason, they forget that. Instead, they talk about the time we went to the homeless shelter. It woke them up and shook them up. Many went into poverty law, or public interest law, or welfare reform law, or lady-in-the-corner law.

The lesson that day goes to the core of peacemaking, as told to me once by Mother Teresa: "Few of us will . . . [ever] be called on to great things, but all of us can do small things in a great way."

I work with a girls' boarding school that is blessed with an enlightened headmistress who cancels classes every Wednesday and sends her students into Washington for internships. This is experiential, not theoretical, learning, not to be flushed away after the last exam. For the past few years, I have had two or three girls from the Madeira School help teach my classes in one of my public high schools—Wilson High which has six police stationed in the halls, each officer carrying a high-powered weapon and wearing a bullet-proof vest.

High school administrators tend to see nonclassroom learning as unproductive. Keep teenagers, especially seniors and juniors who need to be prepped for college, cooped in sterile idea-driven classrooms, especially the advanced placement classrooms that will secure them room and board in Ivy League colleges. Too often we process students as if they were slabs of cheese—enrolled in Velveeta High, on their way to Cheddar University and Mozzarella graduate school.

Serving food to homeless people, tutoring illiterate prisoners, or mentoring a Special Olympics athlete is useful but it can remain idle charity unless twinned with an awareness of politics. At a basic level, and well away from party platforms, focus groups, and candidates' promises, politics is about one reality: who decides where the money goes. Which policy decisions keep more money flowing to military contractors to build weapons and less to building contractors to build affordable housing for the working poor? Which politicians sanction packing our prisons with people who are drug addicted or mentally ill and who need to be treated, not punished? Which lobbies allow tax laws to be written so loopholes get widened for corporations, while rules for home foreclosures get tightened? Which policies allow the Peace Corps and Americorps budgets to languish and let the military budget flourish? Which politicians allowed military spending to rise more than 60 percent since 2001, while every day in the Third World more than 35,000 people die from hunger or preventable diseases?

Why does all that keep happening? Finding answers is the tough part of peace education, learning the connections between the inequities and the structural violence behind them.

A full semester, not a few days in a peace class, could be devoted to the politics of money. The current military budget, according to the Center for Defense Information, a Washington nonprofit staffed mostly by former military officers and Pentagon workers, is $878 billion. Unless you are an astronomer, the number is too large to grasp. Breaking it down, the spending comes to about $2.5 billion a day—a sum that is 10 times more than the Peace Corps budget for a full year. $2.5 billion is still ungraspable. It totes to $28,000 a second. $28,000 . . . $28,000 . . . The seconds tick . . . $28,000 . . . $28,000.

Even that number can remain abstract. It's the government's money, we think, forgetting from whom the government collects it. Depending on your tax brackets, an American family can pay $5,000, $10,000, or often more, in annual federal taxes that is directed by Congress to the military. Martin Luther King Jr., in that same Riverside Church sermon, saw it clearly: "A nation that continues year after year to spend more money on military defense than on programs of social uplift is approaching spiritual death."

Every year some 10,000 citizens break free and refuse to pay federal taxes that go to war. They are not tax cheats or tax evaders. They are acting out of conscience, a kind based on the idea that if killing people is not the way to solve conflicts then so also is paying soldiers to do the killing. Conscientious tax refusers are more than willing to pay their full share for any federal program, except ones that sanction killing in the name of national security. No conscientious tax refuser has ever taken a case to the Supreme Court and won. It's rare that a case gets past a lower court. The reason? Nowhere in the Constitution can the word conscience be found. It's not there, even though you'd think Jefferson or Madison might have slipped in it when the Founders were nodding off after a long day.

After 9/11 peace teachers found ourselves challenged by students who asked, foremost, how should we have responded?

Congress had three options—military, political, and moral—to resolve the conflict. Predictably, the military prevailed. Got a problem? An enemy? Go bomb somebody. The House and Senate both approved bombing the people of Afghanistan, presumably to wipe out the Taliban and al-Qaeda. Out of 535 members of Congress, only one voted no: Barbara Lee of Oakland, California. Her stand brought to mind Jeannette Rankin. On December 8, 1941, the Montanan was the only member of Congress to oppose U.S. entry into World War II, saying as she did in 1917 when voting against entering World War I: "You can no more win a war than win an earthquake."

The political solution was to follow our own nonviolent conflict resolution advice, as when we tell Israelis and Palestinians, or Shiites and Sunnis, or factions in Kenya, or differing sides anywhere: talk, compromise, negotiate, reconcile, and stop killing each other. Sound advice, so why didn't we follow it ourselves and talk to Osama bin Laden or Saddam Hussein? Such a notion is dismissed as surreal or hideously naïve: you can't talk to evil doers, especially satanic ones like bin Laden.

That was the U.S. foreign policy during the Cold War when the evil-doing Chinese Communist government was demonized for its plans of world conquest. But then Richard Nixon went to China. He talked, compromised, negotiated, and reconciled. Today China is not only a major trading partner with the United States but is loaning money to us. Ronald Reagan, who in 1986 called the Soviet Union "the evil empire," went to Moscow soon after. He talked, compromised, negotiated, and reconciled. Russia is no longer an enemy.

Putting aside for a moment their regressive record on other issues, two Republican presidents did indeed provide a model for nonviolent conflict resolution.

A moral solution could have come three days after 9/11 when President Bush, his war council, and members of Congress assembled in the National Cathedral in Washington. Not a pew was empty. Assorted reverends, including Billy Graham and a Catholic cardinal, took to the pulpit to offer prayerful succor to a president who believes that "Our nation is chosen by God and commissioned by history to be a model for the world." At the service's end, the Lord's Prayer was recited, including the most ignored words in history: "Forgive us our trespasses as we forgive those who trespass against us." Three days before, some people did trespass. Were they forgiven? It was the opposite: let's go kill.

The moral solution would have moved us to forgive those behind 9/11, and then ask them to forgive America its long history of invasions that have been far more systematic and violent than the September one-day crime spree. Had Desmond Tutu been invited to speak that day, he might have suggested—as he did five months later in a sermon at St. Paul's Cathedral in Boston—that violent solutions to conflicts are doomed: "The war against terrorism will not be won as long as there are people desperate with disease and living in poverty and squalor. Sharing our prosperity is the best weapon against terrorism."[3]

Much the same thinking has been long advanced by the War Resisters League: "We shall live in a state of fear and terror, or we shall move toward a future in which we seek peaceful alternatives to conflict and a more just distribution of the world's resources."

In 1985, my wife and I founded the Center for Teaching Peace. Supported by foundation grants and a growing membership, our work is to persuade and assist schools at all levels either to begin or expand academic-based programs in peace education. If you want to give peace a chance, first give it a place in the curriculum.

Progress is happening. At one East Coast high school that uses our textbooks, all juniors are required to take a peace studies course. This was once a Catholic military school. In Philadelphia, a publicly funded peace school opened its doors two years ago. "In a city in which too many of our young people and families feel threatened by violence, it's time to study and practice peace," a school official told the *Philadelphia Inquirer*. In Davis, California, the three-year-old Teach Peace Foundation is getting traction.

I heard recently from an English teacher at Niles West High School, in Skokie, Illinois: "I'm writing to let you know that our district, somewhat miraculously, approved a peace studies course . . . I ordered your two collections of peace essays several years ago, and you wrote back an encouraging letter. It took a long time to get a course started here, with many institutional hoops to go through. Two other teachers and I put a proposal together, which was at first rejected. It was too 'social studies' oriented. We are all, incidentally, English teachers. Our second proposal, titled 'The Literature of Peace,' was accepted by the school board. This was the miraculous part."

One of my former Georgetown Law students resigned from the Washington, D.C., bar five years ago to become a high school peace teacher. For several years, Leah Wells, a Georgetown University graduate, was my teaching assistant in two Washington schools and a prison. Then she went to the big leagues, joining the staff here at the Nuclear Age Peace Foundation. She also taught peace courses at a Ventura high school and then put together a widely used 70-page teachers manual. Leah is now going for her doctorate in peace education. I'm proud, too, that my three grown children are involved in social justice work. My son John teaches a peace studies course at Wilson High School, from which he graduated.

Over the years, I've visited hundreds of schools to lecture on peace education, pacifism, and nonviolence. I can report that the hunger to find alternatives to violence is strong and waiting to be satisfied. If members of the peace community don't make it happen, who will?

There's an old Irish saying: The trouble with a good idea is that it soon degenerates into hard work (and it usually is). So let's all become degenerates and get going.

NOTES

1. Berrigan, 1988.
2. McCarthy, 2001.
3. McCarthy, 2010.

CHAPTER 13

When Violence "Works" for 30 Years: The Late Return of Satyagraha to the Northern Irish Peace Process

Marcel M. Baumann

NORTHERN IRELAND AS A GLOBAL FASCINATION

No doubt about it: Too much has been written about the Northern Ireland conflict. There are hundreds and thousands of books, articles, and papers—almost too many to read in a lifetime. The big contradiction of the Northern Ireland conflict, however, is that Northern Ireland is not only one of the most researched conflicts in the whole world, but it is also one of the most misunderstood. This misunderstanding can be described as "peace through demonization":[1] international opinion is dominated by the "Republican interpretation" of the Northern Ireland conflict. If we would believe all the reports of Amnesty International, Human Rights Watch, and countless other groups, those "guilty" and responsible for the Northern Ireland conflict seem undisputed: namely, the Protestant community, the British government, and the Protestant paramilitary organization, the Ulster Volunteer Force (UVF), and the Ulster Defence Association (UDA). Whereas the UVF and the UDA are characterized as "death squads" and even compared with fascist movements, the Irish Republican Army (IRA) is "understood" and characterized as a "movement."

What is usually ignored is the fact that the IRA—the self-styled "defense force" of the Catholic community—has murdered more Catholics than the police and the British army taken together.[2] Sadly, this analytical ignorance and political bias can also be found within "scholarly" work. I therefore do not intend to add to the quantity of research on Northern Ireland which shows "understanding" and "sympathy" with the IRA—and with their political arm called "Sinn Fein"—as well as with the Catholic community at the expense of any understanding for the Protestant perspective. Rather, I want to focus on the dynamics of nonviolence, the violent responses, and the causes of the outbreak of the so-called "Troubles" in 1968.

In this chapter I want to examine the specific scenarios leading to the outbreak of the civil war in Northern Ireland. I will argue that these scenarios are indeed comparable to other cases. I will, thus, try to elaborate on some similarities to South Africa. After analyzing the outbreak of the "Troubles"—and the disappearance of Satyagraha for 30 years—I will explain how it was possible for Satyagraha to "return" to Northern Ireland. This was made possible through the hunger strikes of republican prisoners in 1980 and 1981.

For the analysis of the dynamics and effects of nonviolence and violence the distinction by Michael Nagler between *works* versus "works" becomes important:

> Nonviolence sometimes "works" *and always* works while violence sometimes "works" but never works.[3]

Thus, the specific circumstances in which violence seemed to work and, in fact, "worked" because a civil war raged for 30 years, need to be analyzed. But, the analysis becomes complicated by the fact that, at the same time, nonviolence worked, too; that is, it succeeded in creating the conditions for a process of peaceful conflict resolution.

THE END OF SATYAGRAHA: THE WAY TOWARD "BLOODY SUNDAY" AND THE REVIVAL OF THE IRA

The Paradox of Repression

The specific effects of violence on the consciousness, thinking, or ideology of groups or communities can be explained by the concept of the "paradox of repression." This concept goes back to Smithey and Kurtz;[4] it states that in ethno-political conflicts with an asymmetrical structure, in which the state or regime is "threatened" by non-state groups, overt and repressive violent actions by the state against the non-state groups creates a counterproductive effect: Acts of violence don't weaken or destroy the non-state groups but strengthen them. They become more committed to their cause in the wake of violent repression.

> However, even more relevant than the impact on the non-state groups is the impact repressive state violence has on the wider public, namely on those people who are not yet supporters of the non-state movement. In an ideal situation, the "undecided" sections of society are deeply impressed by watching the state employing overt acts of repression against the non-state groups, which are "civilians" in most cases. Thus, the "undecided" feel more and more compelled to show sympathy or solidarity for the "oppressed" non-state group. As a final result, repressive violence by the state neither "works" nor *works* in those situations. "Paradoxically, the more the regime applies force, the more citizens and third parties are likely to become disaffected, sometimes to such an extreme that the regime disintegrates from internal dissent."[5]

For these effects to happen, there must be an asymmetrical structure of conflict, that is, an imbalance of force and power between the state and the non-state movement. This imbalance must be clearly visible for the undecided public to increase their sympathy and solidarity.[6]

From an analytical perspective it is essential to note that the positive effect of the paradox of repression is not automatic.[7] According to Sharp, similar effects can occur if the non-state groups don't use nonviolent tactics, but violence. Therefore, the paradox of repression can also lead to a strengthening of the *violent* non-state groups. In addition, it can destabilize an existent nonviolent movement and strengthen those groups advocating violent resistance. And this is what happened as a result of measures like Internment in Northern Ireland where the repression culminated in the peak violent experience of "Bloody Sunday"—the same was the case in the South African example of "Sharpeville": overt state repression led to the end of nonviolence against the state or regime.

NV + V = V

The equation NV + V = V was coined by Michael Nagler. It tries to explain the dynamics of escalation leading to the transformation of a nonviolent movement into a "campaign of violence": If violence (V) occurs in the context of an overall nonviolent protest (NV), the protest as a whole ends up being perceived as a *purely* violent conflict. Within the process of violent escalation even a low level of violence may be enough to sabotage the nonviolent movement and transform it into a campaign of violence or "armed resistance." If the input of violence (the variable V) is of a massive scale, the "sabotage effect" is that much greater. These effects can be observed if *mass* violence occurs—what we might call "man-made disasters." Therefore, the equation NV + V = V can be applied as a methodological tool for the following thesis: Mass-scale events of violence have the potential to unleash a "smoldering" or "sleeping" conflict. They usually become crucial turning points, decisive for the outbreak of war. In the words of Friedrich Glasl, we can say that the equation NV + V = V marks the highest level of escalation that he called "together into the abyss."[8] At this highest level of escalation, destructive processes assume a purely negative dynamic: The mutual perceptions of the conflicting parties have hardened, stereotypical views of the "other" dominate, and "win-lose" attitudes evolve.[9]

The Northern Irish conflict erupted violently on October 5, 1968, in Londonderry, when the first violent incidents between the police and demonstrators occurred. Prior to this outbreak of violence the human rights movement Northern Ireland Civil Rights Association (NICRA) had articulated its demand for equal rights for the Catholic community through nonviolent protests and adopted a moderate political ideology. Since the 1950s the Catholic community became more inclined to accept the principle of equality within Northern Ireland than to focus exclusively on the goal of a united Ireland.[10] Thus, the core demands of NICRA were liberal reforms, such as the abolition of discrimination in the allocation of jobs and houses, emergency legislation, and electoral abuses.[11] NICRA's main message was framed as a human rights agenda: it was not about a territorial change for Northern Ireland, that is, to achieve a united Ireland by force, but it was about equal human rights for the Catholic minority within the existing boundaries of the Northern Irish state. Since the partition of the island in 1921, Northern Ireland was ruled by a regional government in which the pro-British Ulster Unionist Party (UUP) governed with an absolute majority until the suspension of the local government in 1972, which means that the Catholic minority was systematically discriminated for almost five decades. But it took until the 1960s for an evolving Catholic middle class to establish a civil rights movement under the leadership of NICRA.

The prevailing mood of the Catholic community in the 1960s was most accurately described by David Trimble in his Nobel Peace Prize-winning lecture in 1998: "Ulster Unionists, fearful of being isolated on the island, built a solid house, but it was a cold house for Catholics."[12]

But in the 1960s Trimble and his party did not have any understanding of or empathy with the Catholic minority's situation.[13] Even more, no Unionist politician would have acknowledged that the Unionist majority rule was indeed a cold house for Catholics.[14] Nor did the Unionist establishment recognize how serious the whole situation was, that is, the potential of a long-lasting civil war.

Even by March 1972 Brian Faulkner, the last prime minister of Northern Ireland, still believed that "the whole spook" of the IRA could be over in just a few weeks.[15] In stark contrast to the repentance expressed by Trimble, Faulkner denied that any discrimination against Catholics existed:

Never, never during the 50-year-rule of the Protestant government, and this I want to emphasize quite clearly, has the Catholic minority been subject to discrimination.[16] This ignorance toward the legitimate demands of NICRA was accompanied by a hostile reaction of the state toward the civil rights movement because it was perceived as a forefront of the IRA. This argument was repeated by William Craig in a documentary by the famous British journalist Peter Taylor.[17] Since it was inspired by similar events in the United States and elsewhere, the "Protestant state" saw the civil rights movement as part of a worldwide, communist-led conspiracy.[18] Put simply, NICRA was a threat to the existence of Northern Ireland.[19]

In this crisis situation of the late 1960s, the British government did not relax the tensions, but made some serious mistakes that further escalated the situation. Harold Wilson's government was under severe pressure because of domestic issues and, therefore, not only showed almost no interest in Northern Ireland,[20] but reacted in a very short-sighted manner because after the deployment of the British Army on August 14, 1969, the British government and the Northern Ireland Assembly thought that the soldiers would have to stay just for two weeks.[21] However, the British troops stayed for the next 38 years and only left Northern Ireland in 2007.

Equally short-sighted was the assessment that the problems in Northern Ireland could be solved very quickly by large-scale military repression. These misconceptions led to the launching of "Internment" (also called "Operation Demetrius") in Republican and Loyalist areas of Belfast and Londonderry on August 9, 1971. In this operation people were arrested and detained without trial because they were suspected of being members of illegal armed groups.[22] Internment caused massive outbreaks of violence in all Republican areas. After the first two days of Internment, 17 persons had died in the disturbances, among them 10 Catholics killed by the British Army. Finally, Internment ended on December 5, 1975. During the whole period a total of almost 2,000 persons had been detained without trial.

The mass protest against Internment organized by NICRA to take place in Londonderry on October 5, 1968, would become the "historic trigger" that started the violent phase of the Northern Ireland conflict. For fear of violent actions and reactions, the then Northern Irish Home Secretary, William Craig, banned parts of the route of the march: within the city walls and within the so-called "Waterside" residential area that was predominantly inhabited by Protestants.[23] To enforce Craig's decision, the police built barriers

and sealed off the banned route. This made the confrontation of the marchers with police forces almost unavoidable. When the march was prevented
from proceeding at the police barriers, street battles between protesters and
police broke out. Seventy civilians and 11 policemen were wounded in the
escalating street battles. After these incidents, violence quickly spread to
other areas of Londonderry and continued well into the night. The "troubles" had erupted.

"THIS IS OUR SHARPEVILLE": "BLOODY SUNDAY" AND THE END OF SATYAGRAHA IN NORTHERN IRELAND

> This afternoon 27 people were shot in this city. 13 of them lay dead.
> They were innocent, we were there. This is our Sharpeville. A moment
> of truth and a moment of shame. And I just want to say this to the
> British government: You know what you have just done, don't you? You
> have destroyed the civil rights movement and you have given the IRA
> its biggest victory it will ever have. All over this city tonight, young
> men, boys will be joining the IRA.[24]

This statement was made by Ivan Cooper, who was one of the leaders of
NICRA and also a member of the British House of Commons. Cooper's reference to "Sharpeville" exemplifies the comparable nature of "man-made
disasters." On March 21, 1960, at least 180 Black South Africans were
injured and 69 killed when South African police opened fire on a peaceful
demonstration by school children who were protesting against the apartheid pass laws in the township of Sharpeville, in the province of Transvaal.
Similar to Bloody Sunday the events of Sharpeville led to the destruction of
the nonviolent resistance against apartheid. Although Sharpeville took
place 11 years before Bloody Sunday, the repercussions were still evident,
since it became a turning point for the struggle against apartheid.[25]

Ronnie Kasrils, a White South African Jew from a rich family and one of the
key ANC supporters in his London exile and later Deputy Secretary of State
for Defence in the first ANC government, reflects on the impact "Sharpeville"
had on him. His personal recollections can be seen as a fairly representative
account of the feelings within the generation of South Africans at that time that
would later be called the *Sharpeville generation*:

> I was extremely angry in the days after the Sharpeville massacre. It was a
> time when one dispute was followed by another one: with my family, with
> my friends, with my colleagues. . . . Outside my immediate environment
> there were not many Whites that show any feelings of sorry—the most
> common sentiment was by contrast: "We should shoot all of them."[26]

Similar to the effects of Bloody Sunday, Sharpeville meant the end of the nonviolent resistance against apartheid. In his autobiography, Kasrils illustrates the changing mood of a whole generation from nonviolence to an acceptance of violence:

> The willingness of the state to use violence, which has been shown, gave the freedom movement an important lecture. All activists in the country asked themselves whether it can really be possible to continue to struggle with nonviolent.[27]

However, the immediate response of the ANC to Sharpeville was to adopt the same traditional nonviolent methods as it had employed since the 1950s. Looking back at the history of nonviolence in South Africa as a whole, it can be traced back to long before the 1950s, as far back as to Mahatma Gandhi's campaign in Natal at the end of the 19th century.[28] Since its foundation in 1912, the ANC was embedded in this tradition of nonviolence. It was the basis for the so-called "defiance campaign" of the 1950s modeled on Gandhi's methods. An essential part of the defiance campaign was the strategy of civil disobedience, that is, to willingly break apartheid laws at the risk of being jailed.[29] A very significant document that substantiated the nonviolent attitude of the ANC was the so-called "Freedom Charter." It employed a very moderate language with the aim of reaching political compromise and reconciliation to achieve a way of peaceful co-existence between the Black and White communities:

> And therefore, we, the people of South Africa, black and white together equals, countrymen and brothers adopt this Freedom Charter. . . . All people shall have equal right to use their own languages, and to develop their own folk culture and customs.[30]

In keeping with the nonviolent tradition, the ANC's immediate reaction to Sharpeville was a national strike that paralyzed the country for several weeks. The apartheid government reacted by calling a state of emergency and also banned the ANC as well as all other anti-apartheid movements.[31]

It is highly disputed whether Sharpeville did in fact mean the turning point in the anti-apartheid struggle as a whole, or in other words, that the ANC's transformation from nonviolence to violence can be interpreted as the first step toward the end of apartheid. The important analytical question is therefore: *Did violence "work" or work in South Africa?*

In the aftermath of Sharpeville it was Nelson Mandela, *the* major ANC figure critical of the nonviolent strategies in the 1950s, who made the case for the transformation of the ANC strategy into an "armed guerilla campaign."

In June 1961 he gave his famous speech at the historic meeting of the ANC Working Committees saying, "The attacks of the wild beast cannot be averted with only bare hands."[32]

Mandela won the argument within the ANC and as a consequence, the party founded an armed wing called Umkhonto we Sizwe ("the spear of the nation"), which on December 16, 1961, declared war against the apartheid state.[33] In return, the apartheid regime reacted with even more repressive measures so that Mandela and several other ANC leaders were arrested at the end of 1964. Those who escaped arrest went into exile or underground.

Because of these developments, scholars like Ackerman and Duvall are quite skeptical whether the renunciation of nonviolence in fact brought the ANC any closer toward liberation saying, "Armed struggle had not brought black people any closer to liberation than the nonviolent campaigns of the 1950s."[34]

More than just skeptical is the analysis of Stephen Zunes, who argues that the abandonment of nonviolence after Sharpeville was indeed counterproductive to the cause of liberation:

> Evidence suggests that the armed struggle may have actually harmed the anti-apartheid movement: the bombing campaign by the ANC's armed wing, Umkhonto We Sizwe (Spear of the Nation), in the early 1960s seriously weakened simultaneous nonviolent campaigns, since the government was able to link them to each other in the eyes of the public and thus justify their repression.[35]

Zunes's central argument is that the "success" of the nonviolent campaign was not "limited" because it was a nonviolent campaign but because of the "limited violence" that occurred within the nonviolent resistance.[36]

As already mentioned in the case of Northern Ireland, the "Irish Sharpeville" happened 11 years later. The events on January 30, 1972, which became known as Bloody Sunday, marked the "point of no return," which prevented any peaceful settlement of the conflict. On that historic day a demonstration against Internment was planned in Londonderry. As on October 5, 1968, parts of the march were declared illegal by the Northern Irish Home Office. And yet again the result was a violent confrontation with the police. The paratroopers of the British army (the so-called "Parachute regiment") were present and opened fire: 13 civilians were killed and another injured person died a few days afterward. Until today the exact circumstances that led the paratroopers to open fire are unclear and disputed.[37]

The British DVD version of the movie *Bloody Sunday* includes a detailed and impressive commentary by Don Mullan, the author of the book *Eyewitness Bloody Sunday.* Mullan was also the co-producer of the movie. At the age of 15 he became an eyewitness of the events. In his personal assessment Bloody Sunday marked the end of the nonviolent resistance because, as a consequence, the nonviolent civil rights movement was destroyed. In Mullan's words, the human rights agenda was violently "suspended" for almost 30 years and was brought back by the peace process in the 1990s. Bloody Sunday allowed the IRA and Sinn Fein to divert attention from the politically moderate attitude of NICRA and put the focus on the armed struggle. Suddenly, the "Northern Ireland problem" was no longer about political and socioeconomic equality for Catholics. After Bloody Sunday the territorial goal of a united Ireland became predominant and never left the agenda.

Because of the *positive* implications Bloody Sunday had unfolded for the IRA, it can be seen as a "pleasing trauma" for the IRA's "campaign of violence." The term *pleasing trauma* is used here as a modification of Volkan's concept of "chosen trauma." According to Volkan, large-scale events of violence can either be enhanced or devalued in a deliberate and arbitrary way.[38] The fact that Bloody Sunday can be seen as a "pleasing trauma" for the IRA was made evident at the annual Bloody Sunday Memorial Lecture in 2000, given by Martin McGuinness, a Sinn Fein politician and former senior member of the IRA at the time of Bloody Sunday. In his lecture, he referred to the 14 people killed on Bloody Sunday as follows: *"They are not victims. They are heroes."*[39] At the end of the 1960s the IRA had no more than a few weapons, only a hundred members, and limited support within the Catholic community. But as Ivan Cooper had predicted in his press statement, Bloody Sunday caused a massive increase in recruitment for the IRA. It became the paradox of repression, since it radicalized the Catholic community.

What is important to recognize is that prior to Bloody Sunday there were quite obvious prospects for peaceful conflict resolution. This was shown when Richard Rose conducted a representative survey of attitudes during the spring and summer of 1968. The results of the survey showed that in 1968 a total of 33 percent of the Catholic community supported the constitution of Northern Ireland, that is, Northern Ireland as part of the United Kingdom. Only 34 percent totally opposed the constitution.[40] So, at that time there was no conclusive evidence of a tendency exclusively toward an armed struggle within the Catholic community. Most of them did *not* completely reject Northern Ireland as a "British state." This attitude within the wider Catholic community changed radically in the aftermath of Bloody Sunday. It became "Northern Ireland's Sharpeville": After Bloody Sunday the British government abolished the Northern Ireland government in March 1972. For the next three decades Northern Ireland was to be governed from London with a British Secretary of State responsible for Northern Ireland affairs.[41]

WHEN NONVIOLENCE "WORKS" AND WORKS: THE IRA HUNGER STRIKES AND THE "CAUTIOUS" RETURN OF SATYAGRAHA TO NORTHERN IRELAND

In addition to the two effects the paradox of repression can unfold—either strengthening or sabotaging a nonviolent movement—a third effect can be observed: An armed group may recognize that the strategy of violence does not work although it had "worked" for some considerable time. Instead, this group realizes that a nonviolent option needs to be developed. Hence, the paradox of repression can also demonstrate chances for ahimsa. A prime example is the hunger strike of 10 Republican prisoners,[42] who starved themselves to death in the Maze prison between 1980 and 1981.

Throughout history, hunger strikes were a common nonviolent method. In the tradition of Gandhi, fasting became the nonviolent action par excellence, as it was the "pure weapon" of a nonviolent struggle. This can be said because fasting is totally nonviolent and inflicts no damage on the enemy in physical or material terms. For Gandhi, politically motivated fasting was the "strongest and most effective weapon" of all nonviolent methods.[43] Directed at the wider and concerned public, the impact of politically motivated fasting can be seen as a sort of propaganda, that is, a nonviolent communication strategy. Ideally, through politically motivated fasting the public is informed, critical awareness is raised and, as a result, a direct effect on the state is achieved.[44]

The hunger strikes of Republican prisoners can be seen as an instrument exerting political pressure, which became a "paradox of repression" that raised the whole Northern Ireland conflict to a completely different level. The immediate trigger to the hunger strikes had nothing to do with the Northern Ireland conflict as such: since the introduction of Internment the status of the prisoners of the paramilitary organizations was highly disputed. The Republican prisoners insisted that they were not just "ordinary criminals" and should therefore not be treated as such. The situation escalated when on March 1, 1976, the prisoners were denied the "special category status" by the British government. The British government adopted a strategy of criminalization by denying them the right and status of "prisoners of war" and labeling and treating them as "ordinary criminals" instead. The prisoners reacted with a "dirty protest" in 1978. They refused to wear the prisoners' clothing, covered themselves in blankets and smeared their excrements on the walls of their cells. After they did not reach any positive reaction from the British government they started their first hunger strike on October 27, 1980.[45] They ended it when they *thought* that the government had met their demands. However, on March 1, 1981, the second hunger strike was started when the prisoners realized that the government had not met their demands and that they had been cheated. This hunger strike finally ended on October 3, 1981, after the British government had given in and 10 hunger strikers had starved themselves to death.[46]

In the political circumstances of 1981, it was clear that the strategy of the hunger strikers could only succeed because the tactics and circumstances were embedded within a certain religious and spiritual set of rules, so that the meaning and "message" could be perceived and understood as legitimate by the Catholic community. One of the most important aspects was the timing to follow the religious and spiritual rules: the first hunger strike was planned to lead to starvation during Christmas, the second during Easter.[47] In West Belfast wall paintings emerged that showed the Virgin Mary holding one of the strikers in her arms. The text below said: "Blessed are those who hunger for justice."[48] During the numerous protests in Republican areas, the hunger strikers were displayed on posters and pictures as crucified persons with a wreath of thorns on their heads, made out of barbed wire from the Maze prison.[49]

The most important consequence of the hunger strikes for the Northern Ireland conflict in general was the politicization of the Republican movement. This process was initiated when the immediate relatives of the hunger strikers founded the so-called Relatives' Action Committee (RAC). RAC quickly grew to a mass movement and established itself as a viable alternative to the "campaign of violence."[50] So the leadership of Sinn Fein watched the development of this alternative movement with great unease; it even led to existential fears because it provoked a deflection from the military war against the British government. In the view of the IRA and of Sinn Fein, the hunger strikes for political status were a dangerous distraction from the "armed campaign" for a united Ireland. The institutionalization of the RAC showed the Catholic community that there was a functioning alternative option to the IRA's "campaign of violence." That's why the IRA was opposed to the hunger strike of its prisoners from the very start. This had serious consequences for the strategy of Sinn Fein. It forced Sinn Fein to organize a conference involving the whole membership in detailed consideration of the prisoners' question. This was when Sinn Fein moved out of its conspirational mode and began to embrace the political process.[51]

The hunger strikes marked the entrance of Sinn Fein into the political process, which started with participation in the elections. The opportunity for politicization was opened by what can be called "fortuna" according to Machiavelli. During the IRA hunger strike, the Unionist representative of the constituency Fermanagh and South Tyrone in the British House of Commons died. Sinn Fein nominated Bobby Sands, one of the strikers, as a candidate against the well-known Unionist hardliner Harry West, who was a

former leader of the UUP. On April 9, 1981, Bobby Sands, already in a coma-
tose condition, gained 30,492 votes, whereas Harry West received 29,046
votes. The turnout was almost 90 percent. Sands died 26 days after his election. The support of Sinn Fein dramatically grew thereafter so that in the
general election of June 1983, the party received 13.4 percent of the vote.

CONCLUSION: SATYAGRAHA CAME BACK LATE TO NORTHERN IRELAND . . . BUT NOT TOO LATE

In retrospect, the politicization of Sinn Fein can be regarded as the result
of the paradox of repression. The huge importance of the hunger strikes
for the peace process in Northern Ireland became evident when both the
British and the Irish government afterward tried to encourage political
conciliation. In the 1970s, all attempts to approach each other had failed, as
had any effort of the two governments to jointly solve the Northern Ireland
conflict. However, it was the electoral rise of Sinn Fein and the international
reactions to the hunger strikes (which were mostly critical of the hard-line
stance of the British government) that made possible the so-called Anglo-
Irish Agreement that was signed by Thatcher and Fitzgerald on November
15, 1985. In general terms, this agreement was a compromise between both
governments whereby, in return for the official recognition by Dublin of the
legitimacy of Northern Ireland, London agreed to consult with the Irish
government on all matters that affected the rights of the Catholic minority.
Subsequently, the Anglo-Irish Agreement led to such dynamics within the
political process that it became a milestone in Northern Ireland's peace
process. Ever since this agreement, it was clear that the conflict was as
much a problem for the British as it was for the Irish government, that is, a
problem that could only be solved collectively.[52] Therefore, the Anglo-Irish
Agreement is seen as the starting point of the peace process that culminated
in the signing of the Good Friday Agreement in April 1998. It formally
ended the civil war in which over 3,600 people were killed. The Good
Friday Agreement enshrined the so-called "consent principle," meaning
that any change to the constitutional status of Northern Ireland could be
only made by the majority vote of its citizens. It further established a
Northern Ireland Assembly with devolved legislative powers on a cross-
community basis.

NOTES

1. Baumann, 2008.
2. Fay et al., 1999.
3. Nagler, 2004.

4. Smithey and Kurtz, 1999.

5. Ibid.

6. Sharp, 1973.

7. Ibid.

8. Glasl, 2002.

9. Ibid.

10. Darby, 1995.

11. Darby, 1995; Smith and Chambers, 1991; Eversley, 1989.

12. Trimble, 2001.

13. Hennessey, 1996.

14. Alcock, 1994.

15. "Der Spiegel," 1972.

16. Ibid.

17. Taylor, 2000.

18. Purdie, 1988.

19. Fitzduff and O'Hagan, 2000.

20. Rose, 1971.

21. Dixon, 2001.

22. Coogan, 1995.

23. Rose, 2001.

24. Greengrass, 2002.

25. Ackerman and Duvall, 2000.

26. Kasrils, 1997.

27. Ibid.

28. Zunes, 1999.

29. Ackerman and Duvall, 2000.

30. African National Congress, 1955.

31. Price, 1991.

32. Ackerman and Duvall, 2000.

33. Meli, 1988.

34. Ackerman and Duvall, 2000.

35. Zunes, 1999.

36. Ibid.

37. Taylor, 2001.

38. Volkan, 1997.

39. The author was present when he made that speech.

40. Rose, 1971; Bew and Patterson, 1985.

41. Darby, 2003.

42. What is very important to recognize is that the hunger strikes *cannot* be qualified as "IRA hunger strikes" because the role of the INLA prisoners should not be ignored: 3 of the 10 prisoners who starved themselves to death were members of the INLA: Patsy O'Hara, Kevin Lynch, and Michael Devine. Indeed, it was often brought to my attention by concerned partiesthat the IRSP expressed its anger on a number of occasions, claiming that the Sinn Fein leadership does not recognize the "sacrifice" of INLA volunteers.

43. Ebert, 1970.

44. Ibid.
45. Arthur, 1997.
46. Coogan, 1995.
47. Arthur, 1997.
48. Ibid.
49. Ibid.
50. Ibid.
51. Ibid.
52. Gillespie, 2000.

CHAPTER 14

HANDS OF PEACE: FROM EPIPHANY TO REALITY

Laura Bernstein

THE EPIPHANY

It was April 2002—six months after the events of 9/11—and Gretchen Grad could not sleep. She saw the United States in mourning over the staggering losses. She saw the country angry and confused. She was deeply disturbed by the way religious faiths were being driven further apart by ignorance and animosity. In that insomniac moment, the basic outline of Hands of Peace (HOP) was born.

Gretchen had never been to Israel. She had never met a Palestinian, nor could she recall ever having met an Israeli. She had no personal ties to the Middle East. But the nighttime epiphany was clear: the Israeli-Palestinian crisis was the one she was being called to address. She envisioned an organization that would bring together young people from the Middle East—to meet, to dialogue, to learn to listen to one another, and to build relationships with one another. Americans would be involved as well, to broaden their understanding of the conflict. Such intimacy would put a human face on "the enemy" and open up a space for new possibilities to emerge. It would be a means of making peace, one relationship at a time.

Gretchen had left her prestigious, well-paid career in finance in 1997 when her second daughter was born. She tried out various combinations of being a stay-at-home mom, and working part-time for an investment firm. None of the options had felt completely satisfying. She wanted to use her abilities to do something more fulfilling. The world of high finance had been heady; the trading floor had provided excitement, accomplishment, and a good income, but did not satisfy the deeper longings she was now experiencing. An expanding involvement with the Glenview Community Church (GCC, a denomination of the United Church of Christ) was pivotal to discovering the joy and soul nourishment of serving others. Gretchen's faith in something larger was deepening.

Rather than being a cause of all this violence and extremism, she felt that faith, in its best form, could be used as a solution to conflict. If she could bring the three monotheistic religions together to work on a small, hands-on approach to healing, then, she believed, bridges could be built and walls taken down. Her home community was fairly multicultural, with churches, synagogues, and a mosque nearby. When her close friend and neighbor, Deanna Jacobson (who is Jewish), agreed to be a partner, this epiphany felt doable.

MAKING IT HAPPEN

Representing Islam was a necessity in this venture. The two women found a Muslim counterpart (Nuha Dabbouseh) through a mosque in a nearby community, who joined them in planning the first summer program. They scraped together funding from friends and relatives, the GCC mailing list, and a few larger donors. They enlisted the support of Bill Taylor, a political science professor from Oakton College who had experience working for Seeds of Peace (SOP), an organization begun in 1993 that brings young people (many are Israelis and Palestinians) from conflict-laden areas to a summer camp in Maine for dialogue.

Gretchen had not known about SOP initially, but came on it fairly quickly while researching and networking her own idea. Through Bill and SOP they found an essential ingredient for starting the program: teenage participants. In July 2003, Hands of Peace brought 12 teenagers to the United States from the Middle East—five Jewish-Israelis, five Palestinians, and two Arab-Israelis. Nine Americans participated as well, largely drawn from the sponsoring congregations—four Jews, three Muslims, and two Christians. That interfaith mix (among both American teens and those from the region) has remained a core value throughout the subsequent years of the organization.

The presence of Americans is another central ingredient to Gretchen's vision of the program: "That came with the epiphany. Part of my frustration was with American adults who seemed so unaware of history, of international relations, of America's role in the world. It was a founding principle that Americans had to be engaged with this; that bringing kids over here and having them live with American families was a way to open up Americans' consciousness—to find out, what goes on in the head of an Israeli? What is it like to be a Palestinian?"

CRISES AND OPPORTUNITIES

As might be expected from a program attempting to effect peacemaking in the volatile Middle East, all has not been smooth sailing. Hands of Peace has been beset with one crisis after another, each an important learning experience and an opportunity for growth.

About six months after the first summer program, the Muslim member of the founding trio pulled out, and the sponsoring mosque left with her. Two years later, the original sponsoring synagogue pulled out of the program as well (unrelated to the synagogue's departure, Deanna also stepped down, needing to devote more time to her family). Accusations that Hands of Peace was insensitive to the Islamic voice and sensibility were followed by Jewish accusations that HOP was pro-Palestinian. When several Palestinians resigned from the organization, the complaint was that HOP had a pro-Israeli bias. As Bill (who became the first executive director of HOP) put it, "If both sides complain, you're doing the right thing. It's inevitable that both sides will see you as biased against them, because they want you to be biased for them."

Nonetheless, these upheavals led to some serious introspection as the organization strove to understand the factors that contributed to the ruptures. One critical factor was a need for more sensitivity to minorities in American culture. Gretchen explains, "As part of the Christian majority, my radar was not well-developed enough to have an appreciation for what people in a minority position in America go through, whether it's American Jews or American Muslims. I think I have a better appreciation for that now." She described how slights can be magnified and mistakes misunderstood in this context: Even an oversight that has no basis whatsoever in faith (issues of dress code, for example) can be perceived through a faith lens and cause considerable trouble.

HOP has sought mightily to maintain its role of neutrality in a conflict that predisposes each group to think that its side is being given short shrift. Political sensitivities are as fraught with tension as are religious and cultural concerns.

Gretchen characterizes the dilemma: "We walk such a razor's edge in this organization, trying not to be partial to one side or the other, trying to provide an open forum for all voices to be heard." She described the futility of being "teeter-tottered" by whichever voice was screaming the loudest, and how ultimately, it was necessary to stop running from one end of the teeter totter to the other to mollify those voices: "Our job is to attract the people who are willing to walk with us along the razor's edge."

Over time, HOP has found enough dedicated people and organizations willing to walk that razor's edge. A new sponsoring mosque and synagogue stepped up and offered their support. Other volunteers replaced those who found the tensions to be unbearable, and a Palestinian who was born in Jerusalem has joined the Board. The Middle East and American staff continues to grow and thrive. And the number of applicants and participants both from the region and the United States has increased yearly with 37 teenagers (referred to as "Hands") participating in the summer of 2008 and 40 participating in the summer of 2009.

ORGANIZATIONAL STRUCTURE AND CHALLENGES

HOP is composed of dedicated volunteers in the United States alongside a small, paid staff both in the Middle East and the United States. The organization is frugal, operating on a bare-bones budget, and requiring sacrifice of time and energy from all who are committed to it. Every resource is carefully considered. No one is in this for the money; everyone who is paid could be making substantially higher salaries elsewhere.

Given the explosive realities in the Middle East, tough challenges confront the organization with some regularity. The violent crisis that occurred in Gaza and Israel in December 2008 and January 2009 is a recent example. As current Executive Director Julie Kanak explained, "We had just come off of an exceptionally successful summer program and we were looking to broaden and expand the follow-up programs in the Middle East. And then the violence erupted. . . . This really rocked many of the participants. The regional coordinators had to spend a lot of time responding to the kids—to their anger, grief, and fear, to all of the questions that this brought back to the surface." The HOP List Serve was another important vehicle for the Hands to express their intense feelings. While the List Serve does not replace face-to-face dialogue with a trained facilitator (and e-mails can become heated and unruly, despite efforts to regulate them), it does allow the Hands to keep communication going. Facilitators and chaperones also got involved during the crisis, contacting individuals when necessary, and older Hands provided support as well.

Trying to keep the conversation from spiraling out of control during this crisis required use of every skill and tool the Hands had learned during the two weeks of the summer program. As Julie described it, "Some of them would refer back to a particular remark a facilitator made or an experience they had, or to the more general feeling of hope they all had on leaving the summer program. They used that as a reminder that when conflict erupts again, you do have a choice. You can choose your behavior—not necessarily your feelings, but what you do with those feelings. Some of the Hands tried to encourage the others to choose to deal with those feelings in a more constructive way." Adding to the anger and hatred that has long been part of the Middle East dynamic or transforming those ingredients and seeking another way to respond is part of that choice: "What keeps me going is seeing and hearing the Hands take this challenge to heart and implement the hard lessons they've learned, even in a most difficult situation."

Other key players in the organization's structure are the summer program director and assistant director, who together manage the multifaceted, two-week summer program, and the four facilitators who run the two morning dialogue groups that are the core of this co-existence endeavor. There are generally 12 to 15 participants in each dialogue group, with two facilitators, one Palestinian and one Jewish. The participants from the region fall into three categories: Jewish-Israelis; Arab Citizens of Israel, who may be either Muslim or Christian; and Palestinians (who are largely Muslim). The American Hands who join them are also a mixture of the three faith traditions. Then there are the XLs, which stands for "Extraordinary Leaders." These are Hands who have been chosen to return for a second year of participation in HOP, and provide leadership and support to the first-year participants. The XLs (the number varies from about 6 to 10) are both from the United States and the Middle East, and include the above ethnic and religious traditions. They form their own dialogue group with two additional facilitators.

Balancing the numbers (and genders) of each constituency and keeping the national and religious identities even enough is an ongoing challenge. Finding host families to house, feed, and chauffeur all these Middle East participants and staff members to their meeting places (even some of the Americans who are not from the immediate area need housing) is another strenuous effort. Talented host family recruiters (all volunteers) have been responsible for this task, and the result has been a wide variety of Americans who have opened their doors and their hearts to this program, to the mutual benefit of all concerned. Often two Hands of different backgrounds will stay with one family, so the intercultural exchange is broadened further.

THE SUMMER PROGRAM

The two-week summer program is a mix of the serious work that dialogue entails, activities that are educational or intercultural in their bent, and those that are just plain fun. The emotional intensity of the morning dialogue sessions is balanced with trips to downtown Chicago, museums, parks, or an outing to a local amusement park. A team-building course helps to create unity and solidarity among these diverse teenagers. A visit to a courthouse where immigrants are sworn in as new American citizens provides a glimpse into the melting pot that is America. Visits to a mosque, a synagogue, and a church are an important interfaith component of the program (and often the first time any of the participants have set foot in a religious setting other than their own). A boat tour and a play, a bowling outing or a pizza party, a night of intercultural cooking and skits—these are examples of some of the enrichment and relaxation that make up the summer's co-existence menu. Down time is woven into the schedule as well, so the Hands and XLs have the opportunity to simply "hang out" with their host families and one another.

Mornings are spent in dialogue sessions with trained facilitators, and these two-and-a-half-hour encounters are the heart of the co-existence program. Here the Hands have the opportunity to explore the conflict in a setting that is safe and allows them the freedom to express their views and explore their identity. They start with less controversial material, getting to know each other and developing some trust and good will. Then they move on to more conflictual topics. Ground rules are set by each group: everyone speaks in English; respect is shown by listening, by not interrupting, by observing confidentiality. However, as Bill Taylor points out, "As soon as somebody's button gets pushed, that's all out the window. You say something that I don't like, I interrupt, I start yelling at you. You're in the middle of what you're saying, so you yell back." Then the facilitators step in and ask, "What did you gain by this? Or, "why don't you repeat what Ahmad or Shira was just saying?" This serves to help the Hands realize that they weren't listening at all because they were so caught up in trying to make their own point. By the end of the two weeks, many of them have learned to listen and respond differently.

Why are these opportunities for dialogue so important? Phil Hammack, former head of facilitation and former program director, speaks to that point on the HOP promotional video, revealing his surprise when traveling to the Middle East and discovering how segregated Israel is from the Palestinian Territories: "There are very few opportunities for Jews and Arabs to come together and have discussions about co-existence because they're not really co-existing. . . . They're living in two separate realities." Unfortunately, the only contact most Palestinians have with Israelis is at security checkpoints where they find themselves on the other side of an Israeli soldier's gun—hardly an opportune time to socialize or to engage in dialogue about the conflict. Similarly, most Israelis only know what they learn about Palestinians from accounts of terrorist attacks, which are not conducive to good will or understanding.

Israeli facilitator Avigail Jacobson comments, "I don't think this conflict can be resolved without the opportunity for Palestinians and Israelis to speak to each other, to listen to each other, to understand each other's narrative." She is pointing to a core dilemma in the conflict: each group has a very different account of what happened historically in the region—of who did what to whom, of who is at fault, of who has suffered most. These conflicting narratives need to be heard and empathized with if there is to be any meeting of hearts and minds, if there is ever to be a new, shared narrative.

Dialogue sessions are conducted with strict confidentiality, but on the promotional video (available on the Web site) we witness an example of the response to a "hot button issue" as the kids discuss whether Israel should rightly be a Jewish state with a Jewish majority, or whether that current reality should be altered to accommodate a Palestinian majority. Tensions rise, passions flair, and you can feel the anguish that infuses both sides of the question. No one side or individual is allowed to dominate, but the complexity of the question of what is fair or possible or desirable lingers. Underneath the anger, there is pain on both sides, and that pain is felt by everyone in the room. The Hands bare their souls in these sessions, and that nakedness and rawness need to be countered by some light heartedness during the rest of the day.

Individuals who may have been totally at odds during the morning dialogue encounters join together in the afternoon activities: handshake games, sightseeing, cultural enrichment programs, and informal gatherings give them a chance to relax and unwind from the morning's tensions and upheavals. A level of intimacy is established during those morning sessions that carries over into the afternoon and evening group activities. That's when they have an opportunity to be teenagers, to explore other parts of themselves and one another, to socialize and enjoy each other.

Assistant Program Director Adam Heffez (who has also been a participant in HOP) sat outside the dialogue sessions in the summer of 2008 to be available to Hands who might walk out of a session for a time-out, if it became too emotional (this role of support person is also available from the chaperones and regional coordinators). When one girl did walk out and reported, "I'm confused!" Adam's response was: "I think 'confused' is the most rewarding and sought-after state of mind we can experience in this type of co-existence. Because 'confused' shows that your long-held truths are being challenged, that you are really thinking about the other side."

THE FOLLOW-UP PROGRAM

As has been observed with many programs of this kind (see the film *Promises*), ongoing contact is essential if there is to be lasting change. The HOP process of dialogue and building relationships therefore continues in the Middle East, where a small but dedicated staff works to bring the Hands together for monthly meetings, usually in Jerusalem. There is also a follow-up program in the U.S. so that participants in both regions have the vital opportunity to join together in their own communities and engage in activities that they find meaningful as they work toward creating a more peaceful world.

But challenges abound—logistical, political, and emotional. Following the crisis in Gaza, tensions were so high that the Middle East regional coordinators chose to hold uninational meetings instead of bringing everyone together immediately. This was helpful in allowing the Hands to process their anger and grief with their own identity group before meeting as a whole.

By all accounts, the follow-up meetings are valuable and sometimes quite powerful. They include Hands from all previous years, so the mix of people is varied. A meeting that occurred just before the 2008 summer program had as its topic the Israeli army, which is a very sensitive matter for all concerned. The young Israeli participants are required to spend two or three years in the army after high school, which can be a source of both pride and conflict for them. The Arab-Israeli and Palestinian Hands generally view the military with mistrust, anger, and fear. Emotions run high on all sides when discussing the army (see the first vignette below).

THE IMPACT OF HOP ON ITS PARTICIPANTS AND STAFF

The following selections from the participants, staff, and host families interviewed for this chapter give a deeper glimpse of the lived realities of HOP.

For 2008 Arab-Israeli XL Nadine Abboud, this potentially inflammatory discussion about the army turned into a source of hope. She described how the session included a Palestinian participant whose family member had set off a suicide bomb in Israel, and an Israeli participant currently serving in an army combat unit. Despite their differences and the heavy emotional load each carried, these two participants "had an incredible dialogue together and respected each other to the end." Nadine was deeply touched by the encounter: "This made me feel that what we are doing is not hopeless at all. I think both of these people, if they didn't have the chance to be in Hands of Peace, could never have reached this level of dealing with the other."

Continued involvement with HOP over a period of years through a variety of modalities helps to strengthen the program's core ingredient of respect for differences. Whether through personal e-mails, the List Serve, face-to-face follow-up, or unstructured meetings between those who have become friends, the HOP community is one that nurtures caring, respectful relationships across cultural divides and among those who otherwise would never have met. As 2008 Jewish-Israeli XL Netta Shalev put it (speaking of her bond with Nadine): "Hands of Peace changed my belief in the power of friendships." Although they disagree on many political issues, they remain close friends: "I realized that arguing between friends and having different opinions doesn't really have anything to do with the friendship, with the relationship that we've built."

Rana Hadad has been a participant, an XL, and most recently joined the staff as a chaperone for the Arab Citizens of Israel (she is a Christian Arab who lives in Haifa). She described how discrimination against Arabs in Israel leads to limited opportunities for jobs and education, as well as hassles with the police (her brother was beaten for no understandable reason). The unspoken quotas in universities and other discriminatory rules make it harder for Arabs to pursue more desirable careers. Prior to HOP, Rana would watch the news with her parents and feel hatred for Israelis whom she saw as the cause of so much suffering. She had no desire to co-exist with them or get to know them (and despite living in a mixed city of Jews and Arabs, there was no real contact between them). But her parents encouraged her to be in the program because they felt it would make her a more mature, responsible person.

At age 14, Rana was the youngest Hand in the first year of HOP's summer program in 2003. And she found herself sharing a bed with a Jewish-Israeli girl: "The first day, we didn't even look at each other. We slept back to back, and we didn't talk; nothing." Neither of them got much sleep that night. Later in the program, as part of a group activity, they sat face to face, closed their eyes, and put their hands on each other's hearts. That experience of feeling one another's heartbeat, alongside everything else that was happening in the program, was transformative: "I got tears in my eyes. Just feeling that the person in front of you is the same as you, just different language, different nationality maybe, or different ID, but she's the same and she's feeling your pain and she's suffering the same way you're suffering . . . I understood now Israelis are not only bad, Israelis are not only soldiers, Israelis are not only in the government. These are people who are exactly the same as me."

She invited Jewish friends to her home to help decorate her Christmas tree, and has sleepovers and social outings that include both Jewish and Arab friends. This is all occurring in an atmosphere where she sees hatred and despair increasing: "Because they're bombing here, killing over there, and people are growing so much hate in their lives . . . people are losing hope." But HOP gave her a different outlook: "I started to believe much more in making change. For the conflict itself, it took on much more meaning for me. I don't want my grandchildren to read about the conflict in newspaper headlines. I want them to read about it in history books."

Rana's sense of hope was sorely tested after a Palestinian suicide bomber destroyed the restaurant co-owned by her cousin and a Jewish partner, a potent symbol of co-existence in Haifa. More than 20 people were killed in the incident. Rana witnessed the carnage immediately afterward, and was struck by the "blood mixed everywhere. You cannot see which blood is Israeli and which is Arab." At the same time, "You could see the Arabs pulling Jews from the restaurant and helping them to go out, and the same exactly for the Jews helping Arabs." This occurred just after Rana's summer as a participant in Hands of Peace, and she initially felt uncertain of what the response would be. She experienced an intense outpouring of support from all her HOP colleagues, Jewish-Israeli and Palestinian alike, all wanting to help in any way they could: "They stood up for me—all of the e-mails, all of the phone calls; they messaged me. Some of them came afterward to see the restaurant where it happened. You could see that they really cared about me and that they hurt with me."

Rather than sinking into bitterness and despair, Rana is hopeful that the Arab Citizens of Israel "can be the bridge between both sides" because they are in a unique position, belonging neither to one side or the other: "For a Palestinian, I'm an Israeli; for an Israeli, I'm a Palestinian. No one recognizes me. For them I don't exist." But for Rana, being "stuck in the middle" has led to a determined resolve to be part of the solution rather than add to the problem. As for her cousin's restaurant, it has been rebuilt and, still co-owned by his Jewish partner, is thriving.

Netta Shalev spoke of HOP's considerable impact on her as a Jewish-Israeli (who has been both a participant and an XL). She came to the program having just had her final history test in school, feeling confident that she knew the facts. Hearing conflicting narratives about those facts was both shocking and broadening: "In the first few dialogue sessions, we had arguments about history issues. And then I discovered the big difference between what we are taught and what they [the Palestinians] are taught about history. . . . It was a shock to see the difference. Then you realize that maybe not everything that *you* know is right, and probably not everything that *they* know is right. So you understand that the history is not really all fact; it's stories. And it could be told by many points of view." This deepened her empathy for the Palestinian narrative. In relation to each side wanting to influence the more neutral American participants to support its view of the conflict, she moved from thinking "How is it possible that you not see that we are right, that what we are saying is the truth, that we are suffering?" to "If I was Palestinian, I would probably think, how can you not see that I am right, that my side of the story is the truth? And after that, I realized that there are two sides of the coin."

Netta gradually began to question some hard-and-fast beliefs that she had held, and to see the danger of stereotypes. She cited an experience during the group visit to the synagogue that opened her mind to some new possibilities. During a discussion with the rabbi, a Palestinian Hand raised a question about something that would apply only to an extremely radical religious group in Israel, a group that Netta considered unimportant because it represents such a small minority of religious Jews. But he asked the question as though it applied to all religious Jews. This opened a door in her consciousness: "Then I realized, if he thinks like that, somebody's probably teaching that the extreme side of the Jews applies to all Jews. So maybe I was taught the extreme side of the Muslims."

This process of questioning, opening, softening "does not mean that you discover that everything that you touch is wrong, and I don't want to be Israeli anymore . . . you come to understand that it's not necessarily bad to be connected [to your identity in a positive way]. While the two sides think differently, we can also be friends, and we can come to compromise." She felt that while she came out of HOP with many questions still unanswered, she also emerged feeling more pride in her Israeli and Jewish heritage.

Jewish-Israeli Bat-Or Hoffman felt that she returned home from HOP "less to the left" politically and more nationalistic in her leanings. Such "identity accentuation," to use the term of social psychologist (and former HOP head of facilitation) Phil Hammack, is not uncommon for participants of coexistence programs who then return to the harsh reality of intractable conflict. This increased identification with one's own group of origin may even be a necessary psychological adaptation for some.

However Bat-Or subsequently became involved in a number of very liberal organizations in Israel that are striving for human rights and justice for the Palestinians. She sees HOP as promoting dialogue without imposing a particular ideology on anyone, but feels concern about those participants who do become "more right wing." Thus, she finds herself in the uncomfortable position of both wanting to protect the Jewish-Israelis in the program from feeling attacked as she did, and wanting them to recognize the mistakes of the Israeli government alongside the realities of Palestinian suffering: "I'm not looking for an easy position. I don't think in the situation we have in Israel and Palestine that there are easy positions."

Bat-Or spoke of her ambivalence toward the state of Israel. She understands why her Hungarian grandfather, fleeing the aftermath of the Holocaust at age 19 after his parents and most of his family were murdered, settled in Israel. He was recruited by a Zionist youth movement: "I don't blame my grandfather for coming here. . . . He wasn't aware of the consequences. Someone else was living in his house [in Hungary]. He had nothing to do, nowhere to go . . . I don't think at that time he thought it [the land of Israel] was his land." At the same time as she feels Israel has the right to exist, she also understands and wants to mitigate the harm done to Palestinians by the occupation: "I see both sides. And it would be easier for me not to see my side because it's the occupier side, it's the oppressor side. But I do see it."

Palestinian Regional Coordinator Hoda Barakat points to the primacy of relationship in describing the impact HOP has had on her. Her attitude toward Israelis prior to involvement in the program was decidedly negative: "I had never been able to communicate with Israeli people before . . . I never had the will to do it . . . because I thought of them as the enemy . . . I couldn't view them as humans." Her views about the conflict have not changed, and her disagreement with the Israeli government remains strong. However, her attitude toward Israelis themselves has altered: "I understand that they see it [the conflict] from a very different perspective, that they have another story that they believe is true. This is where it gets confusing, and you really need to have an open mind. And I see that some people are bad, some people are good, in every culture. So they're not all bad . . . I didn't see it this way before . . . I view Israelis in a new perspective because I worked with great people who really believe in peace."

This powerful shift of perspective began back in Ramallah, when Hoda (whose sister had been both a participant and an XL in the program) agreed to help organize follow-ups for HOP in Jerusalem. There she worked with the Israeli staff and observed the Hands in dialogue sessions. But the change was strengthened when she agreed to become regional coordinator, which involved recruiting Palestinian teens for the summer program, and accompanying them to the United States in the summer of 2008. Being in such close contact with Israelis on a daily basis intensified the process of transformation: "It's a really great staff. Now I understand that there are some very good people in Israel—not all of them, not the government. But I never would have believed that was possible a year ago."

THE FACILITATORS: ALLOWING DIALOGUE TO UNFOLD

Palestinian facilitator Manal Al-Tamimi, who has been on the staff of HOP for three years, has her own perspective on relationship building in the program, which she sees as a series of phases. In the first phase, the teens "learn to look in the eyes of each other" as they become acquainted on a personal level. Then they move little by little toward a group identity. She points to the challenge the Hands face in becoming friends individually when collectively, in relation to the Middle East conflict, they are enemies: "The whole goal is not to create friendship in the first phases. It's even problematic to speak about it in terms of friendship. Real friendship only happens when you manage to go from the personal to the collective to dealing with the fact that you are enemies; *then* you can reach the point of healthy friendship." The contradictions inherent in realizing "that the friend I have is also my enemy" makes the process difficult but rewarding: "Once we deal with the conflicts, once we deal with these contradictions we are living, this is the moment we can have an authentic friendship."

Jewish-Israeli facilitator Tal Dor works together with Manal and agrees that "one goal of the process is to admit that I see the other as my enemy," which is not something the teens often say aloud in the beginning. But another point of the dialogue is to understand the different roles in the power structure of the region. Tal maintains, "Israel is a state that is occupying Palestine, and this creates an unequal power dynamic. . . . This concept of 'enemy' is not an equal concept. This is something the Palestinians come with a need to say and a need to get the Israelis to recognize. . . . While the Israelis come with the need that the Palestinians will recognize their suffering, even if it's not equal." In Tal's view, a successful dialogue "is for the Israeli group to acknowledge their responsibility in the conflict, to see that the power dynamic is not equal, and to understand that we can change." Manal cites a different task for the Palestinians: "Meeting the Israelis and hearing them speak about their suffering alters the feeling that they [the Palestinians] are the only ones suffering. Being the weak side in the power dynamic does not mean that they are not to empathize, and this is the big challenge for the Palestinians."

THE AMERICAN HOST FAMILIES IN THE PROGRAM

The Andersen-O'Brien family has hosted participants every year since the inception of HOP in 2003. Wayne and Sheila (who are both lawyers and judges) have three daughters, Noreen, Maureen, and Mary (ages 12, 13, and 14, respectively). By their account, all have been enormously broadened by the experience. As Wayne puts it, "I don't regard us as givers to the program. We're receivers from the program." And Sheila: "You get an international experience without leaving home." They feel their home has been a refuge from the political struggle for the Hands they host, and make an effort to keep politics out of the mix. The intercultural enrichment has had many dimensions: they've attended services at the mosque and synagogue (they are members of the Glenview Community Church), gone shopping with the teens (Maureen: "Shopping is the international language"), dealt with religious dietary restrictions (Wayne, laughingly: "We suspect the only dietary problems we've run into are an excuse when they don't like what's being served"), and embraced the Hands in their home as surrogate daughters and sisters.

They even agreed to take a male participant one year because they were eager to host a Muslim (prior they had housed Jewish-Israelis and Christian Arabs) and Ihab (declared "darling" by all of them) needed a host family. Sheila described their opening encounter: "He came to our house that day from across the world. And he fell asleep, exhausted, in the La-Z-Boy. So I said, 'Wake up, you have to make sure you sleep tonight; you have a big day tomorrow!' He got up out of his chair, went to the window, faced east, and said his prayers. . . . It was *very* moving."

The family has stayed in touch with their Middle East "children" through the Internet, and as the girls have grown, the participants they host feel like friends as well as big sisters. Noreen was only six the first year they hosted, and Mary hopes to be a Hand in the summer she turns 15. By attending HOP parties and picnics, they've had exposure to a wide variety of other participants and their host families. But the greatest impact is the affection they develop for all those they have met and hosted. When the conflict flares (as it did in Gaza), they are very attuned and concerned for the safety of those they've grown to love. Their faith is part of the equation as well: "We're people of God who want peace . . . and want *life* to be good for others" (Sheila). And Wayne points to the unity underlying the diverse religious traditions in the region: "Looking to the same God in an open way, we think is the key to solving problems."

PROSPECTS FOR PEACE

While there is considerable diversity of opinion regarding the prospects for long-term peaceful co-existence in the region, virtually everyone interviewed regarded the work of Hands of Peace (and other similar organizations) as a small but significant step in that direction. The importance of the approach is only emphasized by the fact that since the second Intifada (which began in 2000), political restrictions have tightened and the social reality has worsened.

As Jewish-Israeli Regional Coordinator Jasmine Tamuz states, "It's a cycle. Israelis make the security, the checkpoints, harder to cross. They put more restrictions on the Palestinians. The Palestinians get more frustrated and more religious and more radical, and they create more hatred with Israelis. Then in return, Israel does all this [increases oppressive security measures]. . . . Before the second Intifada started, there wasn't so much hate. I think it's deteriorating. It's not getting better."

Yet many hold on to the hope that leaders will emerge out of programs like HOP, leaders whose personal experience with co-existence will actively change the political landscape.

Ismail Hummos is a Muslim Palestinian Board member of HOP (born in a small village outside of Jerusalem) who believes that the collective consciousness in the Middle East must shift in order for peace to be possible. But he also regards the organization as "a candle in a very dark world" that may contribute to creating that critical mass of enlarged consciousness: "Call me naïve, but I'm still hoping that out of this little oasis of Hands of Peace, future leaders will be called, men or women who can draw on that personal experience with one another. . . . Because that's really what makes a huge difference. Do you trust the person in front of you, that he's a good person, that she's a human being? Or are you so paranoid and traumatized that you can never invest any faith? That is the crux of the matter here."

Ismail maintains that just as violence and hatred are contagious, so are love, compassion, and good will: "This naïve idea of Hands of Peace is the salvation for the world. Every child that is born in this world is an affirmation that God has not given up on us as human beings. We keep repeating all these mistakes, over and over. But God is the most optimistic Being in the universe. . . . Every time I see a new child smiling at me, innocently, I think, there's God smiling. I think, we've got to get it better with this one. . . . For me, taking part in Hands of Peace is a form of prayer."

CHAPTER 15

THE MOVEMENT TOWARD PEACE IN CRISIS—AND OPPORTUNITY

Michael N. Nagler

Is it possible for a grown person to entertain the hope that we may be able to tilt the balance toward peace in this era of endless wars? I argue that it is not only possible, but necessary. "Not to believe in the possibility of permanent peace," Gandhi said, "is to disbelieve the godliness of human nature" (or, if you prefer, the possibility that we can lead a meaningful, healthy existence). And he goes on to add, "methods hitherto adopted have failed because rock-bottom sincerity on the part of those who have striven has been lacking."[1] Nothing fails like no hope of success. Yet, as Norman Cousins used to say, "Nobody knows enough to be a pessimist"; and Rebecca Solnit pointed out in an article entitled "Acts of Hope," "Who 20 years ago would have pictured a world without the USSR [Union of Soviet Socialist Republics] and with the Internet?"[2]

Norman Cousins's aphorism has very specific applications in the area of war and peace. While there are cases on record of societies that have destroyed themselves by war fighting, there are also some that testify to a mysterious process of recovery by which societies and nations have pulled themselves back from the brink. The Japanese Samurai class as a body threw away the firearms Captain Cook had thoughtfully introduced into feudal Japan when they realized it was overturning their culture and making their life a meaningless bloodbath.[3] Around the turn of the 20th century, the Scandinavian countries simply stopped fighting each other when they spontaneously seemed to have realized there was no reason to continue (which had been true all along); as Boulding puts it, one day they just said "the hell with it."[4] Nobody knows enough to say "it couldn't happen here."

It is not mysterious why societies and nations want peace, given the fact that peace is grounded in, if not identical with, reality itself in the way that St. Augustine was the first to describe in the West (see Volume 1, Chapter 1 of this collection). Nor is it particularly mysterious that nations get so frequently and addictively caught up in wars, given our ignorance of this reality. What is mysterious—and possibly most useful to understand—is how some people suddenly snap out of a symbolic miasma of war and hatred. Sometimes it helps when they can give themselves a reason; the Japanese are said to have believed that the atomic bomb was a more-than-human intervention, which made it psychologically possible for them to surrender. Whether we can actively enable such a conversion or not it is always there, and there is no reason not to believe that such a fit of rationality could happen today on a planetary scale. Bodies heal themselves with a little help from health providers; the Earth itself has scarcely understood restorative processes that we could greatly assist by seeking happiness in ways that do not ravish her resources. Similarly, the drive for "loving community" must be able to assert itself even when, or especially when, it is most suppressed by egotism and unreasoning hatreds. In Gandhi's view Satyagraha ("clinging to truth, soul force") would be the midwife, for that technique does not suppress reason but can "compel reason to be free."[5]

The enormous costs and the pathetic results of modern wars cannot be counted on to break the war-fighting spell by themselves. People who deny global warming can deny anything; but they are a symptom that a deep change is going on that is eroding the underpinnings of the entire war system as a phase of human evolution. In *Stable Peace*, Boulding documented some time ago the dramatic collapse of war's legitimacy, not to mention its penumbra of glory that took place between World Wars I and II; a collapse that was seen in, for example, popular music. There is no doubt now that on one level war has become a creed outworn. But three closely interrelated factors are propping it up: (1) the hard work of dehumanization that the military has learned to add to its training methods since they discovered that a natural inhibition against killing was keeping the majority of combat troops from actually firing their weapons (see Volume 2, Chapter 21), (2) the general level of dehumanization that is, again, artificially propped up by the commercial and materialistic forces in modern culture, and finally (3) the lack of meaning to modern life that makes war an easy substitute, as Chris Hedges has pointed out.[6] None of these factors—at least in their present extreme form—has a long history. We must see to it that they do not have a long future either.

In the case of the most intractable of these three factors or levels—the lack of purpose or meaning sensed by millions of people—a remarkably simple solution suggests itself: to help them understand that, to paraphrase A.J. Muste, we do not need to find a meaning to life to experience peace: peace itself is that meaning. At some point people are going to look at the appalling rates of defection and suicide among modern combat personnel and realize that, as a current slogan has it, "war is not the answer." Then they will be ready to hear that peace is.

We can find hope if we know where to look. In the early phase of modern man's search for peace here in the West—the "Perpetual Peace" tradition that began in the 12th century and counts thinkers like Grotius, Rousseau, Kant, L'Abbé de Saint Pierre, and William Penn in its ranks—the gaze was directed up to princes and then governments. Today, the failure of these "top" institutions to give peace any reality has shifted the attention to what Orville Schell calls the "other superpower:" civil society and even less formally organized embodiments of popular will.[7] It is here that we see a great deal of encouraging change.

For one thing, there is the astonishing *wave of nonviolent movements* set in motion by the campaigns of Gandhi and Martin Luther King, which according to some estimates (and some definitions of nonviolence) have involved more than half the world's population. "In 1989 alone," writes Richard Deats, "thirteen nations comprising 1,695,100,000 people, almost 30 percent of humanity, experienced nonviolent revolutions that succeeded beyond anyone's wildest expectations in every case but China, and were completely nonviolent (on the part of the participants) in every case but Romania and parts of the southern USSR. The nations involved were Poland, East Germany, Hungary, Czechoslovakia, Bulgaria, Romania, Albania, Yugoslavia, Mongolia, the Soviet Union, Brazil, Chile, and China."[8]

Perhaps of even greater significance for the future than these numbers (and the fact that the mainstream media have begun—only begun—to take note and accord some understanding to this phenomenon) are the *new institutions* that, although based on older models to be sure, lend qualitatively greater traction to the great groundswell. Among others can be listed:

- Peace communities have sprung up in highly conflicted areas, particularly Colombia. Some 50 communities, the best known being San José de Apartadó (see Chapter 7 in this volume), which like most of the others was created by refugees from nearby violence, disallow armed actors from entering their premises and refuse to align themselves with any party to the armed struggles around them. Although they have not always been inviolate, as John Lindsay-Poland of the Fellowship of Reconciliation pointed out to me in a recent conversation, they "have become AN institution" that can represent itself with some weight in legal and policy discussions even at the state level. These "islands of peace," as they are sometimes called, intersect with another new peace-keeping and peace building institution referenced several times in this collection:

- Peace teams or nonviolent third-party intervention teams are now referred to usually as Unarmed Civilian Peacekeeping (UCP; see Volume 2, Chapter 8). Places like San José are under constant threat and at times the presence of even a few internationals from a UCP organization can make the difference between their success or failure—to mention but one peacekeeping activity these organizations are carrying out: as the motto of Nonviolent Peaceforce has it, UCP is "what you can say yes to when you say no to war."

- Until quite recently peace movements had to "reinvent the wheel" every time they started. Now systematic and not-so-systematic efforts have begun to communicate lessons learned from the mistakes and successes of earlier, sometimes distant struggles. Largely unknown to the public, a large number of satyagrahis (participants in a Satyagraha, in this case the Indian freedom struggle) came to the United States and a number of Americans went to India to facilitate the Civil Rights movement.[9] In at least one case, the Center for Advanced Nonviolent Actions and Strategies (CANVAS), a formal institution was created (by the Washington-based International Center on Nonviolent Conflict) specifically to coach and assist liberation struggles like those of the "color revolutions" of Eastern Europe.

Not all of this peace innovation has come up from the grassroots. Although "peace law" is increasingly invoked by activists within societies to, for example, protect their right to protest against and even obstruct violence of the state itself, international law has also been advancing, as Professors Cris Toffolo and Ronald Glossop ably describe in Chapters 4 and 5 of this volume. The globalization of justice, while it is far from keeping pace with the globalization of greed and its attendant violence, is happening.

If one were to identify by a single word the reason that these hopeful developments have not coalesced into a revolution in human consciousness and behavior, that word would be *culture*. As a young friend of mine said of the United States in 2001, "we live in a war culture, with a war President, and a war economy." Responding to the growing recognition of culture as the determinant of war or peace, the United Nations dedicated the opening decade of this century to "a culture of peace and nonviolence for the children of the world," and the phrase "culture of peace" is being carried forward in Web sites, online journals, and other formats. *Culture* here means, in the words of a UN declaration, a "set of values, attitudes, modes of behavior, and ways of life that reject violence and prevent conflicts."[10] Therefore, it is potentially of great importance that science, which futurist Willis Harman once called the "knowledge validating system" of modern civilization, has thrown open its lens on human nature and behavior, indeed on those of all forms of life, to take in the attitudes and behavior that constitute a state of peace (see the brief discussion by Ryono and Nagler in Volume 1, Chapter 4). In 2010, the American Sociological Association inaugurated an Altruism and Social Solidarity Section, to cite only one of many examples of the trend. It is doubly unfortunate that, in our culture's retreat from truth, science is far less heeded now than at any time in the modern period. Still, as part of a whole that is struggling to define itself, the discoveries in the realms of altruism, the neuroscience of empathy (especially "mirror neurons," or what one scientist calls "Gandhi neurons" that detect and reflect another's state or intentions), and the mere logic of game theory describing from its formalistic vantage point the robustness of cooperative systems will carry their weight.

THE LAY OF THE LAND

In the academic world of the late 1970s, there was a kind of *samizdat* literature around the exciting concept of the "paradigm shift" that Thomas Kuhn had introduced some 15 years earlier.[11] Discussions of the "prevailing paradigm" versus the "emerging paradigm" circulated widely, though in these discussions peace was, and still is to some extent, a secondary concern at best, prompting me to publish an article called "Peace as a Paradigm Shift" in the *Bulletin of the Atomic Scientists* in 1981.[12]

Since then our understanding of such tectonic cultural shifts and "tipping points" has greatly improved. This is yet another component, potentially, of such a shift itself since, as many have recognized, we cannot wait for or rely entirely on the kind of spontaneous awakening that happened in Scandinavia, or the kind that science itself has recently experienced in opening its lens to the pacific power in nature. We need the huge power of such a groundswell; however, we need to invoke and direct it to some degree by conscious decisions. Too much has to happen too fast for a change of this magnitude to come into play just in the natural course of things. Therefore, let us conclude by looking at some recent studies that help clarify what the strengths and weaknesses of our current situation are with regard to the all-important tipping point from war to a peace economy, a peace culture, and—possibly—a peace president.

One such study was done by social scientists Paul Ray and Sherry Anderson, whose book *The Cultural Creatives* (2001) appeared at a time when military fervor was at high tide and electoral politics in the United States seemed dangerously out of control.[13] They showed that despite appearances there were no less than 50 million Americans—more than enough to change the political balance—who did *not* want the dangerous, demoralizing world into which we were moving. They were ineffective only for one reason: they did not know about each other. The mainstream discourse was so suffocating that even a *majority* can be rendered powerless. But they are there, Ray and Andersen showed, and that was dramatically proven when Junior Senator Barack Obama found a way to mobilize their aspirations.

AN UNPRECEDENTED . . . WHAT?

The work of Ray and Anderson was taken a step further by economist and futurist Paul Hawken, who showed in his book *Blessed Unrest* (2007), that in fact there is a greater social upheaval going on in the world today than at almost any time in history—but it is not (or not yet) a *movement*: "Movements have leaders and ideologies," Hawken writes; "People join movements study these tracts, and identify themselves with a group. . . . This movement, however, doesn't fit the standard model. It is dispersed, inchoate, and fiercely independent. It has no manifesto or doctrine, no overriding authority to check with."[14] And, I would add, no name. Surely "something earth-changing is afoot." Even the informal, serendipitous nature of Hawken's research is a sign of the new character of things. But in terms of the public's awareness so far it is not even *under* foot. For better or for worse—certainly for worse in terms of political effectiveness right now, but possibly necessary for proper incubation before going public—this commotion, or pre-movement, has been very much "under the radar" of the public discourse. As Arundhati Roy famously said of the new world, it portends, "on a quiet day you can almost hear her breathing." But on most any other day, very few indeed seem to hear her speaking.

A succinct version of Hawken's classic statement is reproduced in the following chapter. What we must do to make his observations work for our purposes is to focus them on the critical issue of war and peace, and if possible, suggest a way that the pre-movement could pull itself together and could gain *coherence* without losing its *diversity*.

Like most writers, Hawken focuses almost entirely on the environment. Yet, as environmentalist and physicist Vandana Shiva herself said in a public lecture in 2007, "If you stop the pollution in people's minds, they will stop their pollution of the environment." That inner pollution has as much to do with anger and the lust for power as it does with greed and the lust for possessions.

At any rate, I am among those (we are a minority even in progressive circles) who believe that, if anything, war and peace should be prioritized over environmental concerns—not because they are more important but because they are the most direct contributor to environmental problems. To be perfectly clear, this is not to deny that economic (or ecological) and peace issues are intimately connected. Over two centuries ago, John Woolman made his famous observation, "May we look upon our treasures, and the furniture of our houses, and the garments in which we array ourselves, and try whether the seeds of war have nourishment in these our possessions, or not."[15] My point is, however, that we can solve ecological and economic problems through a focus on war and peace faster than the other way around.

The real revolution for which the world is pining, for which, in my opinion, the political revolutions of 20th century were a misguided attempt, has another yet-undeveloped resource: Gandhi. He was not an ideological anarchist or an ideological conservative; he was, in his own terms, a "practical idealist" who had learned to maintain an attitude of complete impartiality toward every institution of India, whether indigenous or imposed by the Raj, and judged it solely on its merits. Even the most pernicious of institutions that he was faced with—the caste system, he did not feel was necessary or possible to abolish. Rather, it should be purged of the associated value judgment of "high" and "low," so that the unavoidable diversity of people, including their diverse capacities to earn or preserve wealth, could be allowed to go on, indeed appreciated, while the pernicious sense of superiority or inferiority that we often attach to such differences was purged.

A tall order. But not nearly as tall, or as unnatural, he felt, as trying to level human beings in terms of external characteristics like wealth or position. People are all of the same *value*, to be sure: namely, priceless; but we do not have to have the same standard of living, positions of authority, religion, etc., to realize this unity. Even if such a thing were achievable, who would want it? As biologists are aware, the characteristic feature of life, as opposed to insentient matter, is its diversity—or more accurately, when we add a spiritual viewpoint, unity in diversity. Gandhi's goal, therefore, was *heart unity*, which locates unity at a deep, nonphysical level while preserving diversity of almost any characteristics on the surface.

Several writers today have approximated this approach. As the world's large organizations (governmental, corporate, and even educational) collapse, the people of the world who make up the forefront of the change we are discussing tend simply to walk away from them and look for entirely different types of association, such as the "affinity groups" that sprang up during the Spanish Civil War and are now a common format for all manner of protest movements.

The institutions that embodied the old paradigm, the standard corporate model—hierarchical, centralized, and ultimately dehumanizing—are part of the problem. A widely read book by Ori Brafman and Rod Beckstrom, called *The Starfish and the Spider: The Unstoppable Power of Leaderless Organizations*, shows that the most successful recent businesses today (Wikipedia, Google, and others) have not been traditional top-down organizations.[16] These new forms have sprung up more or less from the grass roots, experimentally. Professor and author Clay Shirky has recently shown dramatically that more creative energy arises from loosely coordinated groups, from *cooperative frameworks* that are based on loose-knit, overhead-free, volunteer-driven collective action and what he calls "mass amateurization" than from the classical institutional frameworks.[17] To use the old terminology of Ferdinand Tönnies, it is a case of rediscovering *Gemeinschaft* (informal connections) in the interstices of an exaggerated, and therefore failed, world of *Gesellschaft* (formal stuctures). Some writers, like Janine Benyus and the group around Irvin Laszlo, go a step further and believe that the new organizational forms will even be organic, be "biomimetic" rather than anything designed by our limited intelligence.

The fact that this progressive/spiritual renaissance of ours has to invent its own forms of organization is part of the reason that its progress has been slow, or at any rate invisible: we are inventing a "language" as we go along, while others only have to continue their conversation. Yet this fact also explains the revolutionary potential of the shift. If we really want deep change—and how could we not?—nothing less than an entirely new framework for our thoughts, activity, *and* our relationships can pry the death grip of war from the collective throat of humanity.

But in all this we should not lose sight of the fact that no organizational format, while it may be more or less suitable for a given worldview, can be by itself the leading image or mechanism of the desired change. The revolution that's really trying to happen today is not just wide but deep—it is nothing short of a spiritual revolution. Capitalism, as Karl Marx famously complained, leaves societies mired in the icy water of egotistical calculation, but to reduce egotism in any of its manifestations we need a revolution much deeper than economic.

And this brings us once again to the one person in the modern period who figured out and—remarkably enough—actually put into practice the new paradigm in virtually all its dimensions, including spirituality. Although he did not often speak about the environment, for example, his utter material simplicity and closeness to nature (until the end of his life he enjoyed sleeping outdoors) embodied a life of harmony with the environment that most of us can only dream of. Even though he did not work directly on the war system, the *shanti sena* ("peace army") he invented to keep the peace between communities unfolded into today's UCP. And he did more: his flexible combination of Constructive Programme and Satyagraha (active nonviolent resistance) showed how even the most ruthless and entrenched regimes could be dislodged without perpetuating their violence. I believe that because we have only partially learned the lessons he so painstakingly chalked out over 50 years of intense activity, our own resistance movements have not been anything like as effective. Almost all nonviolent movements since his time—and yes, there have been many—have been either constructive or obstructive, but not both. Finally—and here again so far ahead of his time—he was able to give his titanic struggles strategic direction without inhibiting their diverse, person-centered, and grass roots character. As he said of his glorious successes of the early 1920s, "Mass awakening came no one knows how. Even remote villages were stirred . . . it was true *swaraj* ("freedom, self rule") of the masses attained by the masses."[18]

In their excellent study of the state of the movement (or movement-to-be) Nordhaus and Schellenberger furnish many insights drawn from the recent history of successful social movements in, particularly, the United States. For example the movements all were birthed in preexisting communities of some kind—labor, church, students, or other—that have recently been there only for conservatives and not for those who would move culture and policy toward peace.[19] However, it takes on more importance, if anything, because it explains why the peace movement *and* the environmental movement have had so little traction with the general public. It is the observation that people have become so demoralized today, mainly by the relentless negative images of the mass media, that the "gloom and doom" that is so characteristic of the rhetoric of the left and the environmentalists only further alienates and disempowers them. People can be roused, as Gandhi showed much earlier, only by positive messages (such as Barack Obama's "hope" campaign), and by being challenged to reach *higher* than they think possible. That may seem counterintuitive, but the lower the image of the human being sinks (and that's the specialty of the mass media today), the more we need to challenge ourselves with *higher* aspirations to overcome that negativity and empower ourselves. For this reason we need—and deserve—the signs of hope briefly identified in this chapter.

NOTES

1. Gandhi, 1999.
2. Solnit, 2004.
3. Perrin, 1979.
4. Boulding, 1978.

5. Gandhi, 1999.
6. Hedges, 2002.
7. Schell, 2003.
8. Wink and Deats, 1992; Deats, 2002.
9. Kapur, 1992.
10. UNESCO, 1987.
11. Kuhn, 1962–1970.
12. Nagler, 1981.
13. Ray and Anderson, 2001.
14. Hawken, 2007.
15. Woolman and Gummere, 1922.
16. Brafman and Bergstrom, 2006.
17. Shirky, 2008.
18. Gandhi, 1999.
19. Nordhaus and Schellenberger, 2007.

CHAPTER 16

TO REMAKE THE WORLD

Paul Hawken

Over the past 15 years I have given nearly 1,000 talks about the environment, and every time I have done so I have felt like a tightrope performer struggling to maintain perfect balance. To be sure, people are curious to know what is happening in their world, but no speaker wants to leave an auditorium depressed, however dark and frightening tomorrow is predicted by the scientific studies of the rate of environmental loss. To be sanguine about the future, however, requires a plausible basis for constructive action: you cannot describe possibilities for that future unless the present problem is accurately defined. Bridging the chasm between the two was always a challenge, but audiences kindly ignored my intellectual vertigo, and over time, provided a rare perspective instead. After every speech a smaller crowd would gather to talk, ask questions, and exchange business cards. These people were typically working on the most salient issues of our day: climate change, poverty, deforestation, peace, water, hunger, conservation, and human rights. They came from the nonprofit and nongovernmental world, also known as civil society; they looked after rivers and bays, educated consumers about sustainable agriculture, retrofitted houses with solar panels, lobbied state legislatures about pollutions, fought against corporate-weighted trade policies, worked to green inner cities, and taught children about the environment. Quite

This is an excerpt from chapter 1 in Paul Hawken's book *Blessed Unrest*. New York: Penguin, 2007: 1–6. Reprinted with permission from Penguin.

simply, they had dedicated themselves to trying to safeguard nature and ensure justice. Although this was the 1990s, and the media largely ignored them, in those small meetings I had a chance to listen to their concerns. They were students, grandmothers, teenagers, tribe members, business-people, architects, teachers, retired professors, and worried mothers and fathers. Because I was itinerant, and the organizations they represented were rooted in their communities, over the years I began to grasp the diversity of these groups and their cumulative number. My interlocutors had a lot to say. They were informed, imaginative, and vital, and offered ideas, information, and insights. To a great extent *Blessed Unrest* is their gift to me.

My new friends would thrust articles and books into my hands, tuck small gifts into my knapsack, or pass along proposals for green companies. A Native American taught me that the division between ecology and human rights was an artificial one, that the environmental and social justice movements addressed two sides of a single larger dilemma. The way we harm the Earth affects all people, and how we treat one another is reflected in how we treat the Earth. As my talks began to mirror my deeper understanding, the hands offering business cards grew more diverse. I would get from 5 to 30 such cards per speech, and after being on the road for a week or two would return home with a few hundred of them stuffed into various pockets. I would lay them on the table in my kitchen, read the names, look at the logos, envis-age the missions, and marvel at the scope and diversity of what groups were doing on behalf of others. Later, I would store them in drawers or paper bags as keepsakes of the journey. Over the course of years the number of cards mounted into the thousands, and whenever I glanced at them, I came back to one question: Did anyone truly appreciate how many groups and organizations were engaged in progressive causes? At first, this was a matter of curiosity on my part, but it slowly grew into a hunch that something larger was afoot, a significant social movement that was eluding the radar of mainstream cultures.

So, curious, I began to count. I looked at government records for different countries and, using various methods to approximate the number of environ-mental and social justice groups from tax census data, I initially estimated a total of 30,000 environmental organizations around the globe; when I added social justice and indigenous peoples' rights organizations, the number exceeded 100,000. I then researched to see if there had ever been any equals to this movement in scale or scope, but I couldn't find anything, past or pres-ent. The more I probed, the more I unearthed; the numbers continued to climb as I discovered lists, indexes, and small databases specific to certain sec-tors or geographic areas. In trying to pick up a stone, I found the exposed tip of a much larger geological formation. I soon realized that my initial estimate of 100,000 organizations was off by at least a factor of 10, and I now believe

number between 1 to 2 million or more organizations working toward ecological sustainability and social justice.

By any conventional definition, this vast collection of committed individuals does not constitute a movement. Movements have leaders and ideologies.
People *join* movements, study their tracts, and identify themselves with a
group. They read the biography of the founder(s) or listen to them perorate
on tape or in person. Movements, in short, have followers. This movement,
however, doesn't fit the standard model. It is dispersed, inchoate, and fiercely
independent. It has no manifesto or doctrine, no overriding authority to
check with. It is taking shape in schoolrooms, farms, jungles, villages, companies, deserts, fisheries, slums—and yes, even fancy New York hotels. One of
its distinctive features is that it is tentatively emerging as a global humanitarian movement arising from the bottom up. Historically social movements
have arisen primarily in response to injustice, inequities, and corruption.
Those woes still remain legion, joined by a new condition that has no prece-
dent: the planet has a life-threatening disease, marked by massive ecological
degradation and rapid climate change. As I counted the vast number of
organizations it crossed my mind that perhaps I was witnessing the growth
of something organic, if not biologic. Rather than a movement in the conventional sense, could it be an instinctive, collective response to threat? Is it
atomized for reasons that are innate to its purpose? How does it function?
How fast is it growing? How is it connected? Why is it largely ignored?
Does it have a history? Can it successfully address the issues that governments are failing to: energy, jobs, conservation, poverty, and global warming?
Will it become centralized, or will it continue to be dispersed and cede its
power to ideologies and fundamentalism?

I sought a name for the movement, but none exists. I met people who
wanted to structure or organize it—a difficult task, since it would easily be
the most complex association of human beings ever assembled. Many outside
the movement critique it as powerless, but that assessment does not stop its
growth. When describing it to politicians, academics, and businesspeople,
I found that many believe they are already familiar with this movement,
how it works, what it consists of, and its approximate size. They base their
conclusion on media reports about Amnesty International, the Sierra Club,
Oxfam, or other venerable institutions. They may be directly acquainted with
a few smaller organizations and may even sit on the board of a local group.
For them and others the movement is small, known, and circumscribed; a
new type of charity, with a sprinkling of ragtag activities that occasionally
give it a bad name. People inside the movement can also underestimate it,
basing their judgment on only the organizations they are linked to, even
though their networks can only encompass a fraction of the whole. But after

spending years researching this phenomenon, including creating with my colleagues a global database of its constituent organizations, I have come to these conclusions: this is the largest social movement in all of human history. No one knows its scope, and how it functions is more mysterious than what meets the eye.

What *does* meet the eye is compelling: coherent, organic, self-organized congregations involving tens of millions of people dedicated to change. When asked at a college if I am pessimistic or optimistic about the future, my answer is always the same: If you look at the science that describes what is happening on Earth today and aren't pessimistic, you don't have the correct data. If you meet the people in this unnamed movement and aren't optimistic, you haven't got a heart. What I see are ordinary and some not-so-ordinary individuals willing to confront despair, power, and incalculable odds in an attempt to restore some semblance of grace, justice, and beauty to this world. In the not-so-ordinary category, contrast former Presidents Bill Clinton and George W. Bush.[1] While I was writing this, Bush was snarled in a skein of untruths as he tried to keep the lid on a nightmarish war fed by inept and misguided ambition; simultaneously the Clinton Global Initiative (which is a nongovernmental organization) met in New York and raised $7.3 billion in three days to combat global warming, injustice, intolerance, and poverty. Of the two initiatives, war and peace, which addresses root causes? Which has momentum? Which does not offend the world? Which is open to new ideas? The poet Adrienne Rich wrote, "My heart is moved by all I cannot save. So much has been destroyed I have cast my lot with those who, age after age, perversely, with no extraordinary power, reconstitute the world."[2] There could be no better description of the audiences I met in my lectures.

This is the story without apologies of what is going *right* on this planet, narratives of imagination and conviction, not defeatist accounts about the limits. Wrong is an addictive, repetitive story; Right is where the movement is. There is a rabbinical teaching that holds that if the world is ending and the Messiah arrives, you first plant a tree and then see if the story is true. Islam has a similar teaching that tells adherents that if they have a palm cutting in their hand on Judgment Day, plant the cutting. Inspiration is not garnered from the recitation of what is flawed; it resides, rather, in humanity's willingness to restore, redress, reform, rebuild, recover, reimagine, and reconsider. "Consider" (*con sidere*) means "with the stars"; reconsider means to rejoin the movement and cycle of heaven and life. The emphasis here is on humanity's *intention*, because humans are frail and imperfect. People are not always literate or educated. Most families in the world are impoverished and may suffer from chronic illnesses. The poor cannot always get the right foods for proper nutrition, and must struggle to feed and educate their young. If citizens with such burdens can rise above their quotidian difficulties and act with the clear intent to confront exploitation and bring about restoration, then something powerful is afoot. And it is not just the poor, but people of all races and classes everywhere in the world. "One day you finally knew what you had to do, and began, though the voices around you kept shouting their bad advice"[3] is Mary Oliver's description of moving away from the profane toward a deep sense of connectedness to the living world.

Although the six o-clock news is usually concerned with the death of strangers, millions of people work on behalf of strangers. This altruism has religious, even mythic origins and very practical 18th-century roots. Abolitionists were the first group to create a national and global movement to defend the rights of those they did not know. Until that time, no citizen group had ever filed a grievance except as it related to itself.[4] Conservative spokesmen ridiculed the abolitionists then, just as conservatives taunt liberals, progressives, do-gooders, and activists today by making those four terms pejoratives. Healing the wounds of the Earth and its people does not require saintliness or a political party, only gumption and persistence. It is not a liberal or conservative activity; it is a sacred act. It is a massive enterprise undertaken by ordinary citizens everywhere, not by self-appointed governments or oligarchies.

Blessed Unrest is an exploration of this movement—its participants, its aims, and its ideals. I have been a part of it for decades, so I cannot claim to be the detached journalist skeptically prodding my subjects. I hope what follows is the expression of a deep listening, the subtitle of the book, *How the Largest Movement in the World Came into Being*, cannot be answered by one person. Like anyone, I have a perspective based on biases accumulated over time and a network of friends and peers who color my judgment. However, I wrote the book primarily to discover what I *don't* know. Part of what I learned concerns an older quiescent history that is reemerging, what poet Gary Snyder calls *the great underground*, a current of humanity that dates back to the Paleolithic. Its lineage can be traced back to healers, priestesses, philosophers, monks, rabbis, poets, and artists "who speak for the planet, for other species, for interdependence, a life that courses under and through and around empires."[5] At the same time, much of what I learned is new. Groups are *intertwingling*—there are no words to exactly describe the complexity of relationships.[6] The Internet and other communication technologies have revolutionized what is possible for small groups to accomplish and are accordingly changing the loci of power. There have always been networks of powerful people, but until recently it has never been possible for the entire world to be connected.

Blessed Unrest is an overview that describes how this movement differs from pervious social movements, particularly with respect to ideology. The organizations in the movement arise one by one, generally with no predetermined vision for the world, and craft their goals without reference to orthodoxy. For some historians and analysts, movements only exist when they have an ideological or religious core of beliefs. And movements certainly don't exist in a vacuum: a strong leader(s) is an earmark of a movement and often its intellectual pivot point, even if deceased. The movement I describe here has neither, and so represents a completely different form of social phenomenon.

Editors' Note—Hawken concludes his inspiring account of this new and unprecedented social movement with the claim that it represents a complex social phenomenon that cannot be easily explained or predicted using the scientific language and practices that have been used in the past. The individuals whose work stands out in this potentially transformative movement all try to do good as may have been true in other social movements. But it does not stop there. The people he met who convinced him of something new occurring are people who consider the entire planet, with all its amazing diversity, as sacred, and they want to save it. Hawken concludes, "In total, the movement as I see it results in an inadvertent sense of optimism, an odd thing in these bleak times. I didn't intend it; optimism discovered me."[7]

NOTES

1. At the time this piece was written, George W. Bush was sitting President and the Iraq war had recently begun.
2. Rich, 1993.
3. Oliver, 1986.
4. Hochschild, 2005.
5. Steinman, 1998.
6. Morville, 2005.
7. Hawken, 2007.

CHAPTER 17

SEARCH FOR COMMON GROUND

John Marks and Susan Collin Marks

OUT OF *MAD:* THE RISE OF A PEACEMAKING INSTITUTION

In 1982, the United States and the Union of Soviet Socialist Republics (USSR) were involved in an arms race framed by a nuclear doctrine of mutually assured destruction, or MAD. This deadlock led John Marks to look for a paradigm shift. His defining metaphor was of two boys standing knee deep in a room full of gasoline, arguing over who had the most matches. While most of the world focused on rearranging the mix—on arms control—Marks knew that for the world to be truly safe, the gasoline would have to be drained from the room.

This meant transforming the very framework in which the United States and the USSR related to each other. Marks thus became an advocate of *common security.* Convinced that confrontational, win-lose techniques were not only dangerous, but also ultimately ineffective, he founded Search for Common Ground (Search), a nonprofit organization in Washington, D.C. Search's mission is to find concrete ways to change how the world resolves conflict from adversarial, you-or-me confrontations to you-and-me solutions.

It was a daring vision for that time. The organization was definitely not in line with President Ronald Reagan's characterization of the Soviet Union

An extended version of this article originally appeared in Chris E. Stout, ed., *The New Humanitarian: Inspiration, Innovations, and Blueprints for Visionaries,* Volume 3 (Westport, CT: Praeger, 2008).

as the "evil empire." But in 1989, as the Cold War faded, Search hit the mainstream. It formed a partnership with the Moscow publication *Literaturnaya Gazeta* to establish the Soviet-American Task Force on Terrorism. The results included an unofficial agreement between a former Central Intelligence Agency (CIA) director and the ex-head of counterterrorism for the KGB that outlined how U.S. and Soviet intelligence organizations might work together to combat terrorism. The key recommendation (later published in the task force's book *Common Ground on Terrorism,* 1991) was that the United States and the USSR should "treat terrorism as a problem shared by both superpowers and cooperate wherever possible to eliminate the threat." Although the USSR's KGB accepted the recommendation, the CIA initially rebuffed the effort because it rejected the premise of equivalence with the KGB. As the Gulf War became imminent, the U.S. government needed intelligence on Iraq, and the CIA had little choice but to establish a cooperative relationship with the KGB.

The counterterrorism project was a success, and brought Search credibility. The RAND Corporation, a key Pentagon think tank, became the co-sponsor. The project attracted front-page attention and was the subject of an ABC-TV *Nightline* program. Ted Koppel may have rolled his eyes when he mentioned the name Search for Common Ground, but Marks received an interview, and the *Nightline* host made clear Search's pivotal role in organizing the project.

INTO THE MIDDLE EAST

As Soviets and Americans were finding common ground, the Cold War was ending and Marks realized that the organization needed to expand or it would not survive. Soon an unplanned opportunity presented itself. Two people who were involved in the terrorism project proposed that Search organize a similar project on Lebanon. Marks agreed. He now had the contacts and a model. So, in 1989, he set up the U.S.-Soviet Task Force on Lebanon, recruited a high-level team of American participants, and flew off to Moscow for the first meeting.

Two major lessons emerged from Search's international work. First, violence in Lebanon could not be dealt with without considering the larger Middle East context. Second, rather than pursue a bilateral, U.S.-Soviet strategy, a multilateral, regional approach was needed. Often in Search's work the original concept could be flawed, but Search's receptiveness to adjustments led to success. Marks incorporated these lessons and proposed a multi-track effort to replicate in the Middle East region what the Conference for Security and Cooperation in Europe (now OSCE) had done.

The proposal was not funded until after the first Gulf War. With armed violence raging, liberal American foundations such as Ford, MacArthur, and W. Alton Jones sought a peace plan, and Search's proposal called for a regional structure that would bring together Arabs, Israelis, Iranians, and Turks. Within months, these foundations provided Search with significant funding.

Although seeking common ground in the Middle East was exactly what Search had been doing with the United States and the USSR, the world had changed. Promoting Middle East peace was clearly a mainstream activity. Marks knew Search was operating under new conditions when he received an unsolicited phone call from former Assistant Secretary of State Alfred "Roy" Atherton, asking if he could join the effort. Soon Marks and his colleagues were meeting Yitzhak Rabin, Yasser Arafat, Hosni Mubarak, and Prince Hassan of Jordan. Search needed—and received—official permission to sponsor unofficial meetings, which were often quite successful. In 1993 to 1994, before official peace talks had started, Search sponsored back-channel meetings between former Jordanian and Israeli generals. The generals worked out a series of unofficial agreements that became the basis of the Israeli-Jordanian peace treaty.

BACKING UP A STEP

Marks clearly had come a long way from his arrival in Washington, D.C., in 1966 at age 22. He had hoped for a meaningful Foreign Service career that would end with an appointment as an ambassador. He saw himself working out of an office in the U.S. Embassy building on the Place de la Concorde in Paris. He dreamed about negotiating treaties and driving a sports car around Europe. However, as with so many of his generation, the Vietnam War stood in the way of dreams. Marks was 23 when his draft board refused his deferment to take a diplomatic assignment in London. Intent on staying out of the military, Marks became one of the few members of his generation to go to Vietnam to avoid the draft. He worked as a civilian official in the pacification program in the region east of Saigon.

Then, in 1970, he resigned from the State Department in protest over the U.S. invasion of Cambodia and went to work as executive assistant for foreign policy to U.S. Senator Clifford Case. His main task was to secure passage of the Case-Church Amendment, which in 1973 cut off funding for U.S. military involvement in the Vietnam War. He left the senator's staff in 1973 and co-authored *The CIA and the Cult of Intelligence*, a best-selling exposé about U.S. intelligence abuses. Next, he wrote *The Search for the Manchurian Candidate*, an award-winning book about the CIA's use and misuse of LSD and other experimental behavioral science techniques.

Marks became a minor culture hero, but he was troubled by the adversarial quality of his work—which was mostly defined by what he was against. Instead of throwing monkey wrenches into the old system, he wanted to build a new one.

While Marks was making important life changes, the woman who would become his wife, Susan Collin Marks, was coming of age in South Africa. Susan's mother was one of the first members of Black Sash, a women's human rights organization set up in 1955 to protest the "death of the constitution" under apartheid laws. At age five, she accompanied her mother into black townships, where she witnessed the impact of racism and discrimination. Her mother's activism—of being a white South African—shaped Susan's life. After 1990, when South Africa began its transition from apartheid to democracy, Susan channeled her passion for justice and dignity through peacemaking, peace building, and conflict transformation under the auspices of South Africa's National Peace Accord. She mediated conflicts, intervened in bloody street clashes, took a bullet in the leg while trying to calm a confrontation, facilitated multiple dialogues and policy forums, and helped formulate new policies on community policing.

The guiding principle in Susan's work is a profound compassion inspired by the African principle of Ubuntu, the interconnectedness of all human beings. She believes that when people are provided with the space to be their best, generally they will step into it. Susan would later write a book about the South African peace process titled *Watching the Wind: Conflict Resolution during South Africa's Transition to Democracy*.[1]

COMING TOGETHER

In 1993, Marks traveled to South Africa to produce a TV series called *South Africa's Search for Common Ground*. His co-producer, Hannes Siebert, would later introduce Susan and John to each other. Within 26 hours of meeting, the couple bonded and recognized that they shared a vision. Indeed, the first time John told Susan that he no longer wanted to tear down the old system, but rather to build the new, Susan jokingly accused him of having peeked into her notebooks and stolen her ideas.

By 1994, Susan moved to Washington, married John, and joined Search. They became an effective team, and Search started to grow at the rate of about 20 percent each year. John and Susan became each other's principal advisor, and took to describing their work with the first person plural "we" (which form will be used for the rest of this chapter).

KEEPING HOPE ALIVE: OUR BEST PRACTICES

At Search, we respond to "crisis" by looking for the "opportunity" that lies between the old relationship that is breaking down and the new relationship that is being born. We see the space between as a place for breakthroughs and transformation. As Buckminster Fuller said, "You never change things by fighting the existing reality. To change something, build a new model that makes the existing model obsolete."

One of our core principles is that conflict is a normal part of human interaction, but violence is only one possible response, and not an inevitable one. Indeed, most people, most of the time, find ways to resolve their differences peacefully—within families, at work, and in communities. Even internationally, among states, most disputes are settled amicably. Every day, the world whirrs with cooperation—from telephone and postal services, to shared scientific data, to high-wire diplomacy. Despite awful exceptions, the world is almost always much more at peace than at war.

Unfortunately, however, tens of millions of people are caught up in armed struggles, and millions are still dying every year. We believe that current problems—whether economic, ethnic, or environmental—are simply too complex and interconnected to be settled on a violent, adversarial basis. The Earth is running out of space, resources, and recuperative capacity to deal with wasteful conflict. We continue to search for and often find new ways to empower large numbers of people to make a shift in attitudes and behaviors; but inevitably, our organization has had its share of setbacks. In Liberia, looters sacked our radio studio. The Iraq war diverted much of our African funding. In the United States, both the Left and the Right attacked our Network for Life and Choice on the issue of abortion. Still, we do not give up. In Liberia, we rebuilt our Talking Drum Studio and resumed making radio programs to encourage peace building. We diversified our funding in Africa and looked for new sources. Sadly, however, we had to shut down the Network for Life and Choice.

This is the story of how an abstract idea became a concrete reality, with multiple forms of expression—how it was built, expanded, and sustained; how it lives vibrantly in the hearts and minds of a multi-cultural staff scattered across the planet; and how it continues to reach into societies caught in deadly conflict, bringing inspiration and hope that the violence can and will end.

INSTITUTION BUILDING

Historically, conflict resolution has been the work of committed individuals who sometimes work together in networks or ad hoc partnerships, but for reasons of both temperament and economics, largely avoid organizations. This is the consultant or sole practitioner model. We have developed an alternative. Instead of paying our staff consulting fees by the day, we employ them by the year. In the process, we have made long-term conflict prevention much more affordable. We believe that the most effective way to deal with complex conflicts is for professional peace builders to be engaged on the ground on a full-time, long-term basis.

As Jean Monnet, chief architect of what became the European Union, said, "Nothing changes without individuals. Nothing lasts without institutions." In our view, the principal reason Search has flourished is that we have brought social entrepreneurial skills to the field of conflict resolution, and built an organization with sufficient resources and personnel to tackle multi-layered conflicts that extend across entire countries and regions.

We try to maintain a creative operating environment that is consistent with our vision and the new world we seek to build. We try to avoid a highly centralized system. We want the organization to be a haven for sub-entrepreneurs, who operate autonomously, but within a common ground framework. At the same time, we require strong financial management from headquarters.

This model is full of challenges and contradictions. It requires both innovation and effective administrative and financial systems. We recognize that there is a core tension between flexibility and stability. And we have learned through experience—sometimes the hard way—that an organization like Search requires both.

The passionate, talented people who are drawn to our work are usually stretched to their limits. Violence can flare up and wipe out years of work. Funding often falls through for reasons that have no connection with our work or the conflict at hand, but have to do with the donor's bureaucratic needs.

The question of funding is always an issue. The field of conflict resolution is relatively new. Until 2006, only one American foundation, the William and Flora Hewlett Foundation, provided substantial funding to this area of work and recognized it as a field. However, Hewlett decided to close its program. Through perseverance and ingenuity, we have been able to find funding from governments—European and American—and from multi-lateral agencies such as the European Union and various UN agencies.

BASIC OPERATING PRINCIPLES

Searchers, 350 of them, representing 30 nationalities, come to work at our offices in Africa, the Middle East, Asia, Europe, and the United States. They put their ethnic and religious identities aside and work together to find peaceful ways to deal with differences. They are Israeli and Palestinian, Hutu and Tutsi, Muslim, Buddhist, Jewish, and Christian. They heroically stand for peace—often in the midst of fear and hatred.

One of our basic operating principles is to employ people from all sides of the conflict. This is crucial to our work of reconciling warring parties, since we believe that in order for reconciliation to take place externally, it also must occur internally.

We know that peace is a process, not an event. Although we certainly appreciate those glorious moments when agreements are signed, we recognize that real peace usually occurs after a long, arduous process of reducing fear, building trust, dealing with concerns, and chipping away at stereotypes. Instead of confronting the other side as the enemy, we help people find solutions that benefit all the parties involved.

We avoid parachuting into a conflict, as we believe that real peace building requires a long-term commitment. We use our presence on the ground to develop knowledge and build a network of relationships on all sides. We try to be inclusive and to involve as many partners and allies as practical— including national governments, opposition groups, civil society, security forces, diplomats, international organizations (such as the UN, the World Bank, and the European Union), and—increasingly—the business sector.

We become immersed in the local culture. We believe it is very important to have a profound understanding of where we are. Conflicts are complex, and it takes deep engagement to understand them. In any given country, we try to combine what we have learned elsewhere with native and unique qualities. We work to support and expand indigenous wisdom and creativity. We partner with local peace builders to strengthen their ability to transform their own conflicts, adopting a multipronged, multi-project strategy.

We recognize that each country is different, with a unique history and culture. A standardized, "off-the-shelf" approach simply does not work, and we have no single operating model. Still, we find similarities: everywhere there is a storytelling tradition, and everywhere people in conflict see themselves as victims. In our view, about 50 percent of our toolbox works when we enter a new place, and 50 percent does not—and we never know which 50 percent it will be. The keys are creativity and nimbleness.

Our methodology is rooted in a simple idea stated by South African ANC (African National Congress) leader Andrew Masondo: *understand the differences and act on the commonalities.* Within that framework, we developed a diverse toolbox, which includes such traditional techniques as mediation, training, facilitation, and back-channel negotiations. Because violent conflict is fed by stereotyping, demonizing, and dehumanizing, we also use the tools of popular culture to help reverse this process—what is now called *peace building*. Thus, we produce soap operas that communicate win-win messages of mutual respect, tolerance, nonviolence, and problem solving. We make music videos that have turned into theme songs for entire peace processes. We produce reality TV—with good values. Our toolbox also includes street theater, sport, art, community organizing, and film festivals.

In sum, we are weavers who knit together multiple strands to help mend societies that are torn and broken. We encourage moderate voices, to reduce polarization. We work both top down and bottom up. We promote societal healing across whole countries.

FIELD OFFICES

Our second field office opened in Burundi following the 1994 genocide in Rwanda. In November of that year, Lionel Rosenblatt, then head of Refugees International, challenged us with a question: if we could not take action to help prevent violence in Burundi, which has the same ethnic composition as Rwanda, from becoming a killing field, how could we, in good conscience, call ourselves a conflict prevention organization? We addressed the challenge and traveled to Bujumbura. We talked to everyone we could—Hutus and Tutsis, politicians, civil society leaders, the diplomatic community, religious and business figures, women, youth, teachers, and donors.

Because of the escalating violence, development agencies and other nongovernmental organizations (NGOs) were pulling out of Burundi. Recognizing an immediate need to defuse tension, we identified a key figure to preventing disaster was Ahmedou Ould-Abdullah, the UN secretary-general's special representative. At the time, he worked tirelessly to negotiate, mediate, and cajole to keep the conflict from sliding toward the abyss. Ahmedou became our patron and future board member. He urged that our work be funded by the U.S. Agency for International Development (USAID). Within months, we launched our first activities in Burundi with a budget of more than $1 million a year.

Timing is critical to our work and we employ a mix of instinct, common sense, and good problem solving. In every part of our work, we make careful considerations about where we can bring and/or add value, and how to gain entry. We are dedicated to bringing a compassionate response to the events in our world, and a deep listening ear to the inner voice that draws us closer to understanding.

A CASE IN POINT: BURUNDI

In Bujumbura, we set up a radio production facility, called Studio Ijambo, which means *wise words* in Kirundi, to produce balanced, noninflammatory programming. In Rwanda, hate radio had incited the killers. In neighboring Burundi, which has the same ethnic mix, we hoped to use radio to do the opposite: to defuse violence and build bridges. We recruited a team of journalists— both Tutsis and Hutus. They were often considered traitors to their ethnic group because they were working for what we saw as the common good.

Although we wanted Studio Ijambo to disseminate programming widely and be a resource to the community, we feared that if the studio became a radio station, we would be considered competition to other stations and susceptible to government interference. Thus, we became a production studio, and all the radio stations in the country broadcast our programs. We replicated this studio model in Liberia, Sierra Leone, Angola, Guinea, Congo, and Côte d'Ivoire. The idea was to provide local stations and networks with free, high-quality programming that contained messages of peace and reconciliation. In our peak years in Burundi, we were producing as much as 15 hours a week of original programming.

Our programs were produced by mixed Hutu/Tutsi teams. Acting on their own, these reporters would not have had the same access and protection as they had together. This phenomenon demonstrated both the reality and perception of balanced reporting. In the mid-1990s, when the government and rebel groups cut off contact, we initiated a series of parallel interviews, which allowed the various factions to hear each other's perspectives over the airwaves. We invited rebel leaders to participate in telephone interviews, and we convened roundtable discussions of government, political party, and civil society leaders. Our journalists made a point of traveling to remote corners of the country so that all Burundians felt included in on-air conversations.

The studio set new standards in Burundi for unbiased journalism, and influenced the local radio stations' programming style. The head of Burundi National Radio has credited Studio Ijambo with greatly improving reporting standards throughout the country. Ted Koppel of ABC *Nightline* called the studio "the voice of hope." Eighteen years after its inception, the studio is still going strong.

Our most popular programming was a twice-weekly radio soap opera series called "Our Neighbors, Ourselves." It started in 1996 and led to similar dramatic programming in nine other countries. The series, written by a Burundian playwright, told the story of a Hutu family and a Tutsi family that, during 616 episodes, succeeded in peacefully resolving their disputes. Burundi is a small media market and the series was heard by 87 percent of the population. Indeed, the impact reached the point where our fictional characters became part of national folklore, and we were, in effect, contributing to redefining Burundi archetypes. USAID official Roger Conrad said "You have introduced the vocabulary of peace and reconciliation to the national conversation at all levels, where previously only words of hate and mistrust were heard."

Burundi: Women's Peace Center

Another effective part of our strategy in Burundi was our Women's Peace Center, also established in 1996. The center sought to mobilize women as peacemakers. It worked with thousands of women's associations in organizing, training, and facilitating inter-ethnic dialogue, providing information about women's rights, and helping resettle internally displaced people. It was a venue for societal healing.

Here is one story: Two women, Léonie Barakomeza and Yvonne Ryakiye, were born near each other, but did not know each other. When the fighting broke out in 1993, their community was destroyed. Léonie and her fellow Tutsis fled to one side of the river; Yvonne and the Hutus went to the other. The two met in 1996 through our center and began working together. Unlike most of their neighbors, they were willing to cross the river that separated them. They persisted despite accusations of treason from their respective groups. Eventually, other women followed their example and links grew. With meager means, these women created a women's association and urged people to return home by building 40 brick houses for both Tutsi and Hutu families. Their efforts were recognized when they were nominated, along with eight other Burundian women, for the 2005 Nobel Peace Prize.

Burundi: Youth

Young militia members, paid a few dollars a day by military and political leaders, carried out most of the actual violence in Burundi. In 1999 we started an initiative to provide alternatives for these youths. Originally known as the Working with Killers project, it began when an Italian TV crew asked to use Studio Ijambo to interview two cousins, a Hutu rebel and a Tutsi gang member. They had been enemies for years. Contrary to expectations, the two agreed to stop fighting and team up with a local youth group, Jamaa (Unity). With our support, they began to build an ethnically mixed youth movement called Gardons Contact (Let's Stay in Touch).

Bringing the youth together was not easy. One of the first events we sponsored was a workshop for 30 ethnically mixed youth who gathered on a Saturday afternoon. Participants talked, played cards, and made music. As the evening wore on, no one wanted go to sleep. When the adult staff finally declared that it was time for bed, the youth fell silent. We learned from working with the youth that they did not feel safe sleeping near their enemies. Assurances from the adults, plus fatigue, in the end, won out, and the youth went to bed. In the morning, the Hutu and Tutsi youth woke to look at each other with fresh eyes. They began to talk more deeply, and they discovered a common ground: both felt exploited by political leaders.

This group became the core of our youth activities. The youth organized ethnically mixed soccer tournaments and began to tell their stories through publishing comic books. They communicated the horrors they had seen— for example, watching victims die horrible deaths. The comic books were so compelling that the Burundian Ministry of Education added them to the curriculum material for the country's schools.

Burundi: Domestic Shuttle Diplomacy

We realized that conflict resolution in Burundi would benefit greatly from continuing mediation and facilitation. In 1995 we brought in the late Jan van Eck, a former South African ANC member of parliament, to promote dialogue and help solve problems among leaders of conflicting parties outside of the official peace talks. He worked directly for us for two years, and independently for another 10. During this whole period, Jan spent about half his time in Burundi. He became a widely trusted intermediary, who was in contact with virtually every party to the conflict, including rebel groups with whom almost no one else was talking, and he facilitated many agreements—small and large.

Burundi: Culture

Violent conflict is not purely an intellectual exercise. Therefore, we want to reach people on the emotional level and we make wide use of popular culture. In Burundi, this meant drumming and dancing. We organized national competitions and held giant festivals in Bujumbura. Studio Ijambo employed a full-time disk jockey, and we produced music for peace radio programs. We even enlisted Jamaican reggae star Ziggy Marley, who has a huge following in Burundi, to record public service announcements (PSAs).

CONTINUED EXPANSION

By 1997, we had also established field offices in Ukraine and Angola. Jan Pronk, then the Dutch minister of development cooperation, requested that we launch a Liberian radio studio similar to Studio Ijambo, and the Dutch government offered start-up funding. This offer posed a dilemma for us. We had taken as an article of faith that the availability of funding would not be allowed to drive our programming. After long discussions we came to see that our organizational integrity does not depend on where we work or on whose idea it is to get started. To produce programming with messages of peace—in Liberia or anywhere else—is totally consistent with our vision.

So, we accepted the Dutch grant and established Talking Drum Studio in Liberia. This, in turn, led to more expansion, which occurred because several of our Liberian staff members turned out to be refugees from the war in neighboring Sierra Leone, and from there, once we saw the importance of acting regionally (because African conflicts tend to cross national borders), into Côte d'Ivoire and then Guinea.

This chain of events, in fact, illustrates our methodology: we reacted to an opportunity, learned from experience, and discovered—or stumbled on—a new insight.

MIDDLE EAST

In 1991, we started work in the Middle East with a regional approach. But after the second Palestinian intifada broke out in 2000, there was a need for major changes. As the bloodshed spread, neither Arabs nor Israelis were particularly interested in joint action programs. We went into a period of intense reflection, and we realized that we needed more bilateral programs, aimed at the Israeli-Palestinian conflict. This seemed particularly true after 9/11 when we sensed that the Palestinian-Israeli struggle was at the heart of what was tearing up the Earth.

We (Susan and John) decided to move to Jerusalem for two years to contribute to resolving the conflict. We lived just 70 yards from the Green Line that split the city, and we opened our office in a spare bedroom of our house. In addition to running the Jerusalem office, we were still president and executive vice president of the whole organization. At first, we shuttled between Jerusalem and Washington, D.C., every six weeks, but we could not sustain the pace—nor did we want to be away so often from Jerusalem. In Washington, we had a strong leader, Shamil Idriss, who had started with us as an intern, become head of our Burundi project, and at 27 moved up to be our chief operating officer. We rebuilt the Jerusalem program to meet the changed reality. Producing media seemed to represent one of the few activities where we felt we could make a difference. So we did what is described in the following paragraphs.

CGNews

We built up the Common Ground News Service (CGNews), which offers a selection of solution-oriented, bridge-building articles to newspapers and Web sites around the world and to more than 20,000 individual subscribers every week. We negotiated rights to reproduce articles from leading publications and commissioned original articles from a network of prominent contributors. Our news service now appears in Arabic, Bahasa Indonesia, English, French, Hebrew, and Urdu. Altogether, more than 16,000 of our articles have been reprinted in such places as *Al Hayat* (London), *Ha'aretz* (Tel Aviv), *Christian Science Monitor* (Boston), *Al Quds* (Jerusalem), *Washington Post/Newsweek Online, Jakarta Post, Frontier Post* (Peshawar), *Kuwait Times, Jordan Times, Arab News* (Jeddah), and *Al-Jazeera.com* (Doha).

NONVIOLENCE

Like many people, we felt that if only the Palestinians would practice Gandhian nonviolence, their conflict with Israel would be much more likely to be resolved. So, we commissioned polls among both Israelis and Palestinians—and released them to considerable publicity—showing that the clear majorities of both peoples favored a nonviolent approach but believed that the other side would react with deadly force. We also arranged for the independent Palestinian TV network, called Ma'an and consisting of nine local TV stations, to broadcast a subtitled version of the PBS documentary series *A Force More Powerful*. Our goal was to demonstrate the success of nonviolence in places such as India, South Africa, and the American civil rights movement. Also with Ma'an, we co-produced talk shows in which Palestinians discussed the documentaries.

The Ma'an Network

Ma'an soon became a major partner. Under the leadership of an extraordinary entrepreneur, Raed Othman, we co-produced many additional discussion shows, three multiple-episode soap opera series, and a regular TV news magazine. Also, we collaborated in developing local news shows, originating at member stations. We introduced Raed to international funders, including the Dutch government, which funded the Ma'an News Service, which has grown into Palestine's most-visited Web site.

Television Documentary

During our time in Jerusalem, John conceived, wrote, and produced a four-part TV documentary series portraying what an eventual Palestinian-Israeli peace settlement could look like. The core idea was to examine, in an even-handed way, the aspirations of both Israelis and Palestinians and to show that negotiated settlements are possible. Called *Shape of the Future*, it aired in 2005 and was the first-ever program broadcast simultaneously on

Israeli, Palestinian, and Arab satellite TV. Former President Jimmy Carter commented favorably on the project.

Common Ground Productions

Shape of the Future was one of many TV and radio series produced by Common Ground Productions (CGP), the media production division of Search for Common Ground. CGP was John's vision. From the beginning, he realized that if we were going to be successful in changing how the world deals with conflict, we would need to reach tens of millions of people through media. He was inspired in two different ways: First, in 1979, ABC-TV had turned his book, *The Search for the "Manchurian Candidate,"* into a documentary. John noticed that about 8 million viewers had watched it—which was about 7,970,000 more than had read it! Second, he was struck by a remark attributed to the late *New Yorker* writer A. J. Liebling, who said, "Freedom of the press is guaranteed only to those who own one."

In 1988, John produced a 10-part *Search for Common Ground* series, hosted by NPR's Scott Simon, which aired on over 100 U.S. public television stations. Additional TV series followed in Russia, Sri Lanka, Angola, and South Africa (which led to John meeting Susan).

Nevertheless, in many of the places we work, particularly in Africa, television is seen by only a very small part of the population. Radio is the principal means of communication, so we have made a retro move into radio— in Burundi, Angola, Liberia, Sierra Leone, Congo, Côte d'Ivoire, and Guinea (as well as in Indonesia, Ukraine, Palestine, and Nepal). In all, we have produced thousands of hours of TV drama, radio soap opera, documentaries, call-in shows, and music videos.

In recent years, a term has come into vogue that is now used to describe people like us: social entrepreneurs. Just as a Molière character declared that he had not realized he had been speaking prose his whole life, in our early years, we did not have this term to describe ourselves. Then in 2006, we were named as Skoll Foundation Fellows in Social Entrepreneurship, and we now have a plaque on the wall certifying our profession.

We have, however, developed our own principles of social entrepreneurship:

- **Start from vision:** Our vision is to transform the way the world deals with conflict—away from adversarial, win-lose approaches to non-adversarial, win-win solutions. Everything we do must be consistent— or at least not inconsistent—with our vision.
- **Be an applied visionary:** In order to change the world, it is necessary to break down complicated projects into finite pieces—and to make things happen. We strive to be incrementally transformational.

- **Be prepared to deal with high levels of complexity:** When you intervene in complex systems, such as international conflicts, you can be sure that there will be unexpected results.
- **"On s'engage; et puis on voit":** As Napoleon said, you become engaged, and then you see new possibilities. In our work, this translates into recognizing you cannot plan in advance the various steps to be followed or the results to be achieved.
- **Practice aikido:** In the Japanese martial art of aikido, when you are attacked, you do not try to reverse your assailant's energy flow by 180 degrees, as you would in boxing. You accept the attacker's energy, blend with it, and divert it by 10 or 20 degrees in order to make you both safe. In our work, this means accepting a conflict as it is—while transforming it one step at a time.
- **Make "yes-able" propositions.**
- **Enroll credible supporters:** Social entrepreneurs, who usually operate on the cutting edge, are often seen as marginal—or even crazy. Having prominent supporters can be very helpful.
- **Apply *fingerspitzengefühl*:** This is a German word meaning to have an intuitive sense of knowing—at the tip of your finger. Either you have it or you do not.
- **Demonstrate chutzpah:** Chutzpah is a Yiddish word for nerve or effrontery. In our view, a social entrepreneur needs this characteristic—without being overly pushy or culturally inappropriate.
- **Develop good metaphors and models:** Most people will not shift their attitudes and behaviors if they do not have a good idea of where they are headed. Metaphors and models—compelling stories—are crucial to the reframing process.
- **Have a high tolerance for ambiguity:** If you are uncomfortable with not knowing where you are going and cannot deal well with the unexpected, you probably will not be a successful social entrepreneur.
- **Find trimtab points:** On ships and airplanes, the trimtab, a tiny rudder at the leverage point, can turn the craft with a minimum of effort. Similarly, social entrepreneurs should find the places where their initiatives will have a large impact from a comparatively small input.
- **Be persistent.**

PUTTING IT ALL TOGETHER: THE CASE OF THE UNITED STATES AND IRAN

In 1996, we made a long-term commitment to improving Iranian-American relations, and we have stayed engaged ever since. Although space does not allow us to describe in detail our important work between the United States and Iran, we would like to mention that in February 1998, John and the U.S. national wrestling team flew to Tehran. The American wrestlers marched into the arena, proudly—but without chauvinism—carrying the American flag. The media beamed the scene around the world and contrasted it with the last time the American flag had appeared in Tehran, during the hostage crisis, when it had been burned on a daily basis. We helped to create a vivid, new global image.

When we returned home, President Clinton invited the wrestlers and John to the Oval Office. The president wanted to send a positive signal to Iran, so our visit was filmed and then transmitted to Iran by satellite. We had a vision that "wrestling diplomacy" would end in a breakthrough in relations, but for various reasons involving national egos and not paying enough attention to the needs of the other, the new day never dawned. It has been a heady ride, but we won't give up. About our efforts, a professor at Tehran University put it, "What [Search for Common Ground] has been doing has had a profound effect on the psyche of both the [Iranian] public and the elite. . . . No other activities have had such an effect."

In addition, here is what a key Iranian ambassador said in 2005 about our role in looking for constructive solutions in the nuclear domain:

> I believe you saved our negotiations. Your ideas kept the negotiations going. . . . If there is any outcome of the negotiations that is to the satisfaction of both sides, it will be a derivative of the discussions of this group—with conditions that will make it possible for both sides to accept.

In closing, we would like to describe our mission as it stands today: To transform the way the world deals with conflict: away from adversarial approaches, toward cooperative solutions. Although the world is overly polarized and violence is much too prevalent, those associated with Search remain essentially optimistic. Their view is that, on the whole, history is moving in positive directions. Although some of the conflicts currently being dealt with may seem intractable, there are successful examples of cooperative conflict resolution that can be looked to for inspiration—such as in South Africa, where an unjust system was transformed through negotiations and an inclusive peace process.

NOTE

1. Marks, 2000.

CHAPTER 18

SETTING THE STAGE FOR PEACE: PARTICIPATORY THEATER FOR CONFLICT TRANSFORMATION IN THE DEMOCRATIC REPUBLIC OF THE CONGO

Lena Slachmuijlder

Ongo Benga fled from his home in chaos and confusion. On the front line between opposing armies and local self-defense militias, no safe space remained for ordinary people. Either you joined the war, or you were at constant risk of death. Along with tens of thousands of compatriots, Ongo left behind his house and his land. He fled with the clothes on his back, leaving behind all other possessions. For 10 years he sat in a refugee camp, remembering the horror of the flight, and wondering if he would ever go back and live in peace again in his house, cultivating his land.

When Ongo came back home, he found another family living in his house. Anger welled up inside him, and he thought of whom he could rally around him to chase out these illegal occupants. He would "show them" that even though the residents often called the returnees "cowards," as though they had fled the war rather than fighting it, that he was no coward. "But thanks to the theater performances by Search for Common Ground, I realized that I should rather talk to the people living there. If I used violence, it would only create more problems. I found out that they had bought this land from the local authority. They didn't mean to do me any harm. And so we went together to this local authority to find a solution together. In the end, the local authority recognized what he did, and he gave me another land, where I now live peacefully with my family."

Onga's testimony of choosing dialogue rather than violence echoes many more from the eastern Democratic Republic of Congo. It is in this war-torn zone where Search for Common Ground (known as Centre Lokole locally) has been using the tool of participatory theater for conflict transformation to enable people in conflict to find nonviolent ways of addressing the conflicts in their lives. With support from the Swedish International Development Agency (SIDA) since 2005, Search for Common Ground has become a pioneer in the area of participatory theater for conflict transformation in the DRC.

CONFLICTS ABUNDANT

There is no short supply of conflicts in the zones where Search for Common Ground works. Ten years of war caused nearly 1 million Congolese to flee their homes to neighboring countries, while another 2.5 million became displaced within the DRC. Vast areas of land became abandoned as entire villages fled the violence between local and foreign armies, local self-defense militias, and the minefields they left in their wake.

Now, 10 years later, some of these Congolese are deciding to return home. After a decade in refugee camps in Tanzania, Zambia, Burundi, Rwanda, and Uganda, they return home to a myriad of conflicts. Often, their home was destroyed, and their land either taken over or sold in their absence. Nontangible conflicts are equally important, as issues such as jealousy toward returnees, minimally assisted by the UN High Commission for Refugees or non-governmental organizations, can lead to outright violence. Rumors, stereotypes, and the lack of trust between former neighbors aggravate the situation, complicating the reintegration process of the returnees. As this takes place in a return zone where there is a shortage of schools, water supplies, roads, and livelihood opportunities, the scramble for resources and opportunities pitches residents against returnees and foments a climate of mistrust that easily deteriorates into violence. As well, state-sponsored mechanisms for addressing conflict and injustice are nearly absent: rule of law is absent with impunity prevailing, the DRC does not yet have a professional police force or army, and judiciary mechanisms are corrupt, inadequate, and inaccessible.

UNIQUE, RELEVANT SPIN ON THEATER

It is in this context that Search for Common Ground has developed the tool of participatory theater for conflict transformation. Building on one of the DRC's best known "natural resources"—its creative talent—Search for Common Ground has crafted an appropriate theatrical tool that helps people to live together in peace.

The technique combines various theatrical techniques, including Forum Theater, Playback Theater, and Image Theater, with conflict transformation tools. Actors are trained how to analyze a conflict, how to determine the positions and interests of those in conflict, and what it means to transform a conflict. They are encouraged to analyze the common interests of those in conflict, as it is often by understanding the commonalities of the parties in conflict that one can imagine a way forward.

Using active listening, the first step of this technique is for the actors to enter into a community, talk to diverse members of the population, as well as local authorities, traditional chiefs, and members of the security forces, and begin to understand the conflict dynamics of this community. Based on what they learn, they come back as a group of actors, and share their information. Taking into account the most salient points, the actors begin to develop characters that can tell the stories of what they have heard, as well as a scenario broken up into distinct scenes that will structure the performance.

The actors then perform in public, presenting the reality of the community to the audience. At this point the reaction is already dramatic. "You have presented our lives in your performance," commented a person from Kazimia. "You were able to give us a mirror to look at our lives. I don't know how you could understand all that in such a short time." After the first presentation of the performance, which goes on for approximately 20 minutes, the actors will then bring the participatory techniques into play. They ask for initial comments on the performance, and then rewind the performance back to the beginning. Now, as each scene is replayed, the audience is invited to present alternative reactions by the characters on stage. The conductor, or joker, is one of the actors who plays this role to invite audience participation. *"Who can show us how the military commander could have acted when faced with the angry returnee?" "Who can come up and show us the way this returnee could have responded differently when accused of having stolen the food in her host family?"*

The word "show" is the key. Rather than a conference or seminar, the participatory theater technique enables people from the audience to literally act out a new future. They live through the change from violence to peace for a few short moments; their neighbors and friends watch intently as a new solution to the everyday conflicts is being acted out in front of their eyes. The performance, even with the integration of audience members, keeps its focus, its emotions, its intensity. The message of choosing peace comes through with local expression, from community members themselves, direct to the head and the heart of the audience.

SNOWBALLING IMPACT

Since 2005, Search for Common Ground's participatory theater troupes have performed more than 100 shows, reaching more than 150,000 people in South Kivu province alone. In other provinces, troupes that have been trained in this technique have used it around various conflicts, particularly related to the demobilization and reintegration of former combatants.

In the refugee return zones, Search works closely with local Mediation and Conciliation Committees, run by the local NGO Arche d'Alliance and supported by the UN High Commission for Refugees. "I can see progress since Search for Common Ground has started its work. People are coming to us so that we can help them to mediate, rather than using violence. People who had occupied others' land are finding solutions with the original owners, through dialogue," commented Mayuto Swedi, a member of one such committee in the Katanga village of South Kivu.

In some cases, the ability to mirror the conflicts in the community, and enable a safe space for people to interact and dialogue freely, awakens the conscience of local authorities and security forces. "It's only today that I have understood the problems of Kazimia," testified the military commander of Kazimia, a coastal village in South Kivu province. "You've showed us their problems, and the conflicts they have with the military. It's as though you are from here. I can see how we need to work more closely with the civilians to help them."

REPLICATING SUCCESS

Sharing the experience of this technique in the eastern DRC around the country, the region, and the world is one of Search for Common Ground's goals. With support from SIDA, Search for Common Ground has been able to have the resources to conduct ongoing training of its theater practitioners around the country, in theater techniques and conflict transformation.

Approximately 30 theater troupes have been trained in this technique in the DRC. In September 2006, Search organized a 9-day participatory theater for conflict transformation festival, bringing together actors from Rwanda, Burundi, and around the DRC. A training manual in English and French and an accompanying 30-minute training video was produced and launched in 2007. In 2007, Search for Common Ground's participatory theater work won the Ashoka-Changemaker "Entrepreneuring Peace" Award for "On-the-Ground Innovations for Managing Conflict," selected from 158 entries from 42 countries.

Day by day, performing artists around the DRC are being skilled to build peace. Alphonse Yi-Yegi explains: *"I am helping the population to find solutions to their problems, and to avoid using violence against each other. I didn't really think as an actor that I could really bring people together to understand each other. I am so happy to be doing a work that people appreciate so much that they apply it in their daily lives."*

Transforming these natural human resources into agents of social change is a giant step toward the consolidation of peace and restoration of social cohesion in the DRC. It enables communities to have a technique that enables open and safe dialogue and collective search for solutions without violence.

We are all born onto the stage of life without a rehearsal. Search for Common Ground's participatory theater for conflict transformation enables us to see ourselves in conflict and practice working out ways of responding without resorting to violence. That way, when such a situation actually arises, we'll be better prepared to respond to these conflicts with peace.

CHAPTER 19

THE PLEDGE OF RESISTANCE: LESSONS FROM A MOVEMENT OF SOLIDARITY AND NONVIOLENT DIRECT ACTION

Ken Butigan

Virtually every meaningful social transformation in the history of the United States has resulted from nonviolent movements that have mobilized grassroots "people power." Women's suffrage, the eight-hour work day, steps to curb racial segregation, environmental safeguards, stopping the Vietnam War, limiting nuclear testing—these and many other changes were not made by unprompted power-holders from on high. Instead, they were the direct consequence of broadly based networks of ordinary citizens systematically clamoring for a better world and translating that longing into embodied moral and political action.

As we enter the 21st century, we face widespread economic and social injustice. How are we to build the next great social movement to address these challenges? One important resource that we have at our disposal is the history of *past* progressive nonviolent movements. We need to tell the story of these movements, to analyze how they developed and were nurtured, to weigh their strengths and weaknesses, and to celebrate and defend their accomplishments. By embracing this history as our own, we often discover that the wheel we are so arduously trying to invent was crafted and deployed years before by our movement predecessors.

The Pledge of Resistance is a recent example of the power and possibilities of nonviolence in action. Rooted in the vision and techniques of Mohandas Gandhi and Martin Luther King Jr., the Pledge functioned as the direct-action arm of the U.S. Central America movement in the 1980s and the early 1990s. This chapter will explore the vision, strategy, and nonviolent activities of this initially religious-based grassroots effort that emerged to challenge U.S. intervention in Nicaragua and El Salvador and throughout the region. Then it will suggest a series of lessons that this movement may hold for us as we enter the new millennium.[1]

THE PLEDGE BEGINS

Beginning in the late 1970s, the U.S. Central America movement emerged to respond to U.S. intervention in Nicaragua, El Salvador, Guatemala, and Honduras. The U.S. government backed the Somoza dictatorship in Nicaragua and then launched a military and economic campaign against the revolutionary Sandinista government that came to power in 1979. It supported a death squad regime in El Salvador. Thousands were killed, including Archbishop Oscar Romero. U.S.-backed counter-insurgency campaigns were carried out in Guatemala, and U.S. bases in Honduras dominated that country.

With the inauguration of Ronald Reagan as president in 1981, the war on each of these fronts escalated. Yet with every increase in hostilities, people across the United States increased their opposition. Such widely diverse organizations and efforts as the Sanctuary movement, the Nicaragua Network, the Committee in Solidarity with the People of El Salvador (CISPES), and the Presbyterian Church USA struggled for an end to the bloodbath in Central America.

In the wake of the U.S. invasion of Grenada in 1983, the Pledge of Resistance was born. The Pledge was a commitment that people took to engage in nonviolent civil disobedience or legal protest if the U.S. government invaded Nicaragua or carried out escalations of military action throughout the region. Mobilized in part by *Sojourner* magazine (a progressive Christian periodical and community in Washington, D.C.), the Pledge was launched at a national meeting in Washington in October 1984 attended by representatives of many large peace and justice organizations, many of whom signed on to the project. Within months 42,000 people took the Pledge. By 1987, 100,000 women and men across the United States—organized in 400 local groups—had made this commitment to take nonviolent action. The civil disobedience pledge read:

If the United States invades, bombs, sends combat troops, or otherwise significantly escalates its intervention in Central America, I pledge to join with others to engage in acts of nonviolent civil disobedience as conscience leads me at U.S. federal facilities . . . I pledge to engage in nonviolent civil disobedience in order to prevent or halt the death and destruction which such U.S. military action causes the people of Central America.

There was a similar pledge for those committed to engaging in organized "legal protest."

THE ROOTS OF THE PLEDGE

Both the symbolic and tactical elements of the Pledge of Resistance were rooted in a wide variety of antecedents. Its fundamental impetus can be traced, as so many 20th-century experiments in nonviolent action can, to the vision and tireless activity of Gandhi.

Inheriting and consciously affirming Gandhi's philosophy of *Satyagraha*— a Sanskrit neologism meaning "Soul-Force" or "Truth-Force," this term literally also means "holding firmly to the truth" or "holding firmly to reality"—Pledge organizers called on people throughout the United States to publicly withdraw their consent from U.S. Central America policy. In the spirit of Gandhi, they invited people to demonstrate this opposition in a deeply nonviolent way, including:

- Dramatically vowing to take coordinated and disciplined action together at key moments.
- Willingly facing the consequences of nonviolent action, including potential jail sentences and bodily injury.
- Conducting themselves in a way that respects the sacredness of the opponent, even as they resist the opponent's actions.

The first organizers of the Pledge were deeply steeped in this Gandhian vision, as this definition of nonviolence from one of the movement's founders, Richard K. Taylor, indicates: "Nonviolence is a powerful, active way of working for human liberation that firmly and clearly resists and refuses to cooperate with evil and injustice, while attempting to show goodwill toward all and taking suffering on itself rather than inflicting suffering or violence on others."[2]

Like Gandhi, Pledge activists sought to create a condition in which all parties—the wider public as well as power-holders—would come to see both the truth and the untruth of U.S. actions in Central America and would then fashion a new and more just policy.

The vision and tactics of the Pledge were also rooted in and shaped by the Civil Rights Movement, the Anti-Vietnam War Movement, the Farm Workers Movement, the Anti-Nuclear Movement and the Women's Movement. Many of its organizers had actively participated in these and other nonviolent struggles. They brought to this new effort a conviction of the moral strength and political efficacy of civil disobedience. They drew on tools created in the crucible of these past efforts, including a *public commitment* (the Anti-Vietnam War Movement's "Pledge to Resist Illegitimate Government," as well as the Oxford Pledge of the 1930s, and even Gandhi's "pledge of resistance" that he describes in *Non-Violent Resistance*[3]), *organization* (a model using affinity groups and consensus process that grew out of the Women's Movement and the tradition of the Quakers), and *training* (echoing the Civil Rights Movement's nonviolence training program carried out by Jim Lawson of the Fellowship of Reconciliation for the Southern Christian Leadership Conference).

The Pledge of Resistance wove these and other elements developed by past efforts for change into a movement that sought to create a consensus for a new policy in Central America. Underlying these tactics and processes was a specific strategy to achieve the goal of a "just and lasting peace."

STRATEGY

The Pledge of Resistance was organized to meet two objectives. First, it sought to deter military action, including a full-scale invasion. To this end, it worked to create a climate in which tens of thousands of people would publicly withdraw their consent from this policy, thus eroding the political foundation for it. Second, it sought to create an "emergency response network" to react publicly and visibly to military escalations with nationally coordinated acts of civil disobedience, interfaith services, vigils, marches, and organized communication with policy makers (via phone calls, faxes, telegrams, etc.). These actions were designed to convey to the U.S. government and to the wider public the growing opposition to this policy and the deepening support for a political alternative.

HOW THE PLEDGE WAS ORGANIZED

In seeking to meet these goals, the Pledge was organized on the two mutually reinforcing tracks of national and local work. At a national level, a group of analysts regularly monitored the situation in Central America. When it determined that the United States was about to escalate militarily—or that it had already done so, often in a subtle and covert way—it alerted the

Pledge Signal Group, which then met and decided whether or not to recommend coordinated nonviolent action across the country in response to this increased war-making. (Members of the Signal Group were located throughout the nation; these discussions often took place on conference calls.) If the Pledge Signal Group decided to issue a call for action, this "signal" was routed through 10 regional coordinators to 400 local chapters. Primed ahead of time to respond when such a signal was received, local groups could mount nonviolent demonstrations and make phone calls to the U.S. State Department and Congress in a matter of hours or days. At particularly critical times—for example, when Ronald Reagan dispatched 1,800 troops to the Nicaragua-Honduras border in March 1988 or when six Jesuit priests and their two co-workers were assassinated in San Salvador in November 1989— plans for massive nonviolent civil disobedience were put into action.

Nationwide coordination, supported by a small national office and a national board consisting, at the beginning, of large organizations such as the American Friends Service Committee and, later, Pledge organizers from across the nation, helped sharpen the impact of this protest for government officials and the mainstream press. It also deepened local activists' awareness that they were part of a nationwide movement.

At the same time, this national impact—on the wider public or on the policy itself—was not possible without strong local chapters that, in the long run, proved to be the heart and soul of this movement. Whether they were large organizations (in San Francisco, Chicago, Boston, Los Angeles, St. Louis) or small groups (Fox Valley, IL; Olympia, WA; Burlington, VT; Richmond, VA; Juneau, AK), each found its own way to dramatize the crisis at hand and to urge the wider community to take a stand for a just and lasting peace in Central America.

Locally, groups held nonviolence trainings (in the early months of the Pledge, the San Francisco group sponsored five trainings *a week*), organized Pledge-signers into affinity groups, staged demonstrations to practice for "the emergency," and sat down with policy makers to explain what they were prepared to do if the United States escalated in the region. Moreover, they put in place the infrastructure to sustain their organizations: offices, mailing lists, phone trees, action logistics, media contacts, and contingency plans. They prepared for nonviolent action and, when the moments for action came, they generally carried it out with a sense of dedication and organization. In short, they had transformed unorganized concern into organized and empowered activity.

WHO TOOK PART?

The Pledge was begun by members of the progressive Christian community, and throughout the life cycle of this movement religious organizations continued to play an important role in organizing and deepening this effort. Over the years, however, the Pledge broadened its base, embracing secular organizations and individuals. Though not without its occasional tensions, this bridge-building was one of the reasons the Pledge was able to mount its large and broadly based campaigns and nonviolent actions. Others who played a key role were people who had participated in previous movements, including those listed above. Finally, a key percentage of those who took part included those who had lived in Central America or who had developed bonds with Central Americans, for example, in the Sanctuary Movement.

A common commitment spanning each of these communities was *accompaniment*. That is, the task was not to "lead" the people of Central America, but to walk side by side with them. This generation learned in a new way what labor organizers in the 1930s had known; the importance of solidarity. At the same time, the Pledge saw itself largely as an "anti-intervention" organization. Its job was to resist and transform U.S. foreign policy rather than to either dictate or uncritically support a particular program emerging from the region. The Pledge sought to end U.S. military intervention in Central America so that the people there could make their own choices about their lives and about the future direction of their societies.

KEY PHASES OF THE PLEDGE MOVEMENT

There is no room in this chapter for an exhaustive chronology of the Pledge's effort to transform U.S. policy in Central America. Here, however, is a broad overview of the movement's phases:

The Beginning: 1984–1985

Building on the growing depth and breadth of the larger Central America movement, the Pledge began with unexpected vigor. The San Francisco Pledge, for example, was launched with a "public pledge signing" on the steps of that city's federal building, where 700 people committed themselves to take nonviolent direct action to resist future U.S. intervention. Across the United States, people signed the pledge, took nonviolence trainings, and devised contingency plans—scenarios that pledge-signers would enact if the U.S. government escalated its military action in the region.

Pledge organizers, in spite of this prolonged burst of energy stretching over several months, felt increasingly hamstrung by one of the most significant elements of the Pledge itself: its focus on the future. In the days when the Pledge was first crafted, an invasion of Nicaragua seemed imminent. The power of the Pledge was centered in its proactive and reactive capabilities. However, in that first year, it was unclear which emergency, beyond an outright military landing force storming Nicaragua, would warrant the movement's activation and mobilization. It was a painful irony that, devised to respond to the suffering in Central America, the Pledge could be activated only when the "misery index" (as the authors of the Pentagon Papers, an account of another case of U.S. intervention, phrased such things) went up, and went up dramatically. This was acutely difficult for organizers who, almost daily, received reports of new atrocities in Nicaragua and El Salvador.

The dilemma was solved by making the movement's preparation a very active one, including the staging of a series of nonviolent demonstrations deemed "peace maneuvers" (a conscious counter to the Pentagon's almost continual war maneuvers in Honduras and off the coast of Nicaragua) that became giant role-plays and rehearsals for the future mobilization.

Finally, the Pledge was fully mobilized around two issues: the U.S. economic embargo that the government slapped on Nicaragua in May 1985; and U.S. military and economic aid to the U.S-trained contra rebels who were killing thousands of civilians in the Nicaraguan countryside to destabilize the Sandinista government.

In May 1985, Pledge groups across the United States protested the embargo on Nicaragua. Believing this to be a test by the administration to gauge whether or not the American people would countenance new escalations against Nicaragua, nearly 1,000 people allowed themselves to be arrested from coast to coast in Pledge-sponsored events at local federal buildings. An ongoing campaign to break the embargo was launched.

The Major Contra Aid Battles: 1985–1988

For nearly three years, the Pledge joined with many other organizations to oppose assistance to the Nicaraguan contras. The first major mobilization on this policy took place in June 1985, with relentless activity focused on it at key moments in the Congressional funding cycle in 1985, 1986, and 1987. This effort culminated in the final defeat of military aid on February 2, 1988—when the U.S. House of Representatives narrowly turned it down by two votes—and in skirmishes the following two years over increasingly smaller packages of so-called "humanitarian contra aid."

Iran-Contra and the Maddening Lull: 1987–1988

In November 1986, the White House, maneuvering to control what could have potentially sunk the Reagan presidency, revealed that operatives within the government had been carrying out an illegal covert policy of supplying weapons to the contras using profits from arms sales to Iran. The Iran-Contra scandal confirmed what activists had long suspected: that in spite of the Boland Amendment, which prohibited the United States from making war on Nicaragua, the United States was thoroughly behind this activity. It also confirmed something else: the importance of the Central America movement. Its role in demonstrating the unpopularity of U.S. Central America policy had forced the government to illegally carry on that war clandestinely. Had there been no visible opposition to the policy, there would have been no need for it to go underground.

Ironically, the enormous media exposure that focused on the Iran-Contra policy led many people in the Central America movement to draw the conclusion that this would spell the end of U.S. military adventurism in the region. Participation in nonviolent protests began to fall off. In response, the Pledge organized new campaigns focused on stateside military sites with connections to the war (for example, Fort Bragg in South Carolina; an Army Psychological Operations center in Arlington Heights, Illinois; the Concord Naval Weapons Station in Concord, California) and joined in a large demonstration at the Central Intelligence Agency (CIA) headquarters in Arlington, Virginia.

Furthermore, it flexed its capacity to respond virtually instantly to U.S. escalations. In March 1988, after the congressional defeat of military aid to the contras, President Reagan deployed 1,800 troops to Honduras in an apparent attempt to provoke a Nicaraguan border skirmish and a wider war. In response, the Pledge organized emergency demonstrations across the United States. For three days, these nonviolent protests were the lead story on the national television networks, and the president decided to bring the troops home sooner than previously announced.

El Salvador Redux: 1988–1990

Armed violence in El Salvador had first awakened North Americans to growing U.S. intervention in Central America, with the assassination in March 1980 of Archbishop Oscar Romero and, later that year, of four North American church women working in a barrio of San Salvador. Although tens of thousands of people were being killed in a country the size of the state of Massachusetts—with Salvadoran soldiers using U.S. weapons under the direction of U.S. advisors—the focus on the Central America movement largely shifted to Nicaragua as the Reagan administration escalated its rhetoric and action toward its government.

Seeking to redress this situation, the Pledge joined with CISPES to mount a national campaign focused on El Salvador in 1988. Seventy nonviolent actions were staged in October, culminating in a large nonviolent civil disobedience action at the Pentagon, where 240 people were arrested. From then on, the Pledge focused equally on El Salvador and Nicaragua.

During a military offensive launched by the FMLN (Salvadoran national liberation front) guerrillas in November 1989, the Salvadoran military assassinated six Jesuit priests, their housekeeper, and her daughter in San Salvador. Within 10 days, over 1,000 nonviolent demonstrations were held in response to these horrifying killings, with 2,440 people risking arrest (1,100 people succeeded in actually being arrested) by nonviolently occupying local congressional offices, military bases, and the White House.[4]

This prolonged response transformed U.S. policy in El Salvador. A conservative member of Congress from Texas, whose office had been jammed with concerned citizens engaging in civil disobedience following the killings, vowed never to vote another penny for the Salvadoran government, and his sentiment was shared by many on Capitol Hill who had heard from their constituencies that U.S. policy toward that country must end. The logjam was broken in Congress. This led to an accelerated peace process which, in turn, produced United Nations-sponsored accords ending the war.

Under any circumstances, these heinous crimes would quite likely have provoked outrage, especially among the U.S. Roman Catholic population. But because the Central America movement existed (a movement which, with nine years of experience, had the capacity to field almost instantaneous nonviolent protest in an organized and coherent way), it was able to magnify and dramatize the meaning of these deaths. Structures long in place, including communities of nonviolent direct action located in every part of the country, contributed to the process of transforming disbelief, anger, and grief into means for clarifying and changing U.S. policy in El Salvador.

The Beginning of the End: 1990–1993

On March 24, 1990, the 10th anniversary of the assassination of Oscar Romero, 15,000 people braved a cold and snowy day in Washington to march from the Capitol to the White House to pay respects to the archbishop, to call for an end to U.S. military presence in his war-torn country, and to mourn the Nicaraguan elections which, one month before, had turned the Sandinista Party out of office. As a Central American village was built on Pennsylvania Avenue, an enormous papier-mâché bust of Romero was stationed there, as if the prelate who staked his life on justice and peace was silently contemplating the source of much of the misery of his people— as if a decade later he was gently reminding the policy makers of this world that love is more powerful than death.

More than 620 people were arrested that day. It was the largest single civil disobedience action ever held protesting U.S. Central America policy. It was also the beginning of a new era. The Pledge would continue to maintain a national office for another three years, and would work on a variety of issues, including Haiti, the Gulf War, and a campaign seeking to close the U.S. School of the Americas (which trains soldiers from throughout Latin America). Its life cycle as a movement, however, had begun to change direction, with people beginning to put increasing attention on domestic issues of economic, racial, and sexual justice. The doors of the Pledge's national office closed shortly after a final national gathering of past and present Pledge organizers in August 1993 at a retreat center in rural Virginia.

EVALUATING THE PLEDGE

How are we to assess the impact of the U.S. Central America movement, and its nonviolent direct-action arm, the Pledge of Resistance?

From the outset, it is important to state what the Pledge did *not* accomplish. Most significantly, it did not prevent years of suffering and destruction. The U.S. government's so-called "low-intensity conflict" in Central America—a war relentlessly carried out year after year on political, economic, and military fronts—ground on through the 1980s. Many died and many others were the victims of unspeakable horrors, which they will carry with them all their days. There is sorrow and anguish in knowing that this movement permitted such suffering and destruction to continue as long as it did.

Nevertheless, it is fair to say that this carnage would have been much worse if the U.S. Central America movement had not existed. There are indications that the U.S. government was preparing to invade Nicaragua during this period, but was checked from doing so by a very vocal and active Central America peace movement at home.[5] The firepower that was vented against Panama and Iraq would likely have been used against the Nicaraguan people. If it is true that domestic opposition played a role in hampering these plans, the Pledge, with approximately 15,000 acts of nonviolent civil disobedience and innumerable other public activities, played a key role in strengthening this restraint. At the same time, it seems to have had an impact on other key dimensions of the war, including the March 1988 troop deployment to Honduras; the government's decision to launch a covert war that led to the Iran-Contra scandal; and policy shifts in the aftermath of the assassination of the Jesuits in El Salvador.

Besides these concrete ways that the movement may have directly modified U.S. policy, there are a number of lessons to learn from the history of the Pledge.

First, it is possible to build and sustain over the course of six to nine years a nonviolent social movement made up of people who are not the direct victims of the policy being challenged. Like other movements, the Pledge of Resistance required of

its participants a high level of motivation. It involved constructing and maintaining communities across the country that were prepared to take nonviolent direct action on an emergency basis. This necessitated nonviolence
training, regular meetings, and the creation of a culture that would sustain
such activity, including facing the spiritual and logistical rigors of serving jail
sentences for acts of nonviolent civil disobedience while attempting to carry
on with the demands of one's everyday life. Yet unlike other movements,
Pledge-signers were not the direct recipients of the wars in Central America;
even the Anti-Vietnam War Movement was motivated, in part, by concerns
about the draft. While this suggests an element of self-interest, the phenomenon of the Pledge of Resistance more accurately reflects a case of citizens
taking the responsibility to change what they perceive to be their government's onerous policies. The experience of the Pledge indicates that deeply
rooted movements for social change can be built on the basis of good citizenship and not simply on the grounds of self-interest.

*Second, it is possible to organize both emergency response activities and pro-
active, long-term campaigns and events.* The history of the Pledge of Resistance demonstrates that movements can institutionalize mechanisms that
give it flexibility in responding creatively to events as they occur. This was
rooted in the concept of the "pledge" itself, which represented a commitment to engage in future nonviolent action. Since this activity might take
place literally at a moment's notice, it required Pledge-signers to acquire
nonviolence training and to concoct response plans proactively. The life
cycle of the Pledge indicates that it was able to achieve an effective balance
between "emergency response actions" and fixed-date events. In retrospect,
it seems that these two basic approaches—"emergency alerts" with their
heightened adrenaline, and long-term campaigns and events with their stability and lead time—tended to reinforce and rejuvenate one another.

*Third, it is possible to craft a movement that holds in tension a series of bipolar
oppositions.* The Pledge was home to a variety of political and religious tendencies that were held in creative tension: religious symbols and political
ideology; centralization and local autonomy; emergency response and
planned actions; civil disobedience and legal protest; solidarity commitments and anti-intervention stances; provocative protest and nonviolent
discipline. One of the strengths of this experiment was its ability to draw
together a diversity of organizations and passions, welded together by the
conviction that nonviolent direct action was a key tool in creating the conditions for a social and political transformation of U.S. interventionary policies in Central America.

*Fourth, the Pledge, like many other movements, demonstrates that such phe-
nomena are spiritual journeys as much as political projects.* At bottom, the

Pledge of Resistance was a commitment to human persons: North Americans to accompany—but not re-colonize—Central Americans, and North Americans to work with one another to encourage U.S. society to live up to its stated values of democracy, justice, equality, fairness, and the right to life, liberty, and happiness. Like other spiritual journeys, there were moments of initiation, exhilaration, desolation, and the profound awareness of both the mystery of evil and, at the same time, *the mystery of good in the face of the mystery of evil.* These experiences were shared in a community that sustained itself by acting together and interpreting the meaning of that action for one another and for the larger world. In retrospect, it is possible to speak of the Pledge as a promise people took to become increasingly human together.

A social movement is a kind of language constructed to engender a conversation with its wider society about fundamental issues of injustice and violence. Standing in the traditions of Gandhi and King of active nonviolence, the Pledge of Resistance, as a part of the larger U.S. Central America movement, contributed to this conversation by using the most powerful symbols that human beings have at their disposal: their own vulnerable, achy, resilient, and beautiful bodies. The Pledge was an experiment in active nonviolence that offers both a vision and concrete tools for such future "embodied conversations."

NOTES

1. Smith, 1996.

2. Taylor, 1994.

3. Gandhi, 1951.

4. This is a report prepared by Ken Butigan quantifying hundreds of demonstrations in the wake of these assassinations. See Butigan, 1989.

5. In the first week of June 1985, the *New York Times* ran, on two successive days, stories detailing how every piece was in place for an invasion of Nicaragua. One anonymous source reported that such a military operation would be like "falling off a log." That summer, Pledge organizers were told by Central America policy analysts that they had indications from within the Reagan administration that its invasion plans had been stymied by widespread protests in the wake of the imposition of the embargo and in response to administration efforts to win congressional approval of a package of $37 million in so-called humanitarian aid for the contras.

CHAPTER 20

Money Cannot Be Eaten: Nonviolent Resistance in Struggles over Land and Economic Survival

Rev. José M. Tirado

Only after the last tree has been cut down. Only after the last river has been poisoned. Only after the last fish has been caught. Only then you will find that money cannot be eaten.

—Cree Indian Proverb

Land struggles and resistance to privatization of the commons by indigenous peoples, poor workers, and the disenfranchised, are not historical anomalies. To this day, conflicts over land and resources, and attempts to defend or reclaim the commons continue to be waged.[1] These include struggles in India, Thailand, Brazil, and Papua New Guinea. Within our own culture, Native American resistance to European colonization began shortly after the arrival of Columbus in 1492. Although innumerable treaties were signed with Native tribes ceding control of traditionally used land, these agreements were often constructed unethically, with deceptive intent and, in the end, were abrogated by the insatiable drive for more land for the ever-increasing numbers of European settlers. This struggle did not end until the near complete extinction of Native peoples and, more than 400 years later, the subjugation of their remainders onto reservations by the late 1800s, culminating with the massacre at Wounded Knee in 1890.[2]

African resistance to European colonization and its use of slave labor fared little better, with the forced removal of millions of people due to the slave trade, a period roughly contiguous with the Indian wars in North America, with slavery per se beginning in the 1660s.[3] By 1800, 10 to 15 million Africans were forcibly taken out of Africa as slaves to the Americas, and an incredible *50 million* were estimated lost during slavery's several hundred year era.[4] Yet during the period of American slavery before the Civil War, small-scale armed rebellions and conspiracies in 1800, 1811, 1822, and 1831 occurred that threatened the system.[5] Acts of resistance included "stealing property, sabotage and slowness, killing overseers and masters, burning down plantation buildings, running away."[6] Just how potentially threatening the situation was can be seen in an 1822 attempt that was foiled before it achieved its incredibly ambitious end: the burning down of Charlestown, South Carolina.[7] Thus, resistance was a constant given even then.

But it is not only indigenous resistance that exemplifies the struggle for land and its enormous economic benefits. Resistance carried out by free workers also has played an important role in the history of the West. Indentured servitude in the early history of the United States represented such an important part of the economy that, according to one historian, "Probably half the immigrants to Colonial America were indentured servants,"[8] many working someone else's land for periods of up to seven years. Because of poor working conditions and widespread maltreatment, desertion from their work, strikes, suicide, and occasional conspiracy to outright rebellion characterized much of the period in which indentured servitude existed.[9] This pattern of resistance, often violent, is quite common. The relationship of such resistance to historical issues of land and its control will follow.

RESISTING CONTROL OF THE COMMONS

For more than 9,000 years after the advent of agriculturally settled societies, the lands in which people were born, lived, and died was seen as *a commons* and remained unenclosed. Land, water, and other resources belonged to no one person or group, but to all, and all made use of its supply. According to Schock "for most of human's social history the Earth's resources were used cooperatively and sustainably."[10] He adds that, in fact, "the enclosure of the commons, that is, the taking of common land for private commercial use, can be traced back to 13th century England."[11] That is, despite a 1.5 *million* year presence of humanoids on Earth, the concept of private land ownership is barely *700* years old. Before then, most humans lived in a system whereby the "land and resources [were] held in common and collectively managed by a local community."[12]

During the mid-13th to 18th centuries in England, there were vigorous debates and civil conflicts over the appropriate nature and extent of property rights and resistance to the increasingly concentrated holdings of wealth and property into ever-dwindling numbers of people. By the mid-17th century, there was "open rebellion against enclosures in large areas of the countryside."[13] One group, calling themselves the Diggers, led by Gerrard Winstanley, made impassioned appeals against the idea of property rights:

[S]o long as . . . rulers call the land theirs, upholding this particular property of mine and thine, the common people shall never have their liberty.[14]

According to Winstanley, there would be no need to expropriate land from those who already had it because he believed that the poor should simply "settle the commons and waste land . . . and work them together . . . the Earth become a 'common treasury' providing plenty in freedom for all."[15] Even as late as the 18th century, parts of this system remained as,

[f]or the most part, people had adequate food, shelter, and clothing. . . . Most farming was done on open fields, with families holding the rights to farm small and scattered strips of land. Even those without such rights were able to provide for themselves from the common lands, which provided grazing for their animals, rabbits to eat, and wood for their fires.[16]

Although the Diggers movement was short-lived (vigorously opposed by large landowners, unsurprisingly), Winstanley's ideas were influential to other groups, most notably the anarchist traditions of Peter Kropotkin and those seeking to claim a lineage from the past to their own formalized libertarian ideals.[17] In the mid-18th century, there was also the rise of pacifistic Christian groups like the Russian Doukhobors and the Quakers. The latter group, in addition to their principled stands against the taking of oaths, and resistance to war, also lived lives close to the land in small communities with little or no mechanisms for rule by one group over another and a fairly egalitarian ethos pervading social life. Some referred to and modeled themselves after the earliest Christian communities, where property was "held in common" and "a general distribution as the need of each required" was the practice.[18]

NONVIOLENT RESISTANCE IN RETAINING THE LAND AND IN 20TH- CENTURY CONFLICTS

Others besides Quakers have recommended alternatives to violence, in addition to their cherishing of minimal interference in the free conduct of all members of society—Leo Tolstoy in Russia and Henry David Thoreau in the United States, for example. And in fact, "there is a more global tendency toward using methods of nonviolent action in struggles over land and resources."[19] Thus, there is a fairly long history of Western resistance to land expropriation and forced landlessness, by those who were displaced by laws made by and for ruling elites. These groups were motivated by different concerns, but all shared a deep attachment to the land they lived on and resisted passionately the encroaching system of private ownership of huge swaths of land previously understood as belonging to everyone. (We should note that even Amerindian resistance began nonviolently in the good faith signing of treaties and other accommodationist actions toward their new European-American neighbors.)

It is only when we come to the 20th century that we see a formal theory of nonviolence constructed and specially organized. Later, tactical use was made of nonviolent resistance in struggles over land, and with the economic plight of poor and disenfranchised workers. The first was most dramatically exemplified by the Gandhian *Satyagraha* campaigns for Indian independence and the second, the American Civil Rights struggle after World War II. These two struggles have come to represent the qualitative differences between violent and nonviolent resistance, highlighting the moral questions that arise when violent responses to violent actions are rejected and attempts are made to reconcile differences in a wholly different manner. Struggles over land resources utilizing nonviolent means became a later and most interesting innovation.

Mohandas K. Gandhi (1869 to 1948), an Indian lawyer, became known as the champion of nonviolent resistance and one of the main leaders in India's movement for independence. Gandhi's theories about nonviolence were formulated during his early years in South Africa and centered on the concept of *Satyagraha*, or roughly translated, "truth force." This word combines two Sanskrit words, *satya*, meaning "truth" and *agraha*, meaning "insisting on" or "obstinacy."[20] Satyagraha is not passive resistance as it has sometimes been referred to. (Although Gandhi himself used this phrase in South Africa, he soon gave it up for this neologism of his.) It is instead *a defiant opposition to perceived injustice through an unbending refusal to cooperate*, demonstrating the unethicality of the opponent's position, while stressing the human dignity of one's adversary in an attempt to convert them to one's side, and, if that is not possible, to at least persuade them of one's own humanity. All this was done in the spirit of friendship and common humanity to transform the entire relationship from one of opposition to mutual respect.

Satyagraha seeks to resolve conflict by persuading the adversary . . . that he—we—have much more to gain in harmony than in discord . . . it tries to transform the opponent [regarding them] as a participant in the search for a truthful solution to the conflict.[21] Gandhi came to believe that *passive resistance*, as nonviolent expressions of resistance were usually understood and referred to, was wholly inadequate. For Gandhi, the practitioner of Satyagraha (a *satyagrahi*) engaged in nothing passive at all, in fact, he spoke emphatically about the revolutionarily transformative power a satyagrahi must adhere to and how much more powerful a weapon it was in comparison to violent reaction. This is because the satyagrahi must actively overcome all anger and desire for retribution within their own heart, as well as desiring earnestly to assist the opponent to become one's friend and thus end the cycle of violence.

Gandhi's ideas had a widespread influence in the 20th century, the most well-known example being on the teachings and activities of the Rev. Dr. Martin Luther King Jr. Thrust into the spotlight during the Montgomery bus boycott of 1955 to 1956,[22] Dr. King combined compellingly prophetic speeches and a canny sense of pushing the political envelopes of his day. Thus, while he focused most directly on the struggle for equal civil rights for African Americans, he "[i]ncreasingly . . . came to see himself as advocate for the poor and the oppressed wherever they were."[23] His last major effort, a Poor People's March on Washington, D.C., sadly took place after he was assassinated, indicating what direction he was moving toward and perhaps, where establishment tolerance of his aims would advance no further.

The path of nonviolent resistance is therefore one with dual ideological parents, Eastern and Western. As pacifist David McReynolds put it, "Henry David Thoreau's essay on civil disobedience had been read by Tolstoy, Tolstoy had been read by Gandhi, and Gandhi had been read by Martin Luther King Jr."[24] These two great struggles concentrated on transforming the dominant political structures of their respective countries: independence for India, full equal rights for African Americans in the United States. There were significant social effects of both struggles as well. And while both newly independent Indians and African Americans received some economic benefits, it was the wider political freedom that was the driving spirit. It is an oversimplification of Gandhi's campaigns to suggest a secondary or tertiary place for economic objectives. He hoped satyagrahis would work for all levels of freedom and this included freedom from de facto serfdom for many. He helped form unions and advocated tirelessly for workers' rights. But the broader framework of his activities remained in seeking independence from Britain.

Likewise, in King's case, the struggles for political equality could not long be separated from economic justice: in his later years the Poor People's Campaign and with it, a passionate desire for the "radical redistribution of economic and political power," dominated his thinking.[25]

CURRENT NONVIOLENT RESISTANCE TO RECLAIM THE LAND

In light of the above historical analysis, what is the relationship between nonviolent resistance and present-day struggles over land? If there is just one emblematic and, for this writer, chillingly poignant example of the plight of farmers in the world's land struggles today, it is this single statistic: between 1997 and 2007, over 182,000 farmers committed suicide in India.[26] This figure becomes even more revealing when we look at it as one suicide every 32 minutes from 1997 to 2005, and since 2005, this figure is one *suicide every 30 minutes.*[27] This dramatic figure is still, however, a "huge underestimate"[28] because women farmers, who actually do most of the agricultural work and who are not included since land titles are rarely in their name, are simply regarded as "farmers' wives" and thus excluded from the total. We are looking at what one Indian journalist has described as "the largest sustained wave of such deaths in recorded history."[29] One group that addresses some of the underlying causes of farmers' woes is *Ekta Parishad*.

Begun in 1990, Ekta Parishad (United Forum) is "a Gandhian land rights organization concerned with issues that impact small farmers, landless rural workers, and adivasis (tribal peoples)."[30] They work to redress grievances brought about by the lack of implementation of land distribution laws, governmental agricultural policies, and unequal access of indigenous people to land resources. By organizing and creating solidarity among marginalized peoples, Ekta Parishad then conducts campaigns to put pressure on the government. One of their most important activities is the *yatra*, "an extended journey through the countryside that may last in duration from a few weeks to many months."[31] A "Declaration of Satyagraha" that announces the intents and goals of the trek precedes the yatra, a variant of the spiritual pilgrimages Hindus take. This document summarizes the problems that have prompted the action and the fact that ordinary means have failed to resolve it. A major rally then begins the campaign with speeches given as the main activists and supporters begin the journey. Making repeated stops in different villages, villagers are encouraged to present their grievances while petitions are signed and collected. Finally, reaching the prearranged destination, another rally is held where the thousands of collected petitions are presented to the authorities. Media are contacted along the way, acts of civil disobedience

are carried out, and the entire event may take many months, taking participants through hundreds of villages.[32] The yatra campaigns have had their
successes—in one yatra from 1999 to 2000 more than 150,000 plots of land
were given to landless peasants. They are also significant in part because
they are reviving a government co-opted Gandhian tradition as they focus
on "organizing and promoting the rights and citizenship of people who
have been the most marginalized in Indian society."[33]

In 1984, liberation theology-influenced progressive Catholics and Marxist
activists began the Landless Rural Workers Movement (MST) in Brazil.
Their concerns were the enormous disparities in land ownership and distribution that highlights Brazil as having "one of the highest levels of land inequality in the world."[34] For example, "1.6 percent of the landowners control
roughly half (46.8 percent) of the land."[35] Huge dam building projects, the
expulsion of people from the land for industrial farms, and the indebtedness
of small farmers (a major cause of Indian farmer suicides) caused the rates of
the landless and rural workers to increase beginning in the 1970s. For the
MST, occupying unused land is their strategy of choice. This land must fulfill
two conditions: it "must be classified as not in productive use and therefore
eligible for redistribution, and the land must be suitable for sustaining a community."[36] Once a particular piece of land is chosen, landless people are so-
licited and mobilized. After a series of meetings are conducted, a large
enough group is assembled to begin the next phase, which is the actual occupation. According to Schock,[37] anywhere from 30 to 300 families are typically
assembled to journey to and begin the process of first occupying, then living
together on, the land. This last phase is conducted in secret, the selection of
land, in particular, and when the land is settled, usually after dark, they must
have enough resources to actually begin the process of living on the land
since police may block access to the site once they are discovered to prevent
additional settlers from journeying there. The community then visibly posts
an MST flag, permanent housing is built, and the legal proceedings begin to
have the land transferred legally to the new community.

Although violence in opposing MST settlers occurs, "[t]he MST employs
nonviolent action as a pragmatic means for promoting agrarian reform.
Given the monopoly on violence held by landowners and the state, it would
be suicidal for the movement to respond with violence."[38] Occupations like
this—230,000 of them—have taken place totaling 20 million acres and land
for 350,000 families. In addition, "the MST encourages families to work the
land cooperatively and to engage in organic farming for local markets."[39] As
well, 20 percent of the land is separated out as an ecological reserve. The
MST tactics both enshrine nonviolence into their process and act as a coun-
terweight to industrial, export-oriented farming.

In Thailand, the Assembly of the Poor (*Samatcha khon chon*) is made of many different groups of people displaced by large dam building projects that have been erected to "increase industrialization, promote export-oriented agriculture, and to clear forests of people for commercial forestation." It is a "horizontal network of grassroots organizations and supporting NGOs [nongovernmental organizations]."[40] The main technique of the Assembly is creation of an "encampment" whereby a temporary "rural village" is constructed, near where the official government ministers live and work. Speeches, rallies, and publicity events are staged as the activists live on site for the duration of the encampment. In 1996, 12,000 activists conducted the first encampment that resulted in a stalemate when the government refused to agree to their part of an agreement originally struck. From January 24 to May 2, 1997, a second encampment took place when "25,000 people from 35 provinces . . . demanded that the government adhere to its promises and take action on their grievances."[41] This second encampment succeeded in forcing the government to give compensation to 7,000 families for the loss of their land, cancel one and review five other dam projects, and adopt resolutions ending evictions of forest people from their land.

Although the next government reneged on previous agreements, the subsequent elections in 2001 elected the more favorable government of Thaksin Shinawatra; the Assembly once again placed pressure on the government.[42] (It should be noted that a 2006 military coup, supported by urban and middle-class rebellions that opposed Assembly policies, forced Prime Minister Thaksin out of office. A subsequent encampment that ended in April 2009 raised hopes of his return to power.) Where the Assembly has proved successful is in its decentralized style, a diffuse leadership, and its flexible ability to address local issues. It also advocates local, rural control of resources and remains committed to empowering the country's landless and rural poor.

In Africa a similar pattern of resistance to economic deprivation and land issues exists. As women often bear the largest burdens in the raising of children while participating in the work of the family and community, they are most vulnerable to changes in land ownership and land use. In Nigeria, women have become activists fighting oppression for years. "Realizing the futility of violent action, women of the region have extensively employed nonviolent action."[43] There were many uprisings, including the 1929 Aba women's revolt, the 1984 Ogharefe women's uprising, the 1986 Ekpan women's uprising, and several other movements in the 1990s. In July 2002, a group of Ugborodo women occupied the ChevronTexaco oil platform in Escravos to protest the contamination of both native farmland and the Warri River due to pollution. Subsistence farming and fishing were the main livelihoods in the region and, as both were now ruined, the women felt they had little choice. In addition, oil industry jobs were often given to members of other communities, causing job losses among their husbands, fathers, and sons, adding to the deprivation. On July 8, 2002, more than 700 women took over the oil platform after having been denied a redress of their grievances that they had sought repeatedly. When the occupation began, they were only 150, but as the protest continued more than 2,000 women took part. They later took over the ChevronTexaco airstrip, docks, and stores and "disrupt[ed] the production of about 450,000 barrels of crude oil each day the protest lasted."[44] The company eventually relented and the action was seen as a success. Because these protests united women from various communities and ethnicities, it also had the effect of strengthening opposition to an oppression that had benefitted from their prior disunity.

In Papua New Guinea (PNG), 97 percent of the land in a vast area, which includes 800 different languages and dozens of different cultural and ethnic groups, is regarded as "customary tenured land," that is, land held as a commons. It is land whose "economic aspects" are "to ensure survival of the clan, traditionally through a high level of self-sufficiency," and its "economic aspects" are described as "land [that] is held, securely and in the long term, by the group for the benefit of the group."[45] One can see that in such a system, the people are placed above profit and such a system has reliable staying power in that the long term is considered more important than any short-term commercial gain. Yet it is also true that Papua New Guinea faces increasing pressures to adopt policies that turn the commons into more conventional land distribution. The very government report cited above openly describes the unique and beneficial aspects of the traditional system and declares that "[d]espite the length of tradition, the capitalist system is inexorably infiltrating the traditional economic and social mores of the country."[46] This pattern is apparently spreading. While

[a]lmost half of the people in the world are peasants and small farmers . . . [t]he violation of the rights of peasants have risen dramatically with the liberalization of agriculture that forced farmers to produce for export and to engage in industrial modes of production.[47]

Between international trade agreements such as General Agreements on Tariffs and Trade (GATT) and the North American Free Trade Agreement (NAFTA), and international institutions such as the International Monetary Fund (IMF) and World Bank, there has been a steadily increasing trend among nations to move toward export-oriented farming and land privatization. Because of this, "peasants have disappeared massively all over the world, and a handful of transnational corporations (TNCs) have taken over food production and trade."[48] According to Brecher and Costello, "[b]etween 1968 and 1982, lending by the World Bank increased sixfold. [As a result] huge dam, road, forestry, agriculture, and other development projects . . . displaced millions of poor people and destroyed environments and traditional lifeways for millions more."[49] Several examples of the complex, interrelated, and inexorably debilitating effects of newer development on traditional peoples prove instructive.

In India, for example, an increase in shrimp farming, used primarily for export to Western countries, has proven incredibly destructive. For example, the use of modern, industrial aquaculture to "grow" shrimp consumes inordinate amounts of fish meal. The fish meal itself is taken from destructive to native fish patterns by offshore trawling. In turn, development of "shrimp ponds" has resulted in the destruction of mangroves that have traditionally protected coasts against storm erosion and are a protective ecosystem for other forms of aquatic life.[50] In addition, pesticides and antibiotics that are used to increase production are fed back into the sea or nearby mangroves and farmlands in the form of waste material, adding an unhealthy pollution problem to already struggling areas. Lastly, sea water, used to maintain optimum salinity for the shrimp farms, ends up seeping into farm areas and the water table, causing pollution of drinking water sources, and increasing the salinity of the soil, destroying homes, and causing the displacement of families. All of this is a result of increased shrimp consumption needs in the West and the transformation of more traditional farm practices.[51]

Another example involves the substitution of farm products such as mustard seeds for soybeans, used primarily to make foodstuffs for the West, threatening traditional dietary regimens in India.[52] Adapting the Gandhian concept, a group of women began *Sarson Satyagraha*, or "mustard Satyagraha" to protest new laws protecting the genetically modified soybean industries that have displaced mustard oil production.[53]

BUILDING NONVIOLENT RESISTANCE BEYOND NATIONAL BORDERS

Although most of the world's small farmers and traditional land owners struggle against the overwhelming odds within their own countries, this is not a sustainable strategy for the longer perspective. Resistance to aspects of globalization that displace traditional farmers and those who have lived on community land cannot remain within national borders if it is to be ultimately effective. "An excessive focus on national sovereignty undermines efforts to impose better rules on the global economy" write Brecher and Costello[54] and their words are perhaps more true today than when they wrote them in 1994. Worldwide publicity adds focus and pressure to national states that acts both as a tempering factor in decision-making processes and as a potential recruitment device for allies. The work of Amnesty International is an example of such an organization, and the international attention given to save the Amazon rainforest an example of one issue that transcends national borders and is responsive to international pressure.

It should be noted that resistance patterns have also changed, not necessarily in the success of the struggles but that, "armed guerilla insurgencies . . . declined, while nonviolent strategies for successfully challenging regimes increased."[55] For example, in Bolivia, expansion of privatized ownership of resources, in this case water—and unbelievably enough, rainwater—led to a popular, nonviolent rebellion against the laws passed by the government and the Bechtel corporation. After about a dozen deaths and huge public demonstrations, the government relented, allowing villagers access to and ownership of water resources. But a mentality remains that unless private control (meaning private ownership by people who can profit over what was once free) is accepted, natural resources are "wasted." This is dramatically exemplified by what John Wolfensohn (head of the World Bank at that time) said on April 12, 2000, after the Cochabamba struggle ended, *"free or subsidized delivery of a public service like water leads to abuse of the resource . . . [t]he biggest problem with water is the waste of water through lack of charging"*[56] [emphasis added]. For the billions of people who have lived in natural environments for millennia, such a sentiment would be regarded as absurd and indefensible. Yet it apparently remains a continuing rationale for accumulating control over resources otherwise available freely since the dawn of recorded history.

The use of nonviolence is not limited to societies of democratic governance. Indeed, there are clear examples of its utility in nondemocracies such as Iran, Eastern Europe, and the Philippines.[57] However, there remains the often unspoken suspicion that a fully totalitarian society would not be an efficacious place to engage in such a struggle. Indeed, as Archbishop Desmond Tutu, himself a 1984 Nobel Laureate, said, "[N]onviolence requires that there is a minimum moral standard which is accepted by all the players, as it were, in the game."[58] However, even when movements begin in violent opposition to state or corporate land displacement, there is a tendency to move toward a nonviolent approach as these movements age. The Zapatista uprising in Mexico, inaugurated the day NAFTA took effect, is a clear example of this.

CONCLUSION

What each of the above conflicts shared was a determination to resist private encroachment on their lands, state-sponsored displacement, and rapacious economic dealings that split communities and neighboring peoples. In the face of often overwhelming odds, they resisted and, in many cases, won their struggles. But they shared something else as well: a commitment to nonviolent resistance that provided an effective means of gaining or enforcing a sense of community cohesiveness. In addition to the personal benefits this latter quality is crucial to the maintenance of group identity and a sense of shared community ties necessary for unified action in the future.

This writer makes no claims to fully understanding the enormous sacrifices involved in making decisions to turn to violence, or those painstakingly to avoid it, yet nor do I believe that violence must be abjured 100 percent of the time in all cases, everywhere. Even Gandhi said that, "He who cannot protect himself or his nearest and dearest or their honor by nonviolently facing death, may and ought to do so by violently dealing with the oppressor."[59] For example, the resistance of such movements as the Guatemalan URNG (national revolutionary unit) involved the reluctant taking up of arms to fight back against U.S.-supported terror campaigns that, had they not done so, most likely would have achieved a near genocidal result. As it is, hundreds of thousands were still killed and sickeningly brutalized by a people who "could comfortably have rubbed shoulders with Himmler and Mengele," as author and activist Noam Chomsky has written.[60] Whether they could have succeeded without a civil society in tune with the moral pressure a nonviolent approach might have engendered, is impossible to say. Without the choices they did make, however, many thousands more would most certainly have died.

By resisting nonviolently, others have avoided what conceivably could have become mass slaughters and the possibility of even more violence in a future of recrimination after recrimination. As one author put it, "when challengers employ armed violence in their conflicts with modern states, they tend to become trapped in an escalating spiral of violence that they are unlikely to win."[61] Thus, the use of nonviolence achieves the short-term goal of redressing the particular grievance, and a long-term goal of changing the terms of the struggle itself. It is this component that I regard as the most significant in the resistance to oppression, whether social, political, or economic.

That such resistance is confined to the more underdeveloped nations would belie a recent and inspiring example of the power of nonviolence in other settings. It should be noted that in a roughly contiguous period,[62] two examples of modern society's rebellion against their governments occurred. Between October 2008 and January 2009, as Athens exploded in a rage of violence over the killing of a young protestor, Iceland's economy collapsed. Both societies reacted to this new sense of anger in different ways. Both engaged in resistance to a government whose malfeasance they regarded as eroding its legitimacy. However, while the violence in Greece continued with no significant changes in governance, Icelanders completely withdrew their support and in an unprecedented result, brought about the resignation of their entire government. They then selected a caretaker government until new elections and voted into office a reformist coalition committed to the investigation and punishment of those responsible for Iceland's financial collapse. It may be concluded that even in developed countries there are occasions when, as the systems of greed and misconduct are revealed, the people will "rise in forceful nonviolence to wrest back control of their government."[63]

The struggles against the last remaining possession of a people, the very land they live on, against those who would cavalierly remove them from it replacing a millennia-old lifestyle with mining operations, strip malls, or factories, are emblematic of a world that faces its own moral ruin. No amount of material compensation can replace the contribution of an entire culture to the world's body of "living human documents" as Anton Boisen described individuals.[64] And by removing them from traditional homes and lifestyles, we contribute to the death of spirit, an often debilitating maladjustment to the new world they have been thrust into. For many of those resisting, dying to remain on their land is considered an appropriate sacrifice; killing, however, is not.

The notion of the commons, clearly understood by the indigenous peoples of the Third World resisting the growing privatization of nearly everything around them into commodities they are then forced to purchase, has also been known to those of us in the West. It forms an incredibly rich human heritage, one that has actually been the dominant one during our time on the planet. (One fascinating perspective divides the time humans have been on Earth into an equivalent 24-hour period, noting that agriculture has only been part of that for a pitiful five minutes—before then humans lived as hunter gatherers in small-knit communities.[65]) This heritage is part of the longest-lasting form of human organization, beginning with earliest humans down to the agricultural revolutions of the past 8,000 years or so. When Westerners rediscover their own egalitarian, communalistic past, they may see that native peoples who resist the expropriation of their own land are fighting the same fight our ancestors often fought. Although names such as the Diggers receive scarcely more than footnoted mention in most histories of Western civilization, they represent not only failed rebellions against inequalities in land ownership, but also a memory of a different path we used to take together. This is a path that is still taken by millions of people around the world who are shrinking in strength and numbers daily. Uniting these two strands, therefore, seems to me to be a noble and necessary effort.

If "[s]eparating people from food is violence," as one writer has said,[66] then the continuing displacement of people from their lands that have borne them for millennia represents a form of violence against which we may have no defense. It is a violence against our own common human heritage of mutual benefit and aid, as one philosopher described it.[67] In such a condition, the need of money for food would be considered an abominable anomaly. For as the Cree proverb quoted at the beginning of this chapter relates: money, unlike the produce of the Earth, cannot be eaten.

NOTES

1. Schock, 2007.
2. Brown, 1970.
3. Foner, 1947.
4. Zinn, 1980, 1995.
5. Ibid.
6. Ibid.
7. Ibid.
8. Foner, 1947.
9. Zinn, 1980, 1995.
10. Schock, 2007.
11. Ibid.
12. Ibid.
13. Ibid.
14. Woodcock, 1962.
15. Ibid.
16. Korten, 1995.
17. Woodcock, 1962.
18. *The New English Bible*, 1976.
19. Schock, 2007.
20. Flinders, 1978.
21. Ibid.
22. Buhle et al., 1990.
23. Harding, 1996.
24. McReynolds, 2009.
25. Harding, 1996.
26. Sainath, 2009.
27. Sainath, 2007.
28. Sainath, 2009.
29. Ibid.
30. Schock, 2007.
31. Ibid.
32. Ibid.
33. Ibid.
34. Ibid.
35. Brazil's Landless Workers Movement, 2009.
36. Schock, 2007.
37. Ibid.

38. Ibid.
39. Ibid.
40. Ibid.
41. Schock, 2005.
42. Schock, 2007.
43. George-Williams, 2006.
44. Ibid.
45. Armitage, 2009.
46. Ibid.
47. La Via Campesina, 2009.
48. Ibid.
49. Brecher and Costello, 1994.
50. Shiva, 2000.
51. Ibid.
52. Ibid.
53. Ibid.
54. Brecher and Costello, 1994.
55. Schock, 2005.
56. Andino, 2009.
57. Schock, 2005.
58. Ingram, 1990.
59. Merton, 1965.
60. Harbury, 1994.
61. Schock, 2005.
62. Tirado, 2009.
63. Pilisuk, 2009.
64. Hemenway, 1996.
65. Pilisuk and Rountree, 2008.
66. Ibid.
67. Woodcock, 1962.

CHAPTER 21

SEARCHING FOR DEVELOPMENT WITH HUMAN DIGNITY IN GUATEMALA

Jennifer Achord Rountree

I am riding in the back of a small pickup truck, which serves as taxi service over the mountain from San Lucas Toliman to the neighboring Maya village of Atitlan in the highlands of Guatemala. This rural route takes us through the heart of the coffee-growing region. Along the roadside gather men, women, and children with bags full of the day's pickings. I see a young boy, barefoot, carrying a large bag of coffee on his back. The 125-pound bag surely weighs twice as much as he does. It is an image I will not forget.

THE MAYA

Along with the Olmec, Aztec, and Toltec cultures, the ancient Maya were one of the original Mesoamerican civilizations. For more than 3,000 years they flourished throughout the Yucatan peninsula, Guatemala, and the northern regions of El Salvador and Honduras, and developed advanced methods of engineering, astronomy, mathematics, and stone carving that far surpassed their contemporaries in Europe. An elaborate writing system featured the Maya Long Count Calendar, which the modern Maya observe to this day. The resilience and pride of the present-day Maya, comprised of 21 distinct ethnic groups, is evident in the activism they have shown toward rightfully reclaiming their communal and familial lands, the proliferation of their languages, the celebration of their cultural and spiritual traditions, and in demanding social justice in the face of impunity.

Since colonial times, the Maya have retained their identity as indigenous peoples and have resisted assimilation to ladino culture although they have suffered tremendous exploitation and oppression. Beginning with the colonization of the Spanish, and exacerbated by the production of coffee in the late 19th century, the Maya have been enslaved and exploited for their labor and dispossessed of their communal lands. During the 36-year civil war, the Guatemalan government's policy of genocide toward the Maya resulted in more than 200,000 deaths and millions displaced. During a short intense period of violence in the 1980s, over 400 highland villages were burned to the ground. The Pan-Maya movement that emerged from the Peace Accords in 1996 represented a first step toward a formal recognition of the sovereignty of the Maya people and the gratification of basic human rights; however, the realization of social and economic justice has mostly been thwarted by a corrupt government and a weak judicial system and undermined by foreign interests.

In 2005, the Guatemalan Congress passed the Dominican Republic-Central America Free Trade Agreement (DR-CAFTA) in spite of massive public protest and without a national referendum.[1] DR-CAFTA has effectively eliminated protective tariffs and trade barriers, making 80 percent of U. S. imports duty-free. Since its inception in 2006, it has had detrimental effects in a country where agriculture is the foundation of the economy—nearly one-fourth of its gross domestic product (GDP), two-thirds of its exports, and half of the country's employment.[2] Nearly 70 percent of the people in Guatemala live in poverty; chronic malnutrition affects more than half of all children under 5 years of age, the highest level of malnutrition in Latin America.[3] Centuries of resource extraction and industrial agriculture have ravaged local ecosystems, making them more susceptible to hurricanes and other natural disasters. In October 2005, Hurricane Stan set off flash floods and mudslides that destroyed entire villages around Lake Atitlan in the Guatemalan highlands.

The experience of sociopolitical, economic, and environmental devastation is not unique to the Maya of Guatemala. Land-based populations around the globe are now being plunged into deeper levels of poverty due to the decrease in arable lands through the globalized system of agricultural production and distribution and environmental devastation. Since the United Nations defined the term *Least Developed Countries* (LDCs) in the 1970s to signify severe deprivation of economic and human resources, the number of LDCs has more than doubled, from 24 to 50.[4] LDCs are identified by the criteria of low income (based on a 3-year average of gross national income per capita at or below $900), weak human assets or resources (indicators such as health, nutrition, education, and adult literacy), and economic vulnerabilities (including a dependence on imports and a narrow range of exports and susceptibility to exogenous market conditions).

For the men and women with whom I lived and worked in San Lucas Tolimán, Guatemala, development is about more than increasing their standard of living. The mission statement for Association Ija'tz, a community organization comprised of 62 Maya families, speaks to their desire "to promote democratic participation in the communities of the municipality of San Lucas Tolimán, to foster sustainable development, and to work against the destruction of the ecosystem of Lake Atitlan."[5] Their integrated development is one that reclaims their identities as Maya people, their approach being grounded in the "principles of the Maya cosmovision."[6] Through organic coffee production, agroecological interventions, and other sustainable projects, Ija'tz seeks to bring economic, ecological, and relational well-being to their community.

FUNDAMENTAL HUMAN NEEDS, FREEDOM, AND COMMUNITY DEVELOPMENT

Economic development alone is not the answer in community development. On a national scale, Fisher and Hendrickson[7] point out that Guatemala is not a poor country; it consistently shows more economic growth than neighboring Honduras, Nicaragua, and El Salvador. Yet 87 percent of the population lives in poverty, and 67 percent in extreme poverty, which is defined by the United Nations Development Program as income that is below what is needed for minimal subsistence and caloric intake. Rather, "the problem of poverty in Guatemala is not so much one of wealth as of inequality."[8]

It is for lack of substantive freedoms for most Guatemalans—particularly the 5 million indigenous Mayans—that so many live in poverty. Centuries of colonization were followed by decades of authoritarian regimes, a 36-year civil war, and a slow-to-develop post-war democratic process have severely limited civil rights, access to health care, and opportunities for education for the majority of Guatemalan people.

Ija'tz (which means *seed* in Kaqchikel) began as a seed-saving cooperative and restorative project to redress the local ecology. A few years later, the organization grew into an organic coffee cooperative, a likely economic strategy for development in a highland town that has revolved around the coffee industry for more than a century. However, the Ija'tz community effectively split over the issue of coffee production; several core Ija'tz members left the group to form another community association (Instituto Mesoamericana de Permacultura, or IMAP) to maintain the original focus on restorative agriculture and native seed promulgation. This conflict over economic development versus ecological and cultural restoration represents different understandings of what constitutes freedom and basic (or immediate) and long-term needs.

Coffee production, in Guatemala's history, has been associated with colonialism and foreign development. IMAP's rejection of coffee production as a means of economic development underscores their desire to separate themselves from the legacy of colonialism and free themselves of dependence on global markets. IMAP focuses on restorative agriculture as a means of ecological and cultural revitalization. They emphasize education—training local and nonlocal farmers and groups, women's groups, school children, and foreign students—in permaculture methods, integrating Maya stories along the way. IMAP does not directly promote a specific program for economic development; improved subsistence agriculture is emphasized rather than market production.

At that time the Ija'tz community made the decision to implement the coffee program, most community members were already working as coffee growers and harvesters. Their decision to produce coffee through Association Ija'tz was less about creating a new economic development scheme, and more about coming together as a community, pooling their resources, and creating measures to protect themselves both economically (through the cooperative system and fair trade) and ecologically (by growing organically).

While the coffee program is now the predominant program, Ija'tz has also initiated various health programs in recent years; one program utilizes banana trees to treat disease-carrying grey water, another builds medicinal plant spirals featuring local medicinal plants in the homes of community members and offers workshops on Kaqchikel herbal medicine. A rabbit-breeding program has succeeded in providing new opportunities for income as well as a reliable food source for many San Lucas families.

Ija'tz pursued organic practices for their coffee program after the realization that much of the agrochemical run-off was going into the lake, where several native species of fish and birds have already perished, and where men catch fish to bring to market, and women and young girls bathe, wash their clothes, and collect water for cooking. One of the community's health clinics noted that many people had complained of chronic headaches, and stomach and respiratory problems.[9] When I was there, however, the community was in the process of changing their organic certification to a less rigorous "sustainable" certification, in response to the declining price and demand for organic coffee in combination with declining yields. This decision was the outcome of many months of research and dialogue between community members. Their deliberation emphasizes their attempt to balance economic development with their mission of ecological and human health. The families of

Ija'tz seek to improve their lives through increasing their incomes, but also through protecting and promoting human and ecological health through new (and old) agroecological practices.

PROCESS OF CHANGE AND COMMUNITY DEVELOPMENT

For the Maya and many other land-based peoples, positive change requires the recognition of cultural sovereignty and the peoples' interdependence with the land. The work of two prominent organizations, the Comité de Unidad Campesina and ADIVIMA (the Association for the Integral Development of the Victims of Violence in Maya Achí Verapaz), is noted.

Comité de Unidad Campesina

In Guatemala, community development began during the civil war. The 36-year war began with the U.S.-sponsored overthrow of the democratically elected Arbenz. The overthrow of nationalist president Arbenz occurred in response to his agrarian reform program, which claimed over 550,000 acres of land owned by the U. S.-owned United Fruit Company and redistributed land to more than 100,000 peasants. In the spirit of democracy and freedom from communism, the United States trained and funded the Guatemalan military in a counterinsurgency campaign—a scorched Earth campaign that did not discriminate between guerillas and the indigenous campesinos. By the end of the war, more than 200,000 people were killed and millions displaced.

In the 1970s, liberation theology sparked a popular movement that took several organizational forms. In the highlands, catechists and missionaries organized grassroots "Christian Base Communities" that began to form a network linking different parts of the highlands. Catholic Action leaders organized peasant leagues. By the late 1970s, these groups merged into a national peasant organization called the Comité de Unidad Campesina (CUC). The CUC was formed in 1978 with 20,000 members, becoming the first official organization of peasants and landless Guatemalans. For the next 20 years, the CUC worked for rights to land tenure and organized labor. The group has survived in spite of violent opposition, including the 1980 peaceful occupation of the Spanish Embassy in Guatemala City, when police forces locked the building and burned the activists alive. At the end of the civil war in 1996, the CUC played a critical role in the development of agrarian reform for the Peace Accord. Their most radical proposal was to redefine land ownership and use on the basis of the social function of property, thus directly challenging the government's definition of land ownership since the fall of

Arbenz's government in 1954. Agrarian reform—as well as the economic and social reforms put forward in the Peace Accords—have largely been unrealized; with the 2007 democratic election of Álvaro Colom, it was hoped that more progress would be made toward these major reforms. Land reform continues to be a major issue to this day: an estimated 2 percent of the population own 72 percent of agricultural land.[10] This distribution of land tenure is exactly the same as existed in the country before Arbenz's reforms in the 1940s.

The CUC continues to be active, not only in pushing for land reform, but for protecting and advocating for indigenous communities who continue to be threatened by elite interests—including the interests of the United Fruit Company's successor, Del Monte, which since the 1970s has continued to buy up Guatemalan land. Bandegua, the largest banana exporter in Guatemala (a subsidiary of Del Monte), has a long history of the illegal eviction of Maya communities and is responsible for the killing and intimidation of CUC members representing peasant rights to land and labor.[11]

More recently, the development of the biofuels industry has negatively impacted the Maya Keqchi communities of Alta Verapaz. In July 2008, peasants attempted to rebuild and replant their rightful land in an area known as Finca Los Recuerdos, a region that in years past had become overrun by Ingenio Guadelupe, a biofuel company, which began cutting down trees and replanting sugar cane. The peasants were killed by the company's paramilitary security forces; several CUC members were kidnapped or killed when they demanded the prosecution of those responsible and the clarification of the land title situation.[12]

The extreme hardship that the CUC has endured, however, has not been without success. A community of 135 families in the village of Tzan Siwan, in the state of El Quiche, is celebrating the one year anniversary of the legal communal entitlement to their land. More than a century ago, their land was illegally sold to the wealthy Botrán family, who forced the villagers to work on their farm and to lease their own land. In 1990, the community began their struggle to regain their land. Refusing to pay their lease, and suffering threats of death and displacement in return, the community saw the need to organize with other farmers and to defend themselves. In 2002, community members, now CUC participants, began the process of seeking legal entitlement.[13]

ADIVIMA

ADIVIMA (Asociación para el Desarrollo Integral de las Víctimas de la Violencia en las Verapaces, Maya Achí/Association for the Integral

Development of the Victims of Violence in Maya Achí Verapaz) is a grass-roots community development organization spearheaded by three survivors of the massacres of Maya Achí communities of Río Negro in the early 1980s, when paramilitary forces killed hundreds and displaced thousands during the Guatemalan government's construction of the Chixoy hydroelectric dam, an economic development program sponsored by the World Bank and Inter-American Development Bank. Encouraged by the potential of the Peace Accords, ADIVIMA quickly grew to 800 members who filed requests for exhumations, pressed charges against war criminals, and erected monuments for those who lost their lives.[14]

ADIVIMA has partnered with a number of social justice organizations to strengthen their efforts and to bring their message of peace and justice to an international audience. In 1999, Rights Action, a nongovernmental organiza-tion (NGO) based in Washington, D.C., assisted in the creation of a legal clinic to facilitate members' legal issues, including pressing criminal charges, collecting oral testimony, and organizing a resettlement plan. The Advocacy Project, also based in Washington, has helped bring ADIVIMA's experience and needs to an international audience.

In addition to fighting for human rights, ADIVIMA has also created eco-nomic development projects that utilize the craftsmanship of its participants, including a carpentry shop that builds and sells furniture and an agricultural cooperative that distributes supplies to communities throughout the region. The organization is also investing in its future through the education of its youth. In 2007, the organization initiated a scholarship program for girls, who are less likely than male children to attend school. ADIVIMA's hope for these students is that they will acquire professional skills and return to help their communities.

Many of the female participants, as survivors of the massacres of Río Negro, are in the process of forming a women's weaving cooperative. The cooperative is intended not only as a means of economic development but also as an integral part of the healing process. The women are holding weaving workshops in resettlement communities and in the process are tell-ing their personal stories, honoring their lost loved ones, and reviving the lost art of Maya weaving. A commemorative quilt was completed in the summer of 2008, nearly 30 years after the massacres at Río Negro. The quilt is currently being presented in ADIVIMA's call for reparations. In 2008, Guatemalan president Alvaro Colom signed a breakthrough accord with members of ADIVIMA who lost family members. In this accord, the government acknowledges for the first time that "damages and violations" occurred during the dam's construction and accepts the obligation to offer reparations.[15]

CONSCIENTIZACIÓN AND COMMUNITY DEVELOPMENT

Coffee and Conscientización

Several core members of Ija'tz left the association when the community voted to initiate a coffee cooperative. The majority of Ija'tz' members were already involved in the growing and harvesting of coffee, in a town that has centered on coffee production since the early 20th century. The members who left Ija'tz formed another organization, IMAP, which aims to follow the original vision of ecological and cultural revitalization through agroecological methods.

The split over the coffee issue is a significant one; at the heart of the matter is the history of coffee production in San Lucas Tolimán, and the Guatemala highlands in general. The refusal to support coffee production is a rejection of the legacy of oppression.

Lacking the mineral resources of Mexico or the Andes, the Spanish colonists quickly came to concentrate on agricultural resources for export, including cacao, cotton, indigo, tobacco, and cochineal dye, all of which were produced by the enforced wage labor of the Maya population. The end of Spanish colonial rule was the beginning of a succession of republican dictatorships that opened the doors to foreign development, forging new alliances with British, German, and North American interests. Their economic program stressed the promotion of exports—particularly agricultural exports.

By 1870, coffee was Guatemala's leading export. To meet the labor-intensive demands of coffee production, the state formalized and extended labor laws. As McCreery explains, coffee production did not invent forced wage labor in Guatemala, but "the onset of large-scale coffee production prompted the codification of coercive systems, increased the level and efficiency of these extractions, and generalized forced wage labor to regions of the country and parts of the indigenous population that previously had been little affected."[16] Coffee also had an increasingly detrimental effect on land tenure. Coffee production, which required far larger tracts of land than previous export crops and favored the highland mountain climates of the indigenous population, had a tremendous impact on land ownership. By the mid-1920s, only 7.3 percent of the Guatemalan people owned Guatemalan land.[17]

At the turn of 20th century, San Lucas had a communal land tenure system; there were no land titles, but each family had publicly recognized rights over certain plots of land that could be passed on to heirs but could not be sold. It was during this period that indigenous farmers began to experiment with the production of coffee. The sharp decrease in the corn supply and other subsistence crops provoked a major conflict between subsistence farmers and coffee growers. This conflict was eventually settled by the municipal government, which was still under the traditional control of cofradia, which forbade the production of coffee on communal lands. The coffee growers looked for support outside the municipal government, and returned with a lawyer and an engineer. A compromise was made: San Lucas was re-designed on the colonial grid-pattern; titles to traditional family lands were drawn; and a section of the town's land was set aside for milpa (corn, beans, squash) agriculture only.[18]

By the mid-1970s, 10 fincas existed in the municipality of San Lucas. Like most fincas throughout the country, these were primarily owned by wealthy landowners and managed by an administrator in charge of directing the in-digenous people who lived on the property and constituted the labor force. Many of these workers were from surrounding municipalities who came to San Lucas for work in the fincas. To this day, the economy of San Lucas depends of the exportation of coffee; the land continues to be dominated by a handful of large coffee fincas, with smatterings of private and cooperatively held lands for coffee production as well as small parcels for subsistence agriculture.

The conflict between subsistence farming and coffee production in San Lucas Tolimán has been ongoing for nearly a century. IMAP's rejection of coffee production represents a conscious rejection of the legacy of oppression and dependence on a foreign market. IMAP's emphasis on the subsistence-production of native crops and other plants aims to improve ecological health and promote Maya cultural identity.

For the members of Associacion Ija'tz, however, conscious action regard-ing the legacy of coffee and other nontraditional agriculture in Guatemala does not lead them to the rejection of coffee, but to define and control their own production. Ija'tz members explain that they are insulated from the worst effects of the foreign marketplace through the protections of Fair Trade and other economic and social opportunities provided through their cooperative system. The production of coffee allows them to live year-round to work their land (and the communal land Ija'tz shares)—and not be forced to migrate to the coast to work in the fincas of industrialized agriculture or to the city to work in the maquiladoras (not to mention the United States). Ija'tz members take pride in their sustainable coffee production, and the equipment they have purchased to depulp their own coffee. At the time I was there, they were also researching how to sidestep local coffee coyotes and become direct traders of their own coffee.

Researchers Fisher and Benson show how Maya farmers have turned to the production of nontraditional agriculture through a desire to improve their lives not only in economic terms but also along cultural and moral lines, including community organization and political mobilization, and values associated with family life.[19] In spite of an often declining market price for broccoli, Maya farmers report that broccoli cultivation (a popular crop of "contract" agriculture) has improved their quality of life. Fisher and Benson believe this response is due to farmers' desires to control their means of production and to stay home with their families to work their own land, and to contribute and engage in community and political organizations in addition to their desires to increase their income.

LINKING INNER AND OUTER AWARENESS AND HEALING: ORAL TESTIMONY AND NARRATIVE METHODS

The Commission for Historical Clarification (CEH) describes the nature and brutality of the violence waged by the military against Maya civilians:

> The massacres, scorched Earth operations, forced disappearances and executions of Maya authorities, leaders, and spiritual guides, were not only an attempt to destroy the social base of the guerillas, but above all, to destroy the cultural values that ensured cohesion and collective action in Maya communities.[20]

In addition to the CEH document referenced above, *Guatemala: Never Again*, was based on more than 5,000 testimonies of victims and witnesses of political violence.[21] The study analyzed the collective impact of these many years of violence on the emotional climate and cohesion in Maya communities, showing how the complete lack of institutional structures to protect victims and particularly state-sanctioned violence intensifies the impact of violence on the emotional climate and collective behavior.[22] The group massacres and the public torture of victims in Maya communities by the Guatemalan military were designed to rupture interpersonal relations, fracture communities, and instill a state of fear and terror.

The climate of fear and silence resonates through village communities to this day. Victims and perpetrators exist side by side. As a result of the civil patrols, a method of psychological warfare instituted by the military in which civilians were coerced into policing positions, neighbors and close family members are confronted every day with painful memories as both victims and transgressors. Fear of retaliation prohibits discussion of the past and the expression of past and present suffering.

Testimonio

Throughout Latin America, *testimonio*, urgent narrative accounts of political and social violence, has been an influential medium in bringing awareness of such injustices to international audiences. Nora Strejilevich in Argentina, María Teresa Tula in El Salvador, and particularly Rigoberta Menchú in Guatemala have shared their personal experiences of suffering and emancipation and have spoken out against oppressive forces, becoming international advocates for social justice.

The original Spanish title of Menchú's testimony, *My Name is Rigoberta Menchú and This Is How My Consciousness Was Born* has been translated into 12 languages and has received numerous international awards.[23] The well-known English translation is entitled *I, Rigoberta Menchú, an Indian Woman in Guatemala*.[24] In her testimony, Menchú describes her childhood spent migrating to the coffee fincas on the Pacific coast with her family to work. As a teenager she became influenced by the liberation theology movement within the Catholic Church, becoming active in a burgeoning women's movement and later, in the newly formed Committee for Peasant Unity, the Comité de Unidad Campesina (CUC). Her father and brother were also active members of the CUC; her father died in the famous fire at the Spanish Embassy in 1980, when the Guatemalan military locked CUC activists inside the building and set it on fire. Her brother was later tortured and killed. Within a few years, Menchú lost her parents, two brothers, her sister-in-law, and three nieces and nephews to military forces.

After the death of her family, Menchú became more involved with the CUC, organizing for workers' rights in the plantations of the Pacific coast where she had worked as a child. She also became active in educating the Maya in resistance to massive military oppression. In 1981, Menchú was forced to flee to Mexico, and then to Europe, where she told her story to Elisabeth Burgos-Debray, an anthropologist, who arranged the transcripts. Menchú's testimony brought immediate international attention to the Guatemalan military's clandestine operation and the plight of the Maya.

In 1992, Menchú received the Nobel Peace Prize for her work for social justice and human rights for the Maya. She has lobbied the United Nations to recognize the struggle of indigenous peoples facing discrimination, displacement, and genocide, has served as ambassador of UNESCO, and has created the Rigoberta Menchú Tum Foundation to assist indigenous refugees in their return to Guatemala. In 2004 under the Berger Administration, Menchú served as Goodwill Ambassador to the Peace Accords. Through this appointment, she urged the Spanish court to examine cases of genocide, which has resulted in international warrants for several individuals involved in the abuses of the 1970s and 1980s, including General Ríos Montt.

PARTICIPATORY ACTION RESEARCH: ORAL TESTIMONY AND COMMUNITY NARRATIVE

A number of projects in Guatemala are healing the deep psychological wounds of war through therapies that engage the entire community, combined with civic and political action. These participatory interventions seek to help communities recover by sharing their experiences through oral testimony, creating the opportunity for victims to reclaim their voice and experience and contribute to the collective process of speaking out against impunity. As these examples will show, individual testimony is integrated with methods aimed at healing relationships between community members and reasserting cultural identity.

Equipo de Estudios Comunitarios y Acción Psicosocial (Community Studies and Psychosocial Action Team)

Extending the individual testimony model to the community, Equipo de Estudios Comunitarios y Acción Psicosocial (ECAP) created social spaces for communities to share their experiences, emotions, and conflicts. At times the program concurred with truth commission exhumations of the mass graves. ECAP created support groups for widows, widowers, and orphans. ECAP describes the group focus of their treatment model:

> In groups, members can express their feelings and what bothers them the most. In groups, they can reconstruct their history, express and listen, understand, share and receive/give support and affection. Their testimony, after a long process, is converted into a repairing device. In the case of torture victims, methods range from responsible listening to accompaniment [to trial] and social support. Overcoming the imposed silence through a testimony of what happened allows the victim to gradually register his/her history in an official way. Recognition of the facts returns dignity and self-esteem to the victim.[25]

An important aspect of ECAP's program is its training of participants in listening, communication, conflict resolution, and providing low-level literacy training publications and educational tools. By doing so, ECAP's goal is for communities to sustain collective healing practices and develop their capacity to work together toward common goals.

Between 1995 and 2003, ECAP assisted in the first series of criminal and civil trials in the country's history in which an indigenous community initiated criminal proceedings, and appeals resulted in the eventual condemnation of soldiers directly responsible for the massacre (but absolved their leader).[26] Through their assistance to indigenous communities, they continue to contribute to the slow process against impunity in Guatemala.

Voices and Images: Maya Ixil Women of Chajul

In this PhotoVoice project, 20 Maya women in Chajul interviewed one another, sharing their personal stories that often involved the murder of loved ones, and spoke of the collective experiences they had in their community—the public hanging of a village woman, the destruction of their communal and family fields, and the desecration of their sacred spaces. The iterative process of interview, narrative, and creating and analyzing photographs provided the opportunity to document the atrocities of the past, to grieve, to reclaim their voices, and to regain their sense of place and community. Through group role-play and reflection-action processes the women examined their fears and challenges related to violence, gender, and social oppression that they continue to face. Facilitator M. Brinton Lykes explains:

> For the women, these processes ultimately helped them to problem-solve ways to overcome the barriers that they faced in completing the task, as well as to confront their losses and to develop the self-confidence and interpersonal skills necessary for taking up their new roles in their community.[27]

This project culminated in a publication of their stories and photographs, *Voices and Images: The Maya Ixil Women of Chajul.*[28] On the completion of the project, the women coordinated a new educational program for the children of Chajul in addition to their ongoing participation in a number of local organizational and economic programs.[29]

RESPONSIBILITY AND COMMUNITY DEVELOPMENT

For Ija'tz and many other communities, the Guatemalan government's lack of accountability for the military's abuses during la violencia has created a vacuum of responsibility and fomented a lawless environment where perpetrators roam freely and victims and advocates who dare to speak out face intimidation, torture, and death.

The Guatemalan Commission for Historical Clarification, the truth commission that examined and reported the impact of the 36-year civil conflict in Guatemala, determined more than 90 percent of the humans rights violations and acts of violence during the conflict were attributable to actions by the state, with 85 percent attributable to the Guatemalan military.[30] The Peace Accords of 1996 represent an official but primarily symbolic ending to such violence.[31] For the last 13 years, the Guatemalan Army, paramilitary groups, and organized crime have continued to act with impunity in a seemingly lawless environment. The rate of impunity in Guatemala is 98 percent; only 2 out of 100 cases ever go to trial.[32]

For decades, Guatemalan civil organizations like the CUC, professional organizations such as ECAP, and a number of international human rights organizations have pressed for the incarceration of Ríos Montt and other members of the military, and have been met with intimidation—many have even lost their lives. Even before the 1996 Peace Accords, these organizations have reported how the military groups that carried out Montt's program of genocide were transitioning into clandestine squads with criminal agendas that included kidnapping, extortion, and assassination of personal enemies, business rivals, and the media and human rights advocates who reported their activities.[33] In 2007, after many years of pressure by these human rights groups, the Guatemalan Congress granted the United Nations the authority to investigate and assist in the persecution of current and past state-related abuses. Unfortunately, the International Commission Against Impunity in Guatemala (CICIG), much like the UN-brokered Peace Accords, has thus far been largely ineffective in combating impunity.[34]

Guatemalan President Alvaro Colom, as the first left-leaning president in Guatemala's history since Arbenz in the 1950s, is offering some hope with the establishment of a presidential anti-impunity committee, a panel to review and declassify military archives from the civil war, and an elite, U.S.-trained anti-drug force. As social justice advocates note, committees and panels within the government structure seem unlikely to be able to investigate themselves, and the establishment of an elite, U.S.-trained paramilitary vehicle to combat narcotics trafficking could tempt history to repeat itself. The dilemma for Guatemala is that the military is now being confronted with a more powerful force than itself as drug cartels move southward from Mexico.[35] The hope is that these government-appointed panels and projects will work in conjunction with the CICIG, with the former providing action and the latter maintaining accountability and oversight.

The culture of impunity in Guatemala has fomented a lawless society where the homicide rate is at one of the highest per capita in the world. In 2008, there were 6,200 registered homicides, which translates to 17 deaths per day; only 382 individuals were detained on murder charges.[36] The worsening of homicide statistics in recent years is attributed to the increase in drug-related activity. Drug enforcement analysts believe that traffickers perceive Guatemala as a safe haven for the narcotics trade.

Social justice organizations noted that leaders at the recent Summit of the Americas failed to discuss human rights issues.[37] Impunity was not discussed, yet drug enforcement was; the failure to acknowledge the link between lack of government accountability and responsibility and the inability to protect its citizens is a reflection of the current state of affairs in the United States, where the Obama Administration has failed to identify and charge its own human rights abusers.

Impunity in San Lucas Tolimán

According to popular media sources in Guatemala, the dramatic increases in crime are linked to increased gang activity. During the weeks I spent in San Lucas, not a day passed without a newspaper displaying a photograph of a severed limb or mutilated body. The greater threat to highland Maya communities, however, continues to be the activity of underground paramilitary groups that continue to this day—"social cleansing units" as they are called, which aim to eliminate the so claimed undesirables of society. I had a brief discussion with one member of Ija'tz regarding the activity of Limpieza Sociale, the local social cleansing regime, who informed me that the undesirables targeted by the group include homeless street children, prostitutes, drug users, drug traffickers, brujas (witches), and other marginalized individuals. This member also explained that the local group of Limpieza Sociale extorted money from many of the coffee cooperatives in the region (it was unclear whether Ija'tz was one of those cooperatives). The abuses of paramilitary groups such as Limpieza Sociale reinforce and perpetuate the climate of terror that originated in counterinsurgency tactics during the civil war. The photographs of mutilated and decapitated bodies are more likely the work of such groups, who utilize the media to convey their message.[38]

Guatemala's transition from the worst days of military and paramilitary atrocities is painfully slow and uneven. Entrenched military power prevents a full accounting of the atrocities and blocks reforms that might right the decades of severe poverty. The dearth of economic opportunity enhances the growth of drug trafficking gangs. In light of this reality the amazing courage and ingenuity of the people of Ija'tz and similar communities must be recognized and their efforts assisted.

NOTES

1. Barreda, 2006.
2. Foster, 2006.
3. United Nations World Food Program, 2009.
4. United Nations Conference on Trade and Development, 2007.
5. Asociación Ija'tz, 2007.
6. Ibid.
7. Fisher and Hendrickson, 2003.
8. Ibid.
9. Dudenhoefer, 2004.
10. Krznaric, 2006.
11. Institute for the Study of International Migration, 2002.
12. Rights Action, 2008.
13. Entrepueblos, 2009.

14. The Advocacy Project, 2009.

15. Ibid.

16. McCreery, 1994.

17. Pearcy, 2006.

18. Farrell, 1977.

19. Fisher and Benson, 2006.

20. Guatemalan Commission for Historical Clarification (CEH), 1999.

21. Official Report of the Human Rights Office, 1999.

22. Lykes, et al., 2007.

23. Abram, 1999.

24. Menchú, 1984.

25. Equipo de Estudios Comunitarios y Acción Psicosocial (ECAP), 2009.

26. Lykes et al., 2007.

27. Ibid.

28. Women of ADMI and Lykes, 2000.

29. Lykes, et al., 1999.

30. Guatemalan Commission for Historical Clarification, 1999.

31. The accords consisted of a series of agreements dealing with human rights with particular attention to rights for indigenous peoples, the establishment of a truth commission, the land tenure system, the role of the armed forces, the terms of a ceasefire, the constitutional and electoral regime, the integration of guerrilla forces, and mechanisms for verifying compliance with the agreements. See UNHCR, 2009.

32. United Nations Department of Public Information, 2009.

33. Washington Office on Latin America, 2008.

34. Council on Hemispheric Affairs, 2009.

35. Ibid.

36. Wilson, 2009.

37. Amnesty International, 2009.

38. North American Congress on Latin America, 2008.

PART III

PEACE FROM WITHIN

It is fitting that we conclude these volumes with writings on the area of peace work that is, as many believe, the sine qua non for establishing real peace in the world and at the same time the most difficult to describe in words. Plato, when he set out to describe the constitution of the human soul, used first the model of the ideally constituted state because it was so much easier to see what is outside us. Without wishing to compare ourselves with the author of the *Republic*, we have done something similar in treating the institutions and organizations of peace in the outside world throughout this collection. Now we are attempting to direct the searchlight inward to the mind and perhaps deeper energies that, according to both the wisdom tradition and some aspects of modern science, actually bring those institutions, arrangements, and organizations into existence. "A human being is his or her deep, driving desire," states a famous passage in one of the Upanishads, "for as our deep desire is, so is our will; as is our will, so is our deed; and as is our deed, so is our destiny."[1]

We begin the section with a personal account of meditation by Michael Nagler, who has spent most of his adult life following that practice and drawing on the energy and insight it releases for peace building work without. So has Joanna Macy, our next contributor, who describes how she uses imagery, ritual, and other techniques to encourage people in her many workshops to contact emotionally, but not be overcome by, the despair within themselves that is a natural response to the seemingly hopeless state of the peaceless world. It is a process that leads, when successful, to the availability of positive energy that can be put to work to resolve the problem in whatever way one can. (Several studies have shown that people who work on a problem come to have greater hope in its solvability, and vice versa.)

The remaining four chapters recount the stories of four rather different people, starting from rather different and representative life experiences, who woke up to the reality of what they were doing, and what they could be doing instead, and had a kind of conversion to peace work. (The same trajectory is touched on by other writers in these three volumes, most notably by Daniel Ellsberg [Volume 2, Chapter 3].) Rabbi Michael Lerner also gives an insider's account of another "within"—the peacelessness that sometimes deeply compromises peace movements anywhere when their members lose tolerance and understanding of one another.

Our deepest hope is that many others like Richard Deats, Claude AnShin Thomas, and John Perkins, will provide examples of a similar awakening and that a "tipping point" will be reached so that culture as a whole—the militaristic elements of our national culture in the United States as well as the war culture that has tentacles around the world—will be past history.

—Marc Pilisuk and Michael N. Nagler

NOTE

1. Chhandogya Upanishad, iv.5.5, tr. by Michael Nagler.

CHAPTER 22

ON MEDITATION

Michael N. Nagler

There never was a war that was not inward; I must fight till I have conquered in myself what causes war.

—Marianne Moore

As mentioned in the first chapter of Volume 1, there has been an increasing feeling in many quarters that peace must first come from within, that is, from the consciousness of a person, before it can be established with any stability in the outside world. With that awareness, naturally, comes an increasing interest in getting "in" there to find it. According to Diana Eck, Buddhist centers in the thousands are now spread across the landscape of the United States, partly because their "traditions of meditation appeal to frank, practical Americans";[1] and much the same would go for nominally Hindu schools of meditation (meditation is meditation, after all) and the rediscovery of *lectio divina* and other strands of the practice within Christianity. Here, though, a word of caution may be in order: not everyone who sits still with eyes closed is necessarily meditating, even with the best of intentions. I hold with the classical definition of meditation as "stilling the thought-waves in the mind."[2] Without doing this systematically, and usually on a daily basis for years together, one cannot reliably experience the impressive benefits—and the equally impressive difficulty—of meditation in the meaningful sense of the word. For full disclosure, I have been doing such a practice for most of my adult life under guidance of a well-known teacher who came to Berkeley from South India in the 1960s.[3]

Another good translation for "thought waves" (*cittavritti*) in the definition just cited from Patañjali is "mental *perturbation*" (*vritti*), which points up the direct connection between meditation and peace at the most fundamental level.

Several things happen at once when perturbation rises in the mind (and unfortunately under "normal" circumstances there is almost no time when they do not). First, our own inner peace is disturbed to that extent. Even when the perturbations are "pleasant," the sages discovered, they disturb peace, and inner peace is more than pleasant when we can reach it. Second, this perturbation, or activity, throws up a smoke screen between us and others; we identify with the mind when it is active. If a wave of anger, for example, arises in the mind, we do not say to ourselves, "Ah. Interesting. A wave of anger rising in the mind." If we are normal human beings we say, "I'm angry." One can only stop identifying with the mind—and we do want to do that—when its turmoil subsides.[4] As far as peace goes, the main drawback of such identification is that to identify with *our* mind gets between us and our inherent identification with the minds, the reality, of others. Anyone who understands conflict will recognize at once how this spells trouble.

Third, as the unanimous testimony of the wisdom tradition assures us, we are not our minds, but an even higher reality that is all bliss, the source of love and wisdom. By distracting us from our real self (in Hindu tradition, the Self), which is not separated from the real self of others (are they really "other," in the end?), the restless activity of the mind—well stimulated by modern mass media and advertising—locks us into an identification with the transitory reality of the phenomenal world. This, in turn, causes a vague anxiety. We sense, perhaps not quite consciously, that we are cut off from the source of satisfaction, happiness and peace within us. And this anxiety, in turn, is another source of conflict. We rarely stop to ask, "why am I getting agitated?" The conditioned response is to project our problems outward and chafe, "he or she is agitating me." Affirmations and other kinds of practice that calm the mind can be of some help here, but meditation does more than calm the mind, it *trains* the mind to rest in its native calmness as a permanent condition.

This would be argument enough for the importance of meditation in bringing us to a state of inner peace (the sages would say, bringing us *back* to that native state). Intuition itself would tell us that this is the first step toward peace in interpersonal relationships and eventually the world. But there is more.

Let me here enlist an astute observation of William James that seems way ahead of his time (1890):

> The faculty of voluntarily bringing back a wandering attention over and over again is the very root of judgment, character and will. No one is compos sui if he have it not. An education which would improve this faculty would be the education par excellence. But it is easier to define this ideal than to give practical directions for bringing it about.[5]

It is also, I would add, the very foundation of peace. Here is why. Everyone who meditates in the sense used here will inevitably notice that the dreary practice of bringing the mind back to the designated object of attention, in my case the words of a previously memorized inspirational passage (James's "over and over" is no exaggeration) in some way translates directly into our ability *outside* meditation to bring ourselves back to a state of security and balance when we have been challenged by anger or fear. The Bhagavad Gita gives another classic description of the practice:

> Wherever the mind wanders, restless and
> diffuse in its search for satisfaction without,
> lead it within; train it to rest in the Self. Abiding
> joy comes to those who still the mind.[6]

In meditation, this means returning our attention to whatever we are meditating on; and this digs a track, so to speak, in consciousness so that outside meditation it facilitates bringing it back to the calm, concentrated energy of peace whenever outside circumstances, such as hostile persons, try to jostle us from that state. It is the same process, so that every time we bring our mind back from a distraction—from whatever we *don't* want it to be meditating on—we are creating peace. Or contacting it. Peace is our native state; anger and fear are distractions. That is the eye-opening implication of this experience. This is why mystics, teachers of wisdom, urge meditation on those who would behave nonviolently when faced with agitation; Thich Nhat Hanh explains, "at that crucial moment, even if you know that nonviolence is better than violence, if your understanding is only intellectual and not in your whole being, you will not act nonviolently. The fear and anger *in you* will prevent you."[7]

Other contributors to this book have stressed the importance of the sense of *identity* in peace and war outcomes (see Kimmel [Chapter 6] and Norlander and Marsella [Chapter 7] in Volume 1). With meditation this question takes on a profound significance and one even more pertinent to the question of peace. The question here is not, what label fits on this or that person, but *what is a person*. Let us take an answer supplied by the hierarchical

Figure 22.1 Levels of Being

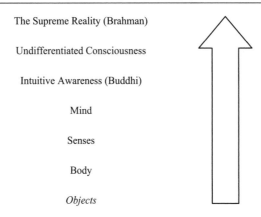

The Supreme Reality (Brahman)

Undifferentiated Consciousness

Intuitive Awareness (Buddhi)

Mind

Senses

Body

Objects

model of the human being offered (Figure 22.1), with minor variations, in the Upanishads, texts that are considered the purest source of the mystical tradition in India (I offer my own translation for some of the terms).

It is interesting that the person in this vision "smears out," as a quantum theorist might say, into realities that are respectively lower (at the bottom) and much greater at the top than what we consider a person, separated by his or her physical boundaries from the rest of creation. More to the point, implicit in the model is an exponential expansion of consciousness as our sense of identity goes upward from stage to stage toward Brahman in the process of meditation. The process even has a direct impact on health; many studies have shown that a robust network of human relationships (or relationships with any living thing, for that matter), confers advantages in almost every parameter of well-being.[8]

Objects are radically separate from one another; on the other end of the hierarchy, Brahman is by definition *advaita*—the state where there is no division, no separateness whatever. In practical terms, then, as we ascend by shifting our sense of identity from level to level we become exponentially more aware of our identity with the life around us. And as the Bhagavad Gita says, "When the seeker sees the divine in all beings he cannot possibly harm another, for [it would be] the Self harming the Self."[9] As our inner vision improves, violence becomes more and more impossible. This is the core significance of meditation for peace; but another consideration is also worth emphasizing.

When one tries to understand a figure like Gandhi—particularly useful because he lived in an era shared with many of us—we can appreciate the power of this practice. Gandhi's thoughts and doings were documented pretty thoroughly from his earliest days, and one quickly gathers from this record and some of his own statements that there is a startling (and as yet largely unused) power for peace creation within every individual. Gandhi was the first to affirm that anyone could do what he had. He was a bit cagey about how he cultivated that power and released it into our world. That reticence was likely for the strategic reason that he did not want people to pedestalize and thus dismiss him, as they very largely have nonetheless done in India. But it is not difficult to glean from some of his sparse statements about his inner life (and from at least one famous photograph[10]) that he practiced meditation, and very deeply, often calling it "prayer." That kind of energy—working 15 hours a day, every day, for 50 years—and the ability to use it (or let oneself be used by it) without fatigue, feeling, as he said to an American journalist, that he was "always on vacation," is often seen in those who carry meditation to a deep level, East or West (see the description of Peace Pilgrim in this volume, Chapter 28).

THE EFFECT ON OTHERS

There are studies carried out by one meditation organization that show, apparently with scientific rigor, that in cities where a certain percentage of the population is practicing their kind of meditation (and not a large percentage, at that) the crime rate drops. Though I personally do not know how to evaluate these studies, they certainly seem to follow an intuitive connection between meditation and the "social field," between inner and outer peace. The text of Patañjali we started from states in another forthright sutra (my translation): "When nonviolence is established (in a person), in his or her (mere) presence hostility falls away."[11]

To sense this connection between meditation and outer peace helps to explain why, per contra, in this most unmeditative of cultures, where we are bombarded by something like 3,000 commercial messages every day,[12] where there is an extremely low image of the human being held before us in print, television, and other media, where violence and self-will are portrayed as normative and exciting, there should be such a dedication to violence and war. Unfortunately, it's a bit hard to know what to do with this insight. Broadcasting encouragements to meditate would not work very well. Even those who took the crude hint would be meditating for the wrong reason. To meditate because someone else told you to, or to meditate to bring about some external result, would be to meditate for a less than perfect motive and in meditation motive and intention are everything. (Though that said, it has often been the case that when one gets a taste of the experience by whatever means, he or she becomes well motivated to pursue it further.)

But there are practical things we can do. Individuals can disengage mentally and in their buying habits from the agitating culture with which we have been so obsessively surrounding ourselves. Then we can take steps to create a supportive environment for anyone intrigued enough to practice meditation and express the great inner resources they contact by that practice in their outward life.

CONCLUSION

That meditation, done reasonably well, can bring a sense of inner peace is not controversial: it is one of the few things about meditation that is generally understood. The argument of this chapter is much more challenging: that at the inner peace that we thereby possess can be translated outwardly into a peace culture, a peace *system*, and that this is the sovereign way, arguably the only way peace can become a stable possession of the human race. It may be fiendishly difficult to practice meditation well—to wrestle down the random impulses of the mind when, as Arjuna bemoans in the Bhagavad Gita (vi.34), you may as well ask us to control the wind. It may demand a special posture, daily practice, a reliable technique, even—a sticking point for many Westerners—a competent teacher. But the benefits are stunning, even if we focus on those that relate most directly to the goal of peace. As we progress along this path the perceived barrier between ourselves and others steadily falls, until we could no more do them injury than we could ourselves. The sense of security correspondingly rises. The drive to get satisfaction from the outside world—with overburdening of the environment, competition, and ultimately violence among its inevitable consequences— subsides as we come in touch with the source of satisfaction within us. The whole "story" of the person as a separate, material fragment doomed to compete for diminishing resources in a meaningless world steadily evaporates. And, finally, our ability to influence others positively rises exponentially— witness Gandhi. It is not for nothing that in ancient India meditation was called *Brahmavidya* "the supreme knowledge." We will be on a secure road to peace when it is so recognized today as well.

NOTES

1. Eck, 2001.
2. Yoga Sutras of Patañjali, I.2. Another translation would be, "suppressing perturbations in consciousness."
3. Easwaran, 1908.
4. Patañjali I.4.
5. James, 1952.

6. Easwaran, 1985.

7. Hanh, 1993.

8. Cobb, 1976; Cassel, 1976; Pilisuk and Parks, 1986.

9. Patañjali, XIII.28 (my translation). The word for 'harm' is *hinaste*, from the same root as h *imsa* and its opposite, *ahimsa*.

10. Easwaran, 1972.

11. Patañjali, II.35 (my translation).

12. Kilbourne, 2004.

CHAPTER 23

DESPAIR WORK

Joanna Macy

We are bombarded by signals of distress—ecological destruction, social breakdown, and uncontrolled nuclear proliferation. Not surprisingly, we are feeling despair—a despair well merited by the machinery of mass death that we continue to create and serve. What is surprising is the extent to which we continue to hide this despair from ourselves and each other. If this is, as Arthur Koestler suggested, an age of anxiety, it is also an age in which we are adept at sweeping our anxieties under the rug. As a society we are caught between a sense of impending apocalypse and an inability to acknowledge it.

Activists who try to arouse us to the fact that our survival is at stake decry public apathy, and rightly so, as apathy, trivialization, and despair itself are encouraged by regimes like our own as tools of oppression. When then-President George W. Bush urged Americans to "go shopping, take the kids to Disney World" in the wake of 9/11 he was in effect disenfranchising us, urging us to stay out of the political system. This is frighteningly reminiscent of Hannah Arendt's characterization of a totalitarian state as one that does not seek to dominate people so much as render them irrelevant. The cause of our apathy, however, is not mere indifference. It stems from a fear of confronting the despair that lurks subliminally beneath the tenor of life-as-usual. A

This chapter originally appeared in Joanna Macy, *World as Lover, World as Self.* Fitchburg, MA: Parallax, 1991; Abridged from the booklet "Despair Work." New Society Publishers, Philadelphia, 1981.

dread of what is happening to our future stays on the fringes of awareness, too deep to name and too fearsome to face. Sometimes it manifests in dreams of mass destruction, and is exorcised in the morning jog and shower or in the public fantasies of disaster movies. Because of social taboos against despair and because of fear of pain, it is rarely acknowledged or expressed directly. It is kept at bay. The suppression of despair, like that of any deep recurrent response, produces a partial numbing of the psyche. Expressions of anger or terror are muted, deadened as if a nerve had been cut.

The refusal to feel takes a heavy toll. Not only is there an impoverishment of our emotional and sensory life—flowers are dimmer and less fragrant, our loves less ecstatic—but this psychic numbing also impedes our capacity to process and respond to information. The energy expended in pushing down despair is diverted from more creative uses, depleting the resilience and imagination needed for fresh visions and strategies. Furthermore, the fear of despair can erect an invisible screen, selectively filtering out anxiety-provoking data. In a world where organisms require feedback to adapt and survive, this is suicidal. Now, when we urgently need to measure the effects of our acts, our attention and curiosity slacken as if we are already preparing for the Big Sleep. Many of us doggedly attend to business-as-usual, denying both our despair and our inability to cope with it.

Despair cannot be banished by injections of optimism or sermons on "positive thinking." Like grief, it must be acknowledged and worked through. This means it must be named and validated as a healthy, normal human response to the situation we find ourselves in. Faced and experienced, its power can be used, as the frozen defenses of the psyche thaw and new energies are released. Something analogous to grief work is in order. "Despair work" is different from grief work in that its aim is not acceptance of loss—indeed, the "loss" has not yet occurred and is hardly to be "accepted." But it is similar in the dynamics unleashed by the willingness to acknowledge, feel, and express inner pain. From my own work and that of others, I know that we can come to terms with apocalyptic anxieties in ways that are integrative and liberating, opening awareness not only to planetary distress, but also to the hope inherent in our own capacity to change.

INGREDIENTS OF DESPAIR

Whether or not we choose to accord them serious attention, we are barraged by data that render questionable the survival of our culture, our species, and even our planet as a viable home for conscious life. These warning signals prefigure, to those who do take them seriously, probabilities of apocalypse that are mind-boggling in scope. While varied, each scenario presents its own relentless logic. Poisoned by oil spills, sludge, and plutonium, the seas are dying; when the plankton disappear (by the year 2010 at present pollution rates, according to Jacques Yves Cousteau), we will suffocate from lack of oxygen. Or carbon dioxide from industrial and automotive combustion will saturate the atmosphere, creating a greenhouse effect that will melt the polar icecaps. Or radioactive poisoning from nuclear reactors and their wastes will accelerate plagues of cancer and genetic mutations. Or deforestation and desertification of the planet, now rapidly advancing, will produce giant dustbowls, and famines beyond imagining. The probability of each of these perils is amply and soberly documented by scientific studies. The list of such scenarios could continue, including use of nuclear bombs by terrorists or nation states—a prospect presenting vistas of such horror that, as former Soviet Premier Nikita Khrushchev said, "The survivors will envy the dead."

Despair, in this context, is not a macabre certainty of doom or a pathological condition of depression and futility. It is not a nihilism denying meaning or efficacy to human effort. Rather, as it is being experienced by increasing numbers of people across a broad spectrum of society, despair is the loss of the assumption that the species will inevitably pull through. It represents a genuine accession to the possibility that this planetary experiment will end—the curtain down, the show over.

SYMPTOMS AND SUPPRESSIONS

In India, at a leprosarium, I met a young mother of four. Her leprosy was advanced, the doctor pointed out, because for so long she had hidden its signs. Fearing ostracism and banishment, she had covered her sores with her sari, pulled the shoulder drape around so no one would see. In a similar fashion did I later hide despair for our world, cloaking it like a shameful disease—and so, I have learned, do others. At the prospect of the extinction of a civilization, feelings of grief and horror are natural. We tend to hide them, though, from ourselves and each other. Why? The reasons, I think, are both social and psychological.

When the sensations aroused by the contemplation of a likely and avoidable end to human existence break through the censorship we tend to impose on them, they can be intense and physical. A friend who left her career to work as a full-time anti-nuclear organizer, says her onslaughts of grief come as a cold, heavy weight on the chest and a sense of her body breaking. Mine, which began years ago after an all-day symposium on threats to our biosphere, were sudden and wrenching. I would be at my desk, alone in my study translating a Buddhist text, and the next moment I would find myself on the floor, curled like a fetus and shaking. In company I was more controlled; but even then, in those early months when I was unused to despair, I would be caught off guard. A line from Shakespeare or a Bach phrase would pierce me with pain as I found myself wondering how much longer it would be heard, before fading out forever in the galactic silences.

In a culture committed to the American dream, it is hard to own up to despair. This is still the land of Dale Carnegie and Norman Vincent Peale, where an unflagging optimism is taken as the means and measure of success. As commercials for products and campaigns of politicians attest, the healthy and admirable person smiles a lot. The feelings of depression, loneliness, and anxiety, to which this thinking animal has always been heir, carry here an added burden: one feels bad about feeling bad. One can even feel guilty about it. The failure to hope, in a country built and nurtured on Utopian expectations, can seem downright un-American.

In a religious context, despair can appear as a lapse of faith. At a vigil before a peace demonstration at the Pentagon, a noted religious leader spoke of the necessity of hope to carry us through. Others chimed in, affirming their belief in the vision of a "new Jerusalem" and their gratitude for having that hope. After a pause, a young man, who planned to participate in the week's civil disobedience actions, spoke up falteringly. He questioned whether hope was really a prerequisite, because—and he admitted this with difficulty—he was not feeling it. Even among friends committed to the same goal, it was hard for him (and brave of him, I thought) to admit despair. Evidently, he feared he would be misunderstood, taken as cowardly or cynical—a fear confirmed by the response of some present.

Despair is tenaciously resisted because it represents a loss of control, an admission of powerlessness. Our culture dodges it by demanding instant solutions when problems are raised. My political science colleagues in France ridiculed this, I recall, as an endemic trait of the American personality. "You people prescribe before you finish the diagnosis," they would say. "Let the difficulties reveal themselves first before rushing for a ready-made solution or else you will not understand them." To do this would require that one view a stressful situation without the psychic security of knowing if and how it can be solved—in other words, a readiness to suffer a little.

"Don't come to me with a problem unless you have a solution," Lyndon B. Johnson is quoted as saying during the Vietnam War. That tacit injunction, operative even in public policy making, rings like the words my mother said to me as a child, "If you can't say something nice, don't say anything at all."

In our culture the acknowledgment of despair for the future is a kind of social taboo and those who break it are considered "crazy," or at least "depressed and depressing." No one wants a Cassandra around or welcomes a Banquo at the feast. Nor are such roles enjoyable to play. When the prospect of our collective suicide first hit me as a serious possibility—and I know well the day and hour my defenses against this despair suddenly collapsed—I felt that there was no one to whom I could turn in my grief. If there were—and indeed there was, for I have loving, intelligent friends and family—what is there to say? Do I want them to feel this horror too? What can be said without casting a pall, or without seeming to ask for unacceptable words of comfort and cheer?

To feel despair in such a cultural setting brings a sense of isolation. The psychic dissonance can be so acute as to seem to border on madness. The distance between our inklings of apocalypse and the tenor of business-as-usual is so great that, though we may respect our own cognitive reading of the signs, we tend to imagine that it is we, not the society, who are insane.

Psychotherapy, by and large, has offered little help for coping with these feelings, and indeed has often compounded the problem. Many therapists have difficulty crediting the notion that concerns for the general welfare might be acute enough to cause distress. Assuming that all our drives are ego-centered, they tend to treat expressions of this distress reductionistically, as manifestations of private neurosis. In my own case, deep dismay over destruction of the wilderness was diagnosed by a counselor as fear of my own libido (which the bulldozers were taken to symbolize), and my painful preoccupation with U.S. bombings of Vietnam was interpreted as an unwholesome hangover of Puritan guilt. Such "therapy," of course, only intensifies the sense of isolation and craziness that despair can bring, while inhibiting its recognition and expression.

Some of the biggest money-makers in the film industry, as Andrée Conrad points out in *Disaster and the American Imagination*, are movies that feature cataclysmic events and violent mass death. Earthquakes, rampaging sharks, and killer bees, blazing skyscrapers and doomed craft in air and sea, loaded with panicked passengers, vie in imageries of terror. Contrived with technical brilliance, these films draw large crowds and large profits. Their appeal, indeed their fascination, stems from an inchoate but pervasive sense of doom in the American public. The scenarios they present give structure and outlet to unformulated fears of apocalypse, and in so doing provide catharsis. But it is a dangerous catharsis, Conrad observes.

Hooking our anxieties onto isolated and unlikely emergencies, frequently handled with technological heroics, these entertainments give their audience, sitting safely in a comfortable theater, the illusion of having dealt with what is bothering them. On fictitious, improbable themes they air and exercise our dread, while habituating us to prospects of mass death and raising our horror threshold another notch. They blur the boundaries between fantasy and reality, making the next day's news seem like more of the same—alarms to be passively watched until the credits appear and we can stop for a beer on our way to bed.

These entertainments constitute a new version of what Geoffrey Gorer in the 1950s called our "pornography of death." He pointed out that, just as the repression of sex in our puritanically conditioned culture produces debased expressions of it, so is our repression of the reality of personal death released in fascination with sadistic violence. By analogous reasoning, disaster films can be seen as pornographies of despair. In the same way that X-rated "adult" flicks cheapen the sexual hungers they trade on, the towering infernos and devouring jaws dull and divert us from the true dimensions of our despair.

Until we get in touch with them, our powers of creative response to planetary crisis will be crippled. Until we can grieve for our planet and its future inhabitants, we cannot fully feel or enact our love for them. Such grief is frequently suppressed, not only because it is socially awkward. It is also denied because it is both painful and hard to believe. At the root of both inhibitions lies a dysfunctional notion of the self. It is the notion of the self as an isolated and fragile entity. Such a self has no reason to weep for the unseen and the unborn, and such a self, if it did, might shatter with pain and futility.

So long as we see ourselves as essentially separate, competitive, and ego-identified beings, it is difficult to respect the validity of our social despair, deriving as it does from interconnectedness. Both our capacity to grieve for others and our power to cope with this grief spring from the great matrix of relationships in which we take our being. We are, as open systems, sustained by flows of energy and information that extend beyond the reach of conscious ego.

VALIDATING DESPAIR

> You can hold yourself back from the suffering of the world: this is something you are free to do, . . . but perhaps precisely this holding back is the only suffering you might be able to avoid.
>
> —Franz Kafka

The first step in despair work is to disabuse ourselves of the notion that grief for our world is morbid. To experience anguish and anxiety in the face of the perils that threaten us is a healthy reaction. Far from being crazy, this pain is a testimony to the unity of life, the deep interconnections that relate us to all beings.

Such pain for the world becomes masochistic only when we assume personal guilt for its plight or personal responsibility for its solution. No individual is that powerful. Certainly by participation in society each shares in collective accountability; but the acknowledgment of despair, like faith, is a letting go of the manipulative assumption that conscious ego can or should control all events. Each of us is but one little nexus in a vast web. As the recognition of that interdependence breaches our sense of isolation, so does it also free our despair of self-loathing.

Our religious heritages can also serve to validate despair and attest to the creative role of this kind of distress. The Biblical concept of the suffering servant, as well as an array of Old Testament prophets, speaks to the power inherent in opening ourselves to the griefs of others. In Christianity the paramount symbol of such power is the cross. The cross where Jesus died teaches us that it is precisely through openness to the pain of our world that redemption and renewal are found.

The heroes and heroines of the Mahayana Buddhist tradition are the bodhisattvas, who vow to forswear nirvana until all beings are enlightened. As the Lotus Sutra tells us, their compassion endows them with supranormal senses: they can hear the music of the spheres and understand the language of the birds. By the same token, they hear as well all cries of distress, even to the moaning of beings in the lowest hells. All griefs are registered and owned in the bodhisattva's deep knowledge that we are not separate from each other.

POSITIVE DISINTEGRATION

The process of internalizing the possibility of planetary demise is bound to bring some psychic disarray. How to confront what we scarcely dare to think? How to think it without going to pieces?

It is helpful in despair work to realize that going to pieces or falling apart is not such a bad thing. Indeed it is as essential to evolutionary and psychic transformations as the cracking of outgrown shells. Polish psychiatrist Kazimierz Dabrowski calls it "positive disintegration." It is operative in every global development of humanity, especially during periods of accelerated change, and, he argues, permits the emergence of "higher psychic structures and awareness." For the individual who, in confronting current anomalies of experience, allows positive disintegration to happen, it can bring a dark night of the soul, a time of spiritual void and turbulence. But the anxieties and doubts are, Dabrowski maintains, "essentially healthy and creative." They are creative not only for the person but for society, because they permit new and original approaches to reality.

What "disintegrates" in periods of rapid transformation is not the self, of course, but its defenses and ideas. We are not objects that can break. As open systems, we are, cyberneticist Norbert Wiener said, "but whirlpools in a river of everflowing water. We are not stuff that abides, but patterns that perpetuate themselves." We do not need to protect ourselves from change, for our very nature is change. Defensive self-protection, restricting vision and movement like a suit of armor, makes it harder to adapt. It not only reduces flexibility, but blocks the flow of information we need to survive. Our "going to pieces," however uncomfortable a process, can open us up to new perceptions, new data, new responses.

ALLOWING OURSELVES TO FEEL

The second requirement in despair work is to permit ourselves to feel. Within us are deep responses to what is happening to our world, responses of fear and sorrow and anger. Given the flows of information circling our globe, they inhere in us already by virtue of our nature as open systems, interdependent with the rest of life. We need only to open our consciousness to these profound apprehensions. We cannot experience them without pain, but it is a healthy pain—like the kind we feel when we walk on a leg that has gone asleep and the circulation starts to move again. It gives evidence that the tissue is still alive.

As with a cramped limb, exercises can help. I have found meditational exercises useful, particularly ones from the Buddhist tradition. Practices designed to increase the capacity for loving-kindness and compassion, for example, are effective in getting us in touch with those concerns in us that extend beyond ego.

In one workshop I led, titled "Being Bodhisattvas," we did a meditation on compassion, adapted from a Tibetan bodhicitta practice. It involved giving oneself permission to experience the sufferings of others (in as concrete a fashion as possible), and then taking these sufferings in with the breath, visualizing them as dark granules in the stream of air drawn in with each inhalation, into and through the heart, and out again.

Afterward one participant, Marianna, described her experience in this meditation. She had been resistant, and her resistance had localized as a pain in her back. In encouraging the participants to open themselves to their inner awareness of the sufferings of others, I primed the pump with some brief verbal cues, mentioned our fellow beings in hospitals and prisons, mentioned a mother with dried breasts holding a hungry infant. . . . That awoke in Marianna an episode she had buried. Three years earlier she had listened to a recording by Harry Chapin with a song about a starving child; she had, as she put it, "trouble" with it. She put away the record never to play it again, and the "trouble" remained undigested. With her recollection of her experience with the song, the pain in her back moved into her chest. It intensified and hardened, piercing her heart. It seemed for a moment excruciating; but as she continued the exercise, accepting and breathing in the pain, it suddenly, inexplicably, felt right, felt even good. It turned into a golden cone or funnel, aimed point downward into the depths of her heart. Through it poured the despair she had refused, griefs reconnecting her with the rest of humanity.

Marianna emerged from this with a sense of release and belonging. She felt empowered, she said, not to do so much as to be—open, attentive, poised for action. She also said that she believed she permitted this to happen because I had not asked her to "do" something about the griefs of others, or to come up with any answers, but simply to experience them.

What good does it do to let go and allow ourselves to feel the pain of our planet's people? For all the discomfort, there is healing in such openness, for ourselves and for our world. To accept the collective pain reconnects us with our fellow beings and our deep collective energies.

ALLOWING IMAGES TO ARISE

To acknowledge our pain for the world and tap its energy, we need symbols and images for its expression. Images, more than arguments, tap the springs of consciousness, the creative powers by which we make meaning of experience. In the challenge to survival that we face now, a strong imagination is especially necessary because existing verbal constructs seem inadequate to what many of us are sensing.

At a week-long meeting of college teachers and administrators, I chaired a working group on issues of planetary survival, and began to explore ways we could share our concerns on an affective as well as cognitive level. I asked the participants to offer, as they introduced themselves, a personal experience or image of how in the past year the global crisis had impinged on their consciousness. Those brief introductions were potent. Some offered a vignette from work on world hunger or arms. A young physicist simply said, very quietly, "My child was born." A social worker recalled a day her small daughter talked about growing up and having babies; with dull shock she encountered her own doubt that the world would last that long.

Some offered images: fish kill washed up at a summer cottage, strip mines leaching like open wounds. Most encompassing in its simplicity was John's image: the view from space of planet Earth, so small as it glittered there that it could be covered by the astronaut's raised thumb. That vision of our home, so finite it can be blotted out by a single human gesture, functioned as a symbol in our week's work. It helped us cut through the verbiage of reports and the temptations of academic one-upmanship, to the raw nerve in us all—desperate concern.

In the sharing of despair that our imagery had permitted, energy was released. As pent-up feelings were expressed and compared, there came laughter, solidarity, and resurgence of commitment to our common human project.

In that same working group on planetary survival, John showed slides of a trek up Mount Katahdin with some of his Yale students. On a ridge between two peaks was a narrow, knife-edge trail they had to cross. It was scary and dangerous because fog had rolled up, blanketing out the destination and everything but the foot-wide path itself. That picture of the trail cutting through the clouds into the unknown became a strong symbol for us, expressing the existential situation in which we find ourselves, and helping us proceed with dogged patience, even though we cannot see more than a step at a time.

Recognizing the creative powers of imagery, many call us today to come up with visions of a benign future—visions that can beckon and inspire. Images of hope are potent, necessary: they shape our goals and give us impetus for reaching them. Often they are invoked too soon, however. Like the demand for instant solutions, such expectations can stultify—providing us with an escape from the despair we may feel, while burdening us with the task of aridly designing a new Eden. Genuine visioning happens from the roots up, and these roots for many are shriveled by unacknowledged despair. Many of us are in an in-between time, groping in the dark with shattered beliefs and faltering hopes, and we need images for that in-between time if we are to work through it.

The first despair work I can recognize as such occurred on a spring weekend toward the end of our military actions in Vietnam. Although I had been active in anti-war protests, I felt sapped that day by a deep sense of futility. To give form to feeling, and tired of words, I worked with clay. As I descended into the sorrow within me, I shaped that descent in the block of clay—cliffs and escarpments plunging into abysses, dropping off into downward-twisting gullies, down, down. Though I wept as I pushed at the clay with fingers and fists, it felt good to have my sense of hopelessness become palpable, visible. The twisted, plummeting clay landscape was like a silent scream, and also like a dare accepted in bitter defiance, the dare to descend into nothingness.

Feeling spent and empty, the work done, my mind turned to go, but then noted what my fingers had, of themselves, begun to explore. Snaking and pushing up the clay cliffs were roots. As they came in focus, I saw how they joined, tough and tenacious, feeding each other in an upsurge of ascent. The very journey downward into my despair had shaped these roots, which now thrust upward, unbidden and resilient. For long moments I traced them, wonderingly, with eyes and fingers.

Quaker-style meetings, where a group sits and shares out of open silence, can let images appear and interact. In one I remember Humpty Dumpty was evoked. Poor old Humpty Dumpty, falling and breaking and all the king's men cannot put him together again. So it is with our outmoded paradigms, our egos and self-concepts: it felt good to give imaginative form to the sense of fragmentation in our time. As we ruminated on that, a voice among us slowly spoke, adding what she saw: From the shattered shell, a bird rose into the air. Eggshells break to reveal new life; I had forgotten that. The very imagery that expressed our pain pointed to the possibility of hope.

Sometimes it takes a while, in the slow alchemy of the soul, for hope to signal, and longer for it to take form in concrete plans and projects. That is all right.

WAITING

So we wait; even in our work, we wait. Only out of that open expectancy can images and visions arise that strike deep enough to summon our faith in them. "The ability to wait," wrote William Lynch, "is central to hope."

Waiting does not mean inaction, but means staying in touch with our pain and confusion as we act, not banishing them to grab for sedatives, ideologies, or final solutions. It is, as a student of mine quoted, "staying in the dark until the darkness becomes full and clear." The butterfly, I am told, eats its way out of the cocoon. In despair, if we digest it, is authenticity and energy to fuel our dreams.

Jacob Needleman suggests that part of the great danger in this time of crisis is that we may short-circuit despair, and thereby lose the revelations that can open to us.

For there is nothing to guarantee that we will be able to remain long enough or deeply enough in front of the unknown, a psychological state which the traditional paths have always recognized as sacred. In that fleeting state between dreams, which is called "despair" in some Western teachings and "self-questioning" in Eastern traditions, a man is said to be able to receive the truth, both about nature and his own possible role in the universal order.

In my own feelings of despair, I was haunted by the question, "What do you substitute for hope?" I had always assumed that a sanguine confidence in the future was as essential as oxygen. Without it, I had thought, one would collapse into apathy and nihilism. It puzzled me that, when I owned my despair, the hours I spent working for peace and environmental causes did not lessen, but rather increased.

One day I talked with Jim Douglass, the theologian and writer who had left his university post to resist nuclear weapons; jailed repeatedly for civil disobedience in this effort, he was leading the citizens' campaign against the Trident submarine base. He had said he believed we had five years left before it was too late—too late to avert the use of our nuclear arsenal in a first strike strategy. I reflected on the implications of that remark and watched his face, as he squinted in the sun with an air of presence and serenity I could not fathom. "What do you substitute for hope?" I asked. He looked at me and smiled. "Possibilities," he said. "Possibilities . . . you can't predict, just make space for them. There are so many." That, too, is waiting, active waiting— moving out on the fog-bound trail, though you cannot see the way ahead.

COMMUNITY

Despair work is not a solo venture, no matter how alone one may feel. It is a process undertaken within the context of community, even if a community of like-minded others is not physically present. Just knowing that one's feelings are shared gives a measure of validation and support.

Many kinds of community can provide the environment for the kind of sharing that despair work involves. The necessary openness and trust can be found in groups devoted to personal or spiritual growth, and also in groups organized for social action. The "affinity groups" that have emerged in the peace and safe-energy movements, and that are based on strategies of nonviolence, set a high priority on mutual support.

My son had a dream one night about the affinity group he belonged to in the anti-nuclear movement in New England. It conveys something of the sense of strength generated in such community. In the dream he and his affinity group are standing together looking out over a darkened city. All is black and cold. Through their linked hands he feels the current of the group's energy. They chant and the current grows stronger; lights begin to appear and soon the city is aglow, empowered by the energy of their trust and commitment. That, in and of itself, seems a fulfillment.

When we face the darkness of our time, openly and together, we tap deep reserves of strength within us. Many of us fear that confrontation with despair will bring loneliness and isolation, but—on the contrary—in the letting go of old defenses, we can find truer community. In the synergy of sharing comes power. In community, we can find our power and learn to trust our inner responses to our world.

CHAPTER 24

EXPERIMENTING WITH NONVIOLENCE: FROM WEST TEXAS TO SOUTH KOREA

Richard L. Deats

I grew up in Big Spring, Texas, a small city in the western part of the state—halfway between El Paso and Dallas, on the route of the Texas and Pacific Railroad and territory that was once Comanche country. One of our neighbors was featured in national ads of "the Marlboro man." I was taught to love God and neighbor, to follow Jesus, to help those in need, to be a good citizen, to save for a rainy day, and not spend more than one has.

I vividly remember Pearl Harbor and can still recall the family sitting in front of the big radio in the living room, listening to President Roosevelt tell us that "yesterday, December 7, 1941, a day which will live in infamy, the United States was suddenly and deliberately attacked by the naval and armed forces of the Empire of Japan." We were at war and all were expected to enter the war effort. At school we collected scrap metal to be used in the rapid shift to a war economy. We collected and made huge balls of tin foil to contribute. Every week I went with my mother to fold bandages for the Red Cross and on Memorial Day I sold red "buddy poppies" for wounded veterans.

I was immersed in church life and heard a lot about love and goodwill, charity and neighborliness. I don't recall ever thinking about the morality of war and the idea of conscientious objection was totally unknown until I was in high school in the late 1940s. Our church was visited by a Methodist Youth Caravan and these older youth challenged us to explore war—and racism—in the light of Jesus's teachings about, as we said in those days, "the Fatherhood of God and the brotherhood of man." As a boy I had lived through the Depression and World War II. After the war, the Cold War, anti-communism, and McCarthyism were overarching national issues. I went with my father once to the Lion's Club luncheon to hear Senator Strom Thurmond, Dixiecrat candidate for president. My father accepted segregation as part of "the southern way of life" but he didn't like the extreme racist sentiments expressed by Thurmond. He worried when I later became involved in civil rights efforts. Afraid I would get hurt, he said, "You don't know how mean these southern racists can be."

When I went away to college, I brought home for weekend visits classmates from Mexico and India and of other races from Texas. My parents were gracious hosts though in retrospect I sensed their discomfort. I began to struggle with the meaning of *all* humanity as God's family. Yet my parents and relatives—and most church-going people for that matter—didn't seem to object to a "good" war or take issue with segregation and Jim Crow laws. These were just a part of our way of life. But the Methodist Youth Fellowship, with the motto "Christ Above All" and the teachings of some of my church-school teachers led me to struggle with these kinds of ethical issues. My dad and brother, patriotic veterans, couldn't understand what troubled me so. But for me, "Love your enemy," "Overcome evil with good," "Turn the other cheek," "Go the second mile," and "Father, forgive them, for they know not what they do" only underscored what is meant when we call Jesus "the Prince of Peace."

My father kept a loaded revolver in his sock drawer. One evening, when I was about 10, I was alone at home with my cousin Peggy. We thought we heard a prowler outside. I got my father's gun and went to the front door and quickly threw it open as I pointed the loaded gun toward the door. Luckily there was no one there but I've often wondered how that might have ended in murder: I was fully prepared to shoot.

In time, my attitudes started changing. I began to have qualms about hunting. We were a big hunting family. We had a gun cabinet and I had my own .22 rifle, 30.06 rifle, and 20-gauge shotgun. Every fall and winter were times of hunting: doves, quail, ducks, and deer. Game was plentiful in parts of South and West Texas. I loved camping out, cooking our meals, sleeping in bedrolls in the tent we pitched the first day. We spent all day walking in the hills hunting deer—whitetail deer in South Texas, blacktail deer in West Texas. My father always insisted we only kill legal game that we would take home and eat. But in time it began to bother me to kill the deer and birds. A turning point came one fall when shooting a doe was legal (ordinarily only male deer with antlers—bucks—could be legally shot). I shot a doe but she was still alive when I reached her. She raised her head and looked at me as she was dying. I cut her throat to end her misery and dragged her back to camp but that was the last time I hunted. It just was no longer a sport to me and the idea of reverence for life was something I would long struggle with. I was to discover that *Erfurcht fur das Leben*, reverence for life, was central to the philosophy of Albert Schweitzer, Alsatian medical doctor in Africa. His writing deeply influenced me.

I entered college with the idea of becoming a doctor, or perhaps a dentist, like my father. However, a growing religious sensibility took place in me and I began to think of studying to be a minister. I went to McMurry College in Abilene, Texas, a Methodist school that had frequent religious services— weekly chapel, religious emphasis week, outdoor early morning services (when the weather permitted), visits to area churches, courses in religion. They all made an impact on me with Jesus becoming the One whom I would follow the rest of my life.

THE FELLOWSHIP OF RECONCILIATION

A turning point occurred when Muriel Lester came to our campus. An English social worker, founder of Kingsley Hall in London's East End, Lester was a "traveling secretary" for the International Fellowship of Reconciliation. A dynamic speaker who had worked with Gandhi in India's freedom struggle and visited many war-ravaged areas in World War II, she talked about the Cold War, McCarthyism, and racism in the light of the Sermon on the Mount. Some on the campus outrageously thought she must be a communist, but I found her nonviolent message challenging, and in the end, transforming. Along with her concern for a just and peaceful world, in her second message she began by saying, "Every breath you take, you take in the spirit of God." She said the outer journey needed to be combined with the inward journey so that there is harmony between our outer and inner lives. The active life is fueled by the inner practice of prayer and meditation. God is nearer than breathing, closer than hands and feet, and God is found in the other, even the stranger and the enemy. Lester summed up her message with these words:

> The job of the peacemaker is to stop war. To purify the world. To get it saved from poverty and riches. To heal the sick. To comfort the sad. To wake up those who have not yet found God. To create joy and beauty wherever you go. To find God in everything and in everyone.

Lester helped me move beyond the false dilemma that focuses either on spirituality that is inner directed, even other worldly, or spirituality that is basically activist. She modeled this in her life, her witness for peace that was rooted in a strong spiritual life.

This led me in 1952 to join the Fellowship of Reconciliation (FOR). The FOR was founded in 1914 in Europe at an ecumenical conference at Lake Constance in southern Germany that was seeking to find ways that Christians, and the European churches they represented, could prevent the war that, as Barbara Tuchman said, everyone knew was coming and no one knew how to stop.

During the conference, however, the war started and everyone had to return home in a continent that was now at war. Two of the delegates, Friederich Sigmund Schultze, Lutheran pacifist and chaplain to the Kaiser, and Henry Hodgkin, Quaker from England, as they parted at the Cologne train station, shook hands and said, "Our nations are at war but we are not. We are one in Christ and we will work for peace." Out of this pledge a conference was held at Cambridge University in December 1914 that led to the founding of the Fellowship of Reconciliation with five convictions:

1. That Love, as revealed and interpreted in the life and death of Jesus Christ, involves more than we have yet seen, that it is the only power by which evil can be overcome, and the only sufficient basis of human society.

2. That, in order to establish a world-order based on Love, it is incumbent on those who believe in the principle to accept it fully, both for themselves and in their relation to others, and to take the risks involved in doing so in a world that does not as yet accept it.

3. That, therefore, as Christians, we are forbidden to wage war, and that our loyalty to our country, to humanity, to the Church Universal, and to Jesus Christ, our Lord and Master, calls us instead to a life service for the enthronement of Love in personal, social, commercial, and national life.

4. That the Power, Wisdom and Love of God stretch far beyond the limits of our present experiences, and that Jesus is ever waiting to break forth into human life to new and larger ways.

5. That since God manifests himself in the world through men and women, we offer ourselves to Him for His redemptive purpose, to be used by Him, in whatever way He may reveal to us.[1]

Refusing to sanction war and killing and transcending the nation state, FOR members sought to sow the seeds of peace throughout that bloody war. Later, influenced by Gandhi, as well as by the teachings of Jewish and Buddhist pacifists, FOR became an interfaith fellowship that honored the nonviolence in all of the world's great religious traditions. It had programs to minister to the victims of war, including conscientious objectors who were treated as traitors, imprisoned, and in certain cases, executed. FOR, with members from a broad cross-section of the churches, both Protestant and Catholic, represented pacifist ecumenism. Pierre Ceresole of the Swiss FOR founded the work camp movement that brought together volunteers from former enemy nations to help heal the broken societies left by the war.

When I joined the FOR decades later, I was led to go to Europe to work with refugees, building houses in Nuremberg, Germany, in a project run by the Quaker International Voluntary Service. This was my first trip to Europe. Even though my heritage was part German, I found that being in Germany and hearing the language spoken at first stirred wartime fears and prejudices. In working side by side with German refugees in building houses, I began to outgrow those feelings when I recalled what a McMurry professor said one day in class, challenging our narrow provincialism: "You don't know what you like. You like what you know." Race, class, ethnicity, language, nationality: there are so many differences that initially at least can create suspicion, caution, and division.

The FOR branch in the United States was begun in 1915 and its efforts included campaigning for the release of imprisoned conscientious objectors (COs) and working for legislation that would recognize the right of COs' beliefs. This effort, carried on by a number of churches and organizations, won the right by a series of incremental benchmarks, from COs in the historic peace churches, to religious COs, to conscientious objectors of particular wars. With the changes in the Soviet nations in the time of Gorbachev, the communists dropped their former opposition to the CO position and the United Nations finally recognized the right of conscientious objection. This development furthered the concept of conscientious objection without specific religious grounding but, instead, from a nonreligious perspective of reverence for life.

The International FOR tried to prevent the advent of World War II with statements, marches, and peace rallies. It sent emissaries of peace such as Anne Seescholz, Muriel Lester, and George Lansbury to world leaders such as Roosevelt, Mussolini, Lloyd George, and even Hitler. It sought to arouse the opposition of nations and churches to the manufacture, sale, and use of weapons of mass destruction.

When the war began, FOR members joined in the nonviolent opposition. In the United States, they formed a project to prevent harsh measures being carried out against American Japanese and ministered to them when they were forcibly relocated to internment camps. FOR members protected Japanese property, businesses, and belongings wherever possible. Widespread, vicious, anti-Japanese prejudice made this work both difficult and absolutely necessary. The International FOR (IFOR) opposed the development of nuclear weapons and the Cold War that started after the end of World War II.

The U.S. FOR particularly worked in helping support and develop the civil rights movement, with education and direct action—sit-ins, marches, rallies, civil disobedience. Jim Lawson and Glenn Smiley held workshops across the South and worked with Martin Luther King Jr. during the Montgomery bus boycott. Jim Lawson, FOR field staffer, led the Nashville movement that helped end Jim Crow laws there. The Journey of Reconciliation, sponsored by FOR and CORE (the Congress of Racial Equality, founded by James Farmer and George Houser) challenged interstate segregation from the North to the Deep South. Houser, the only member of that journey still living, was to become a close friend many years later. Bayard Rustin, another member of the Journey of Reconciliation, was a brilliant black Quaker pacifist who was a popular public speaker and campaign strategist. An open homosexual, he ran afoul of public sentiment and much of the movement, including the FOR, distanced themselves from him—a hurt that was not healed for many years.

The U.S. FOR's motto (attributed to A. J. Muste) is, "There is no way to peace, Peace is the way." This stresses the unity of means and ends for which Gandhi was so famous, and he helped FOR grow in its understanding of nonviolence and of working with its proponents in all the world's faiths. Peaceful means must be used to achieve peaceful ends. Waging war to promote justice and peace contradicts this understanding. Successive wars—in Korea, Vietnam, Iraq, Afghanistan, the wider war on terrorism—have all been opposed by FOR, as each war sows the seeds of future conflicts in the killing and destruction of the present. As Dr. King pointed out, violent conditions are bred in a swamp of misery, poverty, illiteracy, and disease. Bombing those conditions deepens the suffering. The first step should be to drain the swamp and plant seeds of peace for the future.

In 1953, the year after my refugee work in Germany, I spent the summer in a building project at a Methodist Rural Center in Mexico, not far from Mexico City. Having grown up in Texas and taken two years of Texas history as required by our schools (I had one year of U.S. history, two of Texas history, and no other history courses!), I had given little thought to understanding the *Mexican* perspective on Texas. Texas was originally a part of Mexico, as had been much of the western part of what is today the United States. Seeing a Mexican portrayal of its history in Chapultepec Castle was really the first time I had been exposed to something other than an uncritical history of Texas and the southwestern United States. I was surprised to learn that Abraham Lincoln had opposed the war against Mexico, and I was surprised to see powerful paintings in Cuernavaca by Diego Rivera, a Communist, who was not popular in Texas during the Cold War. The extraordinary art, mosaics, and murals in Mexico gave evidence of a rich culture that

I had not anticipated. Discovering Mexico was full of rich surprises. Gogol's advice was right: see the world; you'll never regret it.

Coming home, I decided to go to seminary rather than to medical or dental school. I wanted to immerse myself in biblical and theological study and to draw on that in working for a just and peaceful world. My call to the ministry was leading me step by step into the conviction that I should follow Jesus, the Prince of Peace, wherever that might take me. I was glad that I had a strong education in science, gaining much from both scientific and religious insights and perspectives.

At that time the Methodist Church had a strong, prophetic program for world peace. It worked to develop an effective United Nations and its agencies such as the World Health Organization, the UN Children's Emergency Fund, and the UN Educational, Scientific and Cultural Organization (UNESCO). It was a strong supporter of the work of Eleanor Roosevelt and others who produced the Universal Declaration of Human Rights and the many efforts of the post-war world to move beyond narrow nationalism and to promote efforts to construct a peaceful world. Methodist women built the Church Center for the United Nations that has been used to the present day as headquarters for many peace and justice organizations and a center for related projects, meetings, and conferences.

As a seminary student, I was chosen to participate in the UN-New York Christian Citizenship Seminar sponsored by the student program of the Methodist Board of Missions, edited by Dorothy Nyland. I was introduced to the peace perspective at the United Nations and in the U.S. government; I returned the next year as the student leader of the seminar. The participants met with such leaders as Senators Hubert Humphrey and Wayne Morse. We met with our own senators so I had the privilege of meeting with the then majority leader of the Senate, Texas Senator Lyndon Johnson. I had first seen him when he was campaigning for the Senate by helicopter. There was great excitement as his helicopter landed on the grounds of Big Spring High School.

At the end of the meeting in his Senate office, he telephoned his wife, Lady Bird Johnson, to take me to lunch in the Senate Dining Room. In New York the seminar participants visited various UN agencies and I was especially struck by our meeting with Eduardo Mondlane, great African educator and nationalist leader from Mozambique (tragically, Mondlane was killed in 1969 when he opened a letter bomb in his office). Eleanor Roosevelt met with us in the Methodist offices on Fifth Avenue and gave us her personal perspective on her wide-ranging efforts for peace and world understanding. Her work as one of the writers of the Universal Declaration of Human Rights is a monumental achievement that continues to influence humanity's aspiration for a truly humane world order. The Declaration's focus on individual rights was later complemented by the International Covenant on Economic, Social, and Cultural Rights. The two together move us beyond the individualism of capitalism and the collectivism of communism toward what Walter Muelder of Boston University School of Theology called the "goal of personalistic communitarianism."

NONVIOLENCE: A WAY OF LIFE, A STRATEGY FOR CHANGE

Beginning in the 1920s the Fellowship of Reconciliation began studying and applying the life and example of Gandhi and the Indian freedom struggle in its efforts for racial justice, world peace, and FOR's various efforts to live out the implications of nonviolence for the whole of life. Having lived and worked in Southeast Asia for 13 years before joining the staff of the FOR, I was particularly involved in peace concerns and in situations involving human rights, liberation, oppression, and dictatorship. It meant being prepared to respond to invitations that would come from religious, peace, and human rights organizations, nonviolent underground groups, emerging movements, etc. I was part of an FOR team that went to Wounded Knee at the time of the occupation of Indian land by Native Americans to highlight the injustices the United States perpetrated on their tribe; the Native Americans met with us, but representatives of the U.S. government would not. I led a team to Tunis to meet with Yassir Arafat and leaders of the PLO in response to their request to explore nonviolence in the Palestinian-Israeli struggle. I was asked to be a speaker at a conference on democracy in Bangladesh sponsored by the International FOR branch there. I had extended meetings near the Thai/Burma border with Burmese soldiers fighting the central government; in 2007, I trained Burmese preparing to join the nonviolent monks opposing their oppressive government. With the initial invitation coming from the Little Sisters of Jesus who were working with the poor in metropolitan Manila, I became part of the People Power movement in the Philippines challenging the Marcos dictatorship. As Lithuania became the first Soviet Republic to seek independence, I organized an FOR team to respond to a request from the volunteer militia that was being formed to protect the parliament building from the Soviet Army. The Justice and Reconciliation Committee of the South African Council of Churches invited Walter Wink and me to lead workshops on the gospel and active nonviolence with the anti-apartheid movement. Not allowed to do this in South Africa, we had to meet in an isolated seminary in Lesoto, a tiny, self-governing black republic within South Africa. Hildegard Goss-Mayr and I were asked by the Maryknoll Sisters in Hong Kong to assist them in examining the impact and long-term result of the movement at Tiananmen

Square. In South Korea, in response to the oppression by the Park Dictatorship, a group of missionaries began quietly meeting on Monday nights to examine what was happening and finding ways to support the victims of the dictatorship and get censored news to the outside world. FOR was invited to send a resource person to meet with this group to explore efforts of nonviolent resistance.

I would like to describe the South Korean situation at this point as a representative example of these far-flung efforts.

In 1977, "the Monday Night Group," as it came to be known, invited me to visit South Korea as an outside resource person to contribute to their work. At the time, South Korea was under the brutal military dictatorship of Park Chung-Hee. It was a time of dangerous, ongoing confrontation with the Communist Korean regime in the North. Human rights and other freedoms were being flagrantly violated in the name of national security. The unsettled end of the Korean War left the peninsula bitterly divided, heavily militarized, and under constant provocations from the North and from the South. Public defense of human rights and social justice, a profound matter of conscience for at least a prophetic minority in the churches, schools, and labor unions, met with swift response by the government. Arrest, imprisonment, torture, and even execution, all in the name of national security and anti-communism, became all too common martial law practices. The Korean national intelligence service (KCIA) extended its intrigue and terror throughout the country as well as into the overseas Korean community in Japan, the United States, and other countries. Throughout my stay in the country, I was often followed by KCIA agents so my entire schedule had to be carefully planned.

The Monday Night Group began meeting as a way of sharing information at a time of maximum censorship. They needed a place to hear what was going on. They produced "Fact Sheets" to share with others. They wrote letters abroad to agencies and news services, as well as to local officials. They went with Korean family members to visit prisoners and helped raise funds as needed. They mobilized for action, joining protesters, hiding fugitives, standing with the oppressed as they were able. They prayed together and helped set up prayer services. Much to the consternation of the government, they became a reliable and speedy source of getting information out of the country.

The Korean Student Christian Federation, though having experienced staff arrests and the ransacking of their offices, was making efforts to hold occasional public events. It used my visit to schedule a public lecture on "The Way of Nonviolence." The event was held in the Christian Building, a large office building in Seoul. Even though government agents at the door checked everyone's identification, the hall was packed. In the middle of my address, a woman got up and loudly scolded a man in the audience whom she knew to be a KCIA agent, ordering him to leave the hall. Which he did! I was able to finish my address and be part of a lively question and answer session afterward. I never ceased to be impressed by the strong faith of Korean Christians.

One Sunday I preached at Galilee Church, a congregation that included many family members of imprisoned persons. My translator, the distinguished church leader and ethics professor Lee Oo Jong, spoke in a friendly way to the KCIA agents waiting outside the church. Her genuine goodwill even to the enemy put them to shame.

Many of the women in the church service were part of the project of knitting purple "victory shawls." The shawls were sold, with the proceeds used to buy blankets and warm underwear for prisoners of conscience who suffered greatly in the infamous unheated prison cells. When I left the country, the women gave me a huge box of the shawls to take home and sell on behalf of the prisoners. The luggage examiner at the airport was so amazed at the fluent Korean of my host, Randy Rice, that he just routinely checked my incriminating luggage when my flight was called, much to our surprise and relief.

Although it was a grave crime to criticize the government or the constitution, criticism of government policies could not be stopped. A dramatic example was seen at Seoul's Catholic Myung Dong Cathedral on March 1, 1976, the anniversary of Korea's March 1, 1919, nonviolent movement for independence from Japan. The three-hour mass/prayer service included the proclamation of the "Declaration for Democracy and National Salvation" signed by 18 of South Korea's leading citizens (including Lee Oo Jong, president of Church Women United; Stephen and Timothy Moon, brothers and seminary professors; Ham Suk Hon, the great Quaker patriot who was called the Korean Gandhi; and leading opposition figure and future president Kim Dae Jung). Despite their eminence, all were arrested and brought to trial, accused of plotting to overthrow the government. Their four-month-long trials were not open to the public. Wives stood outside the court wearing black tape crossed over their mouths, symbolic of democracy's death. Another day each woman wore her husband's prison number. And they wore purple, the color of suffering and victory.

The Monday Night Group planned an unpublicized retreat with me in the mountains outside of Seoul at a Christian conference center. We were able to meet free of surveillance so there was a relaxed, open mood to the retreat. We talked about the strong nonviolence tradition in Korean culture and societal practices. We examined the teachings of Jesus, Gandhi, and King and their relevance to a situation of harsh dictatorship. We learned about other nonviolent movements around the world, their struggles and difficulties as well as their achievements and victories among a diverse and growing number of groups.

The greatest emotional outpouring came during the powerful role plays where the group discussed and enacted some of their most difficult experiences, how they had responded and, if they had it to do over again, how they might respond differently.

They talked about plans for the future and were buoyed by fervent singing and prayer. They spoke of their hopes for what was to come and wished for wisdom, faith, and endurance to continue their witness.

The Monday Night Group met regularly over a period of many years, especially in the 1970s and 1980s. As a center of resistance, they demonstrated the power of truth, especially in a society where public information was widely censored with only the government's official point of view allowed. Foreign passports from the various nations represented in the group served as a protective shield that Korean citizens did not have. However, the police, the army, and the KCIA found ways to intimidate the government's critics such as George Ogle, who worked with the Urban Industrial Mission and was deported for his ministry with workers and the poor. During the harsh and lengthy time of his interrogation, Gene Matthews, an American Methodist missionary, and Didier Terstevens, a Belgian priest, maintained a vigil on George's behalf. They subsequently faced their own interrogation for such public actions.

The government learned ways of acting that would not stir up as much public sentiment as expulsion. For example, they began refusing to renew Alien Residence Permits on expiration. This happened to Fr. Jim Sinnot, Jean and Bill Bassinger, and Steve Lavender. Others had their status changed from "missionary" to "teacher," enabling the government to apply both subtle and direct pressure on the schools to control critics.

A huge scandal was the government's anti-communist concocted charge of a "Peoples' Revolutionary Party" plot to overthrow the South Korean government. Eight men were singled out as leaders of the party and a climate of hysteria resulted in the eight being picked up, tortured, interrogated, and executed. Demonstrations at the U.S. Embassy over the issue brought strong media attention to the scandal, although it was not enough to save the lives of those charged. Efforts on behalf of the men and their families were undertaken, resulting in further moves against human rights advocates. Gene Matthews was interrogated for two days by the police and another Methodist colleague, Butch Durst, was interrogated by the KCIA.

Thirty-two years later, the so-called Peoples' Revolutionary Party and the charges against the eight were officially and publicly declared to have been based on false information. This was a vindication of their families and their allies. Although it remains true that "Justice delayed is justice denied." The Brazilians have a term, *firmeza permanente* (persistent firmness), to describe the necessity of holding on to the truth and not giving up, whatever the cost. As Hildegard Goss-Mayr, the Austrian nonviolence scholar points out, this permanent firmness gives power to the powerless and weakens the authority and strength of the repressive forces in a society.

Members of the Monday Night Group stress that whatever they went through was nothing compared to the experiences of the Korean victims of cruel policies during the long struggle for democracy.

POSTSCRIPT

Many years later, in April 2009, I was able to meet with a reunion of the Monday Night Group at the Stony Point Conference Center in New York. All were now retired, though still active in their advocacy for a just and peaceful South Korea. Although the country had moved from dictatorship to democracy, there were still many, many challenges to a fair and just social order.

With a grant from the Korea Democracy Foundation, the Monday Night Group was able to publish a book, *More Than Witnesses: How a Small Group of Missionaries Aided Korea's Democratic* Stentzel et. al., 2006. With essays from most members of the group they told the story of how they chose not silence and neutrality but witnessing in concrete ways for and with the Koreans who were struggling for a just and free society.

I consider it a rare privilege to have been a part of such struggles all over the world. Martin Luther King Jr. wrote from a jail in Birmingham, Alabama, "We are caught in an inescapable network of mutuality, tied in a single garment of destiny. Whatever affects one directly affects all indirectly." These reflections of my life's experience have borne out Dr. King's insight again and again. Embracing the world, I experience a renewed calling and determined hope in my faith journey.

NOTE

1. Brittain, 1964.

CHAPTER 25

TRAINED TO HATE: CONFESSIONS OF A CONVERT TO HUMANITY

Claude AnShin Thomas

For my first 17 years almost all my experiences watered the seeds of violence in me. War was everywhere. I was raised in a small farming community, Waterford, in the northwestern part of Pennsylvania. My father, like most of the men in my town, had served in World War II. When that generation talked about war, they didn't speak truthfully. Unable to touch the deep and profound wounds that war had left inside them, they talked about war like a great adventure. So when I turned 17 and my father suggested that I go into the military, I didn't question him.

I also didn't know much about politics; it wasn't part of my life. Now I understand how important it is to know what is going on in the world. Though no long-term solutions to our world's problems are achieved through political ideologies, I am impacted by them, as is each of us, and we pay a dear price for this ignorance.

Today I understand that my father and the men and women of his generation were filled with illusions and denial about how deeply they were affected by their military service and war experiences. Having come home as the victors, they were thrust into a role: They became the protectors of our culture's denial about the profound and far-reaching impact of war—not just on those who fought, but on all of us. This cultural myth obliged my father's generation not to talk openly or directly about the reality of the individual war experience, and in a sense, for many of them, their inner lives had to be abandoned. Speaking truthfully wasn't encouraged in them or in me. But something unusual happened during and after the war in Vietnam: Many of us could no longer deny reality.

My father was an emotionally hidden person. Most of the time alcohol, tobacco, and other intoxicants provided the bonding agent that held his walls of repression in place. But, as is always the case, repression does not really work as a strategy for dealing with strong emotions. Some of what's hidden squeezes out.

In my town, there was a lake, and in the springtime the water level would rise because of the snowmelt. One day when I was around eight I went out to play. I had been given a new pair of tennis shoes with a clean and distinctive tread. That day I was supposed to be home at four o'clock. But what does a child know about time? When I didn't come home at four, my father got concerned and went looking for me. He went down near the lake and found small footprints going into the water but not coming back. The footprints resembled the tread of my new pair of tennis shoes. He became terrified with the thought that I had fallen into the lake and drowned. He came rushing back, and when he got home, I was already there.

He immediately took me into the bathroom, pulled down my pants, took off his leather belt, and beat me until I was black and blue and bleeding from the middle of my neck to my ankles. In the middle of what he was doing he realized that he was really hurting me, and he stopped beating me and started to doctor the wounds with Mercurochrome. As he was doing this, he said that he had beaten me because he loved me. All the time he was dressing my wounds, he kept repeating that he had done this to me because he loved me. That was the beginning of a long-term association: Love equals violence.

I don't believe that my father's intention was to hurt me. He just could not be afraid, could not stand to feel the reality of his powerlessness, so he expressed his fear through the only feeling he had access to: his rage. Unable to understand or tolerate the intensity of his emotions, he chose to see his problem as external. Then all he needed to do was control the perceived source of his distress. He was violent because he was not able to touch his own suffering. And therefore his suffering was acted out on me in this way.

My father's denial and repression ultimately destroyed him: He died at the age of 53 from a lifestyle that was dominated by his alcoholism, his addiction to cigarettes (50 nonfiltered cigarettes a day), and his general tendencies toward self-destruction. My father did not so much die as was unable to live. I believe that the culture of denial destroyed him, as it destroyed his father, and almost destroyed me. Yet this kind of denial is required to support the myth that war and violence are effective and lasting solutions to conflict.

My father's violence was not the only training ground for war that I experienced growing up. At the age of five, living with my parents in an apartment in Waterford, one day I wanted to ride my bicycle, and my mother didn't want me to. I was excited, and being a kid, I was persistent. My mother's response to this persistence was to push me and my bicycle down a flight of stairs—20 steps. Why I wasn't seriously injured, I don't know. Kids are flexible, perhaps. And they learn quickly.

This wasn't a one-time event. My mother often reacted with violence. One day, for no apparent reason, she placed her hand on the back of my neck, pulled me around, and smashed my face into a wall. Then she said to me that if only I were a better person, she wouldn't have to do that to me. I was being taught through these experiences to block out pain and to trust no one, especially those in authority.

My mother was also unable to have honest access to her feelings, to look at her suffering, and her pain. Like my father her unaddressed feelings turned into violence toward me. I was being taught the tools necessary to be an effective soldier. I became the carrier of the trans-generational effects of war.

I graduated from high school and I directly joined the military because I didn't know what else to do. My father suggested it, and he was my father. Even an absent father remains a powerful figure in a family's life, particularly in a son's. He and his friends who fought in World War II would all sit around and get drunk and tell stories that made war seem glamorous, exciting, and romantic. I not only listened to these stories, I drank them in, longing to be a part of them.

So I believed the stories, without question, listened to my father, without question, and joined the army. But one doesn't need to grow up with a father who is an ex-soldier to hear romantic and misleading stories about war. Popular culture produces endless movies that romanticize and glorify war. They almost never portray the reality of this experience.

And war, whether real or in the movies, is not the only place where a warrior mentality is cultivated. It is also nurtured through sports. I was very talented in all the sports that were offered in school. I actively competed in baseball, football, and wrestling. In fact, the only thing that kept me in school was my athletic ability. And in every sport and on every team, I found this warrior mentality. I developed a romantic vision of what competition, fighting, and battle were like. I envisioned war as just another game.

At the same time, I was extremely insecure, shy, withdrawn, and untrusting. I had the notion that if I went into the military, fought in a war, and received a lot of medals, I would come home a hero, and I would be loved, admired, and cared for. That is how the stories that I read, watched on TV, or saw in the movies went. It would just happen like that, and I wouldn't have to think about anything. "Go into the military," my father said, "it will help make a man out of you." And becoming a man, I thought, would mean being respected and being loved.

I remember the day I left for my military service. My father drove me to the bus station in Erie, Pennsylvania, a distance of about 25 miles from home. I had a little brown Boy Scout suitcase. My name was written on it in black Magic Marker. My father took me to the station, bought me a ticket, and left me. There was no good-bye hug, no handshake, no parting words. He just left me there to wait for the bus, and I went numb.

During basic training I was taught to hate. On the firing range we were shooting at targets that resembled people. We were learning to kill *human beings*. We had to be taught how to do that—that is the work of the military. This work is done in a variety of subtle and not-so-subtle ways. When we were done on the firing range, we were supposed to stack our weapons in a particular way. One day, as I was preparing to place my rifle on the stack, I dropped it. The drill instructor, a sergeant first class, screamed and cursed that I wasn't looking after my rifle properly, that my rifle was the most important thing in my life, because whether I lived or died depended on it.

He was six feet, three inches to my five feet, eight-and-a-half inches. He stood in front of me, his chest jammed up against my face, stabbing me with his finger and screaming obscenities down at me. Then he pulled out his penis and urinated on me, in front of everyone.

I wasn't allowed to wash for two days. I felt shame at such a deep level, I couldn't begin to handle it. Instead, all I felt was rage. I couldn't act it out on him because I would have gone to jail. So I focused my rage on *the enemy*. The enemy was everyone unlike me, everyone who was not an American soldier. This conditioning is an essential ingredient in the creation of a good soldier. Soldiers are trained to see others as dangerous, threatening, and potentially deadly. You dehumanize the enemy. You dehumanize yourself. My military training ultimately taught me to dehumanize a whole race of people. There was no distinction between the Vietcong, the regular Vietnamese army, and the Vietnamese general population.

But if I hadn't been prepared for this military training by the rest of my life, that kind of teaching might not have taken hold. As a young man I was encouraged to fight, to be prejudiced, and be nationalistic. I was taught that the way to solve problems was through violence. If there was a conflict, the strongest person won. I learned this from my mother, my father, my teachers, and my friends.

I volunteered to go to Vietnam because I thought it was the right thing to do. I didn't understand the nature of war or the nature of violence. Three days after I was in-country I began to understand. It was insane. It's difficult to describe what I saw. I could and can still taste and smell it and see the emptiness in everyone's eyes. It was like being in a surreal horror movie.

I was sent to Vietnam "unattached," which meant that I did not have a specific unit assignment. My orders sent me to the Ninetieth Replacement Battalion in Long Binh. Each morning we would get up, make our beds, eat breakfast, and then stand in formation for roll call. We'd then count off by fives or threes or something like that. Some days all the "ones" would get an assignment and ship out, some days the "twos," and so on. For those of us who did not get a unit assignment, there were details such as cleaning latrines, which entailed hauling a cut-down 50-gallon drum from under the toilet seat and then burning the human waste that it contained, or working in the kitchen preparing meals, scrubbing pots, that sort of thing.

One of these details was to clean up some of the huge warehouses full of products for the PX (post exchange) system. The PX is the military version of a Wal-Mart, where soldiers can go to buy food, cigarettes, and so forth. As I had not yet received a unit assignment, I was put on this detail and, bizarrely, spent my first three days in Vietnam destroying thousands of pounds of Milky Way candy bars (which were melting and rotting in the tropical conditions). With the encouragement of a noncommissioned officer in charge, I also "confiscated" (military language for stole) a necklace of cultured Mikimoto pearls, a purchase item that was far beyond my wallet. Two days later I brought them back because I knew that stealing was just wrong. But this confused, corrupt, surreal world of the war was just an extension of my experiences in basic training, where I was formally schooled in the absurd and grotesque reality of violence.

There was no "after the war" for me. My life, as a survivor of Vietnam, was an ongoing war. I isolated myself more and more from other people, took more and more drugs, and lived more and more on the fringes of society.

During all this time, however, I kept looking outside myself for some salvation, for some kind of answer. If I could do the right combination of drugs, the feelings would go away. Or if I could have the right job, I would be okay.

As a result of injuries suffered in a helicopter crash in Vietnam, I required reconstructive surgeries and then physical therapy in a United States army hospital. After I was released from the hospital, in August 1968, I returned to Pennsylvania, started college, and married my high school sweetheart. But I was incapable of intimacy, and the marriage did not last. While attending college, I had many relationships, none of which lasted. I don't know if I had any real intention that they last, but somewhere in my mind I kept telling myself before each encounter that this was the one. I felt what I interpreted as a powerful connection, and that could only mean that physical union was the answer to my problems. We would have sex, then my deadness would return, and I would abandon that woman in search of the next.

I had a son with one of the women that I met in college. When he was a small baby, he slept in a bassinet in the bedroom with his mother and me. When my baby son cried, I became intensely agitated, so much so that I would have to get high or leave the house. I didn't understand why, I just had to get away. I thought I was insane, crazy, that there was something wrong with me. Whenever he cried, I would feel the need to leave, to run. I realize now that there were multiple reasons for my intense reactions to his crying. For one thing, crying, my own or anyone else's, terrified me, was intolerable to me. Sadness had always been a forbidden emotion. But there were also other reasons why his crying caused me to panic, reasons that I wasn't yet ready to acknowledge and wouldn't confront for years to come. But by the time my son was three years old, I felt I couldn't stay there any longer. I left him and his mother. I was completely controlled by my suffering and unaware of how deeply afraid I was of facing what was inside me. I just knew that I couldn't stay still.

At some point, maybe six months into my service in Vietnam, we landed outside a village and shut down the engines of our helicopters. Often when we shut down near a village the children would rush up and flock around the helicopter, begging for food, trying to sell us bananas, pineapples, or Coca-Cola, or attempting to prostitute their mothers or sisters. On this particular day there was a large group, maybe 25 children. They were mostly gathered around the helicopter. As the number of children grew, the situation became less and less safe because often the Vietcong would use children as weapons against us. So someone chased them off by firing a burst from an M60 machine gun over their heads. As they ran away, a baby was left lying on the ground, crying, maybe two feet from the helicopter in the middle of the group. I started to approach the baby along with three or four other soldiers. That is what my nonwar conditioning told me to do. But in this instance, for some reason, something felt wrong to me. And just as the thought began to rise in my head to yell at the others to stop, just before that thought could be passed by synapse to speech, one of them reached out and picked up the baby, and it blew up. Perhaps the baby had been a booby trap, a bomb. Perhaps there had been a grenade attack or a mortar attack at just this moment. Whatever the cause, there was an explosion that killed three soldiers and knocked me down, covering me with blood and body parts.

This incident had been so overwhelming that my conscious mind could not hold it. And so this memory had remained inaccessible to me until that evening in 1990. As I sat there looking at this monk, Vietnam just came rushing back to me—all the unaddressed, repressed thoughts, feelings, and perceptions. I understood for the first time how the war had taken away my ability to have relationships. How the effects of war had prevented me, like my father before me, from having an intimate relationship with my son, or with anyone. I had left my three-year-old son and his mother not because I couldn't stand to be with them, which is what my suffering was telling me, but because I couldn't stand to be in my own skin.

From the time I came home from Vietnam until about a month before I went into a drug and alcohol rehabilitation program in 1983, I carried a gun everywhere. I couldn't feel safe without a gun. I slept with one; I ate with one; I went to school with one; I had one in my car. My sense of safety was completely dependent on this gun. I didn't yet understand that security and safety don't actually come from controlling the world around us (or within us). Later, from my study of the Buddhist teachings, I would learn that true and lasting security can come only from learning to live in harmony with our suffering.

One night in 1978 I found myself sitting on the steps of my house with an unloaded shotgun under my chin, pulling the trigger—click, click, click—screaming and crying, because my pain was so overwhelming. All I wanted was to die—but at the same time, I didn't really want to die, I just didn't know how to live with all this pain. I kept looking outside myself for something to help me, to fix me, to make it better. But nothing was working.

Many times I felt that the men who died in Vietnam were the lucky ones. Those of us who didn't die, who have had to live with the trauma and reality of this experience, continued to pay the price. We were the scapegoats for an entire country, for an entire culture that didn't want to take responsibility for its decisions and actions.

War does not begin with a declaration or end with an armistice. The seeds of war are constantly planted and the harvest is never ending. I experienced the war before the war in my family, then the Vietnam War, and then the war after the war.

The military teaches you to dehumanize, but much in our society also teaches us to dehumanize. And once you dehumanize, once that becomes a habit, it doesn't change easily. When we dehumanize others, we lose our own humanity. This doesn't happen just in the military: It happens through television, in the movies, and in magazines; it happens on the street; it happens in stores and in the workplace. Those who haven't served in the military are confronted with very similar kinds of issues. Think of the shootings in schoolyards, people beating someone to death because the person is gay or road rage. Even just shouting at someone in a checkout line because we can't tolerate the uncomfortable feelings that can arise when we have to wait. In many life experiences, we are dehumanizing others and being dehumanized.

The war in Vietnam, the war in Iraq, the war in Afghanistan, the war on the streets of Los Angeles, Hartford, Denver, Cleveland, or any town, the wars that take place in our homes—what are the seeds of those wars? Vietnam is only an expression of something that begins inside each and every one of us, male or female. We all possess the seeds of violence, the seeds of war.

When I entered a rehabilitation center for drug addiction in 1983, I was able to stop using drugs, stop drinking. After I stopped using drugs including alcohol, the obvious intoxicants, I began to learn what the other intoxicants were that were preventing me from looking at myself. And I began to stop those things also. I stopped using caffeine and nicotine; I stopped eating processed sugar and meat; I stopped going from one relationship to another. I kept coming more and more back to myself, in my commitment to heal, even though I did not understand (in any intellectual way) what it was I was doing.

In 1990 it became impossible for me to hide from the reality of my Vietnam experience any longer. Vietnam was not just in my head; it was all through me. I had talked intellectually about Vietnam, but I had never fully opened myself to the totality of this experience. Now the pain reached a point where it was so great that I wanted only to hide from it, to run from it yet again. My first thought, of course, was to get drunk. When I drink, it covers the pain like a blanket. But under the blanket, inside me, I am full of barbed wire; every time I move, it cuts at me, tears my skin. When I drink, I have the illusion that I have put a buffer between my skin and the barbed wire, but this is not the truth; when I am anesthetized, I am just not so aware of the ripping and tearing. Well, this time I didn't have that drink.

By 1990 I had abstained from drugs and alcohol for seven years. Now there were fewer places to hide from the reality of Vietnam. All my feelings about the war had been tightly repressed until then, and now they were coming to the surface. I couldn't push them away any longer.

At this time I was living in Concord, Massachusetts, and I was in counseling with a social worker, a wonderful, generous woman. When I got to the point where I felt totally overwhelmed by my emotions and wanted to die, she supported me, and in a spiritual way, she held me. I was trapped in the prison of self, confined by guilt, remorse, anxiety, and fear. I became so tormented that I was unable to leave my house. Physically and emotionally, I was under siege, bunkered in. My counselor continued to phone me and gently yet persistently invite me to come to her office. She continued to support the reality that I had *not* gone completely mad and helped me to understand that what was happening to me was the result of getting in touch with my feelings about the war, perhaps for the first time.

At a certain point she told me about a Buddhist monk who had worked with Vietnam veterans and had some success in helping them become more at peace with themselves. She suggested I read some of his books. It was only later that she told me he was Vietnamese. Because I had committed myself to healing, I said: "Sure, okay, I'll read the books," but I wasn't able to, because they were written by a Vietnamese man—the enemy. Every time I would envision reading them, I would think about the monks who opened fire on us.

Six months later someone else, a woman in a therapy group I had joined which was facilitated by this social worker, gave me a catalog from the Omega Institute, a holistic education center in Rhinebeck, New York. One of the pages of this catalog was bookmarked for me. When I opened it I saw a photo of that very same Vietnamese Buddhist monk, and an announcement that he was leading a meditation retreat for Vietnam veterans. Up to that point I had an excellent excuse for not going to see him: He lived in France and I didn't have the money to travel because I was unable to work; I was unemployable. There was, however, a note in the catalog, highlighted for me in yellow, saying that scholarships were available for those in need. I couldn't use the excuse of not having any money. I had made the commitment that I was willing to go to any length to heal, so I had to take this step.

I called to make arrangements to go to the retreat. I explained to the person on the phone that I had a very difficult time being around people. I became anxious and uncomfortable in ordinary social circumstances and needed to be by myself. I also informed the person that I was talking with that I had a very hard time sleeping at night, a polite way of indicating my intensely disturbed sleep pattern. The people at the Omega Institute were nervous about having me, an unstable Vietnam vet, attend this retreat; they called the organizers and asked if it was all right for me to participate. The sponsors said, "We don't turn anyone away." This was the response of the Vietnamese—my enemy. *They* said: "We don't turn anybody away." My countrymen, the people I fought for, wanted to reject me, yet again.

I committed to go and I drove to the retreat on my motorcycle. At that time I was riding a black Harley Davidson. I was dressed in a typical fashion for me: black leather jacket, black boots, black helmet, gold mirror glasses, and a red bandanna tied around my neck. My style of dress was not exactly warm and welcoming. The way I presented myself was intended to keep people away, because I was frightened, really scared.

As I've mentioned before, I suffer from a disturbed sleep pattern that has been a part of my life since a nighttime attack in Vietnam in 1967. Since that time, I haven't slept for more than two consecutive hours in any one night. For years I fought against this fact. You see, my inability to sleep became a symbol to me of how I was no longer "normal," a constant reminder of the war that wouldn't leave me alone. I so much wanted my life to be different from the way it was. My sleeplessness became the central symbol of my not-all-rightness, of my deepest fears that I would never be all right.

In my efforts to live up to my ideas of normal, I held many jobs. On the rare occasions when I could get work, I was not able to hold the job because I just couldn't function as well as people who sleep at night. I was usually tired and distracted, and sometimes I simply couldn't get myself to work on time, because the early hours of the morning had become the only time that I was able to fall asleep.

Part of the reason I had difficulty sleeping was because of my night terrors: the sounds (that aren't there) of artillery firing in the distance, of helicopters on assault, that special look of everything illuminated by artificial light, the sounds of small arms fire, of the wounded screaming for a medic. For me, this is what rises up out of the silence that is special to night. I hated the sun going down. I fought and struggled with my inability to sleep, and the more I fought, the more difficult the nights became. So I turned to alcohol and other drugs (legal and illegal) for relief, but my suffering just got worse.

After I went through drug and alcohol rehabilitation in 1983, I stopped turning to intoxicants (the obvious forms). Looking back, this is probably the single most important event in my life, because it gave me the opportunity to experience my own life and to experience it directly—the only place from which healing and transformation can begin to take place.

Some years after getting sober, I was standing at the kitchen sink in my cottage in Concord, washing dishes. Above the sink was a window through which I could see a row of 50-foot-tall pine trees that lined the driveway. That day as I did the dishes, I was watching a squirrel busy doing whatever it is that squirrels do, when I had a powerful experience. A voice inside me—the voice of awareness—said to me, "You can't sleep, so now what?" I began to laugh. It was a moment of complete acceptance. I finally understood that I just was how I was. To resist, to fight, to attempt to alter the essential nature of my life, was in fact making matters worse, and now I understood that I simply needed to learn how to live with the reality of who I was. In this moment I discovered that it was here, in the midst of suffering and confusion, that healing and transformation can take place, if I can stop trying to escape.

But I'm not special, you know. You can do this, too. You can face your own sorrow, your own wounds. You can stop wanting some other life, some other past, some other reality. You can stop fighting against the truth of yourself and, breathing in and breathing out, open to your own experience. You can just feel whatever is there, exploring it, until you also discover the liberation that comes with stopping the struggle and becoming fully present in your own life. This is the real path to peace and freedom. You could do this for yourself; you could do this for your family. Our whole world will benefit.

CHAPTER 26

Searching for Peace in the Peace Movement: A Lover's Quarrel

Rabbi Michael Lerner

I became an activist for peace in 1965 when I helped organize a teach-in at the University of California, Berkeley, against the Vietnam War, organized demonstrations against the war for the next seven years, served as chair of Berkeley's chapter of the militant Students for a Democratic Society, and was indicted by the Nixon/Mitchell Justice Department as one of the Seattle Seven for "using the facilities of interstate commerce with the intent of inciting to riot" and "conspiracy to destroy federal property." In a gross violation of legal procedures, I was sent to prison at Terminal Island Federal Penitentiary for "contempt of court" and J. Edgar Hoover described me to the media as "one of the most dangerous criminals in America."

Through much of this time I was engaged in a heated debate against those who said, "First we must change ourselves inwardly before we try to change the world."

I said then, and still believe now, that the kind of changes that are needed on the inside cannot be fully accomplished as long as we live in a world that rewards selfishness, materialism, and "looking out for number one" while ridiculing and marginalizing any who believe that the world could be based on caring, generosity, and love. In fact, as I was later to observe in the years that I served as a psychotherapist for the labor movement at the Institute for Labor and Mental Health, the daily experience that most people have in the world of work teaches them that everyone is out for themselves, that they must maximize their own advantage without regard to the consequences for others (if they don't someone else will maximize their advantage at your expense), and that these messages are inevitably brought home into personal life where people increasingly act as maximizers of their own advantage to the detriment of loving and caring relationships and families. I've documented all these dynamics in great detail in my books *The Politics of Meaning*, *Spirit Matters*, and *The Left Hand of God*. I remain committed to the view that challenging the global military industrial complex, democratizing the economy, requiring the media to present the views of the peace movement with equal time to that given to the glorifiers of war, and the elimination of the role of money in elections are necessary components of any strategy to bring peace to our planet.

But there was something importantly right about what those who focused on inward change were trying to say, and I discovered that as well in my work in the peace movement. I'm well aware of the various explanations that contributed to the declining influence of the peace movement in the 1970s, and I won't belittle, for example, the cumulative impact of the killings of John Fitzgerald Kennedy, Martin Luther King Jr., Robert F. Kennedy, dozens of Black Panthers, and demonstrators at Kent State; the impact of the Federal Bureau of Investigation (FBI), National Security Agency (NSA), and local police undercover agents who worked with the Cointelpro campaign to disrupt the peace movement by themselves engaging in and encouraging others to engage in violence, spreading lies about the leaders that sought to show them as racist, sexist, homophobic, or egotistical (to degrees wildly beyond the reality to which everyone in the society already was); and the systematic loss of jobs and careers for those who were most courageous in opposing the Vietnam War (even while some academics who had themselves avoided playing leadership roles or risking their own lives in demonstrations eventually were able to get positions in universities and get their books published). Nor do I underestimate the powerful way in which 9/11 was turned into a "war against terrorism" and played an important role in disempowering a new generation who might have wished to oppose violence of all sorts but who could not deny the reality of the deaths of thousands on American soil.

Yet in my experience there were other self-imposed limitations on our success as a movement that required and still require inner healing and transformation. And it is about those that I have been invited to write this chapter.

The first element of the peace movement's self-disempowerment that I discovered in the 1960s and which still plagues many activists is a persistent disconnect between our call for peace in the world and the way that we treated each other both in our movement and in our personal lives. Our meetings were sometimes characterized by strife that went far beyond the necessary and often helpful clash of ideas; at times there were ruthless attacks on those with whom we disagreed. We labeled others as imperialists, racists, sexists, homophobes, egotists, narcissists, power-hungry, screwed up, neurotic, psychotic, or having the basest of motives when in fact they simply disagreed with our perspective or maybe had not even heard it presented in a plausible manner.

Not surprisingly, then, we attacked those who were not yet part of our movement with disparaging rhetoric. We sometimes even split families and marriages apart on the basis of our political disagreements without adequately weighing in factors like love and caring and generosity of spirit. We tolerated violent discourse and we often were so filled with rage at the immense injustices and the violence in the world—in itself a natural reaction—that we gave too little attention to developing our own capacities to be peaceful and loving human beings. In short, we had missed the first and most important injunction of the spiritual world: to build peace in others, we must be at peace in ourselves.

In our idealism, we overlooked our underdeveloped capacity for compassion. This showed itself in the demand that peace and justice activists made of each other to be the fullest embodiment of our own highest ideals. Over and over again, peace activists who suddenly discover the depths of perversion built into the global capitalist order (with its structural violence that leads to the death through diseases related to malnutrition or inadequate health care of millions of children around the world every year, the sale into sexual slavery or prostitution of millions of children and teenagers seeking a way to feed themselves or their families, and the living in conditions of extreme poverty of at least one-third of the people of the planet, and the death in senseless wars generated by this global system of millions in each of the past several decades) become so outraged at the world they have come to understand that they want to overthrow it immediately. Frustrated in their attempts to do that, they at times turn on themselves and each other, seeing a failure to overcome the very materialism, self-interest, hurtful or aggressive forms of communication and action that they rightly perceive to be making possible the triumph of war on a global scale. This response, of course, tends to create an atmosphere of mutual accusation and self-blaming that makes the peace movement an unpleasant place to be.

So here is what is dangerous about the demand to be the peace in ourselves that we seek in the world or to be the values that we publicly proclaim: if we approach this very correct goal in a way that lacks compassion and a spirit of generosity. As a goal, embodying our highest ideals is absolutely essential. As a demand for immediate change, I've witnessed these goals turned into sledge hammers by which people manage to beat up themselves or each other, creating an atmosphere that makes many people feel defensive and scared. Part of the problem here is that the global culture of capitalism fosters an ethos of immediate gratification: we want what we want when we want it, and the advertising of commodities tends to inculcate in us the feeling that we can have everything and have it now. So if we know that we want ourselves and others to be different, then that should be immediately accomplished, too.

Unfortunately, human beings don't work that way. Changing ourselves is an ongoing process that may often require the assistance of psychotherapy, support groups, spiritual communities, meditation, and a variety of growth practices that sometimes take years to sink in deeply.

What I came to understand in my years as a peace movement activist, social change theorist, psychotherapist, and rabbi is this: if we want to build a new society, we are going to have to start with people who are somewhat less than perfect, maybe quite deficient, and don't fully embody the values they articulate. And the reason for this is simple: there's nothing else on the planet besides people of that caliber, like you and me.

So, if we want to build a peace movement that is actually going to work we need to develop in ourselves and each other a massive amount of compassion for the ways that we are not totally together, and that compassion has to manifest in our organizing, our movement meetings, our demonstrations, and the messages that we put out to the world. This is no easy task, given that the capitalist order fosters exactly the opposite. Getting to compassion requires challenging that tendency toward self-blaming or other-blaming. Ultimately, it requires seeing everyone from the standpoint of the totality of the human experience through history; the way we and others have been formed by the social and economic and cultural assumptions of the era in which we were born; the way that our parents and teachers fostered in us a conception of ourselves and our possibilities that has shaped many of our choices and limited our horizons in various ways; and how chance circumstances may have led some of us to new conceptions and new possibilities for growth while leading others to circumstances in which the same options were not given to them. Or as Phil Ochs beautifully put it, "There but for fortune go you and I." Really getting this and really being able to apply it to everyone, including those who continue to act in hurtful ways, is essential.

Compassion does not mean that we stop our struggle for peace and justice in the name of compassion for those who have chosen militarism and siding with the system that generates global inequalities from which they benefit. Militant but nonviolent demonstrations are not incompatible with compassion. Recognizing the humanity of, say George Bush, Dick Cheney, or Henry

Kissinger, and the way that their lives set the stage for their militarist path does not interfere with me believing that it would be best for the world (and in a way even for them) if they were put in prison for the rest of their lives; nor does it keep me from wishing to close down the weapons' makers and the corporations that are destroying the environment of planet Earth. But it does mean talking about the people involved with a deep understanding and sadness for the ways that their life situations pushed them in hurtful ways.

Similarly, recognizing the ways that we ourselves or others in the movement have been limited by our own conditioning should not be an excuse to avoid the process of self-examination and supporting each other to grow toward our highest selves. But there is a way of doing this that manifests love and caring and compassion, rather than hurtful judgment or public shaming.

So developing an ethos of compassion could be a powerful tool for growing a humane and hence more successful peace movement. Every public demonstration, every public meeting, every conference developed by the peace movement should have a dimension in which the value of compassion is not only articulated, but taught. Nonviolent communication, the ethos of nonviolence, the value of love toward others must become as prominent in our self-presentation and in the actuality of the movement as our analyses of the latest ways in which we expose the perfidies of those who claimed to be for peace and then, after getting power, defaulted toward war, militarism, and power over others.

And this leads to another way in which we need to reconfigure our social change movements, particularly the peace movement. Our peace movement talks a good game when it comes to describing the suffering of people in other parts of the world. I believe that for the most part the caring being expressed is genuine. But the feel of the movement internally is not one of much caring.

I got this most fully after reflecting on my own experience praying at orthodox synagogues, and visiting many evangelical churches that supported right wing politics. Whenever I'd go to more progressive synagogues or churches, I'd hear very enlightened sermons, often articulating peace and social justice messages that resonated with my heart. But after the services, I rarely felt personally engaged by others, and when I was, it was about ideas. Nobody actually seemed to want to know about me and my life and the problems and challenges I was facing. On the other hand, when I went to the orthodox synagogues or to the evangelical churches, I hated much of what was said in the sermons, but afterward I found the people warm and caring about me, asking me if I had a place to go for lunch, if there was anyone in my family or friendship circles who was sick and needed a visit in the hospital, was I single and did I want to meet someone to whom they might be able to introduce me, was I employed, etc. It was a kind of caring I never experienced in the anti-war movement. In fact, had I expressed any of these kinds of personal needs, I might have found myself being denounced for "using" the movement for "merely" personal needs.

A successful peace movement has to give much more attention to these dimensions of human need. We have to show that we not only care about people a few continents away, but also genuinely care about the people who come to our meetings or to our demonstrations. There are ways to do this even with our limited resources, but we first have to have an unambiguous and unambivalent commitment to being a movement that manifests love and caring, and not just good ideas.

And then there's another problem with our movement that I heard over and over again from the middle class and working people I met in my years at the Institute for Labor and Mental Health: the elitism that they perceived as a central reality in the peace movement. I've described many of the aspects of this in my book *The Left Hand of God*, and I only have space here to mention one of those—the condescending and sometimes even overtly hostile attitudes shown by people in the movement toward religious or spiritual practice. Yes, these people had seen the ways that the peace movement invited priests, ministers, rabbis (and more recently imams) to give greetings at peace gatherings. But the culture of the peace movement, they explained to me, is filled with an elitist consciousness toward religious or spiritual people. The Left, they told me (and their primary experience of the Left was through the peace movement), communicates the following message:

> Yes, we need you religious or spiritual people to come to our demonstrations or to vote for peace-oriented candidates. But essentially we believe that you are on a lower level of intellectual or psychological development than those of us who have overcome those kind of irrational ideas and we hope that through hanging out with us more developed types you will eventually be able to transcend your dependency on these irrational beliefs and come to the same high consciousness that we hold.

This is a message that manifests in a thousand different ways. It leads people in the peace movement to explain why they lose elections or why more people haven't joined them yet by reference to the stupidity of the American public or to their fundamental irrationality. And it leads many people who might otherwise want to align themselves with us to feel put-down, disrespected, and hence unwilling to be part of whatever we have to offer.

This impression of elitism has developed over several decades and it will take quite a lot to undo. It doesn't happen simply by having presidential candidates profess their religious commitments, particularly if, once in office, they don't act on the highest loving commands of the religious traditions of which they are part. It requires a whole new attitude among the masses of people who are part of the movement. The religio-phobia that permeates much of the peace movement and other social change movements must be treated the way we've treated sexism, racism, homophobia, anti-Semitism, and Islamo-phobia, namely as an attitude and practice that is destructive to our movement and has no legitimate place within it.

Of course, I don't mean that everyone should become religious. I mean that a full-blooded tolerance of differences between those who are religious and those who are not must permeate our movement so that people no longer feel one-down for being religious, and those who adopt a spiritual practice don't feel that they'd better "keep it to themselves."

And whereas we don't want to impose religion, a peace movement would be wise to actively encourage people to develop some kind of spiritual practice in which they took time each day to develop their capacities to be loving and generous, kind and nurturing to others, ethically and ecologically sensitive, and to respond to the universe with awe, wonder and radical amazement at the grandeur of all that is. I call this a New Bottom Line—and I believe that to the extent that our peace movement becomes a champion for this New Bottom Line that we can become a much more powerful force in challenging the militarism and the military-industrial-educational-media complex in all its various forms.

It would strengthen our movement if some time were given at meetings, for example, to meditation or to guided visualizations about the people who are in need of peace on our planet, or even to a focus on our own resistances to being more fully engaged in the peace struggles, or simply in learning techniques of relaxation, stress reduction, and ways to manifest more loving in our lives. Far from distracting attention from what was supposedly more important, giving 15 minutes to this kind of activity would have a pronounced positive impact in attracting people and sustaining their commitments.

I know that there is much more to be explored here than can happen in this chapter. That's why I helped create *Tikkun Magazine* as a location for this kind of exploration, and also created the interfaith Network of Spiritual Progressives that I co-chair with Benedictine Sister Joan Chittister. Our organization and our magazine are meant to provide a way for people who recognize that this spiritual dimension of human need must become an element in the work of the movements for social change, particularly those focused on peace, environmental sanity, and social justice.

It is through that spiritual focus that I eventually came to understand that one of the great problems facing the peace movement in the 21st century is that it is still perceived by people as a movement that is fundamentally negative—it has a clear idea of what it is against but not so much what it is for. It was through my own spiritual reading of history that I eventually came to recognize that the current peace movement is part of a larger struggle that has been going on for several thousand years, a struggle between two conflicting paradigms about the nature of human reality.

The first paradigm suggests that we are thrown into this universe by ourselves and find ourselves surrounded by hostile others who are seeking their own advantage and will dominate and control us to advance their own self-interest unless we dominate and control them first. We can sometimes make alliances within families, communities, or nations, as long as we understand that we can't really trust other people not to hurt us if that turns out to be in their interests, and the only way we can achieve security is through domination over others who want what we have. I call this paranoid perspective the worldview of fear, domination, and control.

The other contending paradigm argues that we really don't enter the world by being thrown into it, but rather through a mother who provided us with love and good-enough nurturing to make it possible for us to survive when we could not have done that on our own. From that early experience of love emerges a different view of human beings—that they are capable of genuine caring and love, and that we can provide ourselves and each other with security by building mutually caring relationships on the family, local, national, and global levels. I call this the worldview of hope, generosity, and love.

It is my contention that a successful peace movement will be one that makes explicit and embraces this second worldview and explicitly articulates the values of hope, generosity, and love as the foundations for building a world in which peace becomes possible. Such a movement would explicitly challenge the worldview that currently dominates in the Republican and much of the Democratic political parties—that security requires domination. For the Republican and centrist Democrats that domination must be primarily military. For the more moderate and some of the liberal Democrats that domination is meant to take the form of economic and cultural penetration of the world, and diplomatic means, to achieve the domination as well. But the goal is the same: that we get our way in the world and that others let our needs take precedence over theirs.

In contrast, the peace movement needs to articulate a Strategy of Generosity. We must help popularize the notion that our own well-being depends on the well-being of everyone else on earth and the well-being of the planet itself. Our security will best be achieved, we should be arguing, when people around the world can recognize that we really care about them and not just about ourselves.

It was for this reason that we at the Network of Spiritual Progressives developed a campaign for a Global Marshall Plan. The idea is to have the United States and the other G-20 countries dedicate between 2 to 5 percent of their gross domestic product (GDP) each year for the next 20 years to once and for all eliminate global poverty, homelessness, hunger, inadequate education and inadequate health care, and to repair the global environment. Such a program, if implemented in a sophisticated and caring way[1] could do more to defeat "the terrorists" than any war on terrorism will ever accomplish, by drying up the cesspools of hatred that our global system has helped generate. This is one example of what I mean by a Strategy of Generosity.

But here, too, we must balance the inner and the outer. No such strategy can ever work if it is perceived as just another strategy of self-interest on our part. Our caring for others cannot be merely instrumental or it will be a failure—to actually serve our interests, it cannot be pursued solely or even primarily for self-interest reasons. People are too smart for that—they know when they are being condescended to, and they know when they are being manipulated. It will take a huge change in consciousness in our country to achieve what needs to be achieved—namely, that the Strategy of Generosity is implemented because of a genuine spirit of caring, love, and generosity.

That change of consciousness cannot happen without it first being exemplified in our own movement. And that is just one of the many reasons why a focus on inward change must be given serious respect, attention, time, and energy in building the peace movement if we want it to succeed.

That's a big "if" at the end of my last sentence. I've been aware for several decades that one of the disadvantages of being part of the peace movement is that it often attracts people who unconsciously believe that they don't deserve to win, and hence are comfortable building a movement that will attract others who prefer to be part of a group that can righteously critique what is wrong in the world without any hope that they can change it. In fact, their unconscious certainty that they will not ever win leads them to build a movement and public presentations of themselves that guarantee that their unconscious defeatism is confirmed. I know that there is a huge disproportion of power in favor of the elites of this society who favor militarism—I call this real powerlessness. But there is also among many in the peace movement what I call "surplus powerlessness"—a tendency to hold ideas about ourselves, others, and the world that make us believe we are even more powerless than we actually are.

To uproot this powerlessness will require a great deal of inner change; and this is just one more reason why peace movement participants need to attend to the inner life if they want to change the economic and political structures of our global society.

NOTE

1. Please read about it at www.spiritualprogressives.org.

CHAPTER 27

Breaking Out of the Culture of Violence: An Oral History with Former Economic Hit Man John Perkins

Nikolas Larrow-Roberts and John Perkins

NLR: For the record, this is Nikolas Larrow-Roberts [NLR] interviewing Mr. John Perkins [JP]. We are being recorded at California University of Pennsylvania in California, Pennsylvania on February 24, 2009.

Mr. John Perkins has lived many lives. He is well known for his bestsell-
ing exposé, *Confessions of an Economic Hit Man* [2004]. In it, he details his
past covert role as an Economic Hit Man (EHM), while officially working as
a Chief Economist in private industry [specifically, at the engineering firm
Charles T. Main, where he was employed from 1971 to 1981]. Recruited by
the National Security Agency [NSA], Perkins covertly advanced the economic policies of the "U.S. Corporatocracy," which he described in his book
as "a coalition of government, banks, and corporations" that are committed—
by any means necessary—to ensuring that U.S. hegemony prevails."

Opposed to the Vietnam War, he joined the Peace Corps after college,
partly to avoid the draft and partly due to his fascination with Latin America. He had previously been profiled by the NSA, finding out that he had
the perfect skill set of an EHM. With a cover as a highly paid economist
in private industry, Perkins carried out far more clandestine duties,

becoming part of a business class who had built the largest empire in world history. Paradoxically, the devastating economic policies that Perkins brought to countries around the globe were marketed under a humanitarian rubric, such as alleviating poverty. As his conscience grew, so did the inducements—including massive bribes. Eventually, despite financial success, Perkins's disillusionment and shifting values reached a tipping point, causing him to abandon everything he had known. He has gone on to make major changes, becoming an advocate for the oppressed and issues regarding peace, justice, and sustainability.

NLR: Let's start off with some life history. What can you tell me about your upbringing?

JP: I grew up in rural New Hampshire, the son of a teacher in a boy's private boarding school. We never had very much money and lived in a house that was owned by the school. They took very good care of us. From the time I was about four years old, we always ate in the dining room with 200-and-some-odd boys. And yet, I was surrounded by boys who came from very wealthy families from all over the world. Quite a few were from Latin America, as well as from the United States, Asia, the Middle East, Europe, and various places. And so, I grew up with this tremendous desire to travel. I ended up going to that all-boys school, so I had very little contact with women. During Christmas vacation, spring vacation—times like that—I would be stuck in rural New Hampshire shooting baskets by myself in the school gym. All these others kids would go off and would come back with all these very wild stories about parties, orgies—things they had done in New York, Buenos Aries, Paris, and all over the world. I felt so left out of it. That just really spurred my interest and determination to do some of the things that they had done. It had a major impact on me.

NLR: What is the political and religious background of your family?

JP: Politically, my family was Republican, and extremely conservative. Since then, I've often wondered how my dad constantly voted for candidates who threatened to take his pension away—a great benefit of his job. I was raised as a congregational Calvinist. We were sort of the original puritans.

NLR: It's interesting that you use the word "confessions" for the title of your book. It sounds like penance, as if you're seeking some sort of salvation.

JP: Well, that may sound that way, but I didn't look at it like that. I do not seek salvation; I don't think there is any salvation for what I did, or redemption if you want to call it that. I have to live with what I did and I'm not proud of it.

NLR: Do you believe in redemption?

JP: I don't believe in the idea of redemption, but I do believe that we can learn from our past experiences and use those to go forward in doing much better things. That's my determination now; I'm committed to spending the rest of my life to create a sustainable, just, and peaceful world.

NLR: Considering your childhood, your current direction is quite a shift. It's even more dramatic in consideration of your professional role as an EHM, in which you essentially worked under the radar for the U.S. Corporatocracy. I'm sure readers will be curious as to what you are not proud of. How would you, then, describe how imperial power and social control is maintained, and what the role of the EHM is in that?

JP: The way we did it—well, there are many different ways—but typically, we identified a country that we wanted to have control over, usually a country with resources our corporations coveted, like oil. Then we would arrange a huge loan to that country through the World Bank or one of its sisters. But the money doesn't go to the country; it goes to our own companies to build infrastructure projects in that country. These projects could include power plants, industrial parks, or highways—things that will benefit a few very wealthy families, but don't help the poor people who can't afford electricity, and don't have the skills to get jobs in industrial parks, and don't own cars to drive on the highway. And they're left holding a huge debt to the United States—the whole country is and they can't repay it.

Then we go back to the country and say, "Listen, you're in debt to us, so vote with us on the next critical United Nations vote," "Sell your oil to us very cheaply," "Let us destroy the rain forests to take out your oil, then pass laws to make it easy for our oil companies to be profitable," or, "Send troops in support of ours to someplace in the world like Iraq today." That's how we maintain control. In the few cases where heads of state wouldn't accept these deals—like Omar Torrijos in Panama and Jaime Roldós in Ecuador—those leaders are very often taken out by "jackals," either through coups or assassinations.

[Perkins defines "jackals" as Central Intelligence Agency [CIA]-sponsored mercenaries.]

In the few cases where the jackals fail, such as in Iraq, where neither the EHM nor the jackals could succeed with Saddam, we send in the military. There's this whole process that goes on. The first part of it, which is usually successful—the EHM side of it—is very subtle, and it gets less subtle as you go on. The jackals are less subtle than the EHM and certainly the military is the least subtle of all.

NLR: You've mentioned that your determination now is to create a peaceful world. Did this personal transformation happen in one moment—a sort of epiphany—or was it a piecemeal transition over a period of time?

JP: It's fair to say both. When I first got into being an EHM, I just came out of three years of service in the Peace Corps in South America, in the Amazon and the Andes with indigenous people. And before that I had been to business school and I studied macroeconomics. I thought that the things that we were going to do as EHM—for example, building big infrastructure projects—were good for the economies of these countries; macroeconomics teaches you that they are. If you invest hundreds of millions of dollars—or billions of dollars these days—into big infrastructure projects, it usually results in economic growth, and econometrics shows this. And I thought that would be the case.

NLR: What was the case?

JP: Well, Claudine, my mentor and teacher, warned me that I would be in a "dirty business," but a side of me didn't quite believe that. I also figured that I would be different. In fact, the projects that I promoted did increase economic growth. What I didn't realize, and what was never taught in school, is that you can have tremendous economic growth in places like Indonesia—or today China—and yet you're not helping the poor; in fact, they are getting poorer. So the economic "growth" often, in many of these countries, benefits only a relatively few, very wealthy families, and it creates a larger gap between rich and poor and makes more people more poor. I didn't get that for a while.

So, at the beginning at least, I thought that we were going to be doing good things, despite what Claudine had told me. I was young, but as time went on, I began to see the fallacy of this and the lies.

NLR: Can you give an example?

JP: The World Bank has a motto of alleviating poverty, and what I saw more and more is that that wasn't the reality at all. The World Bank was helping the rich become richer. Over time, I saw this more and more and became disillusioned. Toward the very end of my [EHM] career, I *really* came to understand that we were about to exert tremendous pressure on presidents who didn't go along, who I was not able to "bring around," like Roldós and Torrijos.

In fact, ultimately, we assassinated them. And when I say "we" I don't mean "me"; I was not the person involved in that, I had no prior knowledge that it would happen. But I realized that if these presidents didn't give in to me that they are going to have to face the jackals. After 10 years, I really began to "see the light." And then, I did have one very tremendous moment of epiphany; it came after all the rest of the soul searching that had gone on for 10 years.

NLR: Would you tell that story?

JP: I was in the Virgin Islands, sailing on vacation, and I anchored my little sailboat off Saint John Island and climbed up to the top of this hill where there were the ruins of an old sugar cane plantation. As I sat there in this very idyllic setting, watching the sun set over the Caribbean, I suddenly realized that the plantation had been built on the bones of thousands of slaves, and then it struck me that the whole hemisphere was built on the bones of millions of slaves. Then I had to admit to myself that I was an enslaver, that what EHM were doing was a distinct form of modern slavery. At that moment, I decided never to do it again. I went back to my bosses and quit.

NLR: Did your family approve of you working for Main?

JP: Yes, very much; they thought that was great. They didn't see the dark side of it until many years later.

NLR: What about when you quit. What did you tell them?

JP: Well, I was not very close to my mother and my father up to that point. I had some pretty strong disagreements with them. When I quit, I just quit; I told them about it afterward. They didn't have much say in it. Later in life we got back together and became very close, but at that point in my life, I think that they were very shocked. They didn't have any influence over me at all in that part of my life.

NLR: Why do you think that you didn't remain desensitized to socio-political issues like other EHM did?

JP: Mainly because of my time in Ecuador while serving in the Peace Corps, where I saw the other side.

NLR: I've read that, while in the Peace Corps, you recognized the devastation being caused by oil companies. Is it fair to say that you did not yet have an understanding of imperialism and how it subjects everyone, in some way, to its rule?

JP: I think that's fair to say. There's a natural inclination in many of us not to believe that our country and our corporations would do the horrendous things that they're doing. I run into this all the time today. As an EHM, I had a very good life, traveling first-class around the world and staying in great hotels. There's a side to me that really enjoyed that and was in denial. Looking back, I see that there was an inkling that things were wrong. I had been opposed to the war in Vietnam, so I wasn't totally naïve.

People continually come up to me when I'm speaking and signing books and say, "before I read your book, I knew we were doing these things, but I really didn't want to admit it—even to myself—and if I ever talked about it to other people, they told me that I was crazy. And now that I've read your book, I know that it's true and I want to get out there and do something about it." I think that I was in that same frame.

NLR: Did your family see your enlistment in the Peace Corps as an odd choice? After all, here's a Kennedy program . . .

JP: I was determined not to go to Vietnam. My dad was very upset about that. He served in the Navy during World War II, and like so many people, he saw Vietnam as an extension of World War II. I didn't see it that way at all—it was a totally different experience. So my dad was very upset with me for not joining the military. However, he was a Spanish teacher who had a great fascination with Latin America; once he accepted the decision that I wasn't joining the military, he was quite happy that I got a Peace Corps tour in Latin America.

NLR: I'm sure readers will be interested in how your career has transitioned. Can you take us from business school to getting profiled by the NSA, and then later working for Main as an EHM?

JP: During my last year in business school, I was looking for ways to avoid the draft, and I was married to a woman whose father was very high up in the Navy. One of his best friends was very high up in the NSA . . .

NLR: "Uncle Frank?"

JP: Yes. And at that time, NSA employment was draft deferrable—not automatic but likely, at the discretion of your draft board. "Uncle Frank" arranged for me to interview with the NSA. It was an extensive series of interviews, including lie detector tests. They offered me a job as a trainee. At about that same time, I went and heard a Peace Corps recruiter speak. I joined them.

NLR: Why the Peace Corps?

JP: I had always been fascinated with the Amazon and with indigenous people. I had grown up reading a great deal about the Abnakis [who are First Nations, Native North Americans] and the indigenous people of where I had came from, in New England. I knew I had some—although very distant—indigenous blood in me. I also knew that my forefathers had killed Indians and made love with Indians. And I was aware that there was one place in the world where people still lived like that—the Amazon. I talked to the recruiter and he made me think that I had a good chance of going there.

"Uncle Frank" encouraged me to do it. I realize now that that was a very good training ground for what I would later do in life. While I was in the Peace Corps, a senior vice president from Charles T. Main came down and spent time with me and ultimately offered me a job.

NLR: Were you ever made aware of what type of personality or character traits made you a good fit for the NSA?

JP: Well, at the time, I thought I failed. I had been involved in this knife fight at Middlebury College where this Iranian fellow had protected me from this farmer who was trying to beat me up in this bar. The Iranian fellow had pulled a knife on the farmer, and as a result I ended up lying to the police—not telling them what I knew about the Iranian and his knife.

Under a lie detector test at the NSA, I realized that I was probably not going to get away with lying, so I admitted that I was opposed to the war in Vietnam and figured that that would be held against me. Yet, what I later understood was that the opposite was true; they were sort of indifferent whether I was for or against the Vietnam War, but they saw the fact that I was willing to lie to a police officer to protect an associate as very positive. I had no idea, but the Iranian fellow's father was very high up in the Shah's military—he was a General in the Iranian Air Force and a corroborator with our intelligence agencies—namely the NSA and the CIA. They saw the fact that I had befriended him and lied to protect him as something that might come in handy. In fact, it did. Ten years later, he sort of pulled me out of Iran just at the time that it was going to explode.

NLR: Organizationally, I'm curious how EHM would collaborate, if at all, with other government agencies, such as the State Department. Would plausible deniability keep you at a distance? Would the legal and subtle nature of your work bring you together?

JP: When I did encounter U.S. government officials, it was more like the Treasury Department, for instance, on the Saudi Arabia deal. Overseas, it was more likely to be USAID [United States Agency for International Development] people rather than State Department people. When I did come in contact with these people, they were usually pretty high-level, and they were not doing the jobs that I was doing. They were often overseeing policy. For example, the Treasury Department person who came and really got us involved with the Saudi Arabia deal was overseeing this very large amount of money to be paid to consultants like me to basically make the job happen. They weren't actually going to do it. That was typically my experience. The people that were doing that, in every case that I personally know of, were people like me who worked for private corporations; they were not government officials doing it.

NLR: And, the reason for that?

JP: That put a barrier between being able to accuse the government of corrupting officials in other countries. So it was a safety net in a way, and a pretty clever one.

NLR: I'd like to ask about your approach in dealing with presidents and foreign leaders as an EHM at Main. To recapitulate, you were convinced, at first, that what you doing as an EHM was good for some time. But gradually, you were led into accepting the latent inklings that you had. Did you ever try to convince them that the economic policies were truly good for them, or were you more honest in your approach regarding the consequences?

JP: It was a combination, and it would depend on the leaders too. A guy like Omar Torrijos was very savvy, and there wasn't any point in playing games with him. He knew what was going on and he'd call you on it. On the other hand, I met with a lot of government people in Indonesia and in Columbia, where you could sit down and say, "This is really going to be good for your country." And they would say, "Oh, of course it is. We're all doing the right thing here."

I used different approaches for different people. If the person across the table from you is going to go along with it, that made my job easier. With Torrijos, it was pretty tough, and he never did come around, and he was very clear on that from the beginning.

NLR: Can you tell me a story of a time when one of the officials who knew what you were up to either accepted or turned you down?

JP: Well, sure. Torrijos was the prime example. I remember one time when we were on a big sailing yacht, maybe 100 feet long. It was lent to him by a very wealthy person and it was docked on Contadora Island off the coast of Panama—an island where we would take diplomats and corporate executives. Basically anything goes on Contadora and it never leaves Contadora. So, it was whatever you wanted: drugs, booze, women, whatever. Well, I remember being there on this yacht with Omar in a cockpit full of some of his advisors, and there were gorgeous young women in bikinis or less, and lots of rum and cigars being passed around. Well, I'm there specifically to keep working on Omar to "bring him around." And at the same time, he's kind of laughing at me and saying, "Oh, I'm not coming around, I don't need anything else. Look, I've got *this*, you know? I've got a great life, I've got a good house, I've got a good wife, and I've also got this" . . . and he waves his hands around at this cockpit filled with these beautiful women and rum and cigars and he says, "The only thing I don't have is what I need for my people," and he said "those people over there," and he pointed beyond Contadora Island toward Panama, and he says, "They need to be treated justly. You gringos have taken our country away from us, you built this canal and I want my people to get this canal back, and I want your country to pay for the damages you've done here. I want to set an example for all the other people in Latin America and around the world that have been exploited by you— that's what I want. I don't need your money, and why don't you come work for me?" Because—and again he points around this cockpit, and says—"You'll have a lot more fun and you won't make nearly as much money, but who needs the money? You get what money buys and you'll feel that you're doing something good for the poor people of the world."

NLR: Did you think about it?

JP: No, no, I really didn't. I mean that was not an option at that point in my life. Well, I suppose that I sat on this boat and I looked around and I'm thinking about it, but up in the hotel in Contadora there was a young woman who worked for me who was waiting for me there and she was pretty good, too, so I had it good anyway.

NLR: Did you ever reveal any of this to your wife? I mean, I know that your wife got you into some of these arrangements as you said earlier, through "Uncle Frank."

JP: No. No. I had to be *very* careful about that. She couldn't know about Claudine. She couldn't know about any of this. I wasn't supposed to tell anyone about it and I didn't tell anyone about it.

NLR: On a professional level, what would happen to you when you could not get Torrojos, for example, to accept these economic arrangements? Would you describe that as failing in your mission?

JP: First, my job was to bring him around, and so I was failing at my job; and, secondly, I was afraid that if I didn't bring him around, something worse might happen to him. I knew what happened to [President Salvador] Allende in Chile. I knew what had happened to [President Jacobo] Árbenz [Guzmán] in Guatemala and [Prime Minister] Lumumba in the Congo. Torrijos often reminded me of these things.

NLR: Did you learn about the consequences of failure from someone? Was it as if Claudine would say, "You know, John, you are aware of what happens if you fail" or something like that?

JP: At the end, I became very aware. I was actually privy to discussions around a plot to assassinate a leader of an African country. This is part of a book I'm writing now so I can't go into much detail. In the last year or so, I became very aware that Torrijos and Roldós were really at danger. They were not assassinated until I had left, but I became aware that these sorts of things were very likely to happen, and that's when I knew that I had to get the hell out.

NLR: Was the decision to quit being an EHM strictly due to your moral opposition to it, or was there also a professional dimension at play? As you said, you were "failing at your job" in certain respects.

JP: No. I had a staff of several dozen people working for me. They were highly skilled, much more skilled than me—PhDs and MBAs. I was their boss, and our department was doing very well. I was on a course to becoming very rich in the company as everything indicated. As it turned out, the company went bankrupt because of some lousy decisions that were made by Main's president, but that didn't happen till a couple years after I got out. When I left, I had every reason to believe that if I stayed in there, I would do extremely well financially. So, I was failing with Torrijos in Panama, but my department was doing very well all over the world and we had struck this incredible deal in Saudi Arabia. We had projects all over the place.

NLR: You've written about how government essentially serves the interests of business. In terms of social control, what we see today is undeniably a top-down structure. Now, regarding intentional and peaceful social change, do you see peace happening the same way, from the top down? Can you comment about that, namely the top-down versus bottom-up trajectory to positive change?

JP: It has got to come from us, the people, it always has. Slavery didn't end because Abraham Lincoln got in the White House; Lincoln was put in the White House because enough people wanted to end slavery. The Vietnam War didn't end because Nixon was an anti-war person; Nixon ended the war because of pressure put on him—and corporations—to end the war. Apartheid ended because of pressure put on corporations supporting apartheid, and so on and so forth. We force corporations to clean up terribly polluted rivers in this country and to get rid of trans-fats in foods. It's always "we the people" the government follows to make the laws that supervise and regulate it.

NLR: How does that translate into an actionable plan today in bringing about peace?

JP: We have to take the stand. We truly have the first global empire in the history of the world. It's an empire that for the first time hasn't been created by the military for the most part. Unlike every other empire before it, this one has been created through EHM and corporations. That means that it doesn't get changed by military action; it gets changed by the way we vote in the marketplace. That's because every one of these corporations is dependent on you and me and everybody else buying their goods and services. If a critical mass of us let Nike know we're not buying their products because they're made in sweatshops, and we let Patagonia know we're buying their products because they're not, then the sweatshops will go away or get transformed into legitimate factories where people get fair wages.

So the marketplace is really very democratic if we choose to make it democratic, and for the most part we haven't done that up till now, although we have done it in certain instances. If we want to create a world our children will be proud to inherit, if we want to create a truly sustainable, just, and peaceful world, then we've got to pressure the corporations to have that as part of their goal. Right now, their goal is to maximize profits regardless of the social and environmental costs; that is their goal across the board. That's something that Milton Friedman and the Chicago School advocated.

NLR: Can they serve two goals, two gods?

JP: Yeah, we just need to turn that goal around and say, "Listen, it's fine to make profits, but only within the context of creating a sustainable, just, and peaceful world." We don't expect perfection, but I'm only going to buy from companies that are headed in that direction. And when we do that, we have tremendous power; we just need to recognize that. Right now we're seeing how incredibly vulnerable these corporations are. This economic crisis that we're going through now has pointed it out like it's never been pointed out before; it pointed out how the regulatory process is important. I'm sure there is an economist out there who would disagree with me, but it's pretty hard to defend Friedman these days and that whole idea that the sole social responsibility of a corporation is to increase its profits.

NLR: And why is that?

JP: Because we've seen a lot of corporations increase their profits tremendously, but they did so in a way that was incredibly disastrous in the long run.

NLR: And what are your thoughts regarding the ethics of capitalism from the other side of the corporate coin—government?

JP: Starvation, deprivation, and desperation force people sometimes to follow fanatics like Bin Laden. The lack of regulations and the adulation of materialism and overblown salaries cause others to go the route of Bernard Madoff and the many Wall Street executives we read about these days.

NLR: I'd like to ask you about some of the work that you are doing today.

JP: Well yes, very soon after I stopped being an EHM, I formed a company—Independent Power Systems—to develop environmentally good energy projects and we were pretty successful at doing that. This was back in the 1980s. Later on in the 1990s, I founded and co-founded several nonprofit organizations that are dedicated to a sustainable, just, and peaceful world—Dream Change Alliances, for example. And I'm still serving some with some of these nonprofits and getting involved in those activities. But more than anything else, I'm devoting myself to writing and speaking, especially at high schools, colleges, and universities. I'm trying to help young people get a better grasp of what's really going on in the world, how important it is to change it, and how much power we all have in changing it. This Friday night, I'm speaking at Boston University; I'm the keynote opening speaker for the model UN program for 1,300 high school students. This is my life now. It's really working as much as possible with young people to inspire and empower them. The only way my grandson—who is 16 months old—is going to inherit a sustainable, just, and peaceful world, is if every child on the planet inherits the same world.

We've recently become a very small planet. This just happened in the last couple of decades that we've become so tiny. It used to be that nations were very important; today they are not as important. Every one of us on this whole planet faces the same crises: global warming, diminishing resources, species extinction, increasing prices of fuel and foods, the violence that comes out of depravation and starvation, and now this economic crisis. It used to be that Florida had hurricanes, Indonesia had tsunamis, and California had earthquakes, but today we are all facing the same crises and we all are communicating with each other through the Internet and telephones. Everybody knows this, and so we're in a situation that human beings have never ever been in before.

NLR: What does this mean for tomorrow's leaders and visionaries?

JP: Well, it's very exciting. Today's young people have an opportunity like we've never had before, to really create a whole new paradigm and a new philosophy to really look at this world as being a place that we must make peaceful. We essentially have no alternative besides more and more collapse.

NLR: You've noted how you were bothered by a guilty conscience as an EHM, after the epiphany at St. John Island. Psychologically, that realization must bear significant weight.

JP: At Wharton recently, during the Q&A period of one of my talks, a man raised his hand. I called on him and he said, "I'm an economics professor here and I told my students that we're going to hear from an EHM tomorrow. One of my students asked yesterday in class: 'This guy [John Perkins] lived a great life, traveled around the world, living first class, had a wonderful time, and now he's writing books and talking about all the bad things he did. . . . Well, can you tell me why we shouldn't all go out and have a great life and then do that?'" The professor replied, "I couldn't answer him, so I'm asking you, what do you say?" I said, "Well, I *didn't* have a great life; it may look good on paper, but once I understood what I was doing, my conscience was really bothering me. I couldn't sleep at night, I was popping Valium like there was no tomorrow and drinking a lot of alcohol. So, I did not have a great life. I have a great life now, now that I'm out trying to really create a better world." So I look at this audience of MBA students and say, "So don't make the same mistake I did when you graduate. Dig right in and do the right thing to begin with, and then you'll have a great life."

NLR: What a message for an audience of MBAs! What are they going to do now with their lives?

JP: Well, it's interesting. I spoke at Wharton again three years later. And I've seen a huge change. Each time I was there, my agent set up a dinner with 20 or 30 students beforehand. And I said to them, "I want to hear from you—each of you." Well, three years ago, they were all still talking about power and money. Now, almost every one of them talks about social and environmental responsibility.

NLR: It sounds like you found an end to the suffering in living the life that you do now.

JP: I have to live with what I did; however, I feel that having those experiences gives me an advantage toward my personal commitment today.

NLR: Well, John Perkins, even though you're not looking for it, thanks to free will, I think you've done enough to earn your redemption, even as a Calvinist.

JP: Well, I'm glad to hear it. Thank you and good luck.

NLR: You know, if it's possible for an EHM to come to peace and justice, then I'm not sure who that leaves exempt. I thank you very much for your participation with this anthology.

JP: You're welcome. Follow your heart and realize your dreams.

CHAPTER 28

INSPIRING PEACE WORKERS

Marc Pilisuk and Michael N. Nagler

The successful nonviolent overthrow of President Ferdinand Marcos's dictatorship in the Philippines, culminating in February 1986, gave the world a new name for a very old phenomenon: "people power."[1] Whether or not the name helped, the phenomenon has certainly been spreading widely as governments and other "top-down" institutions lose their grip on an increasingly complex reality with which they can only deal in a way that is cumbersome at best and violently oppressive at worst. It could be argued, however, that real peacemaking, especially if it is to be lasting in its effects, comes from an even less formalized "institution," if you will: from "person power." All real contributions to the Peace Movement originate with and are sustained by individuals, sometimes acting in concert but always drawing on their individual energy. As Cardinal Jaime Sin observed of the vast numbers who interposed themselves between the "rebel" soldiers who had defected to the revolution and the contingents Marcos had sent to attack them, "It was amazing. It was 2 million independent decisions. Each one said, in his heart, 'I will do this,' and they went out."[2]

Some personal actions are small, but have a "trim-tab" effect like that of Rosa Parks's refusal to vacate her seat on a Montgomery bus; others remain private and hidden, but nonetheless, as we believe, have their invisible bearing on the overall climate of peace or war. Some are the result of a specific transformative experience, while others arise in the course of a long-term dedication to a life of caring (Rosa Parks had recently gone through a course in justice and resistance at the Highlander Folk School). Some endure deep sacrifice, like the final example in this chapter; but impressive to us are the numbers who find their work for peace the most satisfying and meaningful way to spend their lives.

Because there are obviously so many more of these contributors, sung and unsung, than we could possibly include in even these three volumes, we conclude the set with a few more representative cases, hoping to emphasize the importance of each one of them and ultimately each one of *us* as a strand of something much larger that, taken together, blends into a strong tapestry that enfolds and shelters the experiment of life.

BERTHA VON SUTTNER (COUNTESS KINSKY VON WCHINITZ UND TETTAU, 1843–1914)

Baroness von Suttner was born in Prague, into a family of the declining Austrian nobility and went to work as a governess for the wealthy von Suttner family from 1873 to 1876, during which time she became engaged to engineer and novelist Arthur Gundaccar Freiherr von Suttner. His family, however, opposed the match, and she answered an advertisement from Alfred Nobel in 1876 to become his secretary-housekeeper at his Paris residence. She only remained a week before returning to Vienna and secretly marrying Arthur on June 12, 1876. The couple lived in the Caucasus, where they read, wrote, and studied until they were reconciled to the family and returned to Vienna. Though staying with Nobel for less than a week, the two met occasionally and wrote much, and it was she who encouraged the inventor of dynamite to found the Nobel Peace Prize at the turn of the century.

In the meantime she had become an ardent pacifist, committed to what she called "the greatest of all causes" for the rest of her life; most notably, in terms of her influence on Nobel and millions of others down the years, she wrote perhaps the most successful anti-war novel of all time, *Die Waffen Nieder!* (Lay Down Your Arms!, 1889). Tolstoy compared it to *Uncle Tom's Cabin* (and we might place it alongside Rachel Carson's *Silent Spring* in terms of its consciousness-raising effect). The novel appeared just when the modern peace movement was taking shape as an international entity, and it catapulted von Suttner into fame within and beyond those circles.

A tireless worker for peace in a Europe that had grown apathetic because it was experiencing a brief reprieve from major war, she founded many societies and was a prominent hostess of statesmen and intellectuals at the first Hague Peace Conference in 1899. This conference, called by the Czar to promote disarmament, basically failed at that goal but succeeded in taking steps toward establishing the Permanent Court of Arbitration at The Hague.[3]

This vindicated von Suttner's emphasis on institutions for arbitration rather than relying on disarmament agreements. We may note that 100 years later, when The Hague Conference was reconvened, Americans Mel Duncan and David Hartsough met and vowed to create what is now the Nonviolent Peaceforce (see Christine Schweitzer, Volume 2, Chapter 8). Among relatively minor accomplishments by this central figure at the origins of the modern peace movement, von Suttner became the first woman political journalist in the German language.

During her lifetime, von Suttner received many awards, culminating, of course, with the Nobel Peace Prize of 1905 that had been founded at her instance five years earlier (Nobel himself had not anticipated that it would take that long for her to receive it). She was, needless to say, the first woman to be so honored. An important peace journal was named in her honor and today there are postage stamps, coins, and other memorials to her tireless dedication, while a film entitled *Die Waffen Nieder* by Holger Madsen and Carl Theodor Dreyer was released in Norway in 1914. She died in Vienna a few months before the carnage she had worked so hard to avert.

PEACE PILGRIM (MILDRED NORMAN, 1908–1981)

Sometime in the early 1800s a pious Russian went into his local church to pray the liturgy, heard the words "pray without ceasing" being read from the pulpit (*Thes.* 5:17) and spent the rest of his life wandering the byways of Old Russia with the Jesus Prayer constantly on his lips. Sometime in the 1920s, a young farm girl from Egg Harbor City, New Jersey, read the Golden Rule in a history book and, like the Russian pilgrim before her, unaccountably took it seriously. This was Mildred Norman, later known to the world as Peace Pilgrim, who was to cross the United States on foot seven times before her death, ironically, in an auto accident on her way to a speaking engagement in Knox, Indiana. She carried her mission on a sheet of paper stuffed into her signature blue tunic that was, with the other clothes on her back, all she possessed: *I shall remain a wanderer until mankind has learned the way of peace.* She was what we would call today an "inspirational speaker," but she was far more than that: a wandering *sadhu*, a *parivrajaka* of a type that is familiar in India, was not too uncommon in Old Russia, but unheard of in the United States. And on top of that she was a sadhu with a mission: world peace. Her writings and some scraps of her talks are now given away free by the Friends of Peace Pilgrim, and over 400,000 copies of the book *Peace Pilgrim: Her Life and Work in Her Own Words* and over 1,500,000 copies of the booklet *Steps toward Inner Peace*. Books and booklets have been sent to over 100 countries. The book has been translated into 12 languages and the booklet into over 20. They are an amazing journey of wisdom. It is impossible to document in any other terms how this wise, compassionate woman touched the lives of so many who were fortunate enough to meet and hear from her; but it is impossible not to believe that those encounters have had a profound impact on our lives today.

PETRA KELLY (1947–1992)

Petra Karin Kelly was a woman of great compassion and intensity, a woman whose work continues to be an inspiration to those who strive for the peace, ecological protection, and human solidarity that she worked tirelessly to achieve. Her work arose from a combination of three principles of peace activism. First, issues of peace, social justice, and environmental protection were inseparable. Second was her uncompromising stance on issues of deep principle. She could not accept even a "mild" form of torture or a "safe" level of radioactivity. Third was her belief that these issues came with a mandate to make the political process responsive to them.

Kelly was inspired by the life of Martin Luther King Jr. Her most notable achievement came in 1979, when she was instrumental in founding the German Green Party, called *die Grünen*, the most influential and politically successful of the Green Parties. Formally founded in 1979, it came out of a coalition called "Alliance 90," developed in the 1970s, and came to power in 1983 with the state elections, during which Kelly was elected to the German Bundestag (parliament). The focus of *die Grünen* in its origins was on four main principles as follows: ecology, social justice, grassroots democracy, and nonviolence making it, possibly the only seated party outside India to adopt nonviolence as a leading principle. Her years in Parliament (1983 to 1991) were packed full of activity and accomplishment for herself and her partner, former General Gert Bastian, who left the Army in protest over the stationing of nuclear weapons on European soil in the 1980s. Kelly recognized controversy between the political and spiritual/political wings of the Green movement and was distressed by it. She believed that both wings belong together, complement each other, and are part of each other, that we cannot solve any political problems without also addressing our spiritual ones. For her that meant, above all, respecting all living things and the interrelatedness and interconnectedness of life.

Her intense personal compassion set a pattern for her life as a social activist who created or worked through institutions with lasting impact on sociopolitical culture. She worked with the European Commission in Brussels, Belgium, for 12 years (1971 to 1983), with which she participated in a number of campaigns for peace and environmental justice throughout Germany and surrounding countries. Anti-nuclear issues, feminism, research on childhood cancer, and Tibet (she adopted a Tibetan refugee child) were among her marked concerns. Kelly's book, *Nonviolence Speaks to Power*, based on five influential speeches, was published by the Center for Global Nonviolence in Hawaii in 1992.[4] In 1982 she was honored with the "alternative Nobel Prize," called the *Right Livelihood Award*, and was listed as one of the 1,000 most influential women in Europe. She wrote and spoke consistently on the key issues of ecology, justice, and peace throughout the world.

In October 1992, Kelly was found dead along with Gert Bastian in what was apparently a murder-suicide. The pair had by then lost some political influence but Kelly's death was mourned throughout the peace movement worldwide, and to continue her legacy the Petra Kelly Foundation was founded five years later as part of the Heinrich Böll Foundation. Since 1998, the foundation has presented an annual Petra Kelly Prize for Human Rights, Ecology, and Nonviolence.

THICH NHAT HANH (1926–)

Thich Nhat Hanh is one of the best-known and most highly respected Zen masters in the world today. He is also a brilliant poet, a teacher an author, and an activist for peace and human rights. He was only 16 when he joined the Zen monastery, Tu Hieu Temple, to study Buddhism and was fully ordained as a monk in 1949. Seven years later, he became editor-in-chief of *Vietnamese Buddhism* and later founded the Lá Bối Press. In the 1960s, Thay (as he is popularly and affectionately called) worked tirelessly on behalf of those who were affected by the Vietnam War. His main focus on urging the United States government to withdraw from Vietnam was captured in his moving book, *Lotus in a Sea of Fire*. During this time he founded the School of Youth for Social Services (SYSS) in Saigon, a grassroots organization established to provide relief for institutions, communities, and families that were injured, damaged, or left homeless during the Vietnam War. He also founded the Van Hanh Buddhist University in Saigon. He travelled to the United States to attend Princeton University and spent time as an educator at Cornell and Columbia Universities. He had a significant influence on Martin Luther King Jr., who nominated Thay for the Nobel Peace Prize in 1967.

Some of Thay's most notable achievements have to do with his work in developing Western Buddhism, particularly founding the practice of Engaged Buddhism and coining the term "Interbeing"—all inspired by the integration of traditional meditative practices, dharma teachings, and an active nonviolent civil disobedience. Hanh believes that Buddhist principles reveal the ultimate inter-connectedness of all things and, inspired by the reform movement of Humanistic Buddhism in China, created Engaged

Buddhism as a way to practice this type of integration within his own spiritual community. As he often says, "engaged Buddhism is just Buddhism."

After his peace mission to the United States and Europe in 1966, Thay was exiled from his native Vietnam. It is believed that he significantly influenced U.S. politics and history when he encouraged Martin Luther King Jr. to publicly oppose the Vietnam War. After being exiled by his own government for his efforts to end the violence happening to his own people and to spread Buddhist values of peace, harmony, and diversity around the world, he has continued to live in exile from his home country to this day. In 1982, he founded Plum Village, a Buddhist community in the South of France. He continues to engage with nonviolent civil disobedience efforts to alleviate suffering of the oppressed. He also teaches, writes, spends time in nature, and leads global retreats on "the art of mindful living." According to Thay,

> Everyday we do things, we are things that have to do with peace. If we are aware of our life . . . our way of looking at things, we will know how to make peace right in the moment, we are alive.[5]

KENNETH E. BOULDING (1910–1993)

Kenneth Boulding was an economist, educator, peace activist, poet, devout Quaker, who had an influential role founding both modern peace research and systems science. He was married to Elise Boulding, herself an icon of the peace movement. Boulding was a founder of the Peace Research Movement, an attempt to mobilize all of the social sciences for peace. In 1955, he set up the Center for Advanced Studies in Behavioral Sciences at Stanford University where he met with a small group of scholars asking how to address the fundamental problems of war and peace. As he observed, "The bomb had been dropped. The whole world had changed, as Einstein noted; it's just that we haven't changed."[6] From 1949 to 1967, he was a faculty member of the University of Michigan where he joined Anatol Rapaport and Robert Angell to create The Center for Conflict Resolution and initiated the interdisciplinary *Journal of Conflict Resolution*.

That was the beginning of the peace research movement. Boulding helped then to create the International Peace Research Association and the International Christian University in Japan. Boulding was also a cofounder of General Systems Theory and the spearhead of an evolutionary approach to economics. His broad scholarship brought recognition as an integrator of knowledge and an academician of world stature. He was a president of the American Economic Association, the Society for General Systems Research, and the American Association for the Advancement of Science.

His remarkable creativity and wit were applied to understanding war, peace, and social systems in some extraordinary ways, among them his tongue-and-cheek formulation of Boulding's First Law, that "if something has happened it is possible."[7] The following selection from an interview he gave in 1987 gives something of the flavor of his mind:

War is a public health problem.

The invention of the cannon destroyed the castle and the feudal system. When the weapons were spears and arrows, it made some sense to have a castle or even a city wall. But cannons came about 1500. The feudal system just crumbled. If you stayed in your castle, you got blown up with it. That's what's happened with the nuclear weapons. The United States has lost our "moats."

You could summarize human history in a single sentence: wealth creates power and power destroys wealth. Every empire has been an example of this.

About 85 percent to 95 percent of human activity is peaceful. Peace is plowing and sowing and reaping and making things and being on television and getting married and raising a family and dancing and singing and opera, you know. It is a very large part of human activity, and war is a kind of interruption of this.[8]

And finally: Anyone who thinks that development can expand infinitely in a planet with finite resources must be either insane or an economist.

AUNG SAN SUU KYI (1945–)

Followers of the "Monk's Uprising" in Burma may recall a poignant episode that appeared on news channels showing a crowd of demonstrators stopping at the gate of a mansion, where there soon appears a slender, beautiful woman who looks at the demonstrators without speaking and is soon in tears. Aung San Suu Kyi was born in Rangoon, Burma (we avoid the name Myanmar). Her father, Aung San, had founded the Burmese army and negotiated the country's liberation from colonialism in 1947. He was assassinated the same year, when his daughter was only two, along with his entire cabinet (the assassins, sent by political rivals, have never been identified, much less brought to justice). Daw ("madam") Suu Kyi's mother went on to hold diplomatic positions, including in India, where she took Suu Kyi with her and secured an education for her at Lady Shri Ram College, where she graduated in 1964. She went on to get degrees at Oxford five years later, where she met her future husband, Michael Aris. From there she spent some years at the UN headquarters in New York, but returned to Burma where her mother had fallen ill and decided, courageously, to stay to help the people when the ill-fated student uprising broke out in 1988. In a general election of 1990 she became the General Secretary of the National League for Democracy, which she had helped found and which was voted into power, only to find that the then (and still) ruling military junta would not allow them to form a government. At this point Suu Kyi was placed for the second time under house arrest, where she has remained most of the time until this writing. She was offered freedom if she left the country, but she refused, even to visit her husband Michael (who was terminally ill with cancer) and two sons whom she had seen only five times in the previous five years.

In 1991 she was awarded the Nobel Peace Prize for her courageous, nonviolent opposition to the military rule that still prevails in Burma, one of many peace prizes she has received. Her two sons accepted the prize on her behalf.

Aung San Suu Kyi is regularly described as a leader of the democratic opposition to the extremely oppressive regime in Burma, which of course is true. More to the point, however, she is an extremely courageous nonviolent person whose beliefs and vision come from Mahatma Gandhi and (not unlike Sri Lanka's Dr. A. T. Ariyaratne, founder of Sarvodaya) from her native tradition of Theravada Buddhism. On more than one occasion (again like Dr. Ariyaratne), she has defied what seemed almost certain death to carry out her mission, without a trace of hatred for her opponents; one of these episodes is dramatically rendered in the film *Beyond Rangoon.*

Worldwide protest against her detention coming from the UN itself and other Nobel Prize winners has to this date not prevailed against the regime. She has written several books, one of them *Freedom from Fear and Other Writings* (1995) with Václav Havel, Desmond M. Tutu, and Michael Aris. One of her most famous speeches entitled "Freedom from Fear" begins, "It is not power that corrupts but fear. Fear of losing power corrupts those who wield it and fear of the scourge of power corrupts those who are subject to it." Daw Aung San Suu Kyi, who, like Mahatma Gandhi, has influenced the world and inspired seekers after freedom in her own country and abroad even from behind bars, is a living testimony to that insight. It is a great relief and pleasure to report that on November 13, 2010, Daw Suu Kyi was released from house arrest on the expiry of her latest sentence.

KHAN ABDUL GHAFFAR KHAN (1890–1988)

Badshah ("King") Khan was born in Charsadda, near Peshawar, in what was then the North West Frontier Province (NWFP) of colonial India. His father, Bagram, was a village leader among that Pashtu (Pakhtun, earlier Pathan) community and Abdul Ghaffar received a good education at a British-run school, something unusual at that time because the Mullahs were opposed to it. Indeed, throughout his long life Khan "King" faced opposition from many quarters: hidebound religious authorities, the British, and finally the government of Pakistan that distrusted him because he and his Pashtuns had been opposed to the partition of India and, when it came, voted overwhelmingly to go with India rather than Pakistan. His relations with his fellow freedom fighters in India, except Gandhi himself, turned tragic when they abandoned the Pashtuns to Pakistan—as he said, he was "thrown to the wolves" after going through untold suffering to help their common struggle against British rule.

On graduation from high school he was offered a prestigious commission in The Guides, within the British-run military, but rebuffed the offer when he witnessed a British officer insulting a Pashtun who had just become one. When his mother did not give him permission to follow his older brother to England for higher education, he devoted himself to social uplift, primarily by founding a series of successful schools, beginning with one in Utmanzai, where he was to live much of his later life. He thus anticipated Gandhi's Constructive Program. Khan finally met Gandhi at the All India Congress Party meeting in Calcutta in December 1928. He was, of course, drawn to the man and deeply impressed with his handling of a would-be heckler. Their loving association was to last until the Partition in 1947, with Khan often supporting Gandhi even when other Congress Party members lacked the vision to do so. He soon earned the sobriquet "the Frontier Gandhi," which he refused to own, saying that there was only one Gandhi.

As his engagement with the freedom struggle deepened, he had the stroke of genius to form an "army" of nonviolent Pashtuns—an unheard of concept referring to such a warlike, vengeance-prone people. Perhaps building on Gandhi's idea of the *Shanti Sena*, or "Peace Army," these Khudai Khidmatgars, or "Servants of God," were uniformed, disciplined and devoted unswervingly to their leader because of his spiritual stature—and vowed to follow nonviolence. In April 1930, Khan was arrested in connection with the famous Salt Satyagraha and, on April 23, a large crowd gathered at the Kissa Khahani Bazaar in Peshawar to protest. What followed was nothing short of a miracle, as British troops and armored cars ordered them to disperse and then, when they refused, commenced firing on the unarmed crowd and running over the living and the dead on and off (mostly on) for six hours. Yet the Khudai Khidmatgars, who were more used to giving blows than taking them, held to their nonviolent discipline throughout the horrendous ordeal. After this atrocity their numbers swelled to more than 80,000, making it the largest peace army ever seen before or since.

Khan spent a third of his life imprisoned by one authority or another. When he died at the age of 98, there was a cessation of hostilities on both sides in the Afghan war that was raging at the time so that his funeral procession could go to Jalalabad. He left behind a political party, the Awani League, headed by his son and then his grandson. But his enduring legacy is beyond this or any institution. His life and work served to dispel four damaging myths about nonviolence:

1. Only cowards or "nice" people take to nonviolence. At one point Khan asked Gandhi why his own Pashtuns were still nonviolent while many Hindus had faltered from the faith; Gandhi explained, "we Hindus have always been nonviolent, but we have not always been brave, like you."
2. Nonviolence only works against mild resistance. The British were uncommonly brutal in the NWFP, fearing the nonviolent Khudai Khidmatgars even more than they had the normally violent Pashtuns.
3. Nonviolence cannot be used on a scale that would make it useful in war.
4. Nonviolence cannot find a home in Islam. Khan, like most of his tribesmen, was a devout Muslim to the end of his life, and convinced that the "weapon" of nonviolence had been given by the Prophet himself.

A documentary film, *Badshah Khan, a Torch for Peace*, has been released by Teri McLuhan and is based on Eknath Easwaran's biography, *Nonviolent Soldier of Islam*,[9] and a feature film is in progress at this time in India.

KENULE BEESON SARO-WIWA (1941–.1995)

Ken Saro-Wiwa was a Nigerian author, television producer, businessman, and environmental activist. His satirical TV series Basi & Co was said to be the most watched soap opera in Africa. During the Biafran war (1967 to 1970), he was an administrator for the Port of Bonny near Ogoni in the Niger Delta, and his horror over the violence was reflected in his novels. *On a Darkling Plain* is a diary of his wartime experiences and *Sozaboy: A Novel in Rotten English* is the tale of a naive village boy recruited into the army.

Saro-Wiwa was a member of the Ogoni people, a Nigerian ethnic minority group whose homeland in the Niger Delta suffered extreme environmental damage from crude oil extraction and indiscriminate oil waste dumping. The exploitation of the area by Shell Oil and other multi-national companies was protected by the Nigerian government, which did not enforce environmental laws. The dumping began in the 1950s and exploitation of Ogoni land continues to this day.

Saro-Wiwa began reporting the destruction and was critical of Shell, other multi-national corporations, and the Nigerian government. His concern about the treatment of Ogoni within the Nigerian Federation and his advocacy for greater Ogoni autonomy resulted in his dismissal in 1973 as Regional Commissioner for Education in the Rivers State cabinet. Saro-Wiwa went on to become a spokesperson, and then president, of the Movement for the Survival of the Ogoni People. In this role he led a nonviolent campaign against the degradation of the land and the contamination of the natural waters of Ogoniland.

When this nonviolent campaign gained momentum, Saro-Wiwa was arrested in 1992 and routinely tortured. Amnesty International issued a statement that Saro-Wiwa's arrest was "part of the continuing suppression by the Nigerian authorities of the Ogoni people's campaign against the oil companies" and declared Saro-Wiwa a "prisoner of conscience."[10]

Saro-Wiwa was a vice president of Unrepresented Nations and Peoples Organization (UNPO) General Assembly from 1993 to 1995. UNPO is an international, nonviolent, and democratic organization. Its members are indigenous peoples, minorities, and residents of unrecognized or occupied territories who have joined together to protect and promote their human and cultural rights, to preserve their environments, and to find nonviolent solutions to conflicts that affect them.

In 1995, he was again arrested, charged with murdering public officials, tried in great haste by a special tribunal of the Nigerian military government of General Sani Abacha, and hanged. The charges were unfounded and politically motivated and his execution provoked international condemnation and resulted in Nigeria's suspension from the Commonwealth of Nations for 3–1/2 years.

He was a winner of both the Goldman Environmental Prize and the Right Livelihood Award. His memory lives and as of this writing the case of the Nigerian village farmers against Shell Oil company is being heard in the World Court in The Hague.

Ken Saro-Wiwa's compassion and his frustration were reflected in his book of stories, *Forest of Flowers* (1986).

An old woman had hobbled up to him. My son, they arrived this morning and dug up my entire farm, my only farm. They mowed down the toil of my brows, the pride of the waiting months. They say they will pay me compensation. Can they compensate me for my labors? The joy I receive when I see the vegetables sprouting, God's revelation to me in my old age? Oh my son, what can I do? What answer now could he give her? I'll look into it later, he had replied tamely.

Look into it later. He could almost hate himself for telling that lie. He cursed the earth for spouting oil, black gold, they called it. And he cursed the gods for not drying the oil wells. What did it matter that millions of barrels of oil were mined and exported daily, so long as this poor woman wept those tears of despair? What could he look into later? Could he make alternate land available? And would the lawmakers revise the laws just to bring a bit more happiness to these unhappy wretches whom the search for oil had reduced to an animal existence? They ought to send the oil royalties to the men whose farms and land were despoiled and ruined. But the lawyers were in the pay of the oil companies and the government people in the pay of the lawyers and the companies.

NOTES

1. Schell, 2003; Ash, 2009.
2. Zunes, 1999.
3. See Ron Glossop, Chapter 5 in this volume.
4. Kelly, Paige, and Gilliatt, 1992.
5. Planet Carbon.
6. Boulding, 1987.
7. Ibid.
8. See http://carbontrades.co.uk.
9. Easwaran, 1999.
10. Saro-Wiwa, 1986.

A FINAL WORD

Marc Pilisuk and Michael N. Nagler

Like the surface of the earth, the prevailing war system is a relatively thin and unstable layer that conceals intense energies of greater fluidity beneath its surface-energies that occasionally burst forth. Our journey through the manifold energies and projects that are represented in the chapters of these three volumes did not reveal a single, unified world peace movement but it certainly did reveal wellsprings of activity, more intense, more creative, and more widespread than one would imagine. The bubbling energies appear as contributions to a gigantic wave surging against the barriers that societies have entrenched into laws and ideologies that make inequality, exploitation, and violence appear inevitable. Slowly but with increasing likelihood, individuals and groups of individuals, facing the varied manifestations of that age-old inhumanity, are finding courage, as people have done through history, to rise up against it. But in this generation many more of us are also identifying the existing exploitive system underlying diverse violence and recognizing that this system is failing. And some are daring to view the movements toward peace, justice, and sustainability as a yet-unrealized but potentially unstoppable movement. This emergence is all the more amazing as it comes on the heels of a century in which control over human identity has become all-pervasive and quite often malicious; when the war-propaganda is based, ironically enough, on adaptations of Sigmund Freud's theories about the power of appealing to basic needs and fears; when such propaganda hurled masses of humanity into paroxysms of anti-Semitic hatred, among other examples of targeted dehumanization; and when the self-image of human beings was reduced to "happiness machines that have become the key to economic progress" (to paraphrase President Hoover) came to predominate.[1] The power of such manipulation and control is slowly yielding to a culture in which the better natures of people can assert themselves.

One cannot review the efforts described in these volumes, and the many more that we could not include, without realizing that the wave is powerful and has not yet reached its crest. The power and impact of these healthier alternatives are evident and they are springing up everywhere. They remain seriously under-reported by the mainstream media that instead deliver a constant stream of tragedies, local and national, as though they were singular occurrences rather than looking deeply into the failures of unfettered corporate expansion and the war system. It is an ironically hopeful sign that the failures of that system are becoming apparent to people the world over, despite the impressive capacity of a powerful elite to "spin" the coverage. Some former players of that system, some of whom appear in these pages, have recognized the failure of an unbridled quest for development and unending search for enemies.

A more heartening sign is that the activists described in the final chapter of Volume 3 do not wait for powerful officials to lead them. In ways small and large, people are devoting their creativity, their energy, their dreams, and their quest for a meaningful life to make peace a reality. One cannot come away from the story of these efforts without being heartened by the fact that so many others have stepped forward. We are resourceful and caring custodians of the force of life. The peace movement worldwide is an inchoate but irresitable force. It grows because it must prevail. And if we nurture it, it will.

NOTE

1. See the BBC documentary *Happiness Machines* (2002), available at http://freedocumentaries.org/theatre_med.php?filmID=140.

BIBLIOGRAPHY

Abbé de Saint-Pierre. "Abbé de Saint-Pierre—A European Union: A Project for
Settling an Everlasting Peace in Europe" (excerpted from *Projet de paix perpetu-
elle*). In *Basic Texts in International Relations*, edited and introduced by Evan
Luard. New York: St. Martin's Press, 1992: 441–14.

Abele, Robert P. *The Anatomy of a Deception: A Reconstruction and Analysis of the Decision to Invade Iraq.* Baltimore: University Press of America, 2009.

Abram, Irwin, ed. *Nobel Lecture Series: Peace 1991–1995.* Singapore: World Scientific
Publishing, 1999.

Ackerman, Peter, and Jack Duvall. *A Force More Powerful. A Century of Nonviolent
Conflict.* New York & Basingstoke: Palgrave Macmillan, 2000.

Action Asia. http://HYPERLINK "http://www.actionasia.org/programs/" www
.actionasia.org/programs/.

Adams, Gerry. *The Politics of Irish Freedom.* Kerry: Brandon, 1986.

Advocacy Project. "Association for the Integral Development of the Victims of Violence in the Verapaces, Maya Achi," 2009, www.advocacynet.org/page/adivima.

African National Congress. "The Freedom Charter." Adopted at the Congress of
the People, Kliptown, on June 26, 1955, http.//www.anc.org.za/ancdocs/history/
charter.html.

Aksu, Esref. "Perpetual Peace: A Project by Europeans *FOR* Europeans?" *Peace &
Change* 33, no. 3 (July, 2008): 368–87.

Alcock, Antony E. *Understanding Ulster.* Lurgan: Ulster Society Publications, 1994.

Alston, Philip. Statement by Professor Alston, UN Special Rapporteur on Extrajudicial Executions, "Press Statement. Mission to Colombia," June 8–18, 2009.

Alther, Gretchen, John Lindsay-Poland, and Sarah Weintraub. *Building from the
Inside Out: Peace Initiatives in War-Torn Colombia.* The American Friends Service
Committee, and the Fellowship of Reconciliation, 2004.

Ambi, Madama. Interview by Deva Temple. *Organizer, Feminists for Obama* (November 12, 2009).

American Non-Governmental Organization Coalition for the International Criminal Court. www.amicc.org.

Amjad-Ali, Charles. "Empire and Its Religious Legitimation: Betrayed by a Companion," In *Being the Church in the Midst of Empire: Trinitarian Reflections,* edited by Karen L. Bloomquist, 25–42. Minneapolis, MN: Lutheran University Press, 2007.

Amnesty International. "Summit of the Americas Fails to Address Human Rights," April 20, 2009. http://www.amnesty.org/en/news-and-updates/news/summit-americas-fails-address-human-rights-20090420.

Anderson, Mary B., and Lara Olson. *Confronting War. Critical Lessons for Peace Practitioners.* Cambridge, MA: Collaborative for Development Action, 1999.

Andreopoulos, George, Zehra F. Kabasakal Arat, and Peter Juviler, eds. *Non-State Actors in the Human Rights Universe.* Bloomfield, CT: Kumarian Press, 2006.

Ankerl, Guy. *Coexisting Contemporary Civilizations.* Geneva: INU Press, 2000..

Anthony, David W. *The Horse, the Wheel, and Language.* Princeton, NJ: Princeton University, 2007.

Apple, Michael. *Education and Power.* 2nd. ed. New York: Routledge, 1995.

Archdiocese of Guatemala. *Guatemala: Never Again.* REMHI, Recovery of Historical Memory Project; the Official Report of the Human Rights Office, Archdiocese of Guatemala. New York: Orbis, 1999.

Archibugi, Daniele. *A World of Democracy: Cosmopolitan Perspectives.* Princeton, NJ: Princeton University Press, 2008.

"Armies of Children -Editorials and Commentary- International Herald Tribune." *The New York Times,* October 12, 2006. http://www.nytimes.com/2006/10/12/opinion/12iht-edchild.3132685.html.

Armitage, Lynne. *Customary Land Tenure in Papua New Guinea: Status and Prospects.* http://dlc.dlib.indiana.edu/archive/00001043/00/armitage.pdf.

Arnould, Dominique. *Guerre et paix dans la poesie grecque. De Callinos a Pindare.* New York: Arno Press, 1981.

Arthur, Paul. "Reading Violence: Ireland." In: *The Legitimization of Violence,* edited by David E. Apter. Basingstoke: Macmillan, 1997.

Ash, Timothy Garton, "Velvet Revolution: the Prospects," *New York Review of Books,* December 3, 2009, 20–23.

Asociación Ija'tz. "Misión y Visión." N.d. http://www.ijatz.org.

Bacevich, Andrew J. *American Empire: The Realities and Consequences of U.S. Diplomacy.* Cambridge, MA: Harvard University Press, 2002.

Bajaj, Monisha. "Why Context Matters: The Material Conditions of Caring in Zambia." International Journal of Qualitative Studies in Education, 22(4) (2009): 379–398.

Baker, Martin M., and H. Pence. "Supporting Peace Education in Teacher Education Programs." *Childhood Education* 85, no. 1 (2008): 20–25.

Balch, Thomas Willing. *Emeric Cruce.* Philadelphia: Allen, Lane and Schott, 1900.

Balibar, Ètienne. *We, The People of Europe: Reflections on Transnational Citizenship.* Princeton, NJ: Princeton University Press, 2004.

Banco de datos de derechos humanos y violencia política. *San Josesito de Apartadó: La otra version.* Bogotá, Colombia: CINEP, 2005.

Barlow, Maude. *Blue Covenant: The Global Water Crisis and the Coming Battle for the Right to Water.* Toronto, ON: McClelland & Stewart, 2007.

Barreda, Carlos. "DR-CAFTA Imposition and Poverty in Guatemala." In *Monitoring Report: DR-CAFTA in Year-One: A Report by the Stop CAFTA Coalition*, 2006. http://www.stopcafta.org.

Baumann, Marcel M. "Zwei Friedensprozesse: Nordirland im Schatten seiner Friedensstifter." *W & F Wissenschaft und Frieden* 4 (2008): 28–32.

Beales, A. C. F. *The History of Peace: A Short Account of the Organized Movements for International Peace.* New York: Garland, 1971 [1931].

Bederman, David J. *International Law Frameworks.* New York: Foundation Press, 2001.

Bennett, A. LeRoy. *International Organizations: Principles and Issues.* Englewood Cliffs, NJ: Prentice Hall, 1995.

Bennett, Milton. *Better Together Than A-P-A-R-T Intercultural Communication: An Overview.* Newtonville, MA: Intercultural Resource Corporation, 1996.

Bentham, Jeremy. "Bentham—An International Code" (excerpted from: *A Plan for a Universal and Perpetual Peace*), *Basic Texts in International Relations*, edited and introduced by Evan Luard. New York: St. Martin's Press, 1992, 415–17.

Bernstein, Basil B. *Pedagogy, Symbolic Control, and Identity: Theory, Research, Critique.* Lanham, MD: Rowman & Littlefield, 2000.

Berrigan, Daniel. *Poetry, Drama, Prose.* Maryknoll, NY: Orbis Books, 1988. p. 168–170

Bew, Paul, and Henry Patterson. *The British State and the Ulster Crisis: From Wilson to Thatcher.* London: Verso, 1985.

Biomimicry Institute. *Home.* October 29, 2009. http://www.biomimicryinstitute.org/.

Bird, Kai and Laurence Lifschutz, eds. *Hiroshima Shadow, Writings on the Denial of History and the Smithsonian Controversy.* Stony Creek, CT: The Pamphleteers Press, 1998.

Blakesley, Christopher L., et al. *The International Legal System: Cases and Materials*, 5th ed. New York: Foundation Press, 2001.

Boal, Agusto. "The Role of Spectacle and the Iranian Social Movements Protests." 2009. http://artivism.us/article-on-the-iranian-protests/.

"Bojayá Massacre: Escalating Conflict on Colombia's Pacific Coast. Witness for Peace and Justapaz." May 15, 2002. http://www.witnessforpeace.org/article.php?id=208.

Boulding, Elise. *Building a Global Civic Culture: Education for an Interdependent World.* New York: Teachers College Press, 1988.

Boulding, Elise. *Cultures of Peace: The Hidden Side of History.* Syracuse, NY: Syracuse University Press, 2000.

Boulding, Elise. *The Underside of History: A View of Women through Time.* Boulder, CO: Westview, 1976.

Boulding, Elise and Kenneth Boulding. *The Future: Images and Processes.* Thousand Oaks, CA: Sage, 1995.

Boulding, Kenneth. "Evolutionary Movement toward Peace." In *World Encyclopedia of Peace*, Vol. 1, edited by Ervin Laszlo and J. L. Yoo. Oxford: Pergamon, 1986.

Boulding, Kenneth. *Stable Peace.* Austin: University of Texas, 1978 [1987].

Boulding, Kenneth. *Sonnets from Later Life, 1981–1993.* Wallingford, PA: Pendle Hill Publications. 1994.

Boulding, Kenneth. *Three Faces of Power.* Newbury Park, CA: Sage, 1989.

Bourdieu, Pierre, and Jean Claude C. Passerib. *Reproduction in Education, Society and Culture.* London: Sage, 1977.

Boyte, Harry. "Community Information Commons." In *Rebooting America,* edited by Personal Democracy Forum. New York: Personal Democracy Forum, 2008.

Brazil's Landless Workers Movement, "About Brazil Landless Workers Movement," http://www.mstbrazil.org/?q=about.

Brecher, Jeremy, and Tim Costello. *Global Village or Global Pillage: Economic Reconstruction from the Bottom Up.* Boston: South End Press, 1994.

Brafman, Ori and Bergstrom, Rod. *The Starfish and the Spider: The Unstoppable Power of Leaderless Organizations.* New York: Portfolio, 2006.

Brittain, Vera. *The Rebel Passion.* Nyack, NY: Fellowship Publications, 1964.

Brown, Dee. *Bury My Heart at Wounded Knee: An Indian History of the American West.* New York: Bantam Books, 1970.

Brunson, Russell, Zephryn Conte, and Shelley Masar. *The Art in Peacemaking. A Guide to Integrating Conflict Resolution Education into Youth Arts Programs.* Springfield, IL: National Center for Conflict Resolution Education, 2002.

Buhle, Mari Jo, Paul Buhle, and Dan Georgakas, eds. *Encyclopedia of the American Left.* Urbana and Chicago: University of Illinois Press, 1990.

Butigan, Ken. "The U.S. People Say No." Washington, DC: Pledge of Resistance, December 19, 1989.

Butler, Smedley D. *War Is a Racket: The Antiwar Classic by America's Most Decorated General.* Los Angeles, California: Feral House, 2003.

Canfield, Jack, Mark Victor Hansen, Candice C. Carter, Susanna Palomares, L. Williams, and Bradley Winch. *Chicken Soup for the Soul: Stories for a Better World.* Deerfield Beach, FL: Health Communications, 2005.

Cante, Freddy. "Deficiencias del orden social, acción colectiva contendiente y posibilidades de la noviolencia en Colombia." In *Acción política no-violenta, una opción para Colombia,* edited by F. Cante and L. Ortiz, 25–50. Centro de Estudios Políticos e Internacionales, CEPI. Bogotá: Centro Editorial Universidad.

Cante, Freddy and Luisa Ortiz, eds. *Acción política no-violenta, una opción para Colombia.* Centro de Estudios Políticos e Internacionales, CEPI. Bogotá: Centro Editorial Universidad del Rosario, 2005.

Capeheart, Loretta, and Dragan Milovanovic. *Social Justice: Theories, Issues and Movements.* New Brunswick, NJ: Rutgers University Press, 2007.

"Capitán del Ejército reconoce masacre en San Jose de Apartadó." *El Tiempo,* May 18, 2008. http://colombia.indymedia.org/news/2008/05/86896_comment.php#86994.

Carter, Candice C. "Conflict Resolution at School: Designed for Construction of a Compassionate Community." *The Journal of Social Alternative* 2, no. 1 (2002): 49–55.

Carter, Candice C. *Conflict Resolution and Peace Education.* New York: Palgrave Macmillan, 2010.

Carter, Candice C. "Peace Education through Tele-dramatics Instruction: Implication for Teacher Education." Paper presented for the Peace Education

Special Interest Group at the annual meeting. Chicago: American Educational Research Association, 2007.

Carter, Candice C. "Pro-social Music: Empowerment through Aesthetic Instruction." *Multicultural Perspectives* 5, no. 4 (2003): 38–40.

Carter, Candice C. "Teacher Preparation for Peacebuilding in USA and Northern Ireland." In *Peace Education and Post-Conflict Societies: Comparative Perspectives*, edited by Z. Bekerman, C. McGlynn, and A. Gallagher, 245–58. New York: Palgrave Macmillan, 2007.

Carter, Candice C. "Voluntary Standards for Peace Education." *Journal of Peace Education* 5, no. 2 (2008): 141–55.

Carter, Candice C. "Whither Social Studies? In Pockets of Peace at School." *Journal of Peace Education* 1, no. 1 (2004): 77–87.

Carter, Candice C, and Ravindra Kumar. *Peace Philosophy in Action*. New York: Palgrave Macmillan, 2010.

Carter, Candice C, and Saloshna Vandeyar. *Teacher Preparation for Peace Education in South Africa and USA: Constructing Compassion and Commitment*, edited by C. McGlynn, Z. Zemblas, Z. Bekerman, and A. Gallagher. New York: Palgrave Macmillian, 2009.

Carter, Candice C, and S. Clay-Robinson. "A Review of Youth Literature for Peace Education." Paper presented for the Peace Education Special Interest Group at the annual meeting. San Diego, CA: American Educational Research Association, 2009.

CDA Collaborative Learning Projects. www.cdainc.com/cdawww/default.php.

The Center for Media and Democracy. "The Pentagon's Pundits." n.d. http://www.prwatch.org/pentagonpundits.

Center for Media Democracy's John Stauber. "How Obama Took Over the Peace-Movement." http://www.prwatch.org/node/8297.

"Chain of Extermination Devastates Awa Peoples in Colombia." *Indian Law Resource Center* 2, 2009. http://www.indianlaw.org/en/node/411.

Chatfield, Charles. *Peace Movements in America*. New York: Schocken Books, 1973.

Chatfield, Charles with Robert Kleidman. *The American Peace Movement: Ideals and Activism*. New York: Twayne Publishers, 1992: 180–182.

Chomsky, Noam. *Manufacturing Consent: The Political Economy of Mass Media*. New York: Pantheon Books, 2002.

Clarke-Habibi, Sara. "Transforming Worldviews: The Case of Education for Peace in Bosnia and Herzegovina." *Journal of Transformative Education* 3, no. 1 (2005): 33–56.

Coalition for the International Criminal Court. http://www.iccnow.org.

"Collaborative for Academic, Social, and Emotional Learning." http://www.casel.org/.

Collaborative for Development Action. "Do No Harm." n.d. http://www.cdainc.com/cdawww/project_profile.php?pid=DNH&pname=Do%20No%20Harm.

"Collaborative for Development Action, Theories of Change." http://management-consulting.suite101.com/article.cfm/change-management-using-action-research.

"Comunidad de Paz de San José de Apartadó." Una Política Oficial: El Genocidio Contra San José de Apartadó. March 20, 2005. Prensa Rural. http://www.prensarural.org/apartado20050320.htm.

Conflict Prevention And Post-Conflict Restoration Network. http://cpr.web.cern
    .ch/cpr/.
Conflict Prevention And Post-Conflict Restoration Network. "Peace And Conflict
    Impact Assessment (PCIA) Handbook." Version 2.2 September 2005. http://
    www.reliefweb.int/rw/lib.nsf/db900sid/RURI-6MBNLK/$file/
    PCIA%20Handbook.pdf?openelement.
Conflict Sensitivity Consortium. "Conflict and Policy Assessment Framework."
    Summer, 2000. http://www.conflictsensitivity.org/node/42.
Conflict Sensitivity Consortium. "Conflict and Policy Assessment Framework."
    January, 2000. http://www.conflictsensitivity.org/node/68
Coogan, Tim Pat. *The Troubles: Ireland's Ordeal 1966–1996 and the Search for Peace.*
    London: Hutchinson, 1995.
Cook, Debbie. "Desalination: Energy Down the Drain." *The Oil Drum: Discussions about
    Energy and the Future.* March 2, 2009. http://www.theoildrum.com/node/5155.
Cortes, Carlos E. *The Children Are Watching. How the Media Teach about Diversity.*
    New York: Teachers College Press, 2000.
Council on Hemispheric Affairs, "Combating Impunity, Violence, and Crime in Pres-
    ident Colom's Guatemala," 2009. http://www.coha.org/2009/03/combating-
    impunity-violence-and-crime-in-president-colom's-guatemala/.
Cree Proverb. http://learningtogive.org//search/quotes/Display_Quotes.asp?author_id
    =323&search_type=author.
Crocker, Chester A., Fen Olser Hampson, and Pamela Aall, eds. *Herding Cats: Mul-
    tiparty Mediation in a Complex World.* Washington, DC: United States Institute
    of Peace, 2001.
Crocker, Chester A., Fen Osler Hampson, and Pamela Aall, R. "Taming Intractable
    Conflicts: Mediation in the Hardest Cases. US Institute of Peace," 2004. http://
    www.usip.org/.
*Cronología de agresiones contra la Comunidad de Paz de San José de Apartadó y
    población de la zona, con posterioridad al 7 de agosto de 2002.* Compiled by Comu-
    nidad de Paz de San José de Apartadó Colombia and J. Giraldo, 2008. http://
    cdpsanjose.org/files/cdpsanjose/pdf/CronologiaUribe.pdf.
Cross, Beverly E. "How Do We Prepare Teachers to Improve Race Relations?"
    Educational Leadership 50, no. 8 (1993): 64–65.
Cross, Ryan. *Towards Prevention: Credible Deterrence against the Crimes of the Rome
    Statute. Centre for Foreign Policy studies.* DALHOUSIE University. http://
    www.un.org/Depts/dpa/docs/Prevention%20Report.pdf.
Crucé, Eméric. *The New Cineas.* Translated with introduction by C. Frederick
    Farrell and Edith R. Farrell. New York: Garland Publishing, 1972.
Danesh, H. B., and Sara Clarke-Habibi. "Education for Peace Curriculum Manual:
    A Conceptual and Practical Guide." Vancouver, Canada: Education for Peace
    Institute, 2007.
Darby, John. "Conflict in Northern Ireland: A Background Essay." In *Facets of the
    Conflict in Northern Ireland,* edited by Seamus Dunn, 15–23. Basingstoke: Macmil-
    lan, 1995.
Darby, John. "Northern Ireland: The Background to the Peace Process." 2003.
    http://cain.ulst.ac.uk/events/peace/darby03.htm.

Davis, David Brion. *The Problem of Slavery in the Age of Revolution, 1770–1823*. Ithaca, NY: Cornell University Press, 1975.

Davis, David Brion. *Slavery and Human Progress*. Oxford: Oxford University Press, 1984.

Deats, Richard. *Ambassador of Reconciliation: A Murial Lester reader*. Santa Cruz, CA: Society Publishers, 1991.

Deats, Richard. "The Global Spread of Active Nonviolence." In *Peace is the Way*, edited by Walter Wink. 283–295. Maryknoll, NY: Orbis Books, 2002.

Declaración relativa a la Comunidad de Paz de San José de Apartadó. 2006. HYPERLINK "http://www.cdpsanjose.com" \o "http://www.cdpsanjose.com" \t "_blank" www.cdpsanjose.com.

"Defensores de Derechos Humanos: Bajo el Estigma del Presidente êlvaro Uribe." ALAI. October 23, 2009. http://alainet.org/active/33932&lang=es

De Paul, S. V. "Peace Education in Elementary Teacher Education of Tamil Nadu." In *Peace Philosophy in Action*, edited by Candice C. Carter and Ravindra Kumar. New York: Palgrave Macmillan, 2010.

Department of International Development (DFID). *Preventing Violent Conflict*. 2006. www.dfid.gov.uk.

"Der Spiegel," March 20, 1972. Interview with Prime Minster Brian Faulkner.

Deutch, Morton, Peter T. Coleman, and Eric C. Marcus, eds. *Handbook of Conflict Resolution: Theory and Practice*, 2nd ed. San Francisco: Jossey-Bass, 2006.

Development Co-operation Directorate (DCD-DAC): The Development Assistance Committee (DAC) www.oecd.org/dac http://www.oecd.org/dac.

Department for International Development. "DFID's Conducting Conflict Assessments: Guidance Notes." n.d.

DiMaggio, Anthony R. *Mass Media, Mass Propaganda: Examining American News in the "War on Terror."* Lanham, MD: Lexington Books, 2008.

Dixon, Paul. *Northern Ireland. The Politics of War and Peace*. Basingstoke and New York: Palgrave Macmillan, 2001.

Douglass, James. *JFK and the Unspeakable*. Maryknoll, NY: Orbis Books, 2008.

Dower, Nigel, and John Williams, eds. *Global Citizenship: A Critical Introduction*. New York: Routledge, 2002.

Drescher, Seymour. "Two Variants of Anti-Slavery: Religious Organization and Social Mobilization in Britain and France, 1780–1870." In *Anti-Slavery: Religion and Reform: Essays in Memory of Roger Ansley*, edited by Christine Bolt and Seymour Drescher, 43–63. Kent and Hamden: William Dawsons & Sons and Archon Books, 1980.

Dudenhoefer, David. "Coffee Farmers on Guatemala's Lake Atitlan Go Organic," June 21, 2004. http://www.ens-newswire.com/ens/jun2004/2004-06-21-01.asp.

Easwaran, Eknath. *The Bhagavad Gita*. Tomales, CA: Nilgiri Press, 1985.

Easwaran, Eknath. *Gandhi the Man: The Story of His Transformation*. Tomales, CA: Nilgiri Press, 1972.

Easwaran, Eknath. *Passage Meditation*. Tomales, CA: Nilgiri Press, 1978 (1991, 2008).

Easwaran, Eknath. *Nonviolent Soldier of Islam*. Tomales, CA: Nilgiri Press, 1999.

Ebert, Theodor. *Gewaltfreier Aufstand. Alternative zum Bürgerkrieg.* Freiburg im Breisgau: Rombach, 1970.

Eck, Diana. *A New Religious America.* San Francisco: Harper Collins, 2001.

Education for Peace—World Programme Bosnia and Herzegovina. http://www .efpinternational.org/publications/SDCEvaluationSummary.pdf.

Eisler, Riane T. *Tomorrow's Children: A Blueprint for Partnership Education in the 21st Century.* Boulder, CO: Westview, 2000.

Eisler, Riane T. and Ron Miller. *Educating for a Culture of Peace.* Portsmouth, NH: Heinemann, 2004.

Entrepueblos. "Guatemala: Manifiesto del Nab'e pixab n," April 17, 2009. http:// www.pangea.org/epueblos/index.php?option=com_content&task=view&id=790 &Itemid=150.

Epstein, Edward. "Success in Afghan War Hard to Gauge." *The San Francisco Chronicle,* March 23, 2002. http://www.globalsecurity.org/org/news/2002/ 020323-attack01.htm.

Equipo de Estudios Comunitarios y Acción Psicosocial (ECAP). (n.d.) http://www .ceri-sciencespo.com/themes/re. . ./guatemala_experience.pdf.

European Group on Training (EGT). http://www.europeangroupontraining.eu/.

European Network for Civil Peace Services (EN.CPS) http://www.encps.org/ The_European_Network_for_Civil_Peace_Services.

Evans, Robert R., ed. *Social Movements: A Reader and Source Book.* Chicago: Rand McNally College Publishing, 1973.

Everet, Anna. *Civil Rights Movement and Television.* 2009. http://www.museum.tv/ eotvsection.php?entrycode=civilrights.

Eversley, David. *Religion and Employment in Northern Ireland.* London: Sage, 1989.

Falk, Richard. *Achieving Human Rights.* New York: Routledge, 2009.

Falk, Richard. *The Declining World Order: America's Imperial Geopolitics.* New York: Routledge, 2004.

Falk, Richard. *On Humane Governance: Toward a New Global Politics.* Cambridge, UK: Polity, 1995.

Falk, Richard. *Predatory Globalization: A Critique.* Cambridge, UK: Polity, 1999.

Falk, Richard. "What Comes After Westphalia: The Democratic Challenge." Widener Law Review XIII (No.2), 2007: 243–253.

Falk, Richard, and Andrew Strauss. "On the Creation of a Global People's Assembly: Legitimacy and the Power of Popular Sovereignty." *Stanford Journal of International Law* 36 (2000): 191–220.

Falk, Richard, and Andrew Strauss. "The Deeper Challenges of Global Terrorism: A Democratizing Response." In *Debating Globalization,* edited by Daniele Archibugi, 203–31. Cambridge, UK: Polity, 2003.

Falk, Richard, and Andrew Strauss. "Toward Global Parliament." *Foreign Affairs* 80, no. 1 (2001): 212–20.

Farrell, William T. "Community Development and Individual Modernization in San Lucas Tolimán, Guatemala." PhD dissertation, University of California, Los Angeles, 1977.

Farsetta, Diane, Center for Media Democracy, studies on Pentagon propaganda online at http://www.prwatch.org/pentagonpundits and http://www.prwatch

.org/node/8180. forumZFD | Frieden braucht Fachleute http://www.forumzfd .de/.

Farsetta, Diane. "Debating the Ban on Domestic Propaganda." Center for Media Democracy, February 2, 2009. http://www.prwatch.org/node/8180.

Fay, Marie-Therese, Mike Morrisey, Marie Smyth, and Tracy Wong. *The Cost of the Troubles Study. Report on the Northern Ireland Survey. The Experience and Impact of the Troubles.* Londonderry and Belfast: INCORE, 1999.

Federal Ministry for Economic Cooperation and Development, ed. *Sector Strategy for Crisis Prevention, Conflict Transformation and Peace-Building in German Development Cooperation.* Bonn, Germany, 2005.

Ferguson, Niall. *Colossus: The Price of America's Empire.* New York: Penguin Press, 2004.

Finley, Laura L. "Teaching for Peace in Higher Education: Overcoming the Challenges to Addressing Structure and Methods." *The Online Journal of Peace and Conflict Resolution* 6, no. 1 (2004): 272–81.

Finnis, John. *Natural Law and Natural Rights.* Oxford: Clarendon Press, 1980.

Fisher, Edward F., and Peter Benson. *Broccoli and Desire: Global Connections and Maya Struggles in Postwar.* Stanford, CA: Stanford University Press, 2006.

Fisher, Edward F., and Carol Hendrickson. *Tecpán Guatemala: A Modern Maya Town in Global and Local Context.* Oxford: Westview Press, 2003.

Fitzduff, Mari, and Liam O'Hagan. "The Northern Ireland Troubles." INCORE background paper, 2000. http://cain.ulst.ac.uk/othelem/incorepaper.htm.

Flinders, Timothy. "How Nonviolence Works." In *Gandhi the Man*, edited by Eknath Easwaran, 148–72. Petaluma, CA: Nilgiri Press, 1978.

Foner, Philip S. *History of the Labor Movement in the United States: From Colonial Times to the Founding of the American Federation of Labor.* New York: International Publishers, 1947.

FOR-Colombia. http://www.forcolombia.org/node/4.

Foster, Noah. "CAFTA and Immigration." In *Monitoring Report: DR-CAFTA in Year-One: A Report by the Stop CAFTA Coalition* (2006). http://www .stopcafta.org.

Frank, Thomas. *What's the Matter with Kansas? How Conservatives Won the Heart of America.* New York: Metropolitan Books, 2004.

Freire, Paulo. *Pedagogy of Freedom. Ethics, Democracy, and Civic Courage.* Translated by P. Clarke. Lanham, MD: Rowman & Littlefield, 1998.

Gallie, W.B. *Philosophers of Peace and War: Kant, Clausewitz, Marx, Engels and Tolstoy.* Cambridge: Cambridge University Press, 1978.

Galtung, Johan. *Peace by Peaceful Means. Peace and Conflict, Development and Civilization.* Oslo: Peace Research Institute of Oslo; London: Sage, 1996.

Galtung, Johan. *Maturity Is Needed.* May 2000. http://www.peace2.uit.no/hefp/ final_report/final_report.html.

Galtung, Johan. "The Form and Content of Peace Education." *Infactis Pax* Volume 2 Number 1 (2008): 160–165. http://www.infactispax.org/journal/.

Galtung, Johan. *Transcend and Transform. An Introduction to Conflict Work.* Boulder, CO: Paradigm Press, 2004.

Gandhi, Mahatma. *The Collected Works of Mahatma Gandhi.* (Electronic Book). New Delhi, Publications Division Government of India, 1999, 98 volumes, vol. 68: 23 September, 1935–15 May, 1936.

Gandhi, Mahatma. *Selected writings of Mahatma Gandhi.* Edited by Ronald Frederick and Henry DuncanBoston: Beacon, 1951.

Gandhi, Mahatma. *Collected Works of Mahatma Gandhi,* Vol. 34: 11 February, 1926–1 April, 1926.

García-Villegas Mauricio, and Boaventura Santos. Colombia: El grado cero de la emancipación social? Entre los fascismos socials y la emancipación social. In 2004. Reinventar la democracia Reinventar el Estado 2005, Boaventura de Sousa Santos Buenos Aires: CLACSO 2005 or Quito, Ecuador: Ediciones Abya-Yala 2004.

George-Williams, Desmond. *"Bite Not One Another": Selected Accounts of Nonviolent Struggle in Africa.* Addis Ababa, Ethiopia: University for Peace, Africa Programme, 2006.

German Development Cooperation: Strategy for Peace-Building. "Sector Strategy for Crisis Prevention, Conflict Transformation and Peace-Building." June 2005. http://HYPERLINK "http://www.gtz.de/de/dokumente/en-folder.pdf" \o "http://www.gtz.de/de/dokumente/en-folder.pdf" \t "_blank" www.gtz.de/de/dokumente/en-folder.pdf

Gewirth, Alan. *Human Rights: Essays on Justification and Applications.* Chicago: University of Chicago Press, 1982.

Gewirth, Alan. *Reason and Morality.* Chicago: Chicago University Press, 1978.

Gillespie, Paul. "From Anglo-Irish to British-Irish Relations." In *A Farewell to Arms? From "Long War" to Long Peace in Northern Ireland,* edited by Michael Cox, Adrian Guelke, and Fiona Stephen, 180–98. Manchester, UK: Manchester University Press, 2000.

Giraldo, Javier. "Denuncia sobre San José de Apartadó." *Desde los márgenes.* November 13, 2003. http://www.javiergiraldo.org/spip.php?article53.

Giraldo, Javier. "Carta a la fiscalía 216: Objeción moral y ética." *Desde los márgenes.* March 16, 2009. http://www.javiergiraldo.org/spip.php?article170.

Giroux, Henry. *Schooling and the Struggle for Public Life.* Minneapolis, MN: University of Minnesota, 1988.

Glasl, Friedrich. "Konfliktmanagement." Ein *Handbuch für Führungskräfte und Berater.* Bern: Verlag Freies Geistesleben, 2002.

Glassman, Bernie. *Bearing Witness: A Zen Master's Lessons in Making Peace.* New York: Bell Tower, 1998.

Glazer, Steven. *The Heart of Learning.* New York: Jeremy P. Tarcher/Putnam, 1999.

Glendon, Mary Ann. "The Rule of Law in The Universal Declaration of Human Rights." *Northwestern University Journal of International Human Rights* (July 2004).

Global Partnership for the Prevention of Armed Conflict. http://www.gppac.net.

Glossop, Ronald J. *Confronting War: An Examination of Humanity's Most Pressing Problem,* 4th ed. Jefferson, NC: McFarland & Company, 2001.

Godin, Seth. *Tribes: We Need You to Lead Us.* London: Penguin, 2008.

Goodwin, Jeff, and James M. Jasper, eds. *The Social Movements Reader: Cases and Concepts.* Malden, MA: Blackwell Publishing, 2003.

Governance and Social Development Resource Centre. "Investing in Prevention: An International Strategy to Manage Risks of Instability and Improve Crisis Response." 2005.

Government Offices of Sweden. "Preventing Violent Conflict – Swedish Policy for the 21st Century." 2001. http://www.sweden.gov.se/sb/d/574/a/19894.

Green, Maxene. *The Dialectic of Freedom*. New York: Teachers College, 1988.

Greengrass, Paul (Director). *Bloody Sunday*. Paramount Classics, 2002.

Guatemalan Commission for Historical Clarification (CEH). "Guatemala: Memory of Silence," *Report of the Commission for Historical Clarification Conclusions and Recommendations*, [Point 32], 1999. http://shr.aaas.org/guatemala/ceh/report/english/toc.html.

Gutierrez, Gustavo. *We Drink from Our Own Wells: The Spirtual Journey of a People*. Maryknoll, NY: Orbis books, 2003.

Haavelsrud, Magnus. *Education in Developments*. Norway: Arena, 1996.

Habermas, Jürgen. *The Structural Transformation of the Public Sphere*. Cambridge, MA: MIT Press, 1991.

Habermas, Jürgen. *The Theory of Communicative Action*, Boston: Beacon Press, 1984–1987.

Hall, David, and Emanuele Lobina. *Pipe Dreams: The Failure of the Private Sector to Invest in Water Services in Developing Countries*, 2006. http://www.psiru.org/reports/2006-03-W-investment.pdf.

Hallin, Daniel. *The Museum of Broadcast Communications*. 2008. http://www.museum.tv/eotvsection.php?entrycode=vietnamonte.

Hanh, Thich Nhat. *Love in Action*. Berkeley, CA: Parallax Press, 1993.

Harbury, Jennifer. *Bridge of Courage: Life Stories of the Guatemalan Compañeros and Compañeras*. Monroe, ME: Common Courage Press, 1994.

Harding, Vincent. *Martin Luther King: The Inconvenient Hero*. Maryknoll, NY: Orbis Books, 1996.

Harris, Ian M., and Mary Lee Morridon. *Peace Education*. 2nd ed. Jefferson, NC: McFarland, 2003.

Harvey, David. *The New Imperialism*. Oxford, UK: Oxford University Press, 2003.

Hawken, Paul. *Blessed Unrest: How the Largest Movement in the World Came into Being (and Why Nobody Saw it Coming)*. New York: Penguin, Viking, 2007.

Hauge, Wenge. *Norwegian Peacebuilding Policies: Lessons Learned and Challenges Ahead*, Oslo, Norway: The Royal Norwegian Ministry of Foreign Affairs, 2004.

Hedges, Chris. *War is a force that gives us meaning*. New York: Public Affairs, 2002.

Heidegger, Martin. *The Question Concerning Technology and Other Essays*. Translated and introduced by William Lovitt. New York: Harper & Row, 1977.

Hemenway, Joan E. *Inside the Circle: A Historical and Practical Inquiry Concerning Process Groups in Clinical Pastoral Education*. Decatur, GA: Journal of Pastoral Care Publications, 1996.

Hennessey, Thomas. "Ulster Unionism and Loyalty to the Crown of the United Kingdom, 1912–1974." In *Unionism in Modern Ireland: New Perspectives on Politics and Culture*, edited by Richard English and Graham Walker. London: Macmillan, 1996.

Herman, Edward, and Noam Chomsky. *Manufacturing Consent: The Political Economy of the Mass Media.* New York: Pantheon Books, 1988, 2002.

Hill, Steven. "The World Wide Webbed: The Obama Campaign's Masterful Use of the Internet." *New America Foundation.* April 8, 2009. http://www.newamerica.net/publications/articles/2009/world_wide_webbed_12862.

Hochschild, Adam. *Bury the Chains, Prophets and Rebels in the Flight to Free an Empire's Slaves.* Boston: Houghton Mifflin, 2005.

Holland, Joshua. "Iraq Death Toll Rivals Rwanda Genocide, Cambodian Killing Fields." AlterNet, June 27, 2008. http://www.alternet.org/story/62728/.

Hoppers, Catherine O. *An African Culture of Peace.* May 2000. http://www.peace2.uit.no/hefp/final_report/final_report.html.

Hurd, Elizabeth Shakman. *The Politics of Secularism in International Relations.* Princeton, NJ: Princeton University Press, 2008.

Ingram, Catherine. *In the Footsteps of Gandhi: Conversations with Spiritual Social Activists.* Berkeley, CA: Parallax Press, 1990.

Institute for the Study of International Migration. "Landlessness and Evictions on the Rise in Guatemala." 2002. http://isim.georgetown.edu/pages/Human%20-Rights%20Forum%20Pages/Guatemala.html.

International Alert: Understanding Conflict, Building Peace. http://HYPERLINK "http://www.international-alert.org/" www.international-alert.org/.

International Coalition for The Responsibility to Protect (ICR2P). http://www.responsibilitytoprotect.org/.

The International Development Research Centre. "The Responsibility To Protect: Report of the International Commission on Intervention and State Sovereignty." 2001. http://www.idrc.ca/es/ev-9436-201-1-DO_TOPIC.html.

International Institute for Restorative Practices. 2009. http://www.iirp.org.

International Peace and Development Training Center (IPDTC), Peace Action, Training and Research Institute of Romania (PATRIR), and The Commonwealth Secretariat. *Building Commonwealth Capacity: Workshop on Early Warning and Preventive Measures. Quick Reference Guide,* 2008.

"Investing in Prevention—A Prime Minister's Strategy Unit Report to the UK Government." February 2005. http://www.cabinetoffice.gov.uk/strategy/work_areas/countries_at_risk.aspx.

James, William. *The Principles of Psychology.* Reprinted in *Great Books of the Western World.* Chicago: The Encyclopedia Britannica, 1952.

Jansen, Jonathan. "Race, Education and Democracy after Ten Years: How Far Have We Come?" In *Lessons from the Field: A Decade of Democracy in South Africa.* Institute for Democracy in South Africa (IDASA), Pretoria, 2004.

Jedi Church. *Discuss the Ways of the Jedi Church.* 2009. http://www.jedichurch.org/jedi-church-forums.html.

Jenkins, Tony. "Rethinking the Unimaginable: The Need for Teacher Education in Peace Education." *Harvard Educational Review* 77(3) (2007): 366–370.

Joan B. Kroc Institute. "A Turning Point in International Relations: Establishing a Permanent International Criminal Court." Report of Joan B. Kroc Institute for International Peace Studies, 13 (Fall 1997): 2.

Johansen, Robert, ed. *A United Nations Emergency Peace Service to Prevent Genocide and Crimes against Humanity.* New York: World Federalist Movement-Institute for Global Policy, 2006.

Johnson, Chalmers. *Nemesis: The Last Days of the American Republic.* New York: Metropolitan Books, 2006.

Johnson, Chalmers. *The Sorrows of Empire: Militarism, Secrecy, and the End of the Republic.* New York: Metropolitan Books, 2004.

Johnson, David W., and Roger T. Johnson. "Teaching Students to Be Peacemakers: Results of Five Years of Research." *Peace and Conflict: Journal of Peace Psychology* 1, no. 4 (1995): 417–38.

Jones, Peter. *Rights.* Basingstoke, U.K.: Macmillan, 1994.

Kaldor, Mary. *Human Security.* Cambridge, UK: Polity, 2007.

Kant, Immanuel. "Perpetual Peace: A Philosophical Essay (1795)." In *Early Notions of Global Governance: Selected Eighteenth-Century Proposals for "Perpetual Peace" with Rousseau, Bentham, and Kant unabridged,* edited by Esref Aksu, 180–229. Cardiff: University of Wales Press, 2008.

Kapur, Sudarshan. *Raising up a prophet: the African-American encounter with Gandhi.* Boston: Beacon Press, 1992.

Kasrils, Ronnie. *Steckbrieflich gesucht. Undercover gegen Apartheid.* Essen: Neue-Impulse-Verlag, 1997.

Keck, Margaret, and Kathryn Sikkink. *Activists beyond Borders: Advocacy Networks in International Politics.* Ithaca, NY: Cornell University Press, 1998.

Kelly, Petra Karin, Glenn D Paige, and Sarah Gilliatt, eds. *Nonviolence Speaks to Power.* Publisher: Honolulu : Center for Global Nonviolence Planning Project, Spark M. Matsunaga Institute for Peace, University of Hawaii, 1992.

Kennedy, Helen. "Neda, Young Girl Killed in Iran, Becoming Symbol of Rebellion." June 22, 2009. http://www.nydailynews.com/news/national/2009/06/21/2009-06-21_neda_young_girl_killed_in_iran.html.

Kennedy, Tracy. *Blogging Feminism: Websites of Resistance.* Spring 2007. http://www.barnard.edu/sfonline/blogs/kennedy_01.htm.

Kilbourne, Jean. As quoted in the essay, "Decolonizing the Revolutionary Imagination," by Patrick Rheinborough. *Globalize Liberation: How To Uproot the System and Build a Better World,* June 2004. http://www.smartmeme.org/downloads/sM.DeColonizingImagination.pdf.

Knutsen, Torbjørn. *The Rise and Fall of World Orders.* Manchester, UK: Manchester University Press, 1999.

Kolb, Felix, and, Alicia Swords. "Do Peace Movements Matter?" Commondreams .org. May 12, 2003. www.commondreams.org/views03/may2003.htm.

Korten, David C. *The Great Turning: From Empire to Earth Community.* San Francisco and Bloomfield, CT: Berrett-Koehler and Kumarian Press, 2006.

Korten, David C. *When Corporations Rule the World.* West Hartford, CT and San Francisco: Kumarian Press and Berrett-Koehler Publishers, 1995.

Kraft, Kenneth, ed. *Inner Peace, World Peace: Essays on Buddhism and Nonviolence.* New York: State University of New York, 1992.

Kreis, Steven. *The Printing Press.* May 13, 2004. http://www.historyguide.org/intellect/press.html.

Kreisler, Harry. Conversation with Kenneth Boulding . Institute for International Studies, UC Berkeley, March 16, 1987. http://globetrotter.berkeley.edu/conversations/Boulding/kboulding-con1.html.

Kritz, Neal J., ed. *Transitional Justice: How Emerging Democracies Reckon with Former Regimes. General Considerations.* Vol. I. Washington, DC: U.S. Institute of Peace, 1995.

Krznaric, Roman. "The Limits on Pro-Poor Agricultural Trade in Guatemala: Land, Labor and Political Power." *Journal of Human Development* 7, no. 1 (2006): 111–35.

Kuhn, Thomas. *The Structure of Scientific Revolutions.* Chicago: University of Chicago Press, 1962–1970.

Kuntsler, James Howard. *The Long Emergency.* New York: Grove Press, 2005.

Kurtz, Lester and Jennifer Turpin, eds., *Encyclopedia of Violence, Peace, and Conflict.* San Diego: Academic Press, 1999.

La Via Campesina, *Join the International Day of Peasant's Struggle! Mobilization Kit.* www.viacampesina.org.

Langman, Lauren. "From Virtual Public Spheres to Global Justice: A Critical Theory of Internetworked Social Movements." *Sociological Theory* 23, no. 1 (March 2005): 42–74.

Lazlo, Ervin and John Yoo, eds., *World Encyclopedia of Peace,* Oxford: Pergamon Press, 1986.

Lederach, John Paul. *The Moral Imagination: The Art and Soul of Building Peace.* Oxford and New York: Oxford University Press, 2005.

Lederach, John Paul, and Janice Moomaw Jenner, eds. *A Handbook of International Peacebuilding: Into the Eye of the Storm.* San Francisco: John Wiley & Sons, 2002.

Levering, Ralph B. and Miriam L. Levering. *Citizen Action for Global Change: The Neptune Group and Law of the Sea.* Syracuse, NY: Syracuse University Press, 1999.

Londoño Hoyos, Fernando. May 29, 2009. Interview with a.k.a "Samir." La hora de la verdad [radio show]. Radio Super.

López Martínez, M. "Hacia la institucionalización de la noviolencia. Algunas claves." In *Acción política no-violenta, una opción para Colombia,* edited by. F. Cante and L. Ortiz. Centro de Estudios Políticos e Internacionales, CEPI. Bogotá: Centro Editorial Universidad del Rosario, 2005.

López Martínez, M. "Noviolencia para generar cambios sociales." *Revista Polis 3* (2004): 9. http://www.revistapolis.cl/9/novio.doc.

Lozano, Elizabeth. "We Do Not Bear Children to Feed the War: Gendered Violence and Non-Violent Resistance in Colombia." In *Transformative Communication Studies: Culture, Hierarchy, and the Human Condition,* edited by Omar Swartz. Leicester, UK: Troubador, 2008.

Luard, Evan. *Basic Texts in International Relations.* New York: St. Martin's Press, 1992.

Lykes, M. Brinton, Ana Caba Mateo, Jacinta Chavez Anay, Ana Laynez Caba, Ubaldo Ruiz, and Joan W. Williams. "Telling Stories—Rethreading Lives: Community Education, Women's Development and Social Change among the Maya

Ixil." *International Journal of Leadership in Education: Theory and Practice 2* (1999): 207–27.

Lykes, M. Brinton, Carlos Martín Beristain, and Maria Luisa Cabrera Pérez-Armiñan. "Political Violence, Impunity, and Emotional Climate in Maya Communities." *Journal of Social Issues* 63, no. 2 (2007): 369–85.

Maastricht Treaty. European Union. February 7, 1992. http://www.eurotreaties.com/maastrichtec.pdf.

Mackie, J. L. *Ethics: Inventing Right and Wrong.* Harmondsworth, U.K.: Penguin, 1997.

Mandelbaum, Michael. *The Ideas That Conquered the World: Peace, Democracy, and Free Markets in the Twenty-first Century.* New York: Public Affairs, 2002.

Marks, Susan Collin. *Watching the Wind: Conflict Resolution during South Africa's Transition to Democracy.* Washington, DC: U.S. Institute of Peace, 2000.

Marsden, Bill. "Cholera and the Age of the Water Barons." *The Center for Public Integrity* (February 3, 2003). http://projects.publicintegrity.org/water/report.aspx?aid=44.

Marshall, Thomas H. *Citizenship And Social Class.* Cambridge UK: Cambridge University Press, 1950.

Mathison, David (Ed.). *Be The Media! How to Create and Accelerate Your Message. . . Your Way.* Tiburon, CA: natural E creative Group. 2009. http://bethemedia.com.

McCarthy, Colman. *Strength Through Peace: The Ideas and People of Nonviolence.* Washington, DC.: Center for Teaching Peace. 2001.

McCarthy, Colman "HYPERLINK "http://findarticles.com/p/articles/mi_m1141/is_22_39/ai_99983929/ "War's weapons of mass deception." *National Catholic Reporter.* Nov. 15, 2010. http://findarticles.com/p/articles/mi_m1141/is_22_39/ai_99983929/.

McCreery, David. *Rural Guatemala.* Stanford, CA: Stanford University Press, 1994.

McReynolds, David. "The Philosophy of Nonviolence." http://www.nonviolence.org/issues/philosophy-nonviolence.php.

Meli, Francis. *South Africa Belongs to Us. A History of the ANC.* Harare: Zimbabwe Publication House, 1988.

Melko, Matthew. *52 Peaceful Societies.* Oakville, ONT: Canadian Peace Research Society, 1973.

Menchú, Rigoberta. *I, Rigoberta Menchú, An Indian Woman in Guatemala.* New York: Verso, 1984.

Merriam-Webster Dictionary. "Dialogue." 2009. http://www.merriam-webster.com/dictionary/dialogue.

Merriam-Webster Dictionary. "Debate." 2009. http://www.merriam-webster.com/dictionary/debate.

Merriam-Webster Dictionary. "Discourse." 2009. http://www.merriam-webster.com/dictionary/discourse.

Merton, Thomas, ed. *Gandhi on Non-Violence: Selected Texts From Mohandas K. Gandhi's Non-Violence in Peace and War.* New York: New Directions, 1965.

Milazzo, Linda. "Corporate Media Turned Out for Jena, but Not for Anti-War. Here's Why." Atlantic Free Press. September 23, 2007. http://www.atlanticfreepress .com/news/1/2473-corporate-media-turned-out-for-jena-butnot-for-anti-war-heres-why.html.

Mills, C. Wright. *The Power Elite.* New York: Oxford University Press, 2000, reissue.

Minow, Martha. *Between Vengeance and Forgiveness, Facing History after Genocide and Mass Violence.* Boston: Beacon, 1998.

Montessori, Maria. *Education and Peace.* Translated by Helen R. Lane. Oxford, England: Clio Press, 1992.

Morris, Aldon D., and Carol McClurg Mueller, eds. *Frontiers in Social Movement Theory.* New Haven, CT: Yale University Press, 1992.

Morville, Peter. *Ambient Findability: What We Find Changes Who We Become.* Sebastopol, CA: O'Reilly, 2005.

Muller, J-M. "La noviolencia como filosofía y como strategia." In *Acción política no-violenta, una opción para Colombia,* edited by F. Cante and L. Ortiz. Centro de Estudios Políticos e Internacionales, CEPI. Bogotá: Centro Editorial Universidad del Rosario, 2005.

Mundo, Andino. "Cochabamba Protests of 2000." http://www.mundoandino.com/ Bolivia/Cochabamba-protests-of-2000.

Muravchik, Joshua. "The Past, Present, and Future of Neoconservativism." *Commentary Magazine* (October 2007).

Nagler, Michael, "Peace as a Paradigm Shift," *Bulletin of the Atomic Scientists* (December, 1981).

Nagler, Michael N. *The Search for a Nonviolent Future. A Promise of Peace for Ourselves, Our Families, and Our World.* San Francisco: Inner Ocean, 2004.

National Archives. *Teaching with Documents: FDR's Fireside Chat on the Purposes and Foundation of the Recovery Program.* 2009. http://www.archives.gov/education /lessons/fdr-fireside/.

National Security Strategy of the United States of America. Washington, DC: White House, 2002, 2006.

Naughton, John. *A Brief History of the Internet.* London: Phoenix, 2000.

The New English Bible, Oxford Study ed. New York: Oxford University Press, 1976.

Newmark, Craig. *Commentary: Internet Can Stregnthen Democracy.* August 26, 2008. http://www.cnn.com/2008/TECH/08/26/newmark.democracy/index.html.

Nickel, James. *Making Sense of Human Rights: Philosophical Reflections on the Universal Declaration of Human Rights.* Berkeley: University of California Press, 1987.

Noddings, Nel. "Caring and Peace Education." *Encyclopedia of Peace Education,* 2008: 87–91.

Nordhaus, Ted, and Michael Schellenberger. *Break Through: From the Death of Environmentalism to the Politics of Possibility.* Boston: Houghton Mifflin, 2007.

North American Congress on Latin America. "The Silent Violence of Peace in Guatemala." 2008. https://nacla.org/node/4665.

Nuestros principios en la Comunidad de Paz en San José de Apartadó. 2006. www .cdpsanjose.org.

Nueva arremetida presidencial contra la Comunidad de Paz de San José de Apartado. Corporación Jurídica Libertad (March 22, 2005). http://www.derechos.org/nizkor/colombia/doc/masacre6.html.

Nyheim, David. *Can Violence, War and State Collapse Be Prevented? The Future of Operational Conflict Early Warning and Response Systems.* Paris: OECD-DAC, 2008.

Oetzel, John G., and Stella Ting-Toomey. *The SAGE Handbook of Conflict Communication: Integrating Theory, Research and Practice.* Thousand Oaks, CA: Sage, 2006.

Oliver, Mary. "Journey." In *Dream Work* by Mary Oliver. New York: Atlantic Monthly Press, 1986.

Orwell, George. "A Hanging." In *Shooting an Elephant, and Other Essays.* New York: Harcourt Brace, 1968.

Patrir. *Devastating Development – Costing Lives: The True Impacts of Armed Violence and the Cost of Not Investing in Prevention.* www.patrir.ro.

Patterson, David S. *Toward a Warless World: The Travail of the American Peace Movement 1887–1914.* Bloomington, IN: Indiana University Press, 1976.

Peace Action Training and Research Institute of Romania (PATRIR). http://www.patrir.ro/index.php/en/about-ipdtc.

Peace Pilgrim. Peace Pilgrim: her life and work in her own words: Santa Fe, N.M.: Ocean Tree Books, 1983, 1982.

Peace and Collaborative Development Network. http://HYPERLINK "http://www.internationalpeaceandconflict.org/" www.internationalpeaceandconflict.org/.

Peace Pilgrim. Steps toward inner peace : harmonious principles for human living. Santa Fe, N.M. : Ocean Tree Books, 1993.

Peacekeeping Portal. http://HYPERLINK "http://www.peacebuildingportal.org/" www.peacebuildingportal.org.

Pearcy, Thomas L. *History of Central America.* Westport, CT: Greenwood Press, 2006.

Penn, William. *An Essay towards the Present and Future Peace of Europe by the Establishment of an European Diet, Parliament, or Estate.* Washington, DC: The American Peace Society, 1912 (1693).

Percy, Walker. "Walker Percy Quotes." http://www.goodreads.com/author/quotes/337.Walker_Percy.

Perkins, John. *Confessions of an Economic Hit Man.* New York: Penguin, 2004.

Perkins, John. *The Secret History of the American Empire: Economic Hit Men, Jackals, and the Truth about Corporate Corruption.* New York: Penguin, 2007.

Perrin, Noel. *Giving Up The Gun: Japan's Reversion to the Sword, 1543-1879.* Boston: D.R. Godine, 1979.

Phillips, Peter. "Barack Obama Administration Continues US Military Dominance." http://www.projectcensored.org/articles/story/http-wwwprojectcensoredorg-articlesstory-barack-obama-administration-c/.

Phillips, Peter. *Censored 2008.* New York: Seven Stories Press, 2007.

Phillips, Peter, and Andrew Roth. *Censored 2009.* New York: Seven Stories Press, 2008.

Pianta, Mario. "Democracy versus Globalization: The Growth of Parallel Summits and Moverments." In *Debating Cosmopolitics,* edited by Daniele Archibugi, 232–56. London: Verso, 2003.

Pierce, Paulette. "From Gladiator to Midwife: Birthing 'the Beloved Community' of Partnership in a Black Studies Classroom." In *Educating for a Culture of Peace*, edited by R. Eisler and R. Miller. Portsmouth, NH: Heinemann, 2004.

Pilisuk, Marc, with Jennifer A. Rountree. *Who Benefits From Global Violence and War: Uncovering a Destructive System*. Westport, CT: Praeger Security International, 2008.

Planet Carbon. http://carbontrades.co.uk/.

Popper, Karl R. *The Open Society and Its Enemies*. London: Routledge, 1945.

Postman, Neil. *Amusing Ourselves to Death: Public Discourse in the Age of Show Business*. New York: Viking, 1986.

Powell, Michael. "Barack Obama: Calm in the Swirl of History." June 4, 2008. http://www.nytimes.com/2008/06/04/us/politics/04obama.html.

Powers, Roger and William Vogele, eds., *Protest, Power, and Change: An Encyclopedia of Nonviolence from ACT-UP to Women's Suffrage*. New York: Garland, 1997.

Price, Robert M. *The Apartheid State in Crisis. Political Transformation in South Africa, 1975–1990*. New York: Oxford University Press, 1991.

Prothrow-Smith, Deborah. *Sugar and Spice and No Longer Nice: How We Can Stop Girls' Violence*. San Francisco: Jossey-Bass, 2005.

Public Service Agreement to Reduce the Impact of Conflict through Enhanced UK and International Efforts (October 2007). http://webarchive.nationalarchives.gov.uk/+/http://www.hm-treasury.gov.uk.

Purdie, Bob. "Was the Civil Rights Movement a Republican/Communist Conspiracy?" *Irish Political Studies* 3, no. 1 (1988): 33–41.

Raider, Ellen, Susan Coleman, and Janet Gerson. "Teaching Conflict Resolution Skills in a Workshop." In *The Handbook of Conflict Resolution: Theory and Practice*, edited by P. T. Coleman, M. Deutsch, and E. C. Marcus. San Francisco: Jossey-Bass, 2006.

Ray, Paul and Sherry Anderson. *The Cultural Creatives: How 50 Million People Are Changing the World*. New York: Three Rivers, 2001.

Reardon, Betty A. *Education for a Culture of Peace in a Gender Perspective*. Paris: United Nations Educational, Scientific and Cultural Organization, 2001.

Reardon, Betty A. *Education for Global Responsibility: Teacher-Designed Curricula for Peace Education, K-12*. New York: Teachers College Press, 1988.

"Reflecting on Peace Practice" project of the Collaborative for Development Action (CDA). http://www.cdainc.com/cdawww/project_profile.php?pid=RPP&pname=Reflecting%20Peace%20Practice.

Reid, Cecilie. "Peace and Law—Peace Activism and International Arbitration, 1895–1907." *Peace & Change* 29, nos. 3 and 4 (July 2004): 527–48.

Reinsborough, Patrick. "How to Change Things." In *Globalize Liberation*, edited by David Solnit, 172. San Francisco: City Lights Books, 2004.

Responding To Conflict. http://HYPERLINK "http://www.respond.org/" www.respond.org/.

Responsibility to Protect. "City of San Francisco Adopts Responsibility to Protect Resolution." March 14, 2007. http://r2pcoalition.org/index.php?option=com_events&task=view_detail&Itemid=&agid=15&year=2007.

Reychler, Luc, and Thania Paffenholz, eds. *Peace-Building: A Field Guide.* Boulder, CO: Lynne Rienner Publishers, 2001.

Rheingold, Howard. "Smartmobbing Democracy." In *Rebooting America: Ideas for Redesigning American Democracy for the Internet Age,*" edited by Allison Fine, Micah L. Sifry, Andrew Rasiej, and Josh Levy. New York: Personal Democracy Publishers, 2008. http://rebooting.personaldemocracy.com/node/5484.

Rich, Adrienne. "Natural Resources." In *The Dream of a Common Language: Poems 1974–1977.* New York: W.W. Norton, 1993.

Rights Action. "CUC National Committee Members Attacked by Gunfire and Kidnapped: Biofuel Agrobusinesses Violently Repress Communities," July 10, 2008. http://www.rightsaction.org/urgent_com/CUC_attack_071008.html.

Rorty, Richard. "Human Rights, Rationality, and Sentimentality." In *On Human Rights: The Oxford Amnesty Lectures 1993*, edited by S. Shute and S. Hurley. New York: Basic Books, 1993.

Rose, Richard. *Governing Without Consensus: An Irish Perspective.* London: 1971.

Rosenberg, Marshall. *Life-Enriching Education.* Encinitas, CA: PaddleDancer, 2003.

Rousseau, Jean-Jacques. "Jean-Jacques Rousseau: '*Abstract*' and '*Judgment*' of the Abbe de Saint-Pierre's Project for Perpetual Peace (1756)." In *Early Notions of Global Governance: Selected Eighteenth-Century Proposals for 'Perpetual Peace' with Rousseau, Bentham and Kant unabridged*, edited by Esref Aksu, 95–131, Ch. 11. Cardiff: University of Wales Press, 2008.

Rubin, Elizabeth. "The Prosecutor of the World's Worst." *The New York Times Magazine*, April 3, 2006.

Rummel, R. J. *Death by Government: Genocide and Mass Murder Since 1900.* New Brunswick, NJ: Transaction Publishers, 1994.

Sainath, Palagummi. "Neo-liberal Terrorism in India: The Largest Wave of Suicides in History." *CounterPunch*, December 20, 2009. http://www.counterpunch.org/sainath02122009.html.

Sainath, Palagummi. "Neoliberalism's Price Tag: 150,000 Farm Suicides in India from 1997 through 2005." *CounterPunch*, November 17, 2007. http://www.counterpunch.org/sainath11172007.html.

Salomon, Gavriel, and Baruch Nevo. *Peace Education. The Concept, Principles, and Practices around the World.* Mahwah, NJ: Lawrence Erlbaum, 2002.

Samarasinghe, Stanley, Brian Donaldson, and Colleen. McGinn. *Conflict Vulnerability Analysis. Issues, Tools and Responses.* Arlington, VA: Tulane Institute for International Development, 2001.

Santos, Boaventura de Sousa. *Toward a New Common Sense: Law, Science, and Politics in the Paradigmatic Transition.* New York: Routledge, 1995.

Santos, Boaventura de Sousa, and Mauricio García Villegas, eds. *Emanicipación social y violencia en Colombia.* Bogotá: Grupo Editorial Norma, 2004.

Saro-Wiwa, Ken. "Night Ride," in *Forest of Flowers*, Port Harcourt; Ewell: Saros, 1986.

Scharf, Adria, and Ram Bhagat. "Arts and Peace Education: The Richmond Youth Peace Project." *Harvard Educational Review* 3 (Fall 2007): 379–82.

Schell, Johnathan. *The Unconquerable World: Power, Nonviolence, and the Will of the People.* New York: Metropolitan Books, 2003.

Schock, Kurt. "Nonviolent Struggles to Defend & Reclaiming the Commons." Paper presented at the Annual Meetings of the International Studies Association, Chicago, March 2007.

Schock, Kurt. *Unarmed Insurrections: People Power Movements in Nondemocracies.* Minneapolis: University of Minneapolis Press, 2005.

Scola, Nancy. "Iran Roundup: Inside and Internet-Charged Resistance." June 18, 2009. http://techpresident.com/blog-entry/iran-roundup-inside-internet-charged-resistance.

Search for Common Ground. *Designing for Results: Integrating Monitoring and Evaluation in Conflict Transformation Programs.* http://www.sfcg.org/programmes/ilr/ilt_manualpage.html.

Sharp, Gene. "Desarrollando una alternative realista contra la guerra y otras violencias." In *Acción política no-violenta, una opción para Colombia,* edited by F. Cante and L. Ortiz. Centro de Estudios Políticos e Internacionales, CEPI. Bogotá: Centro Editorial Universidad del Rosario, 2005.

Sharp, Gene. "Nonviolent Struggle: An Effective Alternative." In *Inner Peace, World Peace: Essays on Buddhism and Nonviolence,* edited by Kenneth Kraft, 111–26. New York: State University of New York Press, 1992.

Sharp, Gene. *The Politics of Nonviolent Action.* Boston: B&T, 1973.

Sharra, Steve L. *Breaking the Elephant's Tusk: Teacher Autobiography and Methodology in Peace Education,* 2006. http://www.jsp.st.

Shenkman, Rick. *Just How Stupid Are We? Facing the Truth About the American Voter.* New York: Basic Books, 2008.

Shirky, Clay. *Here Comes Everybody: The Power of Organizing Without Organizations.* New York: Penguin HC, 2008.

Shiva, Vandana. *Stolen Harvest: The Hijacking of the Global Food Supply.* Cambridge, MA: South End Press, 2000.

Shiva, Vandana. *Water Wars: Privatization, Pollution, and Profit.* Cambridge, MA: South End Press, 2002.

Simone, Maria. "Code Pink Alert: The World Wide Web at Work in the Public Sphere." *All Academic.* May 27, 2004. http://www.allacademic.com/meta/p112535_index.html.

Smith, Christian. *Resisting Reagan: The U.S. Central American Peace Movement.* Chicago: University of Chicago Press. 1996.

Smith, David J., and Gerald Chambers. *Inequality in Northern Ireland.* Oxford: Clarendon Press, 1991.

Smith, Dan. *Towards a Strategic Framework for Peacebuilding: Getting Their Act Together—Overview Report of the Joint Utstein Study of Peacebuilding.* Oslo: The Royal Norwegian Ministry of Foreign Affairs, 2004.

Smith, Neil. *The Endgame of Globalization.* New York: Routledge, 2005.

Smithey, Lee, and Lester R. Kurtz. "We Have Bear Hands: Nonviolent Social Movements in the Soviet Bloc." In *Nonviolent Social Movements. A Geographical*

Perspective, edited by Stephen Zunes, Lester R. Kurtz, and Sarah Beth Asher, 96–124. Malden, MA: Blackwell, 1999.

Solnit, Rebecca. "Challenging Empire on The World Stage." *Orion Magazine*, Jan/Feb 2004. http://www.orionmagazine.org/index.php/articles/article/211/.

Solomon, Norman. "The Military-Industrial-Media Complex: Why War Is Covered from the Warriors' Perspective." *Extra!* (July/August 2005), published by Fairness and Accuracy in Reporting (FAIR), on the FAIR Web site at http://www.fair.org/index.php?page=2627.

Stallworth-Clark, Rosemarie. *Transformative Teacher Preparation: Fostering the Development of Teacher Dispositions That Support Peace*, 2006. http://www.jsp.st.

Stauber, John and Sheldon Rampton. *Weapons of Mass Deception: The Uses of Propaganda in Bush's War on Iraq*. New York: Tarcher Penguin, 2003.

Stauber, John and Sheldon Rampton. *Best War Ever: Lies, Damned Lies, and the Mess in Iraq*. New York: Penguin, 2006.

Steinman, Louise. The Call of the Wild: Review of Sleeping Where I Fall by Peter Cayote, Los Angeles Times, June 4, 1998 http://www.petercoyote.com/latimes.html

Stentzel, Jim, ed. More Than Witness: How a Small Group of Missionaries Aided Korea's Democratic Revolution. Seoul: Borea Democratic Foundation, 2006.

Stibel, Jeff. *The Internet as a Brain*. June 23, 2008. http://discussionleader.hbsp.com/stibel/2008/06/the-internet-is-a-brain.html.

Strauss, Andrew. "On the First Branch of Global Governance." *Widener Law Review* XIII, no. 2 (2007): 359.

Stroehlein, Andrew, and Gareth Evans. "A Responsibility To Protect: The World's View." *Open Democracy*, April 4, 2007. http://www.opendemocracy.net/globalization-institutions_government/protect_people_4505.jsp.

Taleb, Nassim Nicholas. *The Black Swan: The Impact of the Highly Improbable*. New York: Random House, 2007.

Tarrow, Sidney. *Power in Movement: Social Movements and Contentious Politics*, 2nd ed. Cambridge, UK: Cambridge University Press, 1998.

Tate, Winifred. *Counting the Dead: The Culture and Politics of Human Rights Activism in Colombia*. Berkeley: University of California Press, 2007.

Taylor, Peter. *Brits: The War Against the IRA*. New York: Bloomsbury Publishing, 2001.

Taylor, Peter. *Loyalists*. New York: Bloomsbury Publishing, 2000.

Tilly, Charles. *Popular Contention in Great Britain, 1758–1834*. Cambridge, MA: Harvard University Press, 1995.

Tirado, José M. "How Iceland Fell: A Hundred Days of (Muted) Rage." *CounterPunch*. January 27, 2009. http://www.counterpunch.org/tirado01272009.html.

Toda Institute for Global Peace and Policy Research. *Full Mission Statement*. August 25, 2008. http://www.toda.org/about/fullmissionstatement.html.

Trimble, David. *To Raise Up a New Northern Ireland*. Speeches and Articles by the Rt. Hon. David Trimble MP MLA 1998–2001. Belfast: Belfast Press, 2001.

UK Department for International Development. "Conducting Conflict Assessments: Guidance Notes." 2002. http://webarchive.nationalarchives.gov.uk/+/http://www.dfid.gov.uk/documents/publications/conflictassessmentguidance.pdf.

UK Department of International Development (DFID). "Preventing Violent Conflict." 2006. HYPERLINK "http://www.dfid.gov.uk" \o "http://www.dfid.gov.uk" \t "_blank" www.dfid.gov.uk, 2006.

UK Government. "Public Service Agreement (PSA 30) for Global Conflict: Reduce the Impact of Conflict through Enhanced UK and International Efforts." October 2007.

UN Department of Economic and Social Affairs. "Developing Capacity for Conflict Analysis and Early Response: A Training Manual." n.d. http://cpr.web.cern.ch/cpr/Library/UNDESA%20Training%20Manual.doc.

UNESCO. *A Practical Guide to the World Decade for Cultural Development, 1988–1997.* Paris: UNESCO, 1987.

UN General Assembly. "Progress Report on the Prevention of Armed Conflict: Report of the Secretary-General." July 18, 2006. http://www.un.org/Depts/dpa/docs/Prevention%20Report.pdf.

UN General Assembly. "Resolution Adopted By The General Assembly: 2005 World Summit Outcome." October 24, 2005. Paragraph 138. http://daccess-dds-ny.un.org/doc/UNDOC/GEN/N05/487/60/PDF/N0548760.pdf?Open Element.

UN Secretary General. "On Anniversary Of Rwanda Genocide, Secretary-General Says Current Challenge Is To Make Responsibility To Protect Operational." April 5, 2007. www.un.org/News/Press/docs/2007/sgsm10934.doc.htm

United Nations Conference on Trade and Development. *Least Developed Countries Report,* 2007.

United Nations. "UN Genocide Post to Full Time." United Press International, April 9, 2007. www.upi.com/International_Intelligence/Briefing/2007/04/09/un_genocide_prevention_post_to_full_time.

United Nations Department of Public Information. Press Conference on International Commission Against Impunity in Guatemala, February 24, 2009. http://www.un.org/News/briefings/docs/2009/090224_CICIG.doc.htm.

United Nations Development Program. *Human Development Report: Beyond Scarcity: Power, Poverty, and the Global Water Crisis,* 2006. http://www.dvgw.de/fileadmin/dvgw/portrait/profil/hdr2006.pdf.

United Nations World Food Program. *Guatemala: Overview,* 2009. http://www.wfp.org/countries/guatemala.

Uribe, Maria Teresa. "Emancipación social en un contexto de guerra prolongada. El caso de la Comunidad de Paz de San José de Apartadó." In *Emanicipación social y violencia en Colombia,* edited by Boaventura de Sousa Santos and Mauricio García Villegas. Bogotá: Grupo editorial Norma, 2004.

Uygur, Cenk. "Conservative Media vs Progressive Media." Posted on The Daily Kos blog, July 1, 2009. http://www.dailykos.com/story/2009/7/1/748854/-Conservative-Media-vs.-Progressive-Media.

Van der Linden, W. H. *The International Peace Movement 1815–1874.* Amsterdam: Tilleul Publications, 1987.

Vélez Rincón, Clara Isabel. "Comunidad de paz dice que el Estado los acosa." El Colombiano. March 22, 2005. http://www.elcolombiano.com/BancoConocimiento/

C/comunidad_de_paz_dice_que_el_estado_los_acosa/comunidad_de_paz_dice_
que_el_estado_los_acosa.asp.

Vidal, Gore. *Imperial America: Reflections on the United States of Amnesia*. New York:
Nation Books, 2005.

Viera, C. *Se recrudece tensión entre el Estado colombiano y Comunidad de paz de San José
de Apartadó*. Inter Press Service, March 6, 2005. http://www.prensarural.org
/vieira20050306.htm.

Volkan, Vamik D. *Bloodlines. From Ethnic Pride to Ethnic Terrorism*. New York:
Farrar & Straus and Giroux, 1997.

Von Glahn, Gerard. *Law among Nations: An Introduction to Public International Law*,
7th ed. Boston: Allyn and Bacon, 1996.

Vongalis-Macrow, Athena. "Rebuilding Regimes or Rebuilding Community?
Teacher's Agency for Social Reconstruction in Iraq." *Journal of Peace Education*
3, no. 1 (2006): 99–113.

Waldron, Jeremy. *Theories of Rights*. Oxford, UK: Oxford University Press, 1984.

Walsh, Gerald G., et al. *St. Augustine, City of God*. New York: Doubleday Image,
1950.

Walvin, James. "The Rise of British Popular Sentiment for Abolition, 1787–1832."
In *Anti-Slavery: Religion and Reform: Essays in Memory of Roger Ansley*, edited by
Christine Bolt and Seymour Drescher, 149–62. Kent and Hamden: William
Dawsons & Sons and Archon Books, 1980.

Wam, Per, and Shonali Sardesai "Conflict Analysis Framework (CAF)." Conflict
Prevention and Reconstruction Team (CRT) Social Development Department,
World Bank. April 11, 2005. http://siteresources.worldbank.org/INTCPR/
214574-1112883508044/20657757/CAFApril2005.pdf.

Washington Office on Latin America. "Advocates against Impunity: A Case Study on
Human Rights Organizing in Guatemala," 2008. http://www.wola.org/organized
_crime/cicig/cicig_advocates_against_impunity.pdf.

Wenden, Anita L. *Education for a Culture of Social and Ecological Peace*. Albany:
State University of New York, 2004.

Whang, Patricia A., and Claudia Peralta Nash. "Reclaiming Compassion: Getting
to the Heart and Soul of Teacher Education." *Journal of Peace Education* 2, no. 1
(2005): 79–92.

Widener Symposium. "Symposium: Envisioning a More Democratic Global System." *Widener Law Review* XIII (No. 2), 2007: i–v, 243–423.

Wilson, Maya. "COHA Concerned about Crime in Guatemala," February 9, 2009.
http://www.guatemala-times.com/news/guatemala/778-coha-concerned-about
-crime-in-guatemala.pdf.

Wink, Walter, and Richard Deats, "Real Grounds for Hope," *Fellowship* January/
February, 1992, p. 2.

Women of ADMI and M. Brinton Lykes. *Voces e Imagenes: Mujeres Ixiles de Chajul
[Voices and Images: Maya Ixil Women of Chajul]*. Guatemala: Magna Terra, 2000.

Woodcock, George. *Anarchism: A History of Libertarian Ideas and Movements*. New
York and Ontario: New American Library, 1962.

Woolman, John, and Amelia Gummere. *The Journal and Essays of John Woolman*,
New York: Macmillan & Co., 1922.

World Health Organization. *Global Water Supply and Sanitation Assessment 2000 Report.* 2000. http://www.who.int/water_sanitation_health/monitoring/global-assess/en/.

World Nuclear Association. *Nuclear Desalination.* November 2008. http://www.world-nuclear.org/info/inf71.html.

World Public Opinion. "Publics Around the World Say UN Has Responsibility to Protect Against Genocide." April 5, 2007. www.WorldPublicOpinion.org.

Zinn, Howard. *A People's History of the United States: 1992–Present,* revised and updated ed. New York: Harper Perennial, 1980/1995.

Zunes, Stephen. "The Role of Nonviolence in the Downfall of Apartheid." In *Nonviolent Social Movements. A Geographical Perspective,* edited by Stephen Zunes, Lester R. Kurtz, and Sarah Beth Asher, 203–30. Malden, MA: Blackwell, 1999.

Zunes, Stephen, "The Origins of People Power in the Philippines." In *Nonviolent Social Movements: A Geographical Perspective,* edited by Stephen Zunes, Lester R. Kurtz, and Sarah Beth Asher. Oxford: Blackwell, 1999.

Zunes, Stephen, Lester R. Kurtz, and Sarah Beth Asher, eds. *Nonviolent Social Movements: A Geographical Perspective.* Malden, MA: Blackwell, 1999, 2007.

INDEX

About the Editors and Contributors

Co-editor **Marc Pilisuk** got his PhD in clinical and social psychology from the University of Michigan in 1961 and went on to teach, research, and write at several colleges, ending up at the University of California and Saybrook University. His various departmental affiliations, psychology, nursing, administrative sciences, social welfare, public health, community mental health, human and community development, city and regional planning, peace and conflict studies, and human sciences, convinced him that academic disciplines could be blinders and should be crossed. He was a founder of the first Teach-in on a University Campus (Michigan) and the Psychologists for Social Responsibility, helped start SANE (now Peace Action), and is a past president of the Society for the Study of Peace Conflict and Violence. He has received several lifetime contribution awards for work for peace. Marc's books cover topics of underlying social issues, poverty, international conflict, and the nature of human interdependence. His most recent, *Who Benefits from Global Violence and War*, uncovered information that was sufficiently shocking to motivate this new undertaking on *Peace Movements Worldwide*.

Co-editor **Michael N. Nagler** was sensitized to issues of peace and justice (the usual term is "radicalized") through folk music and various influences by the time he left his New York birthplace. After attending Cornell University and finishing his BA at New York University, he arrived in Berkeley, CA, in 1960, in time to finish a PhD in Comparative Literature before the advent of the Free Speech Movement. The successes and failures of that movement broadened his outlook such that after meeting a meditation teacher, Eknath Easwaran, late in 1966, he launched a parallel career—inward. Nonviolence, and Gandhi in particular, became a way to carve out a meaningful niche for himself within academia. At Berkeley, he went on to found the Peace and Conflict Studies Program (PACS; now probably the largest in terms of student majors in the United States) and off campus co-founded the Metta Center for Nonviolence (www.mettacenter.org). He also became chair of Peaceworkers (www.peaceworkers.org) and eventually co-chair of the Peace and Justice Studies Association (www.peacejusticestudies.org). He stopped teaching at the university in 2007 to devote his time to Metta and the Blue Mountain Center of Meditation. A frequent speaker on nonviolence and related themes around the world, his most recent recognition is the Jamnalal Bajaj International Award for Promoting Gandhian Values Outside India. His books include *The Upanishads* (with Eknath Easwaran, 1987), *Our Spiritual Crisis* (2004), and *The Search for a Nonviolent Future*, which won a 2002 American Book Award and has been translated into six languages, most recently Arabic.

Maude Barlow is the National Chairperson of the Council of Canadians and Senior Advisor on Water to the President of the United Nations General Assembly. She also chairs the board of Washington-based Food and Water Watch and is a Counselor with the Hamburg-based World Future Council. Maude is the recipient of eight honorary doctorates as well as many awards, including the 2005 Right Livelihood Award (known as the "Alternative Nobel") and the 2008 Canadian Environment Award. She is also the best-selling author or co-author of 16 books, including the recently released *Blue Covenant: The Global Water Crisis* and *The Coming Battle for the Right to Water*.

Marcel M. Baumann is Lecturer at the Department of Political Science, University of Freiburg, and Senior Researcher at the Arnold Bergstraesser Institute for Socio-Cultural Research in Freiburg. His scholarly work is concerned with peace processes and conflict transformation and the topic of political violence. Dr. Baumann has made several research trips to Northern Ireland, South Africa, Macedonia, and Lebanon. In 2004 he was a Visiting Scholar at the University of California at Berkeley.

Laura Bernstein has a BA from Barnard College and an MA from the University of Chicago. She completed post-graduate studies at the Chicago Institute for Psychoanalysis and worked as a child psychotherapist for 10 years. Subsequently, she engaged in rabbinical studies at the Hebrew Seminary of the Deaf (Skokie, Illinois). She is the leader and composer of interfaith chants, the author of poetry and articles on spirituality, and the co-author (with Ron Miller) of *Healing the Jewish-Christian Rift.* She has taught at Common Ground (an interfaith study center in Deerfield, Illinois), where she currently facilitates an ongoing meditation group. For the past three years, she has been an enthusiastic board member of Hands of Peace.

Elise Boulding until her death in 2010 was Professor Emerita of sociology at Dartmouth College. She was born in Oslo, Norway, and earned a PhD at the University of Michigan. A former member of the International Jury of UNESCO (1981 to 1987), she led the move to establish the U.S. Peace Institute in 1984. She was also a founder of the International Peace Research Association and a distinguished member of the Religious Society of Friends (Quakers). Dr. Boulding received numerous honors for her achievements as a scholar and activist in the areas of peace and world order, democracy, and women in society. In 1973, she received the Douglass College Distinguished Achievement Award. She was nominated for the Nobel Peace Prize in 1990, and authored 19 books and hundreds of chapters and articles.

Kai Brand-Jacobsen is a co-founder and Director of the Peace Action, Training, and Research Institute of Romania (PATRIR). He is an expert in mediation; early warning and comprehensive prevention; and reconciliation after violence, post-war recovery, and systemic peace building. He consults widely for governments, foreign ministries, and international and national organizations including the UN and the All Party Parliamentary Working Group (APPG) on Conflict Issues of the British Parliament. His work contributes to governmental, inter-governmental, and nongovernmental organization (NGO) policies and capacities for peace building, humanitarian aid, international development cooperation, and deployment of civil peace services. In cooperation with the International Peace and Development Training Center, Kai works at the invitation of governments, UN agencies, and organizations that have requested training support to design specialized programs customized to meet their specific needs. He has provided more than 260 training programs in 36 countries and has been invited to present more than 600 public talks in 28 countries. From

2005 to 2007 he served on the International Governing Council of Non-violent Peaceforce and in 2007 became a member of the Steering Committee of the European Network of Civil Peace Services. Brand-Jacobsen has taught and lectured at universities across Europe, North America, Latin America, and Asia. He's co-author, with Johan Galtung and Carl Jacobsen, of *Searching for Peace: The Road to TRANSCEND* (2000 and 2002). He is on the executive board of the *Journal of Peace and Development* and an editor of Oxford University Press's *Peace Encyclopedia*. Brand-Jacobsen has worked in Afghanistan, India, Pakistan, Nepal, Sri Lanka, southern Thailand, Burma, Cambodia, Aceh-Indonesia, Russia, Moldova, South Eastern Europe, Mexico, Colombia, Somalia, North America, and the Middle East.

Svetlana Broz, MD, has been a physician since 1992 and volunteered as a cardiologist at the outbreak of the war in Bosnia and Herzegovina. She has continued to work on peace building in the Balkans. In January 1993, she began interviewing for the book *Good People in an Evil Time* (2003). She is the founder and director of NGO Gariwo Sarajevo, president of the Sarajevo city government's Steering Committee for the Garden of the Righteous, honorary president of European Movement in Bosnia and Herzegovina, member of the editorial board of the magazine *Spirit of Bosnia*, adviser at the Institute for Global Leadership at Tufts University and honorary member of the board of Eastern European Service Agency (EESA), San Jose, California. She served as International Advisor of Conflict Management Group, Cambridge, Massachusetts, and is a member of the International Advisory Board of the Center for Macro Projects and Diplomacy, Roger Williams University, Rhode Island. She is the author of two books and many papers and essays, and editor of 10 books about peace building, civil courage, and nonviolence. As a professional lecturer, she delivered more than 1,000 public lectures and media events at over 70 U.S. and European universities.

Ken Butigan, PhD, is a member of the adjunct faculty at DePaul University, Chicago, where he teaches in the Peace, Justice and Conflict Resolution Program, and Loyola University, Chicago. He has published five books, including *Pilgrimage through a Burning World: Spiritual Practice and Nonviolent Protest at the Nevada Test Site* (2003). Since the early 1980s he has been an organizer with a variety of social movements, including those working for a nuclear-free future, freedom for East Timor, and an end to homelessness. From 1987 to 1990 he served as the national coordinator of the Pledge of Resistance, a network of 100,000 people in 400 local groups that organized coordinated nonviolent action for peace in Central America.

In 2006, he was a founder of the Declaration of Peace, a grassroots campaign working for a just and lasting peace in Iraq. Since 1990 Dr. Butigan has been on the staff of Pace e Bene Nonviolence Service, a nonprofit organization promoting nonviolent change in the United States and around the world through education, resources, and action. He created the training project From Violence to Wholeness and collaborated in the development of Engage: Exploring Nonviolent Living, Pace e Bene's comprehensive nonviolence education program. Dr. Butigan was the national coordinator of the Pledge of Resistance from 1987 to 1990. He is currently an adjunct professor at DePaul University and Loyola University, Chicago and on the staff of Pace e Bene Nonviolence Service.

Candice C. Carter, PhD, is an associate professor at the University of North Florida. Her research and scholarship topics include conflict transformation, peace policy, multicultural education, history and social studies instruction, citizenship education, peace education, peace through arts, peace literature, and teacher preparation. She serves in many international and national peace, education, and policy organizations, as well as local ones such as the Florida Center for Public and International Policy. Professor Carter designs and facilitates peace education programs in all levels of education, including the interdisciplinary Conflict Transformation Program at the University of North Florida. Dr. Carter's publications in journals and books include a multitude of topics related to peace and human relations. Her book *Conflict Resolution and Peace Education: Transformations across Disciplines* discusses cases in multiple fields as well as adult education. The books she has co-edited include *Chicken Soup for the Soul: Stories for a Better World* (http://chickensoup.peacestories.info) and *Peace Philosophy in Action*, which present peace actions in many different contexts of the world. Dr. Carter edits the *Journal of Stellar Peacemaking* (www.jsp.st) that incorporates nonfiction, research, and the arts to illustrate peace processes, and she also provides the Peacemaker Site (www.peacemaker.st) with many peace building resources.

Rev. Richard L. Deats, PhD, served as executive director and editor of *Fellowship* magazine at the Fellowship of Reconciliation, where he worked from 1972 to mid-2005. A native of Texas, he taught social ethics in the Philippines at Union Theological Seminary from 1959 to 1972. Long active in the fields of civil rights and peace, he has lectured and led workshops on nonviolence in many countries. He is author of a number of books, including biographies of Martin Luther King Jr., Hildegard Goss-Mayr, and Mahatma Gandhi; he also edited a volume of Muriel Lester's writings and authored a book of humor. He went to Iraq in 2000 with an interfaith delegation and co-led a Friendship Delegation to Iran in May 2006. He taught nonviolence in Burma in 2007 He was a member of the Martin Luther King Jr. Federal Holiday Commission through which the Martin Luther King Jr. national holiday was established. In 2009 he was named to the Rockland Hall of Fame for Human Rights and Civil Rights and Distinguished Alumnus of the Boston University School of Theology.

Richard Falk is Albert G. Milbank Professor Emeritus of international law at Princeton University and Visiting Distinguished Professor in global and international studies at the University of California, Santa Barbara. He is chair of the board of the Nuclear Age Peace Foundation, on the editorial board of *The Nation*, and an honorary editor of *American Journal of International Law* His most recent books are *The Costs of War: International Law, the UN, and World Order after Iraq* (2008) and *Achieving Human Rights* (2009). He is currently serving as Special Rapporteur on the Occupied Palestinian Territories for the UN Human Rights Council.

Ronald J. Glossop, PhD, is Professor Emeritus of philosophical studies at Southern Illinois University at Edwardsville (SIUE). His PhD in philosophy is from Washington University-St. Louis and his BA (summa cum laude) is from Carthage College. He has also taught at Boise State University (Idaho) and Portland State University (Oregon). He is the author of three books: *Philosophy: An Introduction to Its Problems and Vocabulary* (Dell, 1974); *Confronting War: An Examination of Humanity's Most Pressing Problem* (McFarland, 1983, 4th ed. 2001); and *World Federation? A Critical Analysis of Federal World Government* (McFarland, 1993; Esperanto translation *Monda Federacio?* by J. Rapley, 2001). Over 60 of his articles have been published in scholarly publications. He has given lectures in over 10 countries in English and in Esperanto. He is Chair of the St. Louis chapter of Citizens for Global Solutions and a member of its national board of directors and its Political Action Committee. He is president of the American Association of Teachers of Esperanto and Director of the Esperanto organization "Children around the World." Dr. Glossop is an honorary member of Rotary International and a member of Phi Beta Kappa and Phi Kappa Phi.

Paul Hawken is an author of seven books including *The Next Economy* (1983), *Growing a Business* (1987), *The Ecology of Commerce* (1993) and *Natural Capitalism: Creating the Next Industrial Revolution* (co-authored with Amory Lovins, 1999). His most recent book, *Blessed Unrest: How the*

Largest Movement in the World Came into Being, and Why No One Saw It Coming (2007) is the culmination of over a decade of research exploring humanity's extraordinary capacity to address the social and environmental issues of our time. He is the executive director of the Natural Capital Institute, chief executive officer of the Pax Engineering Group, co-founder of Highwater Global Fund, and chairman of Biomimicry Ventures Group. He has served on the board of several environmental organizations including Point Foundation (publisher of the Whole Earth Catalogs), Center for Plant Conservation, Conservation International, Trust for Public Land, and National Audubon Society.

Mickey S. Huff is an associate professor of history at Diablo Valley College and associate director of the Media Freedom Foundation and Project Censored (projectcensored.org), which was the recipient of the 2008 PEN Oakland National Literary Censorship Award. He is Media Freedom International's College and University Affiliates Coordinator, working in conjunction with Project Censored, a former adjunct lecturer in sociology at Sonoma State University, and the previous co-director of the alternative public opinion research agency Retropoll (retropoll.org), in Berkeley, California. Huff has been interviewed by many radio stations and news sources throughout the country and has been published on numerous media and news Web sites and even a few corporate media outlets (that he routinely critiques). He has co-organized and presented at numerous national academic conferences on media and recent historical events on truth emergency and media reform issues in 2008 (see truthemergency.us). He has also given many public addresses at colleges, community halls, and bookstores across the United States on media censorship and American history. Huff was the host of the Modern Media Censorship Lecture Series at Sonoma State University (fall 2008). In spring 2009, he was the Visiting Scholar for the Academic Library at the University of Nebraska, Lincoln, where he sat on a panel and gave a keynote address on media censorship and democracy. His recent publications include co-authoring "Media Reform Meets Truth Emergency" and "Deconstructing Deceit: 9/11, the Media, and Myth Information" in *Censored 2009* (Seven Stories Press); he wrote and edited *Censored 2010* with Dr. Peter Phillips and is working on several articles on the truth emergency, post-9/11 propaganda studies, and collective memory. When he has time, he blogs at mythinfo.blogspot.com and dailycensored.com.

Nikolas Larrow-Roberts grew up in the 1990's punk scene surrounding Pittsburgh, Pennsylvania. He blindly followed his high school guidance counselor's advice to pursue military service rather than higher education. That path led to a transformation in consciousness and the end of his military record. After a few years in the political punk band Despite Best Intentions, he embarked on a journey to become an educator. Nik is pursuing his PhD at Saybrook University and provides faculty professional development at California University (Pennsylvania), where he also serves as an interviewer for the Veterans Oral Histories Project. Currently an adjunct instructor, Nik teaches courses in sociology, criminal justice, and government.

Rabbi Michael Lerner is editor of *Tikkun* magazine: a Jewish and interfaith critique of politics, culture, and society (Web edition at www.tikkun .org) and chair of the interfaith Network of Spiritual Progressives (www .spiritualprogressives.org). He is the author of 11 books including the 1994 national best-seller *Jewish Renewal: A Path of Healing and Transformation*; a book co-written with Cornel West, *Jews and Blacks: Let the Healing Begin*; *The Politics of Meaning: Restoring Hope and Possibility in an Age of Cynicism*; *Surplus Powerlessness: The Psychodynamics of Everyday Life and the Psychology of Individual and Social Transformation*; *Spirit Matters: Global Healing and the Wisdom of the Soul*; *Healing Israel/Palestine; A Path to Peace and Reconciliation*; and the 2006 national best-seller *The Left Hand of God: Taking Back our Country from the Religious Right*. He welcomes feedback at RabbiLerner@Tikkun.org.

Elizabeth Lozano, PhD, is an associate professor in the School of Communication at Loyola University, Chicago, and the Director of the Latin American Studies Program at that institution. She came to the United States in 1987 as a Fulbright scholar and received her PhD in philosophy of communication from Ohio University. Dr. Lozano's areas of expertise are media studies and cultural studies. Her research has focused on the textual analysis of national and international television systems; and the ethnographic study of public comportment in urban settings. Accordingly, Lozano's academic courses range from intercultural communication to new Latin American cinema and global feminisms. From the start of her experience as an "international" researcher in the United States, Lozano has been equally intrigued by pop culture as well as by the quotidian ways in which we construct gender and ethnic identity through communication. In recent years that curiosity has turned into a passion for uncovering the ways in which we collectively "practice violence" or alternatively create ways of nonviolent conflict resolution. Specifically, Lozano is currently studying the ways in which Colombian communities struggle to resist war by means other than war, and the possible relationship between nonviolent resistance and community-enhancing communication practices.

Joanna Macy, PhD, is an eco-philosopher and scholar of Buddhism, general systems theory, and deep ecology. She is also a leading voice in movements for peace, justice, and a safe environment. Interweaving her scholarship and four decades of activism, she has created both a groundbreaking theoretical framework for a new paradigm of personal and social change, and a powerful workshop methodology for its application. Her wide-ranging work addresses psychological and spiritual issues of the nuclear age, the cultivation of ecological awareness, and the fruitful resonance between Buddhist thought and contemporary science. Over the past 30 years many thousands of people around the world have participated in Joanna's workshops and trainings, while her methods have been adopted and adapted yet more widely in classrooms, churches, and grassroots organizing. Her work helps people transform despair and apathy in the face of overwhelming social and ecological crises into constructive, collaborative action. It brings a new way of seeing the world, as our larger living body, freeing us from the assumptions and attitudes that now threaten the continuity of life on Earth. Her books include *Coming Back to Life*; *Widening Circles*, and *World as Lover, World as Self.*

John Marks is president and founder of Search for Common Ground, a nonprofit conflict resolution organization with offices in 18 countries. He also founded and heads Common Ground Productions and has produced or executive-produced numerous TV series around the world. With his wife, Susan Collin Marks, he is a Skoll Fellow in Social Entrepreneurship, and, additionally, he is an Ashoka Senior Fellow. A best-selling, award-winning author, he has been a U.S. Foreign Service Officer, Executive Assistant to the late U.S. Senator Clifford Case, a Fellow at Harvard's Institute of Politics, and a Visiting Scholar at Harvard Law School.

Susan Collin Marks is the senior vice president of Search for Common Ground. She is a South African who served as a peacemaker and peace builder during South Africa's transition from apartheid to democracy. See her book, *Watching the Wind: Conflict Resolution during South Africa's Transition to Democracy* (U.S. Institute of Peace, Washington, DC, 2000.) She serves on numerous boards, including the Advisory Council of the Woodrow Wilson International Center's Project on Africa, and the Abraham Path Initiative. She is the founding editor of *Track Two*, a quarterly publication on community and political conflict resolution. She was portrayed in the PBS documentary *Women on the Frontlines*. In 2006, she launched the *Leadership Wisdom Initiative* to offer leadership development and one-on-one support and coaching to political, institutional, and civil society leaders. Honors include a Jennings Randolph Peace Fellowship (1994 to 1995) at the United States Institute for Peace, the Institute of Noetic Sciences' *Creative Altruism* award in 2005, and a Skoll Fellowship for Social Entrepreneurship in 2006. She speaks, teaches, coaches, mentors, writes, facilitates, and supports peace processes and conflict resolution programs internationally.

Colman McCarthy entered his first career as a columnist for *The Washington Post* in 1969, a position that he held until 1997, being one of the few journalists in the nation to write on nonviolence, pacifism, and peace. He also began teaching nonviolence and peace in 1982, and now in his early seventies continues to teach tirelessly in Washington, D.C., metro area schools and colleges. In 1985 he founded the Center for Teaching Peace, a nonprofit that primarily assists educational institutions seeking to develop peace studies programs, while still writing regularly for the *National Catholic Reporter*. He has received many honorary degrees and awards and is the author of *I'd Rather Teach Peace*, several other books, and countless articles expressing his views as an ethical vegetarian, anarchist, and pacifist, and has become famous for one-liners, like "Unless we teach our children peace, someone will teach them violence," and "Peace is the result of love, and if love were easy we'd all be good at it."

John Perkins, as chief economist at a major international consulting firm, advised the World Bank, United Nations, International Monetary Fund (IMF), U.S. Treasury Department, Fortune 500 corporations, and countries in Africa, Asia, Latin America, and the Middle East. He worked directly with heads of state and chief executive officers of major companies. His latest book, *Hoodwinked* (2009), is a blueprint for a new form of global economics. The solutions are not "return to normal" ones. Instead, Perkins challenges us to soar to new heights, away from predatory capitalism and into an era more transformative than the Agricultural and Industrial Revolutions. *Hoodwinked* details specific steps each of us can take to create a sustainable, just, and peaceful world. *Confessions of an Economic Hit Man*, which spent nearly a year and a half on the *New York Times* best-seller lists and has been published in more than 30 languages, is a startling exposé of international corruption. *The Secret History of the American Empire*, also a *New York Times* best-seller, details the clandestine operations that created the world's first truly global empire. John is founder and board member of Dream Change and The Pachamama Alliance, non-profit organizations devoted to establishing a world our children will want to inherit; has lectured at universities on four continents; and is the author of books on indigenous cultures and transformation, including *Shapeshifting*, *The World Is as You Dream It*, *Psychonavigation*, *Spirit of the Shuar*, and *The Stress-Free Habit*.

Peter Phillips, PhD, is professor of sociology at Sonoma State University and director of Project Censored. He has published 13 editions of *Censored: Media Democracy in Action* (Seven Stories Press). Also from Seven Stories Press are *Impeach the President: The Case against Bush and Cheney* (2006) and *Project Censored Guide to Independent Media and Activism* (2003). In 2009, Phillips received the Dallas Smythe Award from the Union for Democratic Communications. Phillips writes op-ed pieces for independent media nationwide and has published articles in dozens of publications, newspapers, and Web sites. He frequently speaks on media censorship and various socio-political issues on radio and TV talk shows. Phillips has completed several investigative research studies that are available at Projectcensored.org. Phillips earned a BA degree in social science from Santa Clara University and an MA degree in social science from California State University at Sacramento. He earned a second MA in sociology and a PhD in sociology. His doctoral dissertation was entitled "A Relative Advantage: Sociology of the San Francisco Bohemian Club." Phillips is a fifth-generation Californian, who grew up on a family-owned farm west of the Central Valley town of Lodi.

Jennifer Achord Rountree, PhD, is a recent graduate of Saybrook Graduate School and Research Center in San Francisco. Her doctoral research focused on the participatory development project of a Maya community in San Lucas Tolimán, Guatemala. With Dr. Marc Pilisuk, she has co-authored a number of articles and assisted in the writing and research of *Who Benefits from Global Violence: Uncovering a Destructive System* (2008).

Lena Slachmuijlder is the Director of Search for Common Ground (SFCG) in the Democratic Republic of the Congo (DRC). A graduate of Stanford University, she has worked and lived in Africa for the last 20 years as a journalist, human rights defender, media producer, performing artist, and conflict transformation trainer. As director of SFCG's largest program, Lena heads a staff of 75 people in six offices around the country. SFCG in DRC is a multidisciplinary conflict transformation program, involving radio and television production; training; mobile cinema to combat sexual violence; participatory theater; dialogue between youth, civil society, and elected leaders; work with the Congolese army to respect human rights; and joint activities to renew relationships broken by war and conflict. Under Lena's leadership, SFCG programs in Burundi and the DRC have won numerous international awards, including the Ashoka Changemakers Award for innovative on the ground approaches to conflict, and the UNICEF Children's Voices award for children-produced media. She was an international fellow at the Brandeis University Alan B. Slifka Program in Intercommunal Coexistence, "Recasting Reconciliation through Arts and Culture." Lena was born in Katonah, New York, of American-Belgian parents.

Deva Temple is co-founder and director of MUSE: Make Us a Sustainable Earth!, a nonprofit organization dedicated to creating a more sustainable Earth by empowering the public through educational programs that integrate the arts and sciences. She also serves as a researcher and assistant editor of *Peace & Policy* with the Toda Institute for Global Peace and Policy Research. She has worked with several other nonprofits as an organizational development and sustainability consultant. She holds an MA in global leadership and sustainable development, and a graduate certificate in environmental policy, from Hawaii Pacific University, and a BA in psychology from Lewis and Clark College. Her master's thesis focused on the development of values and beliefs among sustainability leaders. Her interests lie in the areas of ethical transformation, feminism, philosophy, systems science, and sustainable development.

Claude AnShin Thomas went to Vietnam at the age of 18, where he received numerous awards and decorations, including 27 Air Medals, a Distinguished Flying Cross, and the Purple Heart. Today he is a monk in the Soto Zen tradition and an active peace maker, speaker, and Zen teacher worldwide. He is also the founder of the Zaltho Foundation, a nonprofit organization that promotes peace and nonviolence.

Rev. José M. Tirado is a poet, priest, and writer completing a PhD in psychology from Saybrook University. His poetry and articles have appeared in such places as Cyrano's Online Showcase, *CounterPunch*, *The International Journal of Transpersonal Studies*, *Dissident Voice*, and *Gurdjieff Internet Guide*. His research interests include politics, Eastern mysticism, Western esotericism, and comparative religious studies. He currently lives in Iceland.

Cris Toffolo, PhD, has been professor and chair of the Justice Studies Department at Northeastern Illinois University in Chicago since 2008. Prior to that, she was an associate professor of political science and director of the Justice and Peace Studies Program at the University of St. Thomas (UST) in Minnesota. Her publications include *The Arab League* (Chelsea House, 2007), *Emancipating Cultural Pluralism* (SUNY Press, 2003), and numerous articles. Dr. Toffolo developed, evaluated, and taught study-abroad programs in Guatemala, Ghana, Bangladesh, and Northern Ireland. In 1997 she received a National Endowment for the Humanities grant to work on ethnicity at the University of Wisconsin-Madison. While on sabbatical in South Africa (2005 to 2006) she was a senior researcher at CARRAS, a human rights nongovernmental organization, for which she conducted research on anti-racism training programs and economic policy. She has won UST's Students of Color Ally Award three times for her work to combat racism, which included founding Teaching Against Racism, a faculty group that explored how to address race issues in the curriculum. Twice she received a UST Bush grant, to work on service learning and inquiry-based education. Other service includes membership on the executive board of the national Peace and Justice Studies Association, and acting as board chair of Higher Education Consortium for Urban Affairs (HECUA). Since 1991 she has been Amnesty International's Pakistan Country Specialist and has provided court testimony in various immigration cases. She received a PhD and MA from Notre Dame; an MA from George Washington University; and a BS from Alma College, cum laude.

ABOUT THE SERIES EDITOR AND ADVISORY BOARD

SERIES EDITOR

Chris E. Stout, PsyD, MBA, is a licensed clinical psychologist and is a Clinical Full Professor at the University of Illinois College of Medicine's Department of Psychiatry. He served as an NGO Special Representative to the United Nations. He was appointed to the World Economic Forum's Global Leaders of Tomorrow and he has served as an Invited Faculty at the Annual Meeting in Davos. He is the Founding Director of the Center for Global Initiatives. Stout is a Fellow of the American Psychological Association, former President of the Illinois Psychological Association, and a Distinguished Practitioner in the National Academies of Practice. Stout has published or presented over 300 papers and 30 books and manuals on various topics in psychology. His works have been translated into six languages. He has lectured across the nation and internationally in 19 countries and has, visited 6 continents and almost 70 countries. He was noted as being "one of the most frequently cited psychologists in the scientific literature" in a study by Hartwick College. He is the recipient of the American Psychological Association's International Humanitarian Award.

ADVISORY BOARD

Bruce Bonecutter, PhD, is Director of Behavioral Services at the Elgin Community Mental Health Center, the Illinois Department of Human Services state hospital serving adults in greater Chicago. He is also a Clinical Assistant Professor of Psychology at the University of Illinois at Chicago. A clinical psychologist specializing in health, consulting, and forensic psychology, Bonecutter is also a longtime member of the American Psychological Association Taskforce on Children and the Family. He is a member of organizations including the Association for the Treatment of Sexual Abusers, International, the Alliance for the Mentally Ill, and the Mental Health Association of Illinois.

Joseph Flaherty, MD, is Chief of Psychiatry at the University of Illinois Hospital, Professor of Psychiatry at the University of Illinois College (UIC) of Medicine and a Professor of Community Health Science at the UIC College of Public Health. He is a Founding Member of the Society for the Study of Culture and Psychiatry. Dr. Flaherty has been a consultant to the World Health Organization, the National Institute of Mental Health, and also the Falk Institute in Jerusalem. He is the former Director of Undergraduate Education and Graduate Education in the Department of Psychiatry at the University of Illinois. Dr. Flaherty has also been Staff Psychiatrist and Chief of Psychiatry at Veterans Administration West Side Hospital in Chicago.

Michael Horowitz, PhD, is President and Professor of Clinical Psychology at the Chicago School of Professional Psychology, one of the nation's leading not-for-profit graduate schools of psychology. Earlier, he served as Dean and Professor of the Arizona School of Professional Psychology. A clinical psychologist practicing independently since 1987, his work has focused on psychoanalysis, intensive individual therapy, and couples therapy. He has provided Disaster Mental Health Services to the American Red Cross. Horowitz's special interests include the study of fatherhood.

Sheldon I. Miller, MD, is a Professor of Psychiatry at Northwestern University, and Director of the Stone Institute of Psychiatry at Northwestern Memorial Hospital. He is also Director of the American Board of Psychiatry and Neurology, Director of the American Board of Emergency Medicine, and Director of the Accreditation Council for Graduate Medical Education. Dr. Miller is also an Examiner for the American Board of Psychiatry and

Neurology. He is Founding Editor of the *American Journal of Addictions*, and Founding Chairman of the American Psychiatric Association's Committee on Alcoholism. Dr. Miller has also been a Lieutenant Commander in the U.S. Public Health Service, serving as psychiatric consultant to the Navajo Area Indian Health Service at Window Rock, Arizona. He is a member and Past President of the Executive Committee for the American Academy of Psychiatrists in Alcoholism and Addictions.

Dennis P. Morrison, PhD, is Chief Executive Officer at the Center for Behavioral Health in Indiana, the first behavioral health company ever to win the Joint Commission on Accreditation of Healthcare Organizations (JCAHO) Codman Award for excellence in the use of outcomes management to achieve health care quality improvement. He is President of the Board of Directors for the Community Healthcare Foundation in Bloomington, and has been a member of the Board of Directors for the American College of Sports Psychology. He has served as a consultant to agencies including the Ohio Department of Mental Health, Tennessee Association of Mental Health Organizations, Oklahoma Psychological Association, the North Carolina Council of Community Mental Health Centers, and the National Center for Heath Promotion in Michigan. Morrison served across 10 years as a Medical Service Corp Officer in the U.S. Navy.

William H. Reid, MD, is a clinical and forensic psychiatrist, and consultant to attorneys and courts throughout the United States. He is Clinical Professor of Psychiatry at the University of Texas Health Science Center. Dr. Miller is also an Adjunct Professor of Psychiatry at Texas A&M College of Medicine and Texas Tech University School of Medicine, as well as a Clinical Faculty member at the Austin Psychiatry Residency Program. He is Chairman of the Scientific Advisory Board and Medical Advisor to the Texas Depressive and Manic-Depressive Association, as well as an Examiner for the American Board of Psychiatry and Neurology. He has served as President of the American Academy of Psychiatry and the Law, as Chairman of the Research Section for an International Conference on the Psychiatric Aspects of Terrorism, and as Medical Director for the Texas Department of Mental Health and Mental Retardation. Dr. Reid earned an Exemplary Psychiatrist Award from the National Alliance for the Mentally Ill. He has been cited on the Best Doctors in America listing since 1998.

.

ABOUT THE SERIES

THE PRAEGER SERIES IN CONTEMPORARY PSYCHOLOGY

In this series, experts from various disciplines peer through the lens of psychology, telling us answers they see for questions of human behavior. Their topics may range from humanity's psychological ills—addictions, abuse, suicide, murder, and terrorism among them—to works focused on positive subjects, including intelligence, creativity, athleticism, and resilience. Regardless of the topic, the goal of this series remains constant—to offer innovative ideas, provocative considerations, and useful beginnings to better understand human behavior.

Series Editor
Chris E. Stout, Psy.D., MBA
Northwestern University Medical School
Illinois Chief of Psychological Services

Advisory Board
Bruce E. Bonecutter, Ph.D.
University of Illinois at Chicago
Director, Behavioral Services, Elgin Community Mental Health Center

Joseph A. Flaherty, M.D.
University of Illinois College of Medicine and College of Public Health
Chief of Psychiatry, University of Illinois Hospital

Michael Horowitz, Ph.D.
Chicago School of Professional Psychology
President, Chicago School of Professional Psychology

Sheldon I. Miller, M.D.
Northwestern University
Director, Stone Institute of Psychiatry, Northwestern Memorial Hospital

Dennis P. Morrison, Ph.D.
Chief Executive Officer, Center for Behavioral Health, Indiana
President, Board of Directors, Community Healthcare Foundation,
Indiana

William H. Reid, M.D.
University of Texas Health Sciences Center
Chair, Scientific Advisory Board, Texas Depressive and Manic
Depressive Association